Journey through Utopia

STUDIES IN THE LIBERTARIAN

AND UTOPIAN TRADITION

JOURNEY THROUGH
UTOPIA

by

MARIE LOUISE
BERNERI

Foreword by George Woodcock

SCHOCKEN BOOKS · NEW YORK

First published in 1950
First SCHOCKEN PAPERBACK edition 1971
Published by arrangement with
Routledge & Kegan Paul Ltd.
Library of Congress Catalog Card No. 71-93316
Manufactured in the United States of America

Note

Marie Louise Berneri died on April 13th, 1949 at the age of thirty-one. Had she lived to see her book in print, she would have wished to acknowledge the advice and encouragement she received from a number of friends in the preparation of the manuscript; and in particular to Garfield Howe who first suggested such a book; to George Woodcock with whom the author discussed the form it should take and who, with Colin Ward, read the manuscript.

I wish to thank the above named and John Hewetson for their help with the proofs of this book and Colin Ward who compiled the Index.

V.R.

April 1950

Acknowledgements

The author is indebted to Messrs. Swan Sonnenschein & Co. Ltd., for permission to include extracts from Richter's *Pictures of the Socialistic Future*, and to Messrs. J. M. Dent & Sons Ltd., for permission to quote from Plato's *Republic*.

Contents

From the First illustrated edition of More's *Utopia*

Foreword

IN *Journey through Utopia*, Marie Louise Berneri has set out to give a description and a critical assessment of the most important (and by this the reader will soon learn that she does not mean necessarily the most famous) Utopian writings since Plato first gave, in his *Republic*, a literary form to the dreams of a Golden Age and of ideal societies which had doubtless been haunting man since the beginning of the conscious discussion of social problems.

A few words of reminiscence are, I think, necessary to explain the form the book has taken. Early in 1948, when the project of publishing a compilation of extracts from celebrated Utopias was put to her, she agreed to undertake the selection, but contended that the plan originally put forward was inadequate, since the celebrated Utopias were in fact easily available in some form or another for those really anxious to read them, and that what was needed was not merely a compilation, but a work that would combine information and commentary, presenting lengthy illustrations, but at the same time discussing them and linking them together in such a way that the development of Utopian thought, and its place in the history of social conditions and ideas, should be clearly demonstrated. Her idea was accepted, with slight modifications, and she set to work with characteristic thoroughness to trace the obscure as well as the familiar Utopias. Even a brief glance through this book and its bibliography will show how successful she was; and it will be seen that some of the Utopias she has rescued from oblivion, like that of Gabriel de Foigny, are both interesting as literature and important as reflections of the social trends of their periods. In some cases no English version existed, and Marie Louise Berneri had to make her own translations from the French or Italian; this was so with Diderot's *Supplement to Bougainville's Voyage* and Cabet's *Voyage to Icaria*, while for Campanella's *City of the Sun* she prepared a new translation based on an Italian version of the original which was some years anterior to the Latin version used by the previous English translator. So far as I have been able to see by referring to the general works on Utopias which existed up to the present, none of them has been so wide in scope as the present volume or has contrived to present its subject in so fresh and stimulating a manner.

In her account of Utopias, Marie Louise Berneri has emphasised the intolerant and authoritarian nature of most of these visions, the exceptions, such as those of Morris, Diderot and Foigny, being only a very slight minority. And she has further pointed to the fact that, although the Marxists have always claimed to be "scientific" as opposed to Utopian socialists, their actual social experiments have in practice tended to take on the generally rigid structure and even many of the individual institutional features of the classic Utopias. Fortunately, the lessons of this development are not being lost on the people of today, whether they are intellectuals or workers. Visions of an ideal future, where every action, as in Cabet's or Bellamy's schemes, is carefully regulated and fitted into a model state, are no longer popular, and it is impossible to consider such a book today achieving the fame which was enjoyed by Bellamy's _Looking Backward_ in the late nineteenth century. It is significant that not only are those writers who are conscious of present-day social evils writing anti-Utopias to warn people of the dangers of going further in the direction of a regimented life, but these very books have the same kind of popularity which the smug visions of a socialist paradise enjoyed before 1914.

Since _Journey through Utopia_ was written, two important books of this kind have been published which Marie Louise Berneri would undoubtedly have mentioned had she been alive to do so. One is Aldous Huxley's _Ape and Essence_, a really macabre vision of a future, after the Atomic war, when the people of California have turned into Belial worshippers and conduct a society which is based on the cult of hatred and evil. It is a work strictly in the Utopian tradition and emphasises its lesson for the present day with a great deal more ferocity than the same author did in his earlier anti-Utopia, _Brave New World_. The second of these new anti-Utopias is the late George Orwell's _Nineteen Eighty Four_, an even more powerful vision of a world destroyed by authority, a kind of extension to a logical conclusion of Plato's

Republic and all the other Utopias which were hostile to human individuality. In Orwell's Airstrip One, all individuality is finally crushed out, and even thought is regulated in a manner which was unimagined by the earlier Utopians. One can speculate with what delight one of the Utopian authoritarians of the past would have seized upon a technique for creating uniformity of thought, for in that day all these things were distant enough to be subjects of armchair visions. Today the nightmares have closed in upon us, the Utopias of the past are taking shape around us, and we realise at last that the most delightful-sounding of these schemes must of necessity become a gruesome prison unless it is based firmly and securely on the foundation of individual freedom, as in the case of that brilliant exception, *News from Nowhere*.

Marie Louise Berneri's book has not merely an academic interest. It is much more than a mere compilation and criticism of Utopias, for it does in fact bring out in a striking way the close and fateful relationship between Utopian thought and social reality, and takes its place among the important books which have appeared in the last few years, warning us, from various points of view, of the doom that awaits those who are foolish enough to put their trust in an ordered and regimented world.

GEORGE WOODCOCK

Without the Utopias of other times, men would still live in caves, miserable and naked. It was Utopians who traced the lines of the first city...Out of generous dreams come beneficial realities. Utopia is the principle of all progress, and the essay into a better future.

Anatole France.

With the Utopia modern Socialism begins

Kautsky.

An acre of Middlesex is better than a principality in Utopia.

Lord Macaulay.

There is no Utopia so wild as not to offer some incontestable advantages.

Auguste Comte.

Utopias are generally regarded as literary curiosities which have been made respectable by illustrious names, rather than as serious contributions to political problems which troubled the age at which they appeared.

H. F. Russell.

A map of the world that does not include Utopia is not worth even glancing at, for it leaves out the one country at which Humanity is always landing. And when Humanity lands there, it looks out, and seeing a better country, sets sail. Progress is the realisation of Utopias.

Oscar Wilde.

Not in Utopia,—subterranean fields,—
Or on some secret island, Heaven knows where!
But in this very world, which is the world
Of all of us,—the place where, in the end,
We find our happiness, or not at all!

William Wordsworth.

Introduction

OUR age is an age of compromises, of half-measures, of the lesser evil. Visionaries are derided or despised, and " practical men " rule our lives. We no longer seek radical solutions to the evils of society, but reforms ; we no longer try to abolish war, but to avoid it for a period of a few years ; we do not try to abolish crime, but are contented with criminal reforms ; we do not try to abolish starvation, but to set up world-wide charitable organisations. At a time when man is so concerned with what is practicable and capable of immediate realisation, it might be a salutary exercise to turn to men who have dreamt of Utopias, who have rejected everything which did not comply with their ideal of perfection.

We shall often feel humble as we read of these ideal states and cities, for we shall realise the modesty of our claims, and the poverty of our vision. Zeno advocated internationalism, Plato recognised the equality of men and women, Thomas More saw clearly the relationship between poverty and crime which is denied by men even to-day. At the beginning of the seventeenth century Campanella advocated a working day of four hours, and the German scholar Andreae talked of attractive work and put forward a system of education which could still serve as a model today.

We shall find private property condemned, money and wages considered immoral or irrational, human solidarity admitted as an obvious fact. All these ideas which could be considered daring to-day were then put forward with a confidence which shows that though they were not generally accepted, they must have been nevertheless readily understood. In the late seventeenth and the eighteenth century we find even more startling and bold ideas concerning religion, sexual relations, the nature of government and of the law. We are so accustomed to thinking that progressive movements begin with the nineteenth century that we shall be surprised to find that the degeneration of utopian thought begins then. Utopias, as a rule, become timid ; private property and money are often judged necessary ; men must consider themselves happy if they work eight hours a day, and there is rarely any question of their work being attractive. Women are placed under the tutelage of their husbands, and children under that of the father. But before utopias became contaminated by the " realist " spirit of our time, they flourished with a variety and richness which may well make us doubt the validity of our claim to have achieved some measure of social progress.

This is not to say that all utopias have been revolutionary and progressive : the majority of them have been both, but few have been entirely revolutionary. Utopian writers were revolutionary when they advocated a community of goods at a time when private property was held to be sacred, the right of every individual to eat when beggars were hanged, the equality of women when these were considered little better than slaves, the dignity of manual work when it was regarded and made a degrading occupation, the right of every child to a happy child-hood and good education when this was reserved for the sons of the nobles and the rich. All this has contributed to make the word "Utopia" synonymous with a happy, desirable form of society. Utopia, in this respect, represents mankind's dream of happiness, its secret longing for the Golden Age, or, as others saw it, for its lost Paradise.

But that dream often had its dark places. There were slaves in Plato's *Republic* and in More's *Utopia* ; there were mass murders of Helots in the Sparta of Lycurgus ; and wars, ex-ecutions, strict discipline, religious intolerance, are often found beside the most enlightened institutions. These aspects, which have often been overlooked by the apologists of utopias, result from the authoritarian conception on which many utopias were built, and are absent from those which aim at achieving complete freedom.

Two main trends manifest themselves in utopian thought throughout the ages. One seeks the happiness of mankind through material well-being, the sinking of man's individuality into the group, and the greatness of the State. The other, while demanding a certain degree of material comfort, considers that happiness is the result of the free expression of man's personality and must not be sacrificed to an arbitrary moral code or to the interests of the State. These two trends correspond to different conceptions of progress. For the anti-authoritarian utopians, progress is measured, as for Herbert Read:

"by the degree of differentiation within a society. If the individual is a unit in a corporate mass, his life is not merely brutish and short, but dull and mechanical. If the individual is a unit on his own, with space and potentiality for separate action, then he may be more subject to accident or chance, but at least he can expand and express himself. He can develop—develop in the only real meaning of the word—develop in consciousness of strength, vitality and joy."

But, as Herbert Read also points out, this has not always been the definition of progress:

"Many people find safety in numbers, happiness in anonymity, and dignity in routine. They ask for nothing better than to be sheep under the shepherd, soldiers under a captain, slaves under a tyrant. The few that must expand become the shepherds, the captains and the leaders of these willing followers."

The authoritarian utopias have aimed at giving shepherds, captains and tyrants to the people, whether under the name of *guardians, phylarchs,* or *samurai.*

These utopias were progressive in as much as they wished to abolish economic inequalities, but they replaced the old economic slavery by a new one : men ceased to be the slaves of their masters or employers, to become the slaves of the Nation and the State. The power of the State is sometimes based on moral and military power, as in Plato's *Republic,* on religion, as in Andreae's *Christianopolis,* or on the ownership of the means of production and distribution as in most of the utopias of the nineteenth century. But the result is always the same : the individual is obliged to follow a code of laws or of moral behaviour artificially created for him.

The contradictions inherent in most utopias are due to this authoritarian approach. The builders of utopias claimed to give freedom to the people, but freedom which is given ceases to be freedom. Diderot was one of the few utopian writers who denied himself even the right to decree that " each should do as he wills"; but the majority of the builders of utopias are determined to remain the masters in their imaginary commonwealths. While they claim to give freedom they issue a detailed code which must be strictly followed. There are the lawgivers, the kings, the magistrates, the priests, the presidents of national assemblies in their utopias ; and yet, after they have decreed, codified, ordered marriages, imprisonments and executions, they still claim that the people are free to do what they like.   It is only too apparent that Campanella imagined himself to be the Great Metaphysician in his *City of the Sun,* Bacon a father of his Salomon's House, and Cabet the lawgiver of his Icaria.   When they have the wit of Thomas More they could express their secret longing with much humour :   " You cannot think how elated I am," he wrote to his friend Erasmus, " how I have grown in stature and hold my head higher ;   so constantly do I imagine myself in the part of sovereign of Utopia ;   in fact I fancy I am walking with the crown of corn-ears upon my head, wearing a Franciscan cloak, and carrying the corn sheaf as a sceptre, attended by a great throng of the people of Amaurote."   Sometimes others have to point out the inconsistencies of their dream, as when Gonzalez in *The Tempest* tells his companions of the ideal commonwealth which he would like to create on his island :

> Gonzalez: I' the commonwealth I would by contraries
>   Execute all things ;   for no kind of traffic
>   Would I admit ;   no name of magistrate ;
>   Letters should not be known ;   riches, poverty
>   And use of service, none ;   contract, succession
>   Bourn, bound of land, tilth, vineyard, none ;
>   No use of metal, corn or wine or oil ;
>   No occupation, all men idle, all ;
>   And women too, but innocent and pure ;
>   No sovereignty :—
> Sebastian: Yet he would be king on't.
> Antonio: The latter end of his commonwealth
>   Forgets the beginning.

Another contradiction of authoritarian utopias consists in asserting that their laws follow the order of nature when in fact their code has been arbitrarily constituted.   Utopian writers, instead of trying to discover the laws of nature, preferred to invent them, or found them in the " archives of antient prudence."   For some of them, like Mably or Morelly, the code of nature was that of Sparta, and instead of basing their utopias on living communities and on men as they have known them, they built them on abstract conceptions.   This is responsible for the artificial atmosphere prevalent in most utopias : Utopian men are uniform creatures with identical wants and reactions and deprived of emotions and passions, for these would be the expression of individuality. This uniformity is reflected in every aspect of utopian life, from the clothes to the time-table, from moral behaviour to intellectual interests. As H. G. Wells has pointed out : " In almost every Utopia—except, perhaps, Morris's *News from Nowhere*—one sees handsome but characterless buildings, symmetrical and perfect cultivations, and a multitude of people, healthy, happy, beautifully dressed, but without any personal distinction whatever. Too often the prospect resembles the key to one of those large pictures of coronations, royal weddings, parliaments, conferences and gatherings in Victorian times, in which, instead of a face, each figure bears a neat oval with its index number legibly inscribed."

The setting of the utopia is equally artificial. To the uniformed nation must correspond an uniform country or city. The authoritarian love of symmetry causes utopians to suppress mountains or rivers, and even to imagine perfectly round islands and perfectly straight rivers.

" In the utopia of the National State (says Lewis Mumford) there are no natural regions ; and the equally natural grouping of people in towns, villages and cities, which, as Aristotle points out, is perhaps the chief distinction between man and the other animals, is tolerated only upon the fiction that the State hands over to these groups a portion of its omnipotent authority, or ' sovereignty ' as it is called, and permits them to exercise a corporate life. Unfortunately for this beautiful myth, which generations of lawyers and statesmen have laboured to build up, cities existed long before states—there was a Rome on the Tiber long before there was a Roman Imperium—and the gracious permission of the state is simply a perfunctory seal upon the accomplished fact. . . .

" Instead of recognising natural regions and natural groups of people, the utopia of nationalism establishes by the surveyor's line a certain realm called national territory, and makes all the inhabitants of this territory the members of a single, indivisible group, the nation, which is supposed to be prior in claim and superior in power to all other groups. This is the only social formation which is officially recognised within the national utopia. What is common to all the inhabitants of this territory is thought to be of far greater importance than any of the things that bind men together in particular civic or industrial groups."

This uniformity is maintained by a strong national State. Private property is abolished in Utopia, not merely to establish equality among the citizens or because of its corrupting influence, but because it presents a danger to the unity of the State. The attitude towards the family is also determined by the desire to maintain an unified State. Many utopias remain in the Platonic tradition and abolish the family together with monogamous marriage, while others follow Thomas More and advocate the patriarchal family, monogamous marriage and the bringing up and education of children within the fold of the family. A third group effect a compromise by retaining family institutions but entrusting the education of the children to the State.

When Utopias want to abolish the family it is much for the same reasons as they want to abolish property. The family is considered as encouraging selfish instincts and as having therefore a disintegrating influence on the community. On the other hand the advocates of the family see in it the basis for a stable State, the indispensable cell, the training ground for the virtues of obedience and loyalty required by the State. They rightly believe that the authoritarian family, far from presenting a danger by inculcating individualist tendencies in the children, accustoms them, on the contrary, to respect the authority of the father ; they will later obey just as unquestioningly the orders of the State.

A strong State necessitates a ruling class or caste holding power over the rest of the people, and, while builders of ideal commonwealths took great care that property should not corrupt or disunite this ruling class, they did not see, as a rule, the danger of the love of power corrupting and dividing the rulers and oppressing the people. Plato was the chief offender in this respect. His Guardians were entrusted with all the power in the city, while Plutarch was aware of the abuses which could be carried out by the Spartans, but offered no remedy. Thomas More put forward a new conception : that of a State representing all the citizens, except for a small number of slaves. His régime was what we would call democratic ; that is to say, power was exercised by the representatives of the people. But these representatives had the power of administrating the laws rather than framing them, since all the major laws had been given to the country by a law-giver. The State therefore administered a code of laws which the community had not made. Furthermore, in view of the centralised nature of that State, the laws are the same for every citizen and every section of the community, and do not take into account varying personal factors. For this reason, some utopian writers, like Gerrard Winstanley, were opposed to the community delegating its power to a central body, for fear that it would in fact lose its liberty, and wanted it to retain its autonomous government. Gabriel de Foigny and Diderot went even further by abolishing governments altogether.

The existence of the State also necessitates two codes of moral behaviour, for the State not only divides people into classes but also divides humanity into nations. Loyalty to the State often demands the negation of the feelings of solidarity and mutual aid which naturally exist between men. The State imposes a certain code of behaviour governing the relations between the citizens of the commonwealth and another governing the relations between the citizens and the slaves or the " barbarians." All that is forbidden in relations between equals is allowed towards those who are considered inferior beings. The utopian citizen is gentle and courteous towards his peers but cruel to his slaves ; he loves peace at home but carries out the most ruthless wars abroad. All the utopias which follow in Plato's footsteps admit this duality in man. That this duality exists in society as we know it is true enough, but it may seem curious that it should not have been eliminated in a " perfect society." The universalist ideal of Zeno who, in his *Republic*, proclaimed the brotherhood of men of all nations, has rarely been adopted by utopian writers. The majority of utopias accept war as an inevitable part of their system, as indeed it must be, for the existence of a national State always gives birth to wars.

The authoritarian Utopian State does not allow of any personality strong and independent enough to conceive of change or revolt. Since the utopian institutions are considered as perfect, it goes without saying that they cannot be capable of improvement. The Utopian State is essentially static and does not allow its citizens to fight or even to dream of a better utopia.

This crushing of man's personality often takes a truly totalitarian character. It is the law-giver or the Government which decides the plan of cities and houses ; these plans are prepared according to the most rational principles and the best technical knowledge, but they are not the organic expression of the community. A house, like a city, may be made of lifeless materials, but it should embody the spirit of those who build it. In the same way utopian uniforms may be more comfortable and attractive than ordinary clothes, but they do not allow for the expression of one's individuality.

The Utopian State is even more ferocious in its suppression of the freedom of the artist. The poet, the painter, the sculptor must all become the servants and propaganda agents of the State. They are forbidden individual expression either on aesthetic or moral grounds, but the real aim is to crush any manifestation of freedom. Most utopias would fail the " test of art " suggested by Herbert Read :

Plato, as is too often and too complacently recalled, banished the poet from his Republic. But that Republic was a deceptive model of perfection. It might be realised by some dictator, but it could only function as a machine functions—mechanically. And machines function mechanically only because they are made of dead inorganic materials. If you want to express the difference between an organic progressive society and a static totalitarian régime, you can do so in one word : this word *art*. Only on condition that the artist is allowed to function freely can society embody those ideals of liberty and intellectual development which to most of us seem the only worthy sanctions of life.

The Utopias which pass this test are those which oppose to the conception of the centralised State, that of a federation of free communities, where the individual can express his personality without being submitted to the censure of an artificial code, where freedom is not an abstract word but manifests itself concretely in work, whether that of the painter or of the mason. These utopias are not concerned with the dead structure of the organisation of society, but with the ideals on which a better society can be built. The anti-authoritarian utopias are less numerous, and exerted a lesser influence than the others, because they did not present a ready-made plan but daring, unorthodox ideas ; because they demanded each of us to be " unique " and not one among many.

When the utopia points to an ideal life without becoming a plan, that is, a lifeless machine applied to living matter, it truly becomes the realisation of progress.

1

Utopias of Antiquity

GREEK philosophical and political thought possesses such a richness and variety as to make it the greatest source of inspiration for utopian writers throughout the ages. The legends of the Golden Age, the descriptions of ideal states belonging to a mythical past or to a distant future, the theoretical writings on the art of government, have all had a profound influence on the builders of ideal commonwealths, from Thomas More to H. G. Wells.

It is not always easy to determine which works can be considered as utopias, for the difference between imaginary and historical accounts is sometimes a very tenuous one. Plato himself, to whom later writers have most often turned, has left works which contain various forms of utopian thought. The *Timaeus* and the *Critias* are both descriptions of mythical societies and of ideal commonwealths, the *Republic* lays down the basis for an ideal city of the future, and the *Laws* that of a second-best state. In Aristotle we find the frame of an ideal constitution and also an account of the institutions governing many Greek states ; in Diodorus Siculus, historical accounts of early communities and legends of the golden age ; in Zeno a study of governments and a sketch of an ideal republic, and in Strabo and Plutarch a fairly accurate description of society as it had existed in Crete and Sparta.

Among these works, those which come nearer to the definition of an ideal commonwealth and to which, at the same time, subsequent utopias have been most indebted, are Plato's *Republic* and Plutarch's *Life of Lycurgus*. Both represent the authoritarian and communistic trends of Greek thought, but their influence on later thinkers has often been tempered by the reformist " petty-bourgeois " ideas of Aristotle or the libertarian and cosmopolitan ideals of Zeno. If our aim were to trace the influence of Greece on utopian thought rather than to present schemes of ideal commonwealths, their works should have been considered here. It may also seem an arbitrary choice to include the *Republic* and leave out the *Timaeus*, the *Critias* and the *Laws*, but, as Alexander Gray has remarked, " there is an immensity of Plato as there is

9

an immensity of Shakespeare," and the limitations of a short
survey are necessarily somewhat arbitrary.

PLATO

The Republic

THE period in which Plato wrote *The Republic* was one of decline
in Greek history.   The Peloponnesian war (431-404 B.C.) had
ended with the crushing defeat of Athens, and the independent
cities which had taken part in it were weakened by the long
struggle and by internal factions.   Their lack of unity rendered
them vulnerable to foreign aggression and had allowed the
military and authoritarian state of Sparta to triumph over them.
Plato was twenty-three years old when the war came to an end,
leaving Athens in a state of political and economic exhaustion.
It is understandable, therefore, that his writings should show such
an interest in political and social questions, and that he should
have attempted to draw some lessons from the defeat of Athens
and the victory of Sparta.

The mind of the defeated is often fascinated by the power of
the conquerors, and when Plato came to build his ideal city he
turned to Sparta for a model.   He did not, of course, imitate that
model slavishly, but his Republic is more similar to the authoritarian organisation of Sparta than to the liberal institutions
which the other Greek cities had enjoyed during the preceding
centuries.   To the spirit of independence and extreme individualism which characterised Greek life, Plato opposed the conception
of a strong and homogeneous state based on authoritarian
principles.

The Sophists, against whom Plato directed his most persistent
and bitter attacks, had sought a solution to the disintegration of
Greek life along opposite lines.   Their cure was not less, but
more freedom.   They turned to the traditional belief in a Golden
Age when men lived in a state of complete freedom and equality,
and they put forward the theory that it was with the birth of
political institutions that men had lost that freedom and happiness
which belonged to them as a " natural right."   In his *Nationalism*

and Culture, Rudolf Rocker described this social conception thus :

It was especially the members of the Sophist school who in their criticism of social evils used to refer to a past natural state where man as yet knew not the consequences of social oppression. Thus Hippias of Elis declares that " the law has become man's tyrant, continually urging him to unnatural deeds." On the basis of this doctrine Alkidamas, Lykophron and others advocated the abolition of social prerogatives, condemning especially the institution of slavery, as not founded upon the nature of man, but as arising from the enactments of men who made a virtue of injustice. It was one of the greatest services of the much maligned Sophist school that its members surmounted all national frontiers and consciously allied themselves with the great racial community of mankind. They felt the insufficiency and the spiritual limitations of the patriotic ideal and recognised with Aristippus that " every place is equally far from Hades."

These ideas were taken up later by the Cynics, who considered the institutions of the State as being opposed to the natural order of things and denied class and national distinctions, and by the school of Stoics, founded by Zeno of Kittion, who refused to submit to external compulsion but followed the " inner law " which revealed itself in nature. In Zeno's ideal commonwealth there were to be no states or political institutions, but complete freedom and equality for all human beings, while marriage, temples, law-courts, schools and money were to be abolished. Zeno did not, however, confuse freedom with license or irresponsibility. He believed that human social instinct has its roots in communal life and finds its highest expression in the sense of justice, and that man combines a need for personal freedom with a sense of responsibility for his own actions.

Plato represented a reaction against the major trends of philosophical thought in his time, for he believed in moral and external compulsion, in inequality and authority, in strict laws and immovable institutions, and in the superiority of the Greeks over the " barbarians." Though his influence on modern thought has been far greater than that of the other philosophers, there were times when thinkers proclaimed, like the Stoics, the " natural right " of men to complete freedom and equality.

Like the Sophists and the Stoics, however, Plato was convinced that his institutions were in accord with the law of nature, but, for him, nature had created some men to rule and others to be ruled.

In *The Republic* he says :

The truth established by nature is that he who is ill, whether he be rich or poor, ought to wait at the doctor's door, and every man who needs to be ruled, at the door of him who can rule.

Having denied that each man is to be his own ruler and established the necessity of a ruling class, Plato logically wished to establish a strong government, strong not only by the power it would have over the mass of the people but by its moral and intellectual superiority and its internal unity. The rulers or guardians of his ideal Republic are not to be chosen for their birth or their wealth but for the qualities which predispose them to their task ; they must be men of good stock, good physique, good mind and good education. This is how Socrates explains to Glaucon the essential qualities of the guardians :

" Then," I said, " because the work of our guardians is the most important of all, it will demand the most exclusive attention and the greatest skill and practice."

" I certainly think so," he said.

" And will it not need also a nature fitted for this profession?"

" Surely."

" Then it will be our business to do our best to select the proper persons and to determine the proper character required for the guardians of the city?"

" Yes, we shall have to do that."

" Well, certainly it is no trivial task we have undertaken, but we must be brave and do all in our power."

" Yes, we must," he said.

" Do you not think, then," I said, " that so far as their fitness for guarding is concerned, a noble youth and a well-bred dog are very much alike?"

" What do you mean?"

" I mean, for example, that both must be sharp-sighted, quick of foot to pursue the moment they perceive, and strong enough to make captures and overcome opposition when necessary."

" Yes," he said ; " all these qualities are required."

" And since they are good fighters, they must certainly be brave."

" Surely."

" But will either horse or dog or any animal be brave if it is not spirited? Have you not observed that spirit is unconquerable and irresistible? Every soul possessed by it will meet any danger fearless and unshrinking."

" I have noticed that."

" Then we are quite clear as to what must be the bodily characteristics of our guardians?"

" Yes."

" And as to their mental qualities, we know they must be spirited."

" Certainly."

" Then, Glaucon," I said, " with such natures as these, how are they to be prevented from behaving savagely towards one another and the other citizens?"

" By Zeus," he said, " that will not be easy."

" Still we must have them gentle to their fellows and fierce to their enemies. If we can't effect that, they will prevent the enemy from destroying the city by doing it first themselves."

" True," he said.

" What then are we to do?" I said. " Where shall we find a character at once gentle and high-spirited? For a gentle nature is surely the antithesis of a spirited one?"

" So it appears."

" Nevertheless, if either is lacking, we shall certainly not have a good guardian. But this combination is apparently unattainable, and so you see it follows that a good guardian is an impossibility."

" It looks like it," he said.

I was perplexed, but reflecting on what had gone before I said, " We certainly deserve to be in difficulties, for we have forsaken the simile we set before ourselves."

" What do you mean?"

" Have you noticed that natures are to be found possessed of those opposite qualities, for all that we thought them non-existent?"

" Where?"

" In many animals, but perhaps best in that with which we compared our guardian. Well-bred dogs, you surely know, are naturally of that disposition—as gentle as possible to their friends and those whom they know, but the very opposite to strangers."

" Yes, I know that."

" Then," I said, " we may assume that the character we seek in our guardian is possible, and not contrary to nature?"

" I think we may."

" Do you think, then, that there is another quality indispensable to the guardian? The spirited element is not enough ; he must be of a philosophical nature as well."

" What are you saying?" he said. " I don't understand."

" You will notice this other quality in dogs," I said. " It certainly is surprising in the creatures."

" What quality?"

" Why, when dogs see a stranger, without any provocation they get angry ; but if they see someone they know, they welcome him, even though they have received no kindness at his hands. Have you never wondered at that?"

" I have hardly thought of it before. But that certainly is how they behave."

" Well, but this instinct in the dog is a very fine thing, and genuinely philosophical."

" In what way?"

" Why, he distinguishes between a friendly and an unfriendly face, simply by the fact that he knows the one and is ignorant of the other. Now, how could the creature be anything but fond of learning when knowledge and ignorance are its criterion to distinguish between the friendly and the strange?"

" How indeed?"

" Well, but is it not the same thing to be fond of learning and to be philosophical?" I asked.

" It is," he said.

" Then shall we confidently apply this to man? If he is to be gentle to his friends and acquaintances, he must be by nature philosophical and fond of learning."

" Let us do so," he said.

" Then he who is to be a good and noble guardian of our city will be by nature philosophical and spirited, and quick and strong."

This body of guardians will be chosen by a small number of men who are true philosophers and know who is a fit person to compose the ruling class. Plato does not explain very clearly how this government of philosophers is to come into being but merely says that in his Republic, either the philosophers must become kings or the kings philosophers. Having assumed then that the reins of government have been put into the hands of the philosophers, their first task must be to select those who are to become guardians and this is how it will be done :

" Then we must discover who are the best guardians of the doctrine that is in them, that they must do whatever they think at any time best for the city. We must watch them from their earliest childhood, and set them tasks in which there are the strongest temptations to forget or be cheated out of their devotion

to the city. We must select those that are tenacious of memory and hard to deceive, the others we must reject. Do you agree?"
" Yes."
" We must impose upon them, too, labours, and vexations, and contests, and watch for the same things there."
" You are right," he said.
" Then," I said, " we must prepare for them a contest of the third kind, a trial in resistance to witchcraft, and watch them then. As men try whether colts are easily frightened by taking them near noises and alarming sounds, so we must bring our men, while still young, into the midst of terrors, and then again plunge them into pleasures, testing them more hardly than gold is tested in the fire ; and if one appears in all things gracious and a resister of enchantment, if he is a good guardian of himself and the music he has learnt, if he bears himself in all his trials with rhythm and harmony, such a man would be of the greatest service to himself and to the city. Therefore we must elect as ruler and guardian of the city him who as boy and youth and man has been tested and has come out without stain, and render him honours in life and after death, giving him the highest rewards of public burial and other memorials. The others we must reject. Some such method as that, Glaucon," I said, " seems to me the best for the election and appointment of rulers and guardians. I give the outline only without accurate details."
" My opinion is much the same," he said.
" Then is it really most correct to give these the name of perfect guardians, inasmuch as they watch over both enemies without and friends at home, taking care that the first shall be unable, and the second unwilling, to do harm ; and to call the young men, whom we formerly counted as guardians, auxiliaries, and upholders of the doctrines of the rulers?"

Once the guardians have been chosen they must be invested with authority and that authority will be all the more respected if it is believed to be of a predestined character. By means of a myth or, as Plato calls it, a " necessary lie " or a " noble false-hood," the rulers must be persuaded that they belong to a superior class, that they are *born* to be leaders, and what is more important, the rest of the citizens must be coached into believing that they are born to be ruled and that these class distinctions are all part of a divine scheme. Rather shyly, because he is afraid that his " noble falsehood " may not be easily accepted, Socrates expounds to Glaucon his ingenious myth :

" You in this city are all brothers," so we shall tell our tale to them, " but God as he was fashioning you, put gold in those of you who are capable of ruling ; hence they are deserving of most reverence. He put silver in the auxiliaries, and iron and copper in the farmers and the other craftsmen. For the most part your children are of the same nature as yourselves, but because you are all akin, sometimes from gold will come a silver offspring, or from silver a gold, and so on all round. Therefore the first and weightiest command of God to the rulers is this—that more than aught else they be good guardians of and watch zealously over the offspring, seeing which of those metals is mixed in their souls; if their own offspring has an admixture of copper or iron, they must show no pity, but giving it the honour proper to its nature, set it among the artisans or the farmers ; and if on the other hand in these classes children are born with an admixture of gold and silver, they shall do them honour and appoint the first to be guardians, the second to be auxiliaries. For there is an oracle that the city shall perish when it is guarded by iron or copper. Can you suggest any contrivance by which they may be made to believe this story?"

" No," he said, " I see no hope of succeeding with your original citizens, but possibly their sons and their descendants, and subsequent generations, might believe it."

Once the guardians have been selected and invested with authority, the task remains to regulate their lives so as to ensure the greatest unity among them. This is achieved by requiring them to share their goods, their houses and their meals. Furthermore the guardians will not know any greed or covetousness which might sow dissension among themselves and distract them from their tasks :

In the first place, no one shall have any private property, unless it is absolutely necessary. Secondly, no one shall have dwelling-place or storehouse which any one who pleases may not freely enter. To supply the proper necessities of men who are warrior athletes, and both prudent and courageous, they shall receive from the other citizens a fixed reward for their guardian-ship, large enough to support them for a year and leave nothing over. They shall live in common, taking their meals at the public tables, as in an army. As for silver and gold, we shall tell them that they have the divine metals always in their hearts, given them by the gods, and have no need of men's silver and gold ; nay, that it is an act of impiety to pollute their possession of the divine gold by conjoining it with the mortal ; for many unholy deeds are done for the common currency, but the coinage in their souls is unsullied. They alone in all the city are not allowed to handle or touch silver and gold, or to be under the same roof with it, or hold it in their hands, or drink out of gold and silver vessels; this will be their salvation, and the salvation of the city. But if at any time they acquire land or houses or money of their own, and are men of business and farmers instead of guardians, they will become the hated masters instead of the allies of the other citizens.

The city will be best governed when " the largest number of men agree in applying these words, 'mine' or ' not mine ' to the same thing." There must be communion in pleasure and pain, for " individuality in these feelings is a dissolving force." This unity must be particularly strong among the guardians, and for this reason there must be a community of wives and children so that " in every one he meets he will think he has a brother or sister, or father or mother, or son or daughter, or grandchild or grandparent." This law " will do still more to make them true guardians, and prevent the disruption of the city which would result if each man gave the name of 'mine' not to the same but to different things ; if all took what they could for themselves, and dragged it off to their different private houses ; if each called a different wife and different children his own, and thus implanted in the city the individual pleasures and griefs of individuals . . . . . "

Marriages, or it would be more exact to say, sexual unions, are to be carried out according to strict eugenic principles and here again Plato has recourse to the use of " necessary lies ":

" Then you, the lawgiver, as you have selected the men, will select the women, choosing as far as possible those of a similar nature, and place them together. Both sexes will live together, with common houses and common meals, no one possessing any private property ; and associating with one another in the gymnasia and in the rest of their daily life, they will be led, I imagine, by an inherent necessity to form alliances. Do you not think that this will be the inevitable?"

" Yes," he said ; " not by geometric but by lovers' necessity, which, perhaps, is stronger than the other in its power to persuade and constrain the mass of men."

"You are right," I replied. "But next, Glaucon, promiscuous unions or anything of that kind would be a profanation in a state of happy citizens, and the guardians will not allow it."

" No, it would not be just," he said.

" Then clearly we shall next see to making the marriages as sacred as possible, and this sanctity will attach to those which are most advantageous."

" Most certainly."

" How then will they be most advantageous?   Tell me this, Glaucon.   I see that you have in your house hunting dogs and a great many game birds.   Tell me, I conjure you, have you paid any attention to their unions and breeding?"

" In what respect?" he said.

" Firstly, though they are all well bred, are there not some which are, or prove themselves to be, the best?"

" There are."

" Then do you breed from all alike, or are you anxious to breed as far as possible from the best of them?"

" From the best of them."

" Then do you breed from those that are very young or very old, or as far as possible from those that are in their prime?"

" From those in their prime."

" And if you did not breed in this way, are you of opinion that the stock of birds and dogs would greatly deteriorate?"

" I am," he said.

" What is your opinion in regard to horses and other living creatures?" I said.   " Would it be different with them?"

" The idea is absurd," he said.

" Good heavens, my dear friend," I said, " what surpassing excellence we need in our rulers, if the same principles apply to the human race !"

" They certainly do," he said.   " What then?"

" Because," I said, " they will have to administer a great deal of medicine.   You know that for cases where medicine is not needed, and the constitution will respond to a diet, we think a quite ordinary doctor good enough ; but when medicine has to be administered, we know that a much more courageous doctor is needed."

" True.   But what is your point?"

" This," I answered.   " It seems that our rulers will have to administer a great quantity of falsehood and deceit for the benefit of the ruled.   For we said, if you remember, that all such practices were useful in the form of medicine."

" Yes, and we were right," he said.

" And the rightness of it seems to find special application in marriages and the begetting of children."

" In what way?"

" From our admissions," I said, " it follows that the best of both sexes ought to be brought together as often as possible, the worst as seldom as possible, and that we should rear the offspring of the first, but not the offspring of the second, if our herd is to reach the highest perfection, and all these arrangements must be secret from all save the rulers if the herd of guardians is to be as free as possible from dissension."

" You are perfectly right," he said.

" We must then have statutory festivals, at which we shall bring together the brides and bridegrooms. There should be accompanying sacrifices, and our poets must compose strains as honour of the marriages which take place. But the number of marriages we shall place under the control of the rulers, that they may as far as possible keep the population at the same level, having regard to wars and disease and all such ravages, and also taking care to the best of their power that our city become neither great or small."

" You are right," he said.

" They must invent, I fancy, some ingenious system of lots, so that those less worthy persons who are rejected when the couples are brought together may on each occasion blame their luck, and not the rulers."

" Certainly," he said.

" And surely to our young men who acquit themselves well in war or other duties we may give, along with other rewards and prizes, a more unrestricted right of cohabitation in order that there may be a colourable excuse for such fathers having as many children as possible."

" You are right."

" Then the children as they are born will be taken in charge by the officers appointed for the purpose, whether these are men or women, or both. For of course offices also are common to men and women."

" Yes."

" The children of good parents, I suppose, they will put into the rearing pen, handing them over to nurses who will live apart in a particular portion of the city ; but the children of inferior parents and all defective children that are born to the others they will put out of sight in secrecy and mystery, as is befitting."

" Yes, they must," he said, " if the race of guardians is to be pure."

" And will not these officers also superintend the rearing of the children, bringing the mothers to the nursery when their breasts are full, and taking every precaution to prevent any woman knowing her own child, and providing wet-nurses if the mothers are not enough ; and will they not take care that the mothers do not give too much time to suckling the children, and assign night watches and all troublesome duties to nurses and attendants?"

" As you describe it," he said, " child-bearing will be a very easy matter for the wives of the guardians."

" So it ought to be," I said. " Let us now discuss the next point in our proposals. We said that children must be born from parents in their prime."

" True."

" Then do you agree with me that on an average a woman is in her prime for twenty years, and a man for thirty?"

" Which twenty, and which thirty?" he said.

" For a woman," I said, " the proper time is to begin at twenty years and bear children for the city until she is forty ; for a man the proper time to begin is when he has seen ' the swiftest prime of his running ' go by, and to beget children for the state until fifty-five."

" Yes," he said, " in both cases that is the period of their prime both in body and mind."

" Therefore if a man above or below these ages meddles with the begetting of children for the commonwealth, we shall declare this to be a transgression both impious and unjust ; he is raising up a son for the state who, though his birth be secret, will not be born the child of the sacrifices and prayers which the priests and priestesses and the whole city will offer, when on each occasion of marriage they pray that the children may be ever better and more useful than their good and useful parents ; but he will be born in darkness, the child of dire incontinence."

" You are right," he said.

" And the same law will apply," I said, "if a man who is still of an age to be a father meddles with a woman of marriageable age when the ruler has not joined them. We shall say that he is giving to the city a child that is a bastard, unauthorised and unholy."

" You are perfectly right," he said.

" Then I fancy that when the men and women have passed the age of having children we shall, of course, leave them at liberty to associate with whosoever they please ; except that a man must not associate with his daughter or his mother, or his grand-daughter, or grandmother ; and the women we shall allow to associate with any one but a son or a father, or grandson or grandfather ; and all this only after we have exhorted them to be very careful that no child, if one should be so conceived, should see the light ; but if one should by any chance force its way to the light, they must dispose of it on the understanding that such an offspring is not to be reared."

" These are certainly reasonable proposals," he said. " But how will they distinguish one another's fathers and daughters, and the relations you have just mentioned?"

" They will not do so," I said. " But all the children that are born in the tenth month, and also in the seventh, after a man's bridal day, will be called by him, if male his sons, and if female his daughters, and they will call him father, and similarly he will call the offspring of his generation grandchildren, and they again will call him and his fellow-bridegrooms and brides grandfathers and grandmothers ; and, lastly, those born in the time when their fathers and mothers were having children will be called brothers and sisters, so that in accordance with what we said a moment ago, they will not associate with one another ; but the law may allow the union of brothers and sisters if the lot falls in that way and the priestess of Apollo approves."

" Quite right," he said.

" Such, then, Glaucon, is the community of wives and children for the guardians of your city."

The wives of the guardians having been freed from the task of bringing up children and looking after their family, are able to share the duties of their husbands in governing the city. " Do you agree," Socrates asks Glaucon, " to this community of women with men in education, in the care of the children and guardianship of the other citizens, and that they must both remain in the city and go out to war, guard and hunt with them like dogs, and as far as possible take their full share in everything, and that by so doing their actions will be most desirable and not contrary to the natural relations of male and female or their natural Community." And Glaucon dutifully replies " I agree."

The relations between men and women must not be allowed to have a disturbing effect on the life of the community. Plato conceives only of love between people of the same sex but, even then, it must be devoid of passion, " true love really consists in loving in a temperate and musical spirit that which is orderly and beautiful." " And," says Socrates to Glaucon, " in the city we are founding you will lay down a law that the lover may kiss his beloved, may frequent his society and embrace him, as though he were his son, if he so persuade him, for beauty's sake, but in all else his relations with the person he affects shall be such that they shall never be suspected of going beyond this. If he acts otherwise, he shall draw upon himself the reproach of bad taste and vulgarity."

The government of Plato's ideal commonwealth is thus to be carried out by a particularly gifted class of men and women who have renounced property and material privileges, who marry and procreate in the best interests of the state, who scorn passions and individuality of feeling. But even among the guardians there are some who are more fitted to govern than others. Those who have a more philosophical nature will be the rulers while the others, who are less intelligent but more inclined to violent sports, will become the auxiliaries or soldiers and will form a regular, professional army :

" Our city will need to be still greater, and by no small amount either, but by a whole army. It will defend all the substance and wealth we have described, and will march out and fight the invaders."

" Why," he said, " are they not capable of doing that themselves?"

" Certainly not," I said, " if you and the rest of us were right in the principle we agreed upon when we were shaping the city. I think we agreed, if you remember, that it was impossible for one man to work well at many crafts."

" True," he said.

" Well," I said, " does not the business of war seem a matter of craftsmanship?"

" Yes, certainly," he said.

" Then ought we to be more solicitous for the craft of shoemaking than for the craft of war?"

" By no means."

" But did we not forbid our shoemaker to attempt to be at the same time a farmer or a weaver or house-builder? He was to be a shoemaker only, in order that our shoemaking work might be well done. So with all the others : we gave each man one trade, that for which nature had fitted him. Nothing else was to occupy his time, but he was to spend his life working at that, using all his opportunities to the best advantage and letting none

go by. And is not efficiency in war more important than anything else? Or is it such a simple profession that a farmer or a
shoemaker, or any other craftsman, can be a soldier in the
intervals of his craft, though no one in the world would find that
practice in his leisure moments or anything short of studying the
game from his youth, would make him a good draught or dice
player? Is he to take up a shield, or any other of the weapons
and tools of war, and in a single day to become an efficient
antagonist in a heavy-armed engagement or in any other kind of
battle, though the mere handling of any other tools will never
make a craftsman or an athlete, and though tools are useless to
the man who has not acquired the special knowledge and gone
through the proper training for their use?"

There is a passage, at the beginning of *The Republic*, which seems
to indicate that Plato believed that in a truly ideal city there
would be no army, for people would lead a simple existence and
would not require to increase their territory to satisfy their needs.
It is the desire for luxury which creates wars. Socrates has been
explaining that cities originate because by nature no man is
self-sufficient and he has therefore to associate with other men
who have the same needs but different capacities to supply these
needs. These men will lead a leisurely and peaceful life :

" Let us consider what will be the manner of life of men so
equipped. Will they not spend their time in the production of
corn and wine and clothing and shoes? And they will build
themselves houses ; in summer they will generally work without
their coats and shoes, but in winter they will be well clothed and
shod. For food they will make meal from their barley and flour
from their wheat, and kneading and baking them they will heap
their noble scones and loaves on reeds or fresh leaves, and lying on
couches of bryony and myrtle boughs will feast with their children, drink wine after their repast, crown their heads with garlands,
and sing hymns to the gods. So they will live with one another
in happiness, not begetting children above their means, and
guarding against the danger of poverty or war."

Here Glaucon interrupted and said : " Apparently you give
your men dry bread to feast on."

"You are right," I said ; " I forgot that they would have a
relish with it. They will have salt and olives and cheese, and
they will have boiled dishes with onions and such vegetables as
one gets in the country. And I expect we must allow them a
desert of figs, and peas and beans, and they will roast myrtle

berries and acorns at the fire, and drink their wine in moderation. Leading so peaceful and healthy a life they will naturally attain to a good old age, and at death leave their children to live as they have done."

" Why," said Glaucon, " if you had been founding a city of pigs, Socrates, this is just how you would have fattened them."

" Well, Glaucon, how must they live?"

" In an ordinary decent manner," he said. " If they are not to be miserable, I think they must have couches to lie on and tables to eat from, and the ordinary dishes and dessert of modern life."

" Very well," I said, " I understand. We are considering, apparently, the making not of a city merely, but of a luxurious city. And perhaps there is no harm in doing so. From that kind, too, we shall soon learn, if we examine it, how justice and injustice arise in cities. I, for my part, think that the city I have described is the true one, what we may call the city of health. But if you wish, let us also inspect a city which is suffering from inflammation. There is no reason why we should not. Well, then, for some people the arrangements we have made will not be enough. The mode of living will not satisfy them. They shall have couches and tables and other furniture ; rich dishes, too, and fragrant oils and perfumes, and courtesans and sweetmeats, and many varieties of each. Then again we must make more than a bare provision for those necessities we mentioned at the first, houses and clothes and shoes. We must start painting and embroidery, and collect gold and ivory, and so on, must we not?"

" Yes," he said.

" Then we must make our city larger. For the healthy city will not now suffice. We need one swollen in size, and full of a multitude of things which necessity would not introduce into cities. There will be all kinds of hunters and there will be the imitators ; one crowd of imitators in figure and colour, and another of imitators in music ; poets and their servants, rhapsodists, actors, dancers and theatrical agents ; the makers of all kinds of articles, of those used for women's adornment, for example. Then, too, we shall need more servants ; or do you think we can do without footmen, wet-nurses, dry-nurses, lady's maids, barbers, and cooks and confectioners, besides? Then we shall want swineherds too ; we had none in our former city— there was no need—but we shall need them along with all the others for this city. And we shall need great quantities of all kinds of cattle if people are to eat them. Shall we not?"

" Surely."

" Then if we lead this kind of life we shall require doctors far more often then we should have done in the first city?"

" Certainly."

" Then I dare say even the land which was sufficient to support the first population will be now insufficient and too small?"

" Yes," he said.

" Then if we are to have enough for pasture and ploughland, we must take a slice from our neighbours' territory. And they will want to do the same to ours, if they also overpass the bounds of necessity and plunge into reckless pursuit of wealth?"

" Yes, that must happen, Socrates," he said.

" Then shall we go to war at that point, Glaucon, or what will happen?"

" We will go to war," he said.

It is curious to see that, though Socrates seems to be reluctant to " inspect a city which is suffering from an inflamed constitution," he does not attempt to persuade his listeners to give up their desire for a more comfortable life, and accepts its consequences, which are war and the need for a permanent army.

Plato deals at great length with the education of the guardians and indeed with education in general ; as it has been pointed out, *The Republic* is, among other things, a treatise on education. Education is divided, in the traditional Greek manner, between gymnastic, which includes military training, and music. Of music, Lowes Dickinson remarks, " We have to remind ourselves that the term in Greek was far more comprehensive than it is with us, and included all moral, aesthetic, and intellectual culture." The education of the future ruler, however, must go beyond gymnastic and music, his mind must be trained to think and rise above the senses by the study of mathematical sciences, so that he will then be able to devote himself to the study of real philosophy, which is called dialectic :

" Calculation, then, and geometry, and all those preliminary studies which must pave the way for dialectic, should be set before our guardians when they are boys, and in such a fashion as will not seem compulsory."

" Why so?"

" Because," I said, " the free man should learn no study under bondage. And while enforced bodily labours do no harm to the body, study forced on the mind will not abide there."

" True," he said.

" Then, my excellent friend, train your children in their studies not by compulsion but by games, and you will be better able to see the natural abilities of each."

" What you say is reasonable," he said.

" Do you remember," I said, " that we declared that even in battles the children must be taken on horseback to look on, and must be taken near the fighting line if safety allowed, and have their taste of blood like puppies?"

" I remember," he said.

" Then he," I said, " who in all those toils and studies and alarms proves himself the readiest on every occasion will be put on a select list."

" At what age?" he asked.

" When they are released from the necessary gymnastics," I answered. " For in the two or three years occupied in those it will be impossible to do anything else. For weariness and sleep are foes to study. And at the same time the proficiency shown in gymnastics will be one of our tests, and that not the least important."

" Surely," he said.

" Then after this," I said, " from their twentieth year those who have been selected shall have special privileges, and the studies which they have come across at random in their education as children, they must now bring together so that they will have a general view of their kinship with one another and with the nature of Being."

" Yes," he said, " such knowledge alone is abiding in those who possess it."

" And it is also," I said, " the best test of a dialectical or non-dialectical nature. For the power of seeing things as a whole distinguishes the dialectician."

" I agree," he said.

" Then you will have to watch these tests," I said, " and see who best come up to our requirements, and are persevering in their studies, and persevering in battle and the other duties the law imposes upon them ; and then when they are past thirty you must select those out of ' the selected,' and give them greater privileges, and by testing their power in dialectic examine which of them can do without his eyes and his other senses and approach in truth to real being."

" Then for the acquisition of dialectic, is it sufficient if the student perseveres in constant and intense study to the exclusion of everything else, in the same way as he was disciplined in bodily exercises, but for twice the number of years?"

" Do you mean six or four?" he asked.
" It is of no consequence," I said. " Say five. And after that you will have to force them down into the cave again, and compel them to take command in war and in such offices as pertain to the young, in order that they may not come short of others in practical experience. And still in these pursuits also you must test them and see whether they abide steadfastly every kind of temptation, or whether they give way in anything."
" What time do you give for this?" he asked.
"Fifteen years," I said. " And when they are fifty, those who have come safely through, and have always triumphed throughout in word and deed, must at last be taken to the goal; they must be compelled to look upon that which gives light to all, and turn the gleam of their soul upon it and see the real good; then using that as the pattern for the rest of their life, they must take their turn in ordering city and individuals and their own lives ; the most of their time they will spend in philosophy, but when their turn comes, they will endure the toil of directing politics and being rulers for the sake of their city, regarding such action not as anything noble but as a compulsion laid upon them; and so each generation, having trained up others like to themselves whom they can leave to be the city's guardians, will depart to the islands of the blest and dwell there. The city shall establish monuments and sacrifices to them, if the Pythian allows, honouring them as demi-gods, if not as happy and divine."
" You have finished off your ruling men most beautifully, Socrates, like a sculptor," he said.
" And the ruling women, also, Glaucon," I replied; "for don't imagine that anything I have said applies any more to men than to women, so long as we have women of adequate natural gifts."

We have, until now, dealt almost exclusively with the selection, the education and the institutions governing the guardians whose task is to rule and defend the city. We have said nothing about the questions of production and distribution, about the peasants, artisans and tradesmen without whom the city could not live. Plato is little concerned with them, for he thought that if a state had a good government the rest could take care of itself. *The Republic* is more the description of an ideal ruling class than of an ideal commonwealth, for it says little about the producers, who seem to be left to their old institutions. It is the task of the philosophers to legislate about matters concerning the " common people":

" Then in heaven's name," I said, " what of those market troubles about contracts which the various classes make with one another in the market, and, if you please, about the contracts of craftsmen; what of libels, assaults, the bringing of lawsuits, and the empanelling of juries, and all such exaction or payment of dues as may be necessary in markets and harbours, and, in a word, all market, city, and harbour regulations, and the like— are we to venture to legislate in these matters?"

" No," he said, " in these matters there is no need to dictate to true men. They will easily find for themselves most of the legislation required."

One searches in vain in *The Republic* for some indication of how the class of producers are to govern their lives ; there are only a few hints, which indicate that private property has not been abolished and that monogamy and family life are allowed to exist in the old way. Aristotle seems to have been amply justified in criticising Plato for having determined nothing about the main body of the State which is composed, not of the guardians, but of the mass of the other citizens. These citizens, according to Plato, would have left all the matters of the State in the hands of the Guardians, in exchange for whose administrative work they would provide the bare necessities of existence.

From a Marxist point of view it would seem paradoxical that Plato should have given no economic power to his Guardians. They possess no property, are not allowed to touch gold and silver, and if they are paid in kind it is clear that they are badly paid, for they are not allowed to indulge in luxury. The producers on the other hand have all the economic power, though they are deprived of all political power. " The necessary consequence," says Aristotle, " is that there will be two States in one and two States mutually hostile," and enlarging on this view Alexander Gray remarks : " An age which has been, and is being increasingly taught the importance of economic power, will have little difficulty in deciding which of the two mutually hostile States will enter the contest with most advantage."

However unrealistic Plato's division between economic and political power may appear at first sight, it would be a mistake to think that the Guardians are completely at the mercy of the rest of the citizens, who would be in the position to starve them if they had a mind to do so. If the Guardians do not possess economic

power they have military power, being the only citizens trained
for war. It is not difficult to foresee that if the husbandmen
refused to supply them with food the Auxiliaries would soon force
them to do so. There are several passages which show that
Plato did not imagine that the affairs of his ideal republic would
always run smoothly, and that the Auxiliaries would have to
defend the State not only against foreign aggression but internal
revolts. For example, when the Guardians examine which is the
best place in the city for establishing their camp, they select a
site from which they can not only repel attacks from without
but also " control any disobedience to the law within the city. . . ."
  One must also remember that, in the eyes of the people, the
Guardians are endowed with a kind of divine power, they are
made of gold, they are a chosen people. That such a myth could
be believed is shown by the fact that for centuries Kings were
thought to be the representatives of God upon earth. Plato has
clearly perceived that a State could be created by placing the
productive classes under the tutelage of a caste owing its power to
military and religious domination. Throughout history one
sees that the existence of a State implies the division of society
into classes, but that the ruling class does not necessarily owe its
power to its economic wealth but to an ideology which clothes it
with a superior power, maintained by the use of armed forces.
  Plato has been described as being " in some respects the greatest
of revolutionaries, in others the greatest of reactionaries". It
would be perhaps more exact to say that he is the greatest ex-
ponent of totalitarianism. Though his ideal state is ruled by
philosophers, there is no more freedom in it then if it were ruled by
gauleiters. In fact there is less freedom, because philosophers can
crush freedom much more effectively, being more able to detect
any non-conformist idea. They are prepared to allow a certain
latitude in matters of little importance such as trade, but in
matters of art and education, that is to say, in all that relates to
intellectual freedom, they are completely ruthless. No innovation
can be introduced in teaching because it would be a subversive
influence :

  " The overseers of the city must devote themselves to this
principle, preserving it from secret destruction, and guarding it
with all care—the principle, namely, that there shall be no
innovation of the established order in gymnastic and music. They

must watch over this with all possible care, fearing when they hear
such words as

> For men more praise
> That which is newest of the minstrel's lays

lest, perchance, someone thinks the poet means, not new songs,
but a new fashion of songs, and praises that. But he must
neither praise such a novelty nor understand this to be the poet's
meaning. He must beware of changing to a new kind of music,
for the change always involves far-reaching danger. Any alteration in the modes of music is always followed by alteration in the
most fundamental laws of the state. So says Damon, and I
believe him."

" You may put me down also as a believer," said Adeimantus.

" Then," I said, " here it would seem, in music, the guardians
must erect their guard-house."

" The first beginnings of lawlessness in music are very hard to
detect," he said.

" Yes, it is looked on as an amusement which can do no harm."

" All it does," he said, "is gradually to establish and quietly to
insinuate itself into manners and customs. From these it issues
in greater force and penetrates men's mutual dealings ; from
mutual dealings it advances, with the utmost insolence, Socrates,
to laws and constitutions, till in the end it overturns all things
public and private."

In the Republic of Plato all music, literature, architecture and
painting must conform to certain ethical standards. Art ceases
to be the expression of individual personality and is made to
serve only the interests of the State. It is the State which
determines what is good and evil, what is beautiful or ugly.
Musical instruments and rhythms which "express meanness and
pride, or madness or other evils" must be forbidden. Poets must
be compelled " to impress upon their poems only the image of
the good or not to make poetry " and if they do not conform they
must be asked to leave the city. Painting, weaving, embroidery,
architecture and other crafts must all show good rhythm and
good harmony, but by this Plato obviously means the approved
rhythm, the approved harmony.

Plato saw very clearly the relation between art and ethics or,
as we would say now, art and politics. Though he claims to be
defending truth and beauty it is clear that he wants to preserve
the stability of the State from the subversive influence of free art.

The architecture of a house as well as a poem can manifest certain tendencies which he called good or evil, that is to say, conformist or revolutionary.

With the rise of the modern totalitarian states we have become familiar with the view that the artists may be considered as dangerous enemies of the state, not merely because of the ideas they express but because of the form which their art may take. In recent years works of art have been destroyed or banned because they were considered a manifestation of bourgeois decadence, and writers, poets, and musicians have been "purged" for being counter-revolutionary or petit-bourgeois. It is not an accident that the description of Plato's Republic should begin and end with an attack on the freedom of the artist, which is really an attack on the freedom of thought, for there were no books or Press in Plato's time and men's ideas could only manifest themselves through their teaching or their literary and artistic productions. It is always the first task of every totalitarian government to suppress that freedom and to try to make the artist into a tool of the state with the result that, under totalitarian régimes, art invariably stagnates or degenerates. Art can only reach its highest expression when it is allowed maximum freedom, as can be seen by the wealth and the diversity of the artistic productions of Ancient Greece. If, instead of being a loose federation of free cities, Greece had been a totalitarian republic such as Plato imagined, Homer, Sophocles, Aristophanes and Plato himself would not have been able to produce their masterpieces.

This would in itself be sufficient to make us hope fervently that a system of society such as the one described in *The Republic* shall never become a reality. But the lack of intellectual freedom is not the only unattractive feature of Plato's ideal commonwealth. The idea that each man is gifted for one task and one task only, leading to the artificial division of the citizens into producers, soldiers and rulers, is completely divorced from the most elementary psychological observation. Some men are certainly more gifted for certain tasks than others, but the same man may be able to carry out several activities equally efficiently, and his many-sided interests generally result in the enrichment of his personality. Nor can Plato convince us that *by nature* some men are born to rule and others to be ruled, for throughout history, we find examples of flourishing societies where the affairs of the community were carried out by all its members. And one cannot but applaud Erasmus who, under the mask of Folly, pokes fun at Plato for putting so much faith in the rule of philosophers :

And next to these is cry'd up, forsooth, that goodly sentence of Plato's : " Happy is that Commonwealth where a Philosopher is Prince, or whose Prince is addicted to Philosophy." When yet if ye consult Historians, you'll find no Princes more pestilent to the Commonwealth than where the Empire has fallen to some smatterer in Philosophy or one given to Letters. To the truth of which I think the Catoes give sufficient credit ; of whom the one was ever disturbing the peace of the Commonwealth with his hair-brain'd accusations ; the other, while he too wisely vindicated its liberty, quite overthrew it. Add to these the Bruti, Cassii, nay Cicero himself, that was no less pernicious to the Commonwealth of Rome than was Demosthenes to that of Athens. Besides M. Antoninus (that I may give ye one instance that there was once a good Emperour, for with much ado I can make it out) was become burthensome and hated of his subjects, upon no other score that he was so great a Philosopher. But admitting him good, he did the Commonwealth more hurt in leaving behind him such a Son as he did, than ever he did it good by his own Government. For these kind of Men that are so given up to the study of Wisdome are generally most unfortunate, but chiefly in their children ; Nature, it seems, so providently ordering it, lest this mischief of Wisdome should spread farther among mankind. For which reason 'tis manifest why Cicero's Son was so degenerate, and that wise Socrate's children, as one has well observ'd, were more like their Mother than their Father, that is to say, Fools.

One may also question Plato's idea that family institutions cannot be reconciled with the existence of a totalitarian state, in view of the observations of sociologists, which show that in primitive societies where the state has not made its appearance family institutions are generally non-existent. The family, far from being inimical to the state, is necessary to its stability, for children who are brought up to respect the authority of the father will accept more readily the authority of the state. Modern totalitarian régimes which had begun by trying to break up family life, soon re-instated family institutions, realising that they offered a better guarantee to the security of the state.

If Plato seems to have been obsessed by the fear that riches, or even mere comfort, may corrupt his Guardians he was completely unaware that, in the words of Lord Acton, " power corrupts, absolute power corrupts absolutely." There is nothing, in his ideal republic, which provides a check on the authority of the rulers and we do not see what would prevent his Auxiliaries from behaving like the Spartans who, according to Plutarch, took great delight in butchering their slaves.

It is rather puzzling that Plato's *Republic* should have aroused such admiration and, paradoxically, it has been chiefly admired by men whose principles were completely opposed to those of Plato. It has been praised by poets who would have been banned from it, by revolutionaries who fought for the abolition of serfdom and seemed to have been unaware that Plato's régime was based on slavery; it has been extolled by democrats in spite of the fact that one can hardly conceive a more despotic rule than that of the Guardians; it has been praised as an example of a communist society, when it is clear that the community of goods only applies to the ruling class and that private property is concentrated in the hands of a class, which, contrary to Marxist doctrines, does not hold any political power.

The enthusiasm which many enlightened thinkers have shown for Plato's *Republic* can be explained partly by the fact that they attributed to him ideas which they wished he had held, and partly because, having little experience of totalitarian states, they could not visualise their disadvantages. Unfortunately for us, we can have few illusions as to the merits of a totalitarian state, however wise it claims to be, and we begin to feel that each of us may be his own best guardian.

PLUTARCH
Life of Lycurgus

SPARTA rivals Athens in its influence on utopian thought, and just as Athens has come to be identified with Plato's Republic, Sparta has been seen chiefly through the idealised description, written by Plutarch in the first century B.C., of Lycurgus who, according to tradition, was the lawgiver of Sparta. Plutarch himself says that nothing " certain and uncontroverted is known,

least of all the times in which he lived," and that it is even possible
that there were two Lycurguses in Sparta, at different times.
The institutions attributed to this semi-mythical figure lasted,
according to Plutarch, for five hundred years.

However, whether Plutarch's account is based on historical
facts, or whether it is his own creation, is of little importance here.
We are merely concerned with the influence of the laws and
institutions he described on later ideal constitutions and utopias ;
and that influence could not have been greater had Lycurgus
really lived.

When Lycurgus assumed the direction of the affairs of Sparta
he had spent many years travelling in Crete, Asia and Egypt,
where we are told that he had acquired political knowledge in a
scientific manner : " just as physicians compare bodies that are
weak and sickly with the healthy and robust." He was furthermore in the fortunate position of being supported both by the
Lacedaemonians, who were dissatisfied with the rule of the
Kings, and by the Kings themselves who hoped that " in his
presence they would experience less insolence amongst the
people." They soon discovered that he was not a mild peace-
maker or a timid reformer, but that he was bent on carrying out
a complete revolution, for he believed : " that a partial change,
and the introduction of some laws, would be of no sort of
advantage : but, as in the case of a body diseased and full of
bad humors, whose temperament is to be corrected and new
formed by medicines, it was necessary to begin a new regimen."

His seizure of power followed the now familiar pattern of a
putsch, except for the consultation of the oracle at Delphi
(dictators nowadays generally consult some " foreign power ").
He ordered thirty of the principal citizens to appear armed in
the market-place at break of day, " to strike terror into such as
might desire to oppose him." He succeeded in intimidating the
kings who gave him their support and he immediately formed a
senate composed of twenty-eight members (the men who had
assisted him in his enterprise, i.e. his Party) who, together with
the two kings, formed a body of thirty members. Later, to fill
up any vacancy " he ordered the most worthy men to be selected,
of those that were full threescore old " and these were elected by
the assembled people.

The senate, sharing " in the power of the kings, too imperious and unrestrained before, and having equal authority with them, was the means of keeping them within the bounds of moderation, and highly contributed to the preservation of the state. For before it had been veering and unsettled, sometimes inclining to arbitrary power, and sometimes towards a pure democracy ; but this establishment of a senate, an intermediate body, like ballast, kept it in just equilibrium, and put it in a safe posture : the twenty-eight senators adhering to the kings, whenever they saw the people too encroaching, and, on the other hand, supporting the people, when the kings attempted to make themselves absolute." We are not told how the senate was endowed with such admirable impartiality.

The senate was assisted by the assembly of the people, which had no right of debate but was invested with the power to ratify and reject what might be proposed to them by the senate and the kings. Lycurgus (via the Delphic oracle) ordered that the people should have their assemblies in the open ; he thought halls of " no advantage to their councils, but rather a disservice ; as they distracted attention, and turned it upon trifles, on observing the statues and pictures, the splendid roofs, and every other theatrical ornament."

Having settled the question of government, Lycurgus turned his attention to social problems. He was struck by the inequality between rich and poor, and determined to carry out a redistribution of the land. This inequality, as we shall see, shocked him more for political reasons than for humanitarian ones : property exerted an evil influence on the rich and had a disturbing effect on the stability of the state. This attitude is very remote from that of modern socialists, who are more concerned with the empty stomachs of the poor than with the corrupting influence of riches on the wealthy. But Lycurgus, in spite of those socialists who want to see in him an ancestor, was not the defender of the dispossessed, the slaves or helots, and his redistribution of wealth was carried out *within* the ruling class. He aimed at bringing the " small bourgeoisie " and the " capitalist class " to the same level so as to create a united, homogeneous body, and not at abolishing classes or castes. If this is overlooked the following account acquires a strong communistic flavour :

A second and bolder political enterprise of Lycurgus was a new division of the lands. For he found a prodigious inequality, the city overcharged with many indigent persons, who had no land, and the wealth centred in the hands of a few. Determined, therefore, to root out the evils of insolence, envy, avarice, and luxury, and those distempers of a state still more inveterate and fatal, I mean poverty and riches, he persuaded them to cancel all former divisions of land, and to make new ones, in such a manner that they might be perfectly equal in their possessions and way of living. Hence, if they were ambitious of distinction they might seek it in virtue, as no other difference was left between them but that which arises from the dishonour of base actions and the praise of good ones. His proposal was put in practice. He made nine thousand lots for the territory of Sparta, which he distributed among so many citizens, and thirty thousand for the inhabitants of the rest of Laconia. But some say he made only six thousand shares for the city, and that Polydorus added three thousand afterwards; others, that Polydorus doubled the number appointed by Lycurgus, which were only four thousand five hundred. Each lot was capable of producing (one year with another) seventy bushels of grain for each man, and twelve for each woman, besides a quantity of wine and oil in proportion. Such a provision they thought sufficient for health and a good habit of body, and they wanted nothing more. A story goes of our legislator, that some time after returning from a journey through the fields just reaped, and seeing the shocks standing parallel and equal, he smiled, and said to some that were by, " How like is Laconia to an estate newly divided among many brothers!"

Lycurgus then proceeded to divide movable property but here he was less successful in " persuading " the Lacedaemonians, and he had to adopt indirect measures which rendered money more or less of no value :

First he stopped the currency of the gold and silver coin, and ordered that they should make use of iron money only, then to a great quantity and weight of this he assigned but a small value ; so that to lay up ten *minae*, a whole room was required, and to remove it, nothing less than a yoke of oxen. When this became current, many kinds of injustice ceased in Lacedaemon. Who would steal or take a bribe, who would defraud or rob, when he could not conceal the booty ; when he could neither be dignified by the possession of it, nor if cut in pieces be served by its use? For we are told that when hot, they quenched it in vinegar, to make it brittle and unmalleable, and consequently unfit for any other service. In the next place, he excluded unprofitable and superfluous arts ; indeed, if he had not done this, most of them would have fallen of themselves, when the new money took place, as the manufactures could not be disposed of. Their iron coin would not pass in the rest of Greece, but was ridiculed and despised ; so that the Spartans had no means of purchasing any foreign or curious wares ; nor did any merchant ship unlade in their harbours. There were not even to be found in all their country either sophists, wandering fortune-tellers, keepers of infamous houses, or dealers in gold and silver trinkets, because there was no money. Thus luxury, losing by degrees the means that cherished and supported it, died away of itself ; even they who had great possessions, had no advantage from them, since they could not be displayed in public, but must lie useless, in unregarded repositories. Hence it was, that excellent workmanship was shown in their useful and necessary furniture, as beds, chairs, and tables ; and the Lacedaemonian cup called *cothon*, as Critias informs us, was highly valued, particularly in campaigns: for the water, which must then of necessity be drank, though it would often otherwise offend the sight, had its muddiness concealed by the colour of the cup, and the thick part stopping at the shelving brim, it came clearer to the lips. Of these improvements the lawgiver was the cause ; for the workmen having no more employment in matters of mere curiosity, showed the excellence of their art in necessary things.

Plutarch's remarks on the Lacedaemonians' cup have a very modern ring and could almost serve as a definition of " functional art.' There was, however, little opportunity for artistic expression in Sparta, and the following ordinance of Lycurgus gives an idea of the severity of that Spartan austerity which has become proverbial :

Another ordinance levelled against magnificence and expense directed that the ceilings of houses should be wrought with no tool but the axe and the doors with nothing but the saw. For, as Epaminondas is reported to have said afterwards, of his table, " Treason lurks not under such a dinner," so Lycurgus perceived before him, that such a house admits of no luxury and needless splendour. Indeed, no man could be so absurd as to bring into a dwelling so homely and simple, bedsteads with silver feet, purple coverlets, golden cups, and a train of expense that follows these : but all would necessarily have the bed suitable to the room, the coverlet of the bed and the rest of their utensils and furniture to that.

Austerity is a familiar feature of most utopias, and we have
seen that Plato considers temperance one of the essential virtues
of the citizens of his republic. In Sparta, however, austerity was
not merely welcomed on ethical grounds ; it was a necessity, for
the Lacedaemonians lived in a constant state of war or readiness
for war. Anticipating modern dictatorships, Lycurgus realised
that a dictatorial régime can survive only if war is made a
permanent institution. The sharing of the land, the levelling of
incomes were not only necessary to a war economy ; they were
also designed to keep up war morale. The expediency of these
measures has been tested again in recent years when we have
seen conservative statesmen adopt regulations enforcing a
certain equality of responsibilities and sacrifices, without which
war morale could not have been maintained. The only difference
is that Sparta carried out her conscription of persons and wealth,
her rationing and common feeding with a thoroughness which
has probably never been equalled by any country at war.

There seems to have been a limit even to the patience of the
Lacedaemonians, and they revolted when Lycurgus obliged them
to take their repasts in common. We see that here again practical
considerations were of secondary importance :

Desirous to complete the conquest of luxury, and exterminate
the love of riches, he introduced a third institution, which was
wisely enough and ingeniously contrived. This was the use of
public tables, where all were to eat in common of the same meat,
and such kinds of it as were appointed by law. At the same time
they were forbidden to eat at home, upon expensive couches and
tables, to call in the assistance of butchers and cooks, or to fatten
like voracious animals in private. For so not only their manners
would be corrupted, but their bodies disordered ; abandoned to
all manner of sensuality and dissoluteness, they would require
long sleep, warm baths, and the same indulgence as in perpetual
sickness. To effect this was certainly very great ; but it was
greater still, to secure riches from rapine and from envy, as Theo-
phrastus expresses it, or rather by their eating in common, and
by the frugality of their table, to take from riches their very being.
For what use or enjoyment of them, what peculiar display of
magnificence could there be, where the poor man went to the same
refreshment with the rich? Hence the observation, that it was
only at Sparta where Plutus (according to the proverb) was kept
blind, and like an image, destitute of life or motion. It must

further be observed, that they had not the privilege to eat at
home, and so to come without appetite to the public repast ;
they made a point of it to observe any one that did not eat and
drink with them, and to reproach him as an intemperate and
effeminate person that was sick of the common diet.

There were fifteen persons to a table, or a few more or less.
Each of them was obliged to bring in monthly a bushel of meal,
eight gallons of wine, five pounds of cheese, two pounds and a
half of figs, and a little money to buy flesh and fish. If any of
them happened to offer a sacrifice of first fruits, or to kill
venison, he sent a part of it to the public table: for after a sacrifice
or hunting, he was at liberty to sup at home: but the rest were
to appear at the usual place. . . . Children also were introduced
at these public tables, as so many schools of sobriety. There
they heard discourses concerning government, and were instructed in the most liberal breeding.

The same thoroughness and disregard for people's individual
freedom were present in all of Lycurgus's laws, which accompanied the citizen from the cradle (and even before) to the grave.
Lycurgus began the education of youth " at the very source,
taking into consideration their conception and birth." For this
reason marriage was carried out, not according to the inclinations
of the individual, but in the interest of the state. Although the
idea that the love of the family should not supersede the love of
the state is not expressed as clearly in the *Life of Lycurgus* as it was
to be later by Campanella in the *City of the Sun*, it is evident that
the unity of the citizens must not be broken by too strong ties
between men and women. Just as envy is eliminated by the
levelling of fortunes, jealousy is prevented by allowing husbands
to share their wives with men capable of producing healthy
offspring. And even after marriage the men lead a batchelor's
life, sleeping in dormitories and meeting their wives only for
sexual intercourse.

This is how Lycurgus justified " extra-marital " relations :

When he had established a proper regard to modesty and
decorum with respect to marriage, he was equally studious to
drive from that state the vain and womanish passion of jealousy ;
by making it quite as reputable to have children in common with
persons of merit, as to avoid all offensive freedom in their own
behaviour to their wives. He laughed at those who revenge with
wars and bloodshed the communication of a married woman's

favours; and allowed, that if a man in years should have a young wife, he might introduce to her some handsome and honest young man, whom he most approved of, and when she had a child of this generous race, bring it up as his own. On the other hand, he allowed, that if a man of character should entertain a passion for a married woman on account of her modesty and the beauty of her children, he might treat with her husband for admission to her company, that so planting in a beauty-bearing soil, he might produce excellent children, the congenial offspring of excellent parents. For, in the first place, Lycurgus considered children, not so much the property of their parents as of the state ; and therefore he would not have them begot by ordinary persons, but by the best men in it. In the next place, he observed the vanity and absurdity of other nations, where people study to have their horses and dogs of the finest breed they can procure either by interest or money ; and yet keep their wives shut up, that they may have children by none but themselves, though they may happen to be doting, decrepit or infirm. As if children, when sprung from a bad stock, and consequently good for nothing, were no detriment to those whom they belong to, and who have the trouble of bringing them up, nor any advantage, when well descended and of a generous disposition. These regulations tend-ing to secure a healthy offspring, and consequently beneficial to the state, were so far from encouraging that licentiousness of the women which prevailed afterwards, that adultery was not known amongst them.

If Lycurgus discouraged love, as we understand it, between men and women he did, on the other hand, take great pains to see that women should be sexually attractive to men, and instituted public dances and other exercises of naked young maidens in the presence of the young men, not only " to take away the excessive tenderness and delicacy of the sex, the con-sequence of a recluse life," but also because these exercises were incentive to marriage. If this failed to have the desired effect on the young Spartans and they persisted in refusing to get married, " some marks of infamy were set upon those that continued bachelors, for they were not permitted to see these exercises of the naked virgins ; and the magistrates commanded them to march naked round the market-place in the winter, and to sing a song composed against themselves, which expressed how justly they were punished for their disobedience of the laws."

But even when marriage took place, Lycurgus did not leave

the union to follow its natural course, but laid down an elaborate routine :

In their marriages, the bridegroom carried off the bride by violence ; and she was never chosen in a tender age, but when she had arrived at full maturity. Then the woman that had the direction of the wedding, cut the bride's hair close to the skin, dressed her in man's clothes, laid her upon a mattrass, and left her in the dark. The bridegroom, neither oppressed with wine nor enervated with luxury, but perfectly sober, as always having supped at the common table, went in privately, untied her girdle, and carried her to another bed. Having stayed there a short time, he modestly retired to his usual apartment, to sleep with the other young men ; and observed the same conduct afterwards, spending the day with his companions, and reposing himself with them in the night, nor even visiting his bride but with great caution and apprehensions of being discovered by the rest of the family ; the bride at the same time exerted all her art to contrive convenient opportunities for their private meetings. And this they did not for a short time only, but some of them even had children before they had an interview with their wives in the daytime. This kind of commerce not only exercised their temperance and chastity, but kept their bodies fruitful, and the first ardour of their love fresh and unabated ; for as they were not satiated like those that are always with their wives, there still was place for unextinguished desire.

We see that Lycurgus attached more importance to regulating the consummation of the marriage than to the choice of the partners. Unlike Plato, he seemed to have allowed his citizens a certain latitude in deciding with whom they could produce beautiful children. If they happened to be mistaken, the fault could always be rectified for " it was not left to the father to rear what children he pleased, but he was obliged to carry the child to a place called Lesche, to be examined by the most ancient men of the tribe, who were assembled there. If it was strong and well-proportioned, they gave orders for its education, and assigned it one of the nine thousand acres of land ; but if it was weakly and deformed, they ordered it to be thrown into the place called Apothetae, which is a deep cavern near the mountain Taygetus ; concluding that its life could be no advantage either to itself or to the public, since nature had not given it at first any strength or goodness of constitution."

Parents were not, of course, at liberty to educate their children
as they pleased :

As soon as they were seven years old, Lycurgus ordered them
to be enrolled in companies, where they were all kept under the
same order and discipline, and had their exercises and recreations
in common. He who showed the most conduct and courage
amongst them, was made captain of the company. The rest
kept their eyes upon him, obeyed his orders, and bore with
patience the punishments he inflicted ; so that their whole
education was an exercise of obedience. The old men were
present at their diversions, and often suggested some occasion of
dispute or quarrel, that they might observe with exactness the
spirit of each, and their firmness in battle.

As for learning, they had just what was absolutely necessary.
All the rest of their education was calculated to make them subject
to command, to endure labour, to fight and conquer. They
added, therefore, to their discipline, as they advance in age ;
cutting their hair very close, making them go barefoot, and play,
for the most part, quite naked. At twelve years of age, their under
garment was taken away, and but one upper one a year allowed
them. Hence they were necessarily dirty in their persons, and
not indulged the great favour of baths, and oils, except on some
particular days of the year. They slept in companies, on beds
made of the tops of reeds, which they gathered with their own
hands, without knives, and brought from the banks of the
Eurotas. In winter they were permitted to add a little thistle-
down, as that seemed to have some warmth in it.

The education of elder boys was more ruthless, but not unlike
that of some English public schools :

At this age, the most distinguished amongst them became the
favourite companions of the elder ; and the old men attended
more constantly their places of exercise, observing their trials of
strength and wit, not slightly and in a cursory manner, but as
their fathers, guardians, and governors : so that there was
neither time nor place where persons were wanting to instruct
and chastise them. One of the best and ablest men of the city
was, moreover, appointed inspector of the youth : and he gave
the command of each company to the discreetest and most
spirited of those called Irens. An Iren was one that had been two
years out of the class of boys : a Melliren one of the oldest lads.
This Iren, then, a youth twenty years old, gives orders to those
under his command in their little battles, and has them to serve

him at his house. He sends the oldest of them to fetch wood, and the younger to gather pot-herbs : these they steal where they can find them, either slily getting into gardens, or else craftily and warily creeping to the common tables. But if any one be caught, he is severely flogged for negligence or want of dexterity. They steal, too, whatever victuals they possibly can, ingeniously contriving to do it when persons are asleep, or keep but indifferent watch. If they are discovered, they are punished not only with whipping, but with hunger. Indeed, their supper is but slender at all times, that, to fence against want, they may be forced to exercise their courage and address.

The education of women was not neglected, but was directed to improve their bodies rather than their minds : " He ordered the virgins to exercise themselves in running, wrestling and throwing quoits and darts ; that their bodies being strong and vigorous, the children afterwards produced from them might be the same ; and that, thus fortified by exercise, they might the better support the pangs of child-birth, and be delivered with safety." They also praised or criticised the men, and we are told that " they were not excluded from their share of bravery and honour." There is, however, no indication that they took a direct part in the administration of the state, as in Plato's *Republic*, and it seems that the great power they had acquired in the past, on account of the frequent expeditions of their husbands, was curbed rather than increased.

There is little to say about the organisation of work in Sparta, for the Lacedaemonians were essentially a leisured class, and probably the only nation where work was practically forbidden. They engaged in unproductive work such as military exercises, teaching, learning and trade, but the task of providing for their daily needs was left to their slaves, the Helots. Though many enthusiastic admirers of Sparta seem to overlook it, the Lacedaemonian society was based on slavery and adult citizens could not work with their hands even if they wished to do so :

The discipline of the Lacedaemonians continued after they were arrived at years of maturity. For no man was at liberty to live as he pleased ; the city being like one great camp, where all had their stated allowance, and knew their public charge, each man concluding that he was born, not for himself, but for his country. Hence, if they had no particular orders, they employed themselves in inspecting the boys, and teaching them something useful, or in learning of those that were older than themselves. One of the greatest privileges that Lycurgus procured his countrymen, was the enjoyment of leisure, the consequence of his forbidding them to exercise any mechanic trade. It was not worth their while to take great pains to raise a fortune, since riches there were of no account : and the Helots, who tilled the ground, were answerable for the produce above-mentioned. To this purpose we have a story of a Lacedaemonian, who, happening to be at Athens while the court sat, was informed of a man who was fined for idleness; and when the poor fellow was returning home in great dejection, attended by his condoling friends, he desired the company to show him the person that was condemned for keeping up his dignity. So much beneath them they reckoned all attention to mechanic arts, and all desire of riches!

Lawsuits were banished from Lacedaemon with money. The Spartans knew neither riches nor poverty, but possessed an equal competency, and had a cheap and easy way of supplying their few wants. Hence, when they were not engaged in war, their time was taken up with dancing, feasting, hunting, or meeting to exercise, or converse. They went not to market under thirty years of age, all their necessary concerns being managed by their relations and adopters. Nor was it reckoned a credit to the old to be seen sauntering in the market-place ; it was deemed more suitable for them to pass great part of the day in the schools of exercise, or places of conversation.

On this question of the slaves, Plutarch's boundless admiration for Lycurgus is put to a severe strain. The mass murders of Helots carried out as a sport by young Spartans, even if they took place after Lycurgus's time, throw a sinister light on Sparta's ideal institutions. And Plutarch has to admit that, in some respects, they treated their slaves with great inhumanity : " Sometimes they made them drink till they were intoxicated, and in that condition led them to the public halls, to show the young men what drunkenness was. They ordered them to sing mean songs, and to dance ridiculous dances, but not to meddle with any that was genteel and graceful." By these methods of direct, if somewhat crude, propaganda the two " races " were kept apart.

" Those who say that a freeman in Sparta was most a freeman, and a slave most a slave," says Plutarch, " seem well to have considered the difference of states." As to the second part of his statement, one can only agree, but it is doubtful whether men who hold others in slavery, and can insult, torture or kill them at will, deserve the appellation of free men.

It is not surprising to hear that these " free men " were in fact themselves prisoners in their own country :

He would not permit all that desired to go abroad and see other countries, lest they should contract foreign manners, gain traces of a life of little discipline, and of a different form of government. He forbad strangers too to resort to Sparta, who could not assign a good reason for their coming ; not, as Thucydides says, out of fear they should imitate the constitution of that city, and make improvements in virtues, but lest they should teach his own people some evil. For along with foreigners come new subjects of discourse ; new discourse produces new opinions ; and from these there necessarily spring new passions and desires, which, like discords in music, would disturb the established government. He, therefore, thought it more expedient for the city to keep out of it corrupt customs and manners, than even to prevent the introduction of a pestilence.

That Lycurgus should have been " charmed with the beauty and greatness of his political establishment " and that he should have rejoiced at his own work " like the Deity when he had created the world," does not surprise us. A lawgiver is as un-critical towards his own laws as he expects other people to be submissive to them. What is more surprising is the influence Sparta has had on so-called progressive thought. Revolution-aries, humanitarians, reformists and communists, from Harrington to Mably, from Campanella to Marat, from Napoleon to Stalin, have all sought inspiration from this most perfect example of a totalitarian state.

ARISTOPHANES

BEFORE we leave Greece we should glance at the satirical utopias of Aristophanes, because their influence on utopian thought has only been second to that of the utopias they set out to ridicule.

Aristophanes' plays give us, furthermore, an idea of how the general public received the schemes of the great philosophers. Their reactions must have been very different from those of the pupils in the gymnasia, always ready to discuss and accept new ideas, with the enthusiasm and the lack of prejudice of youth.

Though Aristophanes presents a distorting mirror to the public
opinion of the time, there is a ring of authenticity in his plays.
His personages talk about Plato's communism very much as
most people do to-day about Bolshevism (or about anarchism).
The majority of the ancient Greeks, like the majority of modern
men, probably dismissed communism as a state of society where
" women belong to everybody," " nobody will do any work,"
" everyone will get drunk and over-eat."   Aristophanes laughs
and sneers with them, but he occasionally puts forward some
better arguments in favour of communism than Plato himself.
Praxagora, who leads a revolution of women which is going to
abolish property and institute a reign of plenty, makes a more
convincing propagandist than Socrates.   This is how she describes
to her husband, Blepyros, how she will bring about this happy
and free society :

Prax.	The rule which I dare to enact and declare,
	Is that all shall be equal and equally share
	All wealth and enjoyments, nor longer endure
	That one should be rich, and another be poor,
	That one should have acres, far-stretching and wide,
	And another not even enough to provide
	Himself with a grave : that this at his call
	Should have hundreds of servants, and that none at all.
	All this I intend to correct and amend :
	Now all of all blessings shall freely partake,
	One life and one system for all men I make.
Blep.	And how will you manage it?
Prax.	First, I'll provide
	That the silver, and land, and whatever beside
	Each man shall possess, shall be common and free,
	One fund for the public ; then out of it we
	Will feed and maintain you, like housekeepers true,
	Dispensing, and sparing, and caring for you.
Blep.	With regard to the land, I can quite understand,
	But how, if a man have his money in hand,
	Not farms, which you see, and he cannot withhold,
	But talents of silver and Darics of gold?
Prax.	All this to the stores he must bring.
Blep.	But suppose
	He choose to retain it, and nobody knows ;
	Rank perjury doubtless ; but what if it be?
	'Twas by that he acquired it at first.

Prax.	I agree.
	But now 'twill be useless ; he'll need it no more.
Blep.	How mean you?
Prax.	All pressure from want will be o'er.
	Now each will have all that a man can desire,
	Cakes, barley-loaves, chestnuts, abundant attire,
	Wine, garlands, and fish : then why should he wish
	The wealth he has gotten by fraud to retain?
	If you know any reason, I hope you'll explain.
Blep.	'Tis those that have most of these goods, I believe,
	That are always the worst and the keenest to thieve.
Prax.	I grant you, my friend, in the days that are past,
	In your old-fashioned system, abolished at last ;
	But what he's to gain, though his wealth he retain,
	When all things are common, I'd have you explain.
Belp.	If a youth to a girl his devotion would show,
	He surely must woo her with presents.
Prax.	O no.
	All women and men will be common and free,
	No marriage or other restraint there will be.
Blep.	But if all should aspire to the favours of one,
	To the girl that is fairest, what then will be done?
Prax.	By the side of the beauty, so stately and grand,
	The dwarf, the deformed, and the ugly will stand ;
	And before you're entitled the beauty to woo,
	Your court you must pay to the hag and the shrew.
Blep.	For the ladies you've nicely provided no doubt ;
	No woman will now be a lover without.
	But what of the men? For the girls, I suspect,
	The handsome will choose, and the ugly reject.
Prax.	No girl will of course be permitted to mate
	Except in accord with the rules of the state.
	By the side of her lover, so handsome and tall,
	Will be stationed the squat, the ungainly and small.
	And before she's entitled the beau to obtain,
	Her love she must grant to the awkward and plain.
Blep.	O then such a nose as Lysicrates shows
	Will vie with the fairest and best, I suppose.
Prax.	O yes, 'tis a nice democratic device,
	A popular system as ever was tried,
	A jape on the swells with their rings and their pride.
	Now, fopling, away, Gaffer Hobnail will say,
	Stand aside ; it is I have precedence to-day.

Blep.   But how, may I ask, will the children be known?
         And how can a father distinguish his own?

Prax.   They will never be known : it can never be told ;
         All youths will in common be sons of the old.

Chremes A nuisance much greater than this might befall you.

Blep.   How so?

Chremes If the skunk Aristyllus should call you
         His father, and seize you, a kiss to imprint.

Blep.   O hang him! Confound him! O how I would
         pound him!

Chremes I fancy you soon would be smelling of mint.

Prax.   But this, sir, is nonsense : it never could be.
         That whelp was begotten before the Decree.
         His kiss, it is plain, you can never obtain.

Blep.   The prospect I view with disgust and alarm.
         But who will attend to the work of the farm?

Prax.   All labour and toil to your slave you will leave ;
         Your business 'twill be, when the shadows of eve
         Ten feet on the face of the dial are cast,
         To scurry away to your evening repast.

Blep.   Our clothes, what of them?

Prax.   You have plenty in store,
         When these are worn out, we will weave you some
         more.

Blep.   Just one other thing. If an action they bring.
         What funds will be mine for discharging the fine?
         You won't pay it out of the stores, I opine.

Prax.   A fine to be paid when an action they bring!
         Why, bless you, our people won't know such a thing
         As an action.

Blep.   No actions! I feel a misgiving.
         Pray what are " our people " to do for a living?

Chremes You are right : there are many will rue it.

Prax.   No doubt.
         But what can one then bring an action about?

Blep.   There are reasons in plenty : I'll just mention one.
         If a debtor won't pay you, pray what's to be done?

Prax.   If a debtor won't pay. Nay, but tell me, my friend,
         How the creditor came by the money to lend?
         All money, I thought, to the stores had been
         brought.
         I've got a suspicion, I say it with grief,
         Your creditor's surely a bit of a thief.

Blep.	Now that is an answer acute and befitting.
	But what if a man should be fined for committing
	Some common assault, when elated with wine ;
	Pray what are his means for discharging that fine?
	I have posed you, I think.
Prax.	Why, his victuals and drink
	Will be stopped by command for awhile ; and I guess
	That he will not again in a hurry transgress,
	When he pays with his stomach.
Blep.	Will thieves be unknown?
Prax.	Why how should they steal what is partly their own?
Blep.	No chance then to meet at night in the street
	Some highwayman coming our clokes to abstract?
Prax.	No, not if you're sleeping at home ; nor, in fact,
	Though you choose to go out. That trade, why pursue it?
	There's plenty for all : but suppose him to do it,
	Don't fight and resist him ; what need of a pother?
	You can go to the stores, and they'll give you another.
Blep.	Shall we gambling forsake?
Prax.	Why, what could you stake?
Blep.	But what is the style of our living to be?
Prax.	One common to all, independent and free,
	All bars and partitions for ever undone,
	All private establishments fused into one.
Blep.	Then where, may I ask, will our dinners be laid?
Prax.	Each court and arcade of the law shall be made
	A banqueting hall for the citizens.
Blep.	Right.
	But what will you do with the desk for the speakers?
Prax.	I'll make it a stand for the cups and the beakers ;
	And there shall the striplings be ranged to recite
	The deeds of the brave, and the joys of the fight,
	And the cowards' disgrace ; till out of the place
	Each coward shall slink with a very red face,
	Not stopping to dine.
Blep.	O, but that will be fine.
	And what of the balloting booths?
Prax.	They shall go
	To the head of the market-place, all in a row,
	And there by Harmodius taking my station,
	I'll tickets dispense to the whole of the nation,

Till each one has got his particular lot,
And manfully bustles along to the sign
Of the letter whereat he's empanelled to dine.
(Ecclesiazusae).

Plato's commonwealth was designed for super-men who despised the joys of the table, of laughter, of poetry, of music and of love-making. Praxagora's utopia is that of ordinary people who, fortunately, do not believe that beautiful women or men should be wooed merely for the sake of the beautiful children they can produce, and that man becomes wicked if he enjoys some of the less noble pleasures of life. Her communism is not one of austerity but of abundance with "cakes, barley-loaves, chestnuts, abundant attire, wine, garlands and fish."

Because Aristophanes has made fun of Socrates and Plato he has often been described as a reactionary. G. Lowes Dickinson, for example, has said of him that he was the defender of "instinctive life... of the old religion, the old habits and the old traditions," and he has seen in the *Clouds* the essence of the better Toryism. One feels more inclined to believe that Aristophanes only defended the old institutions when he was afraid that the new ones, put forward by authoritarian philosophers, would be worse than the old. In the *Birds* he not only ridicules Greek mythology but also a frustrated, power-seeking politician, who succeeds in using the birds to satisfy his "imperialistic" aspirations. Before the arrival of Peisthetarius, an Athenian adventurer, the Birds were leading a somewhat primitive but happy and carefree life and their time passed "like a perpetual wedding day." Their King describes their life in these words :

.... Time passes smoothly enough ;
And money is out of the question. We don't use it.
We have our field sports. We spend our idle mornings
With banqueting and collations in the gardens,
With poppy-seeds and myrrh.

The first task of the Athenian politician and demagogue is to awaken the pride of the Birds and convince them that they are superior to the gods and should rule the earth. Their gullible king makes himself the advocate of Peisthetarius and tells the birds to follow the example of the "civilised" nations :

Look on earth! behold the nations, all in emulation vieing,
Active all, with busy science engineering, fortifying ;
To defend their hearths and homes, with patriotic industry,
Fencing every city round with massy walls of masonry :
Tactical devices old they modify with new design ;
Arms offensive and defensive to perfection they refine ;
Galleys are equipped and armed, and armies trained to
  discipline.

And the birds, infused with " nationalist " spirit, set about constructing a city in their atmospheric domain, bigger and stronger than Babylon. They succeed in frighting the gods but they do not gain by it ; they have to spend their time building, fortifying, guarding the city, and their life is no longer a perpetual wedding-feast.

It is difficult not to sympathise with Aristophanes' satire on the town-planners, moralists and philosophers whose ideas went against the instinctive life of the people. And in spite of all its simplicity, the Kingdom of the Birds appears as a more pleasant place than the Republic.

2

Utopias of the Renaissance

FROM the Greek ideal commonwealths we now pass to those of the Renaissance. This does not mean that during this gap of fifteen centuries the mind of man had ceased to be interested in building imaginary societies, and a complete survey of utopian thought should describe its manifestations during the Roman Empire and even more during the following period which is generally, and unjustly, called the Dark Ages. In many legends of that time one finds that the utopian dream assumes a primitive form as in the early Greek myths.

With the theological thought of the Middle Ages the ideal commonwealths are projected in the next world either, in the mystic and philosophic manner of St Augustine's *De Civitate Dei*, or in the poetical and naive fashion of the narrative of the great Irish traveller St Brendan. This intrepid monk tells how, during one of his travels, his ship was driven towards the north, and how after fifteen days he and his companions reached a country where they saw cathedrals of crystal and where day followed day without night and they landed on an island which was the abode of the blessed. Though in this 6th century legend, Utopia is identified with Paradise, the combination of actual travels with the vision of an ideal island is a feature which will be found in many later utopias.

If the utopian writers of the Renaissance owe a great deal to Greek philosophy they are also indebted to the Christian Fathers and to later theologians. St Thomas Aquinas's *De Regimine Principum*, written during the 13th century, contains some passages which are worth quoting because they express ideas common to almost all the utopias of the Renaissance. Firstly that human happiness is dependent on ethical principles as well as material comfort :

For an individual to lead a good life two things are required. The first and most important is to act in a virtuous manner, for virtue is that by which one lives well ; the second, which is secondary and as it were instrumental, is a sufficiency of those bodily goods whose use is necessary to an act of virtue.

The self-sufficiency of the city and surrounding country is the ideal to be achieved :

Now there are two ways in which an abundance of food-stuffs can be supplied to a city. The first is where the soil is so fertile that it nobly provides for all the necessities of human life. The second is by trade, through which the necessities of life are brought to the town from different places. But it is quite clear that the first means is better. For the higher a thing is the more self-sufficient it is ; since whatever needs another's help is by that very fact proven inferior. But that city is more fully self-sufficient which the surrounding country supplies with all its vital needs, than is another which must obtain these supplies by trade. A city which has an abundance of food from its own territory is more dignified than one which is provisioned by merchants. It is safer, too, for the importing of supplies can be prevented whether owing to the uncertain outcome of wars or to the many dangers of the road, and thus the city may be overcome through lack of food.

St Thomas Aquinas perceived the disruptive effect of commerce upon the community :

Again, if the citizens themselves devote their lives to matters of trade the way will be opened to many vices. For since the object of trading leads especially to the making of money, greed is awakened in the hearts of citizens through the pursuit of trade. The result is that everything in the city will be offered for sale ; confidence will be destroyed and the way opened to all kinds of trickery ; each one will work only for his own profit, despising the public good : the cultivation of virtue will fail, since honour, virtue's reward, will be bestowed upon everyone. Thus in such a city civic life will be corrupted.

It would have been impossible for the Renaissance writers to model their ideal commonwealth entirely upon those of the Greek thinkers, for the structure of the society they had before their eyes was fundamentally different from that of ancient Greece. The Athenian or Spartan city, with its watertight division between citizen and slaves, its primitive economy based almost exclusively on agriculture, could not be transplanted into the society of the sixteenth century without undergoing some radical changes.

The most important change was in regard to manual labour. For Plato manual work was merely a necessity of life and should be left to the slaves and artisans, while a special caste busied itself with the affairs of State. The experience of the mediaeval city had shown, on the contrary, that the whole community was capable of governing itself through its guilds and city councils, and this community was entirely composed of producers. Thus work had acquired an important and respected position which it did not altogether lose with the breaking up of communal institutions.

All the utopists of the Renaissance insist that work is a duty for all citizens and some of them, like Campanella and Andreae, maintain that all work, even the most menial, is honourable. Nor was this a mere statement of principle ; it was reflected in the institutions which gave equal rights to the labourer as to the craftsman, to the peasant as to the school-master. These utopian institutions deprived work of its mercenary character by abolishing wages and trade, and they further endeavoured to make work pleasant by reducing the number of working hours. These institutions, which strike us as modern, had in fact existed in the mediaeval city where hired labour was practically non-existent and where manual labour was no token of inferiority, while the idea that work must be pleasant was a current one and was well expressed in this mediaeval Kuttenberg Ordinance which says : " Every one must be pleased with his work, and no one shall, while doing nothing, appropriate for himself what others have produced by application and work, because laws must be a shield for application and work."[1] The utopian idea of a short working day which to us, accustomed to think of the past in terms of the nineteenth century, seems a very radical one, does not appear such an innovation, if it is compared with an ordinance of Ferdinand the First relative to the Imperial coal mines, which settled the miner's day at eight hours. And according to Thorold Rogers, in fifteenth century England men worked forty-eight hours a week.

During the fourteenth and fifteenth centuries the cities gradually lost their independence, their prosperity began to decline and soon the most abject poverty prevailed generally among working people. But the experience of the free cities was not lost and was consciously or unconsciously assimilated in the constitution of ideal states.

The utopias of the Renaissance introduced, however, some important innovations. The mediaeval city had not succeeded

---

[1] Quoted by Peter Kropotkin in *Mutual Aid*.

in allying itself with the peasantry and this had been one of the chief causes of its decay. The peasant had remained in a condition of slavery and, though in England serfdom had been abolished, in most European countries the peasants were enduring conditions not dissimilar from those of the Helots in Sparta. The utopian writers of the sixteenth and seventeenth century realised, as St Thomas Aquinas had done, that a stable society must integrate the town and the countryside, craftsmen and peasants, and that agricultural work should be given an honoured position equal to that of the other crafts.

The importance given in utopian writings to the scientific cultivation of the land was probably inspired by the work done by the monasteries in this field. Other features of monastic life, such as the rigid time-tables, the meals taken in common, the uniformity and austerity of clothes, the considerable amount of time devoted to study and prayer were also included in the constitutions of ideal cities.

Of more importance than the experiences of the past, however, is the direct influence that the movements of the Renaissance and the Reformation have had on utopian thought. This influence is a complex one for, though the utopias of Thomas More, Campanella and Andreae embody to a great extent the spirit of the Renaissance, they are also a reaction against it.

The splendid artistic and scientific movement of the Renaissance was accompanied by a disintegration of society. The assertion of man's individuality, the development of his critical faculties, and the widening of knowledge, had consolidated the destruction of the collective spirit of the Middle Ages and undermined the unity of the Christian world. The Renaissance furthermore had led to the formation of a class of " intellectuals " by creating a division between the worker and the technician, the craftsman and the artist, the mason and the architect. A new aristocracy was born ; not, at first, based on wealth and power, but on intelligence and knowledge. Burckhardt, the brilliant apologist of the Renaissance, admits that this movement " was anti-popular, that through it Europe became for the first time sharply divided into the cultivated and the uncultivated classes."

This division quickened the disintegration of society. The rising power of the nobles and the kings was no longer held in

check by the Communes, and led to continuous and exhausting
warfare.   The old associations had been broken up and nothing
had come to take their place.   The condition of the people
grew increasingly worse until it reached that abject poverty so
powerfully described in More's *Utopia*.

The utopias of the Renaissance represented a reaction against
its extreme individualism and were an effort to create a new unity
among nations.   For this purpose they sacrificed the most
cherished conquests of the Renaissance ; Thomas More the
scholar and humanist, the patron of painters and friend of
Erasmus, produced an utopia where the lack of individuality is
evident—from the uniformity of the houses and clothes to the
adherence to a strict routine of work; where artistic manifestations
are completely absent ; where the " unique " man of the
Renaissance is replaced by a " standard " man.   Except for
Rabelais, who is in a category of his own, all the other utopian
writers are as parsimonious as More, in their allowance of
personal freedom.

If these utopias represented a reaction against the movement
of the Renaissance they also anticipate its logical outcome.   The
development of the individuality had taken place in a minority
at the expense of the majority.   A cathedral built according to
the plan conceived by one artist, more clearly expresses his
individuality than one built by the common efforts of an
association, but the workmen who execute the plan have less
chance to develop their personalities.

In the political sphere the initiative also passed from the
people to a few individuals.   The condottieri, the princes, kings
and bishops, dispensed justice, waged wars, contracted alliances,
regulated commerce and production : all tasks which had been
previously undertaken by the communes, guilds or city councils.
The Renaissance which had allowed the development of the
individual also created the state which became the negation of
the individual.

The utopias of the Renaissance try to offer a solution to the
problems facing a society in the process of evolving a new form
of organisation.

As has often been pointed out, the discovery of the New World
gave a new impetus to utopian thought, but it played only a
secondary role, and one can safely assume that had More never

read Vespucci's travels he would have imagined an ideal common-wealth in a different setting, like Campanella or Andreae who did not bother to consult travel books before they described their ideal cities. The main impetus came from the need to replace the associations, and the philosophical and religious systems of the Middle Ages, with new ones.

Next to the utopias we find, as we did in Greece under similar circumstances, the elaboration of ideal constitutions which sought a solution in political reforms rather than in the establishment of a completely new system of society. Among the creators of ideal constitutions of that period, Jean Bodin probably exerted the greatest influence. This French philosopher strongly resisted the temptation of wishing to build " a Republic in the imagination and without effect such as those which Plato and Thomas More, the chancellor of England, have imagined." He believed, like Aristotle, that private property and family institutions should remain untouched, but that a strong state should be created which would be able to maintain the unity of the nation. At the time when Bodin wrote his *Republic* (1557), France was torn by religious wars, and there began to grow up a movement in favour of a monarchical state which would be strong enough to prevent religious struggles but which would at the same time allow political and religious freedom. Bodin's theories on the state answered these preoccupations and his works were read with interest all over Europe. He himself translated *La République* into Latin in 1586, when it had already been translated into Italian, Spanish and German. His ideas seem to have met with similar interest in England, for when Bodin came to this country in 1579 private lectures were held both in London and Cambridge to explain his work.

We have only included in this section works which can be defined as ideal, imaginary commonwealths or communities, rather than those which, like Bodin's *Republic*, are treatises on government or politics. Though the utopias which follow were all conceived by thinkers who had been profoundly influenced by the ideas of the Renaissance they are, in many respects, widely dissimilar. Thomas More abolishes property but retains family institutions and slavery; Campanella, though a staunch Catholic, wants to abolish marriage and the family; Andreae borrows many of his ideas from More and Campanella but puts his faith in a new religious reformation which would go deeper than that inspired by Luther; Bacon wants to preserve private property and a monarchal government but believes that the happiness of mankind can be achieved through scientific progress.

SIR THOMAS MORE

Utopia

WHEN Sir Thomas More wrote his *Utopia* he took great delight in trying to mystify his readers, and he seems to have succeeded beyond his expectations, for even to-day, over four hundred years after its publication and in spite of all the learned commentaries written around it, this book is still considered, by some, as an enigma.   Is it to be taken merely as an amusing satirical work, or can More's ideas be identified with those of his Utopians?   These questions have a purely academic interest, but it might help the understanding of *Utopia* to remember that it was written in a transitory period of history when the movement of the Renaissance was giving birth to that of the Reformation with its profound social and political upheavals.

At that moment it was still possible to hope that the much needed economic and religious reforms could be carried out in a peaceful manner.   A few years later this hope had to be abandoned, and it became obvious that reforms would be carried out only through violence and schisms, and the Chancellor of England, who condemned heretics to the stake and was himself to die for his religious beliefs, could no longer have conceived a society where the greatest religious tolerance was observed.

Although More wrote during the lull which preceded the storm, he was acutely aware of the social and political problems that demanded a solution.   But he was no practical reformer, and the solution he offered was completely divorced from realities. It was an escapist dream and at the same time a means to satirise the institutions and governments under which he lived.

Utopia is the work of a scholar and reflects More's wide reading; consequently the sources to which it can be attributed are innumerable.   The most obvious influence is that of the works of Plato and Plutarch, and of St Augustine's *De Civitate Dei*, on which More had delivered public lectures, and from which the conception of penal and corrective slavery as a substitute for capital punishment, is believed to be derived.

As for the setting of More's *Utopia*, commentators are more divided. It is generally assumed that it was inspired by the account of Amerigo Vespucci's travels which had been published in 1507. This clue was furnished by More himself, for his hero, the Portuguese Hythlodaye, who is given the task of describing the commonwealth of Utopia, is alleged to be one of the twenty-four men whom Vespucci left behind at Cape Frio on his fourth voyage. The island of Utopia was supposed to have been discovered somewhere between Brazil and India. G. C. Richards, in the introduction to his translation of *Utopia* into modern English, also suggests that More met some mariner at Antwerp who gave him an account of Japan and he points out the similarities which exist between the position and shape of More's imaginary island and that of Japan, and between the physical appearance of the Japanese and the Utopians. In recent years a new theory has been put forward according to which More may have been acquainted with the Inca civilisation and used it as a model for his own commonwealth.[1]

All these theories do not necessarily exclude one another. The

[1] This theory has been put forward by Prof. H. Stanley Jevons in *The Times Literary Supplement* (Nov. 2nd, 1935) and again in the *Tribune* (Feb. 13th, 1948). He believes that " accounts of the Incas probably reached Spaniards who from 1510 onward had settled permanently on the Isthmus of Panama.

" Vasco Nunez de Balboa made friends with the natives to learn from them all he could about the country and its products, and he reached the Pacific Ocean 100 miles southward in 1513. His full account of his discoveries reached the King of Spain the following year, and More began writing *Utopia* in 1515. It seems probable that trade along the Pacific coast led to the inhabitants of Central America being informed about the Inca empire, which they described as a place reached by sea. This corresponds with More's account of Raphael Hythlodaye's travels, first by land and then by sea. It appeared to me probable that a traveller or mariner returned to Spain from Panama with the party bringing Vasco de Balboa's report, and that he subsequently met More in Antwerp."

A similar theory has been put forward in America by Arthur E. Morgan in a book entitled *Nowhere was Somewhere* (published by the University of North Carolina Press). Mr Morgan attempts to show, by a detailed comparison of More's *Utopia* with the available information about Inca institutions, that the resemblances are far too great to be purely accidental.

H. W. Donner thinks that More must have been acquainted also with Peter Martyr's work *De Orbo Novo* (1511) in which a rosy account is given of the West Indies and of the island of Cuba.

influence of Greek and Roman writers is unmistakable, as also
is that of St Augustine and other Fathers of the Church whom
More had assiduously studied before his journey to the
Netherlands. In Antwerp he may have met some mariner or
traveller and heard him relate stories of the Inca Empire or of
Japan which gave him the idea for the setting of his Utopia.

But *Utopia* is neither a replica of Plato's or Plutarch's ideal
commonwealths, nor a second-hand description of the Inca
civilisation of Peru before the Spanish conquest. It is an original
production, in as much as More has been able to combine the
teachings of classical writers with the widening of horizons
brought about by the discovery of the New World, and the
Renaissance. However much More may have been influenced
by Greek philosophers, or by a dim knowledge of the Inca régime,
his Utopia answers the preoccupations of his time and of his
country.

Utopia is divided into two books which were written at different
times, but it is not known for certain which was written first. The
second book, which contains the description of the Utopian
commonwealth, was probably begun during More's stay in the
Netherlands, in 1515, where he went as a member of the embassy
to Flanders to settle what he describes as "weighty matters in
dispute with His Serene Highness Charles, King of Castile." It
was then that he met Peter Gilles, the friend and host of Erasmus,
for whom he conceived a great friendship and to whom his *Utopia*
was dedicated.

When More returned to London, he completed his work and
sent it to Erasmus, on the 3rd September 1516, asking him to get
it printed and to provide it with "high recommendations, if
possible not only from scholars but also well-known public men."
Erasmus executed his task, with the help of Gilles, and the book
was printed in Louvain and appeared at the end of 1516.[1] It
was extremely well received and two more editions followed
almost immediately, one printed by Gilles de Gourmont in Paris
at the end of 1517 and the other printed by Froben of Basle in
March, 1518. Yet another appeared in November 1518.

Though Erasmus loyally endeavoured to introduce More's book
to the European scholars with whom he was in contact, he does
not seem to have approved of it entirely, and provided a preface

---

[1] *Utopia* was written in Latin and an English translation did not appear until
1551 ; a French translation had already appeared in 1550.

only to the third edition, in which he turned his misgivings into an elegant compliment : " I have always hitherto been exceedingly pleased with all my friend More's writings, but on account of our close friendship, I somewhat distrusted my own judgement. But now I see that all learned men unanimously subscribe to my opinion, and even more warmly admire the man's pre-eminent genius—not that they have more affection, but they have greater discernment—I am quite inclined to approve of my verdict, and shall not hesitate in future to express my opinion."

Erasmus and More had a common outlook on many questions. They both believed in the need for a reform of the Church in a liberal and humanist sense and without a schism ; both had a great admiration for Greek philosophy and hated scholastic doctrines ; both attacked the tyrannical power of the clergy and the monarchy ; both believed that before a better society could be created man had to shed his selfishness, covetousness and pride. But it is unlikely that Erasmus would have been much attracted by More's "state communism." In one of his adages he asks, " Should we deprive the rich of their wealth?" and he answers, " No, all revolutions are impious. I want them to shed their riches themselves or at least that they should be detached from their riches and possess them as if they did not possess them." This represents the traditional Christian attitude towards property and Erasmus is merely echoing the Christian Fathers. More also wanted a " change of heart," but he believed that if the institutions were to be changed by some lawgiver the moral progress of mankind would be facilitated.

Erasmus could also have been little attracted by the strictly regulated society of More ; it smelt too much of the monastery, against which he had written some of his most virulent pages. If he was opposed to an artificially regulated life he was equally against depriving man of his natural instincts and passions to transform him into a rational automaton. More's ideal men are completely inhuman in that they are incapable, or are forbidden, to have any feelings other than those dictated by certain laws ; they are all like the " wise man " whom Erasmus had ridiculed in his *Praise of Folly* :

...And much good to them with this Wise Man of theirs ; let them enjoy him to themselves, love him without Competitors, and live with him in Plato's Common-Wealth, the Countrey of

Ideas, or Tantalus's Orchards. For who would not shun and startle at such a man, as at some unnatural accident or Spirit? A Man dead to all sense of Nature and common affections, and no more mov'd with love or Pity than if it were a Flint or Rock ; whose censure nothing escapes, that commits no errors himself, but has a Lynx's eyes upon others ; measures every thing by an exact Line, and forgives nothing ; pleases himself with himself onely ; the onely Rich, the onely Wise, the onely Free Man, and onely King ; in brief, the onely man that is every thing, but in his own single judgment onely ; that cares not for the Friendship of any man, being himself a friend to no man ; makes no doubt to make the Gods stoop to him, and condemns and laughs at the whole Actions of our Life? And yet such a Beast is this their perfect Wise Man. But tell me pray, if the thing were to be carri'd by most voices, what City would chuse him for its Governour, or what Army desire him for their General? What Woman would have such Husband, what Good-fellow such a Guest, or what Servant would either wish or endure such a Master?

The *Praise of Folly* contains many passages which show that Erasmus's admiration for Plato did not blind him to his authoritarian philosophy, which More on the other hand accepted almost in its entirety.

The first book of *Utopia* is, in part, a description of the conditions which prevailed in England at the beginning of the sixteenth century but, in the main, it is a discussion of two problems which occupied More's mind at the time. The first was a personal one: should he enter the service of the King, and more generally, should philosophers help kings with their advice and experience and thereby endeavour to benefit the commonwealth? The other problem was one of penal reform. More, through his office as a lawyer, had a close knowledge of the administration of "justice" and must have been strongly perturbed by the liberal use of the death penalty even for petty thefts. He had seen that so far from it acting as a deterrent, crimes against property were increasing daily and it was natural that he should try to find a better way of dealing with them.

These questions are discussed in a conversation between Peter Gilles, Raphael Hythlodaye,[1] a philosopher and a scholar, with a passion for exploring foreign countries, and More himself. In the garden of More's house, in Antwerp, Hythlodaye begins to

[1] This name is from Greek words which mean "Knowing in Trifles."

tell his companions of his voyages and of the customs he has met among the strange nations he has visited. After listening to him for a while Peter Gilles expresses his surprise that a man with such experience of world affairs should not attach himself to the court of some king, whom he could entertain with his learning and experience of countries and people and whom he could assist with counsel, thereby serving public interest.

Hythlodaye replies that not only would he lose his independence by doing so, but also he would not be promoting the public interest in entering the service of kings, for " most princes apply themselves more to affairs of war than to the useful arts of peace; and in these I neither have any knowledge, nor do I much desire it ; they are generally more set on acquiring new kingdoms, right or wrong, than on governing well those they possess." He then goes on to denounce the evils of courts and their indifference towards the sufferings of the people. When he visited England he learned that thieves were everywhere condemned to death and " were hanged so fast, that there were sometimes twenty to one gibbet," and he remarked that this manner of dealing with thieves was "neither just in itself nor good for the public ; for as the severity was too great, so the remedy was not effectual ; simple theft not being so great a crime that it ought to cost a man his life, no punishment how severe soever being able to restrain those from robbing who can find out no other way of livelihood. . . .There are dreadful punishments enacted against thieves, but it were much better to make such good provisions by which every man might be put in a method how to live, and so be preserved from the fatal necessity of stealing and of dying for it."

But, instead of providing the people with a means of livelihood, men who come back from the wars maimed, infirm or too old to work, are forced to steal, beg or starve. Nor do noblemen discharge their obligations towards those who served them better than the state :

There is a great number of noblemen, that are themselves as idle as drones, that subsist on other men's labour, on the labour of their tenants, whom, to raise their revenues, they pare to the quick. This indeed is the only instance of their frugality, for in all other things they are prodigal, even to the beggaring of themselves: but besides this, they carry about with them a great number of idle fellows, who never learned any art by which they may gain their living ; and these, as soon as either their lord dies, or they themselves fall sick, are turned out of doors ; for your lords are readier to feed idle people, than to take care of the sick ; and often the heir is not able to keep together so great a family as his predecessor did.   Now when the stomachs of those that are thus turned out of doors, grow keen, they rob no less keenly ; and what else can they do? for when, by wandering about, they have worn out both their health and their clothes, and are tattered, and look ghastly, men of quality will not entertain them, and poor men dare not do it; knowing that one who has been bred up in idleness and pleasure, and who was used to walk about with his sword and buckler, despising all the neighbourhood with an insolent scorn, as far below him, is not fit for the spade and mattock : nor will he serve a poor man for so small a hire, and in so low a diet as he can afford to give him.

The enclosure of lands is another of the main causes of the poverty and vagrancy of the people :

The increase of pasture by which your sheep, which are naturally mild, and easily kept in order, may be said now to devour men, and unpeople, not only villages, but towns ; for wherever it is found that the sheep of any soil yield a softer and richer wool than ordinary, there the nobility and gentry, and even those holy men the abbots, not contented with the old rents which their farms yielded, nor thinking it enough that they, living at their ease, do no good to the public, resolve to do it hurt instead of good.   They stop the course of agriculture, destroying houses and towns, reserving only the churches, and enclose grounds that they may lodge their sheep in them.   As if forests and parks had swallowed up too little of the land, those worthy countrymen turn the best inhabited places in solitudes ; for when an insatiable wretch, who is a plague to his country, resolves to inclose many thousand acres of ground, the owners, as well as tenants, are turned out of their possessions, by tricks, or by main force, or being wearied out with ill usage, they are forced to sell them.   By which means those miserable people, both men and women, married and unmarried, old and young, with their poor but numerous families (since country business requires many hands), are all forced to change their seats, not knowing whither to go ; and they must sell almost for nothing their household stuff, which could not bring them much money, even though they might stay for a buyer.   When that little money is at an end, for it will be soon spent ; what is left for them to do, but either to steal and so

be hanged (God knows how justly), or to go about and beg? And
if they do this, they are put in prison as idle vagabonds ; while
they would willingly work, but can find none that will hire them,
for there is no more occasion for country labour, to which they
have been bred, when there is no arable ground left.

To punish theft by death is not only unjust and ineffectual,
it is also conducive to greater crimes : " It is plain and obvious
that it is absurd, and of ill consequence to the commonwealth,
that a thief and a murderer should be equally punished, for if a
robber sees that his danger is the same, if he is convicted of theft
as if he were guilty of murder, this will naturally incite him to
kill the person whom otherwise he would only have robbed, since
if punishment is the same, there is more security, and less danger
of discovery, when he that can best make it is put out of the way ;
so that terrifying thieves too much, provokes them to cruelty."
The most convenient way for punishing crime is to be found in
the method which was in use among the old Romans who " condemned such as they found guilty of great crimes, to work their
whole lives in quarries, or to dig in mines with chains about
them," or in the method used by the Polylerits[1] who oblige the
thieves to repay the owner what they have taken from him and
then condemn them to hard labour " but are neither imprisoned,
nor chained, unless there happened to be some extraordinary
circumstances in their crimes." To prevent them from escaping
" they all wear a peculiar habit, of one certain colour, and their
hair is cropped a little above their ears, and a piece of one of their
ears is cut off."
Hythlodaye suggests that such methods should be adopted in
England, and More, impressed by the wisdom of his alter-ego,
renews Gilles' advice that he should persuade himself not to shun
the courts of kings, and invokes Plato for whom Hythlodaye
professes a great admiration : " Your friend Plato thinks that
nations will be happy, when either philosophers become kings,
or kings become philosophers ; it is no wonder if we are so far
from that happiness, while philosophers will not think it their
duty to assist kings with their councils." Hythlodaye does not
accept this reproach and he too quotes Plato to support his point
of view : " They are not so base-minded (said he) but that they

[1] An imaginary people whose name in Greek means " much nonsense."

would willingly do it ; many of them have already done it by their books, if those that are in power would but hearken to their good advice. But Plato judged right, that except kings themselves became philosophers, they who from their childhood are corrupted with false notions, would never fall in entirely with the councils of philosophers, and this he himself found to be true in the person of Dionysius."

This is an almost prophetic passage, though Thomas More could not foresee that Henry VIII would treat him with even less gratefulness than Dionysius, according to tradition, treated Plato. It is also interesting because it would lead one to believe that the ideal commonwealth of Utopia is to be ruled by philosophers, but this idea is not developed in the second part of the book and seems to indicate that More's conception of an ideal state underwent a change in the period which separated the composition of the two books.

Hythlodaye then goes on to denounce the passion of kings for wars, which they carry out in a dishonest manner, by not respecting treaties, by obtaining subsidies on false pretences and debasing the coinage at home, by intrigues and bribery. A philosopher would feel compelled to reproach a king for these actions, but if he did so he would be immediately dismissed. But More is still not convinced and maintains that, providing the philosopher is a clever politician he can have some influence on princes. This argument forces Hythlodaye to reveal the whole of his thought : kings not only need to be good philosophers to rule wisely ; the whole structure of society must be changed :

To speak plainly my real sentiments, I must freely own, that as long as there is any property, and while money is the standard of all other things, I cannot think that a nation can be governed either justly or happily : not justly, because the best things will fall to the share of the worst men ; not happily, because all things will be divided among a few (and even these are not in all respects happy), the rest being left to be absolutely miserable. Therefore when I reflect on the wise and good constitution of the Utopians, among whom all things are so well governed, and with so few laws ; where virtue hath its due reward, and yet there is such an equality, that every man lives in plenty ; when I compare with them so many other nations that are still making new laws, and yet can never bring their constitution to a right regulation, where notwithstanding every one has his property ; yet all the laws that they can invent have not the power either to obtain or preserve it, or even to enable men certainly to distinguish what is their own from what is another's ; of which the many lawsuits that every day break out, and are eternally depending, give too plain a demonstration ; when, I say, I balance all these things in my thoughts, I grow more favourable to Plato, and do not wonder that he resolved not to make any laws for such as would not submit to a community of all things : for so wise a man could not but foresee that the setting all upon a level was the only way to make a nation happy, which cannot be obtained so long as there is property: for when every man draws to himself all that he can compass, by one title or another, it must needs follow, that how plentiful soever a nation may be, yet a few dividing the wealth of it among themselves, the rest must fall into indigence. So that there will be two sorts of people among them, who deserve that their fortunes should be interchanged ; the former useless, but wicked and ravenous ; and the latter, who by their constant industry serve the public more than themselves, sincere and modest men. From whence I am persuaded, that till property is taken away there can be no equitable or just distribution of things, nor can the world be happily governed: for as long as that is maintained, the greatest and the far best part of mankind will be still oppressed with a load of cares and anxieties. I confess without taking it quite away, those pressures that lie on a great part of mankind may be made lighter ; but they can never be quite removed. For if laws were made to determine at how great an extent in soil, and at how much money every man must stop, to limit the prince that he might not grow too great, and to restrain the people that they might not become too insolent, and that none might factiously aspire to public employments; which ought neither to be sold, not made burthensome by a great expense, since otherwise those that serve in them would be tempted to reimburse themselves by cheats and violence, and it would become necessary to find out rich men for undergoing those employments which ought rather to be trusted to the wise. These laws, I say, might have such effects, as good diet and care might have on a sick man, whose recovery is desperate : they might allay and mitigate the disease, but it could never be quite healed, nor the body politic be brought again to a good habit, as long as property remains ; and it will fall out as in a complication of diseases, that by applying a remedy to one sore, you will provoke another ; and that which removes the one ill symptom produces another, while the strengthening one part of the body weakens the rest.

To this More objects that " men cannot live conveniently, where all things are common," and Gilles refuses to believe " that any nation in that new world, is better governed than those among us," and to prove his case Hythlodaye proceeds to describe the wise and prosperous commonwealth of Utopia.

The second book begins with a description of the island and of its cities :

The island of Utopia[1] is in the middle two hundred miles broad, and holds almost at the same breadth over a great part of it; but it grows narrower towards both ends. Its figure is not unlike a crescent : between its horns, the sea comes in eleven miles broad, and spreads itself into a great bay, which is environed with land to the compass of about five hundred miles, and is well secured from winds. In this bay there is no great current, the whole coast is, as it were, one continued harbour, which gives all that live in the island great convenience for mutual commerce ; but the entry into the bay, occasioned by rocks on the one hand, and shallows on the other, is very dangerous.

But they report (and there remains good marks of it to make it credible) that this was no island at first, but a part of the continent. Utopus that conquered it (whose name it still carries, for Abraxa was its first name) brought the rude and uncivilised inhabitants into such a good government, and to that measure of politeness, that they now far excel all the rest of mankind ; having soon subdued them, he designed to separate them from the continent, and to bring the sea quite round them.

There are fifty-four cities in the island, all large and well built: the manners, customs, and laws of which are the same, and they are all contrived as near in the same manner as the ground on which they stand will allow. The nearest lie at least twenty-four miles distance from one another, and the most remote are not so far distant, but that a man can go on foot in one day from it, to that which lies next it.

The cities present a monotonous resemblance and Amaurot, the capital, is an improved version of London. This description betrays a lively interest in town improvement :

[1]The word Utopia is derived from the Greek and means Nowhere. Similarly Utopus means "he who has no people." Amaurot, the capital, is the "shadowy town " and the river Anider, " Waterless." Of the use of these facetious Greek names G. C. Richards remarks that More meant those acquainted with Greek to see through his fiction, while he desired to keep it up for everyone else as shown by his introduction to the second edition.

He that knows one of their towns, knows them all, they are so like one another, except where the situation makes some difference. I shall therefore describe one of them ; and none is so proper as Amaurot ; for as none is more eminent, all the rest yielding in precedence to this, because it is the seat of their supreme council ; so there was none of them better known to me, I having lived five years altogether in it.

It lies upon the side of a hill, or rather a rising ground : its figure is almost square, for from the one side of it, which shoots up almost to the top of the hill, it runs down in a descent for two miles to the river Anider ; but it is a little broader the other way that runs along by the bank of that river. There is a bridge cast over the river, not of timber, but of fair stone, consisting of many stately arches : it lies at that part of the town which is farthest from the sea, so that ships without any hindrance lie all along the side of the town. There is likewise another river that runs by it, which though it is not great, yet it runs pleasantly, for it rises out of the same hill on which the town stands, and so runs down through it, and falls into the Anider. The inhabitants have fortified the fountain-head of this river, which springs a little without the towns ; that so if they should happen to be besieged, the enemy might not be able to stop or divert the course of the water, nor poison it ; from thence it is carried in earthen pipes to the lower streets ; and for those places of the town to which the water of that small river cannot be conveyed, they have great cisterns for receiving the rain-water, which supplies the want of the other. The town is compassed with a high and thick wall, in which there are many towers and forts ; there is also a broad and deep dry ditch, set thick with thorns, cast round three sides of the town, and the river is instead of a ditch on the fourth side. The streets are very convenient for all carriage, and are well sheltered from the winds. Their buildings are good, and are so uniform, that a whole side of a street looks like one house. The streets are twenty feet broad ; there lie gardens behind all their houses ; these are large but enclosed with buildings, that on all hands face the streets ; so that every house has both a door to the street and back door to the garden. Their doors have all two leaves, which, as they are easily opened, so they shut of their own accord ; and there being no property among them, every man may freely enter into any house whatsoever. At every ten years end they shift their houses by lots. They cultivate their gardens with great care, so that they have both vines, fruits, herbs, and flowers in them; and all is so well ordered, and so finely kept, that I never saw gardens anywhere that were both so fruitful and so beautiful as theirs. And this humour of ordering their gardens so well, is not only kept up by the pleasure they find in it, but also by an emulation between the inhabitants of the several streets, who vie with each other ; and there is indeed nothing belonging to the whole town that is both more useful and more pleasant. So that he who founded the town, seems to have taken care of nothing more than of their gardens ; for they say, the whole scheme of the town was designed at first by Utopus, but he left all that belonged to the ornament and improvement of it, to be added by those that should come after him, that being too much for one man to bring to perfection.

The land is the principal source of wealth in Utopia, as it was in England at that time, and the Utopians cultivate their land skilfully and none of it is allowed to go to-waste. They have not, however, a specific class of peasants or farmers ; there is a complete integration, or better, identity, between city and country workers for each citizen is both in turn. Agricultural work is carried out as a form of military service, which each citizen undertakes for a period of two years. This would appear to be too short a time to acquire sufficient experience to cultivate the land efficiently, but the inhabitants of Utopia are trained in agriculture long before they join the " land army " :

Agriculture is that which is so universally understood among them, that no person, either man or woman, is ignorant of it ; they are instructed in it from their childhood, partly by what they learn at school, and partly by practice ; they being led out often into the fields, about the town, where they not only see others at work, but are likewise exercised in it themselves.

In the towns families are composed of not more than seventeen members, but while some of their members are sent to work on the land they belong to households of less than forty members :

They have built over all the country, farmhouses for husband-men, which are well contrived, and are furnished with all things necessary for country labour. Inhabitants are sent by turns from the cities to dwell in them ; no country family has fewer than forty men and women in it, besides two slaves. There is a master and a mistress set over every family ; and over thirty families there is a magistrate. Every year twenty of this family come back to the town, after they have stayed two years in the country ; and in their room there are other twenty sent from the town, that they may learn country work from those that have been already one year in the country, as they must teach those that come to them the next from the town. By this means such as dwell in those country farms are never ignorant of agriculture, and so commit no errors, which might otherwise be fatal, and bring them under a scarcity of corn. But though there is every year such a shifting of the husbandmen, to prevent any man being forced against his will to follow that hard course of life too long ; yet many among them take such pleasure in it, that they desire leave to continue in it many years. These husbandmen till the ground, breed cattle, hew wood, and convey it to the towns, either by land or water, as is most convenient. They breed an infinite multitude of chickens in a very curious manner ; for the hens do not sit and hatch them, but vast number of eggs are laid in a gentle and equal heat, in order to be hatched, and they are no sooner out of the shell, and able to stir about, but they seem to consider those that feed them as their mothers, and follow them as other chickens do the hen that hatched them.[1]

The close relationship between town and country is further strengthened by the free exchange of goods and by periodically drafting citizens to the land when extra labour is required :

When they want anything in the country which it does not produce, they fetch that from the town, without carrying anything in exchange for it. And the magistrates of the town take care to see it given them ; for they meet generally in the town once a month, upon a festival day. When the time of harvest comes, the magistrates in the country send to those in the town, and let them know how many hands they will need for reaping the harvest ; and the number they call for being sent to them, they commonly despatch it all in one day.

The whole island of Utopia is a federation of cities and the land which surrounds them :

Every city sends three of their wisest senators once a year to Amaurot, to consult about their common concerns ; for that is chief town of the island, being situated near the centre of it, so that it is the most convenient place for their assemblies. The jurisdiction of every city extends at least twenty miles : and where the towns lie wide, they have much more ground: no town

---

[1] The use of incubators does not seem, in fact, to have altered the filial instincts of chickens.

desires to enlarge its bounds, for the people consider themselves rather as tenants than landlords.

Each city is composed of roughly 100,000 inhabitants who, for electoral and administrative purposes, are divided into four sectors and within each sector into groups of thirty families. Every thirty families elect each year a magistrate whom they call Syphogrant. Over every ten Syphogrants with their families there is a Tranibore, who is elected annually but is not changed without good reason. The whole body of Syphogrants, who number 200 and form a kind of Senate, appoint the prince of the city from one of the four candidates previously named to them by the people ; the prince holds office for life, unless he be suspected of aiming at tyranny. He is assisted by a council or cabinet composed of twenty Tranibors and two Syphogrants :

The Tranibors meet every third day, and oftener if necessary, and consult with the Prince, either concerning the affairs of the state in general, or such private differences as may arise sometimes among the people ; though that falls out but seldom. There are always two Syphogrants called into the council-chamber, and these are changed every day. It is a fundamental rule of their government, that no conclusion can be made in anything that relates to the public, till it has been first debated three several days in their council. It is death for any to meet and consult concerning the state, unless it be either in their ordinary council, or in the assembly of the whole body of the people.[1]

These things have been so provided among them, that the Prince and the Tranibors may not conspire together to change the government, and enslave the people ; and therefore when anything of great importance is set on foot, it is sent to the Syphogrants ; who after they have communicated it to the families that belong to their divisions, and have considered it among themselves, make report to the senate ; and upon great occasions, the matter is referred to the council of the whole island.

The magistrates seem to be chosen rather for the confidence they inspire in the families which elect them than for their know-

---

[1]It is not clear if this sentence means that it is death for any member of the government to meet and consult outside the council and senate or if this applies to the whole population as it has been sometimes understood to mean. In G. C. Richards' translation this sentence has a less ominous sound : " To take counsel on matters of common interest outside the Senate or the electoral body is considered a capital offence."

ledge and intellectual gifts. There is, however, an indication that in the choice of priests, tranibors and princes, special regard is given to knowledge, whether it has been acquired by scholars or craftsmen :

Exemption (from work) is allowed to those, who being recommended to the people by the priests, are by the secret suffrages of the Syphogrants privileged from labour, that they may apply themselves wholly to study ; and if any of these fall short of those hopes that they seemed at first to give, they are obliged to return to work. And sometimes a mechanic, that so employs his leisure hours, as to make a considerable advancement in learning, is eased from being a tradesman, and ranked among their learned men. Out of these they choose their ambassadors, their priests, their Tranibors, and the Prince himself ; anciently called their Barzenes, but is called of late their Ademus.

In Utopia the family is not only the political but also the economic unit of society :

As their cities are composed of families, so their families are made up of those that are nearly related to one another. Their women, when they grow up, are married out ; but all the males, both children and grandchildren, live still in the same house, in great obedience to their common parent, unless age has weakened his understanding ; and in that case, he that is next to him in age comes in his room. But lest any city should become either too great, or by any accident be dispeopled, provision is made that none of their cities may contain above six thousand families, besides those of the country round it. No family may have less than ten, and more than sixteen persons in it ; but there can be no determined number for the children under age. This rule is easily observed, by removing some of the children of a more fruitful couple to any other family that does not abound so much in them.

The oldest man of every family, as has been already said, is its governor. Wives serve their husbands, and children their parents, and always the younger serves the elder. Every city is divided into four equal parts, and in the middle of each there is a market-place : what is brought thither, and manufactured by the several families, is carried from thence to houses appointed for that purpose, in which all things of a sort are laid by themselves ; and thither every father goes and takes whatsoever he or his family stand in need of, without either paying for it, or leaving anything in exchange.

All the inhabitants, with the few exceptions already mentioned, are engaged in some useful trade, and work ceases to become a burden when the hours of labour are reduced and ample time for leisure is allowed :

Besides agriculture, which is so common to them all, every man has some peculiar trade to which he applies himself, such as the manufacture of wool, or flax, masonry, smith's work, or carpenter's work ; for there is no sort of trade that is in great esteem among them...

The same trade generally passes down from father to son, inclinations often following descent ; but if any man's genius lies another way, he is by adoption translated into a family that deals in the trade to which he is inclined : and when that is to be done, care is taken not only by his father, but by the magistrate, that he may be put to a discreet and good man. And if after a person has learned one trade, he desires to acquire another, that is also allowed, and is managed in the same manner as the former. When he has learned both, he follows that which he likes best, unless the public has more occasion for the other...

The chief, and almost the only business of the Syphogrants, is to take care that no man may live idle, but that everyone may follow his trade diligently : yet they do not wear themselves out with perpetual toil, from morning to night, as if they were beasts of burden, which as it is indeed a heavy slavery, so it is everywhere the common course of life amongst all mechanics except the Utopians ; but they dividing the day and night into twenty-four hours, appoint six of these for work ; three of which are before dinner ; and three after. They then sup, and at eight o'clock, counting from noon, go to bed and sleep eight hours. The rest of their time besides that taken up in work, eating and sleeping, is left to every man's discretion ; yet they are not to abuse that interval to luxury and idleness, but must employ it in some proper exercise according to their various inclinations, which is for the most part reading. It is ordinary to have public lectures every morning before daybreak ; at which none are obliged to appear but those who are marked out for literature ; yet a great many, both men and women of all ranks, go to hear lectures of one sort or other, according to their inclinations. But if others, that are not made for contemplation, choose rather to employ themselves at that time in their trades, as many of them do, they are not hindered, but are rather commended, as men that take care to serve their country. After supper, they spend an hour in some diversion, in summer in their gardens, and in winter in the halls where they eat ; where they entertain each other, either with music or discourse.

Here More foresees that many objections would be raised at his shortening of the working day and he explains how this can be done with arguments which clearly show that his idea is not an " utopian " one :

The time appointed for labour is to be narrowly examined, otherwise you may imagine, that since there are only six hours appointed for work, they may fall under a scarcity of necessary provisions. But it is so far from being true, that this time is not sufficient for supplying them with plenty of all things, either necessary or convenient ; that it is rather too much ; and this you will easily apprehend, if you consider how great a part of all other nations is quite idle. First, women generally do little, who are the half of mankind ; and if some few women are diligent, their husbands are idle : then consider the great company of idle priests, and of those that are called religious men ; add to these all rich men, chiefly those that have estates in land, who are called noblemen and gentlemen, together with their families, made up of idle persons, that are kept more for show than use ; add to these, all those strong and lusty beggars, that go about pretending some disease, in excuse for their begging ; and upon the whole account you will find that the number of those by whose labours mankind is supplied, is much less than you perhaps imagined. Then consider how few of those that work are employed in labours that are of real service ; for we who measure all things by money, give rise to many trades that are both vain and superfluous, and serve only to support riot and luxury. For if those who work were employed only in such things as the conveniences of life require, there would be such an abundance of them, that the prices of them would so sink, that tradesmen could not be maintained by their gains ; if all those who labour about useless things, were set to more profitable employments, and if all they that languish out their lives in sloth and idleness, every one of whom consumes as much as any two of the men that are at work, were forced to labour, you may easily imâgine that a small proportion of time would serve for doing all that is either necessary, profitable, or pleasant to mankind, especially while pleasure is kept within its due bounds.

Working hours can be shortened not only by distributing work more equally but by avoiding waste of man-power :

But besides all that has been already said, it is to be considered that the needful arts among them are managed with less labour than anywhere else. The building or the repairing of houses among us employ many hands, because often a thriftless heir suffers a house that his father built to fall into decay, so that his successor must, at a great cost, repair that which he might have kept up with a small charge : it frequently happens, that the same house which one person built at a vast expense, is neglected by another, who thinks he has a more delicate sense of the beauties of architecture ; and he suffering it to fall to ruin, builds another at no less charge. But among the Utopians, all things are so regulated that men very seldom build upon a new piece of ground; and are not only very quick in repairing their houses, but show their foresight in preventing their decay : so that their buildings are preserved very long, with but little labour ; and thus the builders to whom that care belongs are often without employ-ment, except the hewing of timber, and the squaring of stones, that the materials may be in readiness for raising a building very suddenly, when there is any occasion for it.

A certain austerity is also necessary ; one cannot have leisure and at the same time indulge in extravagant tastes :

As to their clothes, observe how little work is spent in them : while they are at labour, they are clothed with leather and skins, cast carelessly about them, which will last seven years ; and when they appear in public they put on an upper garment, which hides the other ; and these are all of one colour, and that is the natural colour of the wool. As they need less woollen cloth than is used anywhere else, so that which they make use of is much less costly. They use linen cloth more ; but that is prepared with less labour, and they value cloth only by the whiteness of the linen, or the cleanness of the wool, without much regard to the fineness of the thread : while in other places, four or five upper garments of woollen cloth, of different colours, and as many vests of silk, will scarce serve one man; and while those that are nicer think ten too few, every man there is content with one, which very often serves him two years. Nor is there anything that can tempt a man to desire more ; for if he had them, he would neither be warmer, nor would he make one jot the better appearance for it. And thus, since they are all employed in some useful labour, and since they content themselves with fewer things, it falls out that there is a great abundance of all things among them : so that it frequently happens, that for want of other work, vast numbers are sent out to mend the highways. But when no public undertaking is to be performed, the hours of working are lessened. The magistrates never engage the people in unnecessary labour, since the chief end of the constitution is to regulate labour by the necessities of the public, and to allow all the people as much time as is necessary for the improvement of their minds, in which they think the happiness of life consists.

We have already seen that in Utopia there is no private property, no money nor wages. Each citizen receives according to his needs and here again More forestalls the inevitable objections which would be voiced against such a system, and he points out that it is a feeling of economic insecurity which induces people to accumulate more goods than they can use :

There is no reason for giving a denial to any person, since there is such plenty of everything among them ; and there is no danger of man's asking for more than he needs : they have no inducements to do this, since they are sure that they shall always be supplied. It is the fear of want that makes any of the whole race of animals either greedy or ravenous....

The builders of Greek imaginary commonwealths had banished family institutions as being antagonistic to the unity of the state. Thomas More was too much a " family man " to abide by the verdict of Athens or Sparta, but he must have seen the danger that the Utopian family, closely knit by the authority of the elder member and by common work, might destroy the homogeneity of the community. It was probably to offset this danger that he introduced the institution of common repasts, though he did not make them compulsory as Lycurgus had done. It will be noticed that in regard to meals More relents somewhat from his austere principles :

At the hours of dinner and supper, the whole Syphogranty being called together by sound of trumpet, they meet and eat together, except only such as are in the hospitals, or lie sick at home. Yet after the halls are served, no man is hindered to carry provisions home from the market-place ; for they know that none does that but for some good reason ; for though any that will may eat at home, yet none does it willingly, since it is both ridiculous and foolish for any to give themselves the trouble to make ready an ill dinner at home, when there is a much more plentiful one made ready for him so near hand.

They sit at three or more tables, according to their number ;

the men sit towards the wall, and the women sit on the other side, that if any of them should be taken suddenly ill, which is no uncommon case amongst women with child, she may, without disturbing the rest, rise and go to the nurse's room, who are there with the sucking children ; where there is always clean water to hand, and cradles in which they may lay the young children if there is occasion for it, and a fire that they may shift and dress them before it.

All the children under five years old sit among the nurses, the rest of the younger sort of both sexes, till they are fit for marriage, either serve those that sit at table ; or if they are not strong enough for that, stand by them in great silence, and eat what is given them ; nor have they any other formality of dining. In the middle of the first table, which stands across the upper end of the hall, sit the Syphogrant and his wife ; for that is the chief and most conspicuous place ; next to him sit two of the most ancient, for there go always four to a mess. If there is a temple within the Syphogranty, the priest and his wife sit with the Syphogrant above all the rest : next them there is a mixture of old and young, who are so placed, that as the young are set near others, so they are mixed with the more ancient ; which they say was appointed on this account, that the gravity of the old people, and the reverence that is due to them, might restrain the younger from all indecent words and gestures. Dishes are not served up to the whole table at first, but the best are first set before the old, whose seats are distinguished from the young, and after them all the rest are served alike. The old men distribute to the younger any curious meats that happen to be set before them, if there is not such an abundance of them that the whole company may be served alike.

Thus old men are honoured with a particular respect ; yet all the rest fare as well as they. Both dinner and supper are begun with some lecture of morality that is read to them ; but it is so short, that it is not tedious nor uneasy to them to hear it ; from hence the old men take occasion to entertain those about them, with some useful and pleasant enlargements ; but they do not engross the whole discourse so to themselves, during their meals, that the younger may not put in for a share : on the contrary, they engage them to talk, that so they may in that free way of conversation find out the force of every one's spirit, and observe his temper. They despatch their dinners quickly, but sit long at supper ; because they go to work after the one, and are to sleep after the other, during which they think the stomach carries on the concoction more vigorously. They never sup without music;

and there is always fruit served up after meat ; while they are at
table, some burn perfumes, and sprinkle about fragrant ointments
and sweet waters : in short, they want nothing that may cheer
up their spirits : they give themselves a large allowance that way,
and indulge themselves in all such pleasures as are attended with
no inconvenience.

The Utopians have not only abolished money and trade
amongst themselves ; they have also succeeded in depriving gold,
silver and precious stones of their magic and corrupting power.
They invented an ingenious method by which they were able to
preserve them and use them occasionally in trade, with foreign
countries, without attaching any value to them, and even
regarding them with contempt :

They eat and drink out of vessels of earth, or glass, which make
an agreeable appearance though formed of brittle materials :
while they make their chamber-pots and close-stools of gold and
silver ; and that not only in their public halls, but in their
private houses : of the same metals they likewise make chains
and fetters for their slaves ; to some of which, as a badge of
infamy, they hang an ear-ring of gold, and make others wear a
chain or a coronet of the same metal ; and this they take care, by
all possible means, to render gold and silver of no esteem. And
from hence it is, that while other nations part with their gold and
silver, as unwillingly as if one tore out their bowels, those of
Utopia would look on their giving in all they possess of those
metals, (when there were any use for them) but as the parting
with a trifle, or as we would esteem the loss of a penny. They find
pearls on their coast ; and diamonds and carbuncles on their
rocks ; they do not look after them, but if they find them by
chance, they polish them, and with them they adorn their
children, who are delighted with them, and glory in them during
their childhood ; but when they grow to years, and see that none
but children use such baubles, they of their own accord, without
being bid by their parents, lay them aside ; and would be as
much ashamed to use them afterwards, as children among us,
when they come to years, are of their puppets and other toys.

As is to be expected in a state where the family plays such an
important role, great care is taken to make marriage as stable as
possible and, though divorce is permitted, adultery is punished
by slavery and sometimes death :

Their women are not married before eighteen, nor their men

before two-and-twenty, and if any of them run into forbidden
embraces before marriage they are severely punished, and the
privilege of marriage is denied them, unless they can obtain a
special warrant from the Prince. Such disorders cast a great
reproach upon the master and mistress of the family in which they
happen, for it is supposed that they have failed in their duty.
The reason of punishing this so severely is, because they think
that if they were not strictly restrained from all vagrant appetites,
very few would engage in a state in which they venture the quiet
of their whole lives, by being confined to one person, and are
obliged to endure all the inconveniences with which it is
accompanied. In choosing their wives they use a method that
would appear to us very absurd and ridiculous, but it is constantly
observed among them, and is accounted perfectly consistent with
wisdom. Before marriage some grave matron presents the bride
naked, whether she is a virgin or a widow, to the bridegroom ;
and after that some grave man presents the bridegroom naked to
the bride. We indeed both laughed at this, and condemned it
as very indecent. But they, on the other hand, wondered at the
folly of the men of all other nations, who, if they are but to buy
a horse of a small value, are so cautious that they will see every
part of him, and take off both his saddle and all his other tackle,
that there may be no secret ulcer hid under any of them ; and
that yet in the choice of a wife, on which depends the happiness
or unhappiness of the rest of his life, a man should venture upon
trust, and only see about a hand's-breadth of the face, all the rest
of the body being covered, under which there may lie hid what
may be contagious, as well as loathsome. All men are not so
wise as to choose a woman only for her good qualities ; and even
wise men consider the body as that which adds not a little to
the mind ; and it is certain there may be some deformity covered
with the clothes as may totally alienate a man from his wife when
it is too late to part with her. If such a thing is discovered after
marriage, a man has no remedy but patience. They therefore
think it is reasonable that there should be good provision made
against such mischievous frauds.

There was so much the more reason for them to make a
regulation in this matter, because they are the only people of
those parts that neither allow of polygamy, nor of divorces,[1]
except in the case of adultery, or insufferable perverseness ; for
in these cases the Senate dissolves the marriage, and grants the
injured person leave to marry again ; but the guilty are made

---

[1] In view of what follows, G. C. Richards' translation seems more exact :
" matrimony is seldom broken except by death unless it be for adultery..."

infamous, and are never allowed the privilege of a second marriage. None are suffered to put away their wives against their wills, from any great calamity that may have fallen on their persons ; for they look on it as the height of cruelty and treachery to abandon either of the married persons when they need most the tender care of their comfort, and that chiefly in the case of old age, which as it carries many diseases along with it, so it is a disease of itself. But it frequently falls out that when a married couple do not well agree, they by mutual consent separate, and find out other persons with whom they hope they may live more happily. Yet this is not done without obtaining leave of the Senate, which never admits of a divorce, but upon a strict inquiry made, both by the senators and their wives, into the grounds upon which it is desired ; and even when they are satisfied concerning the reasons of it, they go on but slowly, for they imagine that too great easiness in granting leave for new marriages would very much shake the kindness of married people. They punish severely those that defile the marriage-bed. If both parties are married they are divorced, and the injured persons may marry one another, or whom they please ; but the adulterer and the adulteress are condemned to slavery. Yet if either of the injured persons cannot shake off the love of the married person, they may live with them still in that state, but they must follow them to that labour to which the slaves are condemned ; and sometimes the repentance of the condemned, together with the unshaken kindness of the innocent and injured person, has prevailed so far with the Prince that he has taken off the sentence ; but those that relapse after they are once pardoned are punished with death.

More must have had a poor opinion of the intricacies of the legal system and the artifices of lawyers, for he deals with them in a drastic manner :

They have but few laws, and such is their constitution that they need not many. They very much condemn other nations, whose laws, together with the commentaries on them, swell up to oblige men to obey a body of laws that are both of such a bulk, and so dark as not to be read and understood by every one of the subjects.

They have no lawyers among them, for they consider them as a sort of people whose profession is to disguise matters, and to wrest the laws ; and therefore they think it is much better that every man should plead his own cause, and trust it to the judge, as in other places the client trusts it to a counsellor. By this means they both cut off many delays, and find out truth more certainly ; for after the parties have laid open the merits of the cause, without those artifices which lawyers are apt to suggest, the judge examines the whole matter, and supports the simplicity of such well-meaning persons, whom otherwise crafty men would be sure to run down : and thus they avoid those evils which appear very remarkably among all those nations that labour under a vast load of laws. Every one of them is skilled in their law, for as it is a very short study, so the plainest meaning of which words are capable is always the sense of their laws.

Their law does not determine the punishment for other crimes; but that is left to the Senate, to temper it according to the circumstances of the fact. Husbands have power to correct their wives, and parents to chastise their children, unless the fault is so great that a public punishment is thought necessary for striking terror into others. For the most part, slavery is the punishment even of the greatest crimes.

We have, so far, shown the brighter side of life in Utopia. The abolition of property and wages, the rational integration of agriculture and industry, the reduction of working hours and the opportunities given for study may well arouse our admiration. It would be more difficult to be attracted by the strict timetable which governs work, leisure and sleep for, as Rabelais said, " can there be any greater dotage in the world than for one to guide and direct his course by the sound of a Bell, and not by his own judgment and discretion?" Nor would the laws governing marriage suit our modern taste, and women might well think that " to obey and serve their husbands " is not exactly their idea of utopia.

More's Utopia contains, however, some even more shocking features. There is a class of slaves not as numerous or cruelly treated as in Lycurgus's Commonwealth, but the institution exists nevertheless. Though work is not carried out by the slaves alone, all the community being employed in some kind of useful labour, none of the free citizens do what More considers to be " dirty work." The slaves do not form a caste as they did in ancient Greece, but are recruited in the following manner :

They do not make slaves of prisoners of war, except those that
are taken in battle ; nor of the sons of their slaves, nor of those
of other nations : the slaves among them are only such as are
condemned to that state of life for the commission of some crime,
or, which is more common, such as their merchants find condemned to die in those parts to which they trade, whom they
sometimes redeem at low rates ; and in other places have them
for nothing. They are kept at perpetual labour, and are always
chained, but with this difference, that their own natives are
treated much worse than others ; they are considered as more
profligate than the rest, and since they could not be restrained
by the advantages of so excellent an education, are judged worthy
of harder usage. Another sort of slaves are the poor of the
neighbouring countries, who offer of their own accord to come
and serve them ; they treat these better, and use them in all
other respects as well as their own countrymen, except their
imposing more labour upon them, which is no hard task to those
that have been accustomed to it ; and if any of these have a
mind to go back to their own country, which indeed falls out but
seldom, as they do not force them to stay, so they do not send
them away empty-handed.

If the death penalty is rarely inflicted in Utopia, it is for reasons
of expediency rather than on humane or ethical grounds :

For the most part, slavery is the punishment even of the
greatest crimes; for as that is no less terrible to the criminals
themselves than death, so they think the preserving them in a
state of servitude is more to the interest of the commonwealth
than killing them.

It is surprising, in view of the obvious advantages which this
method presents, from the point of view of governments, that it
has not been applied on a great scale until the present day. But
when it was applied it was on a scale and with such results that
even More could not have foreseen. Armies of slaves numbering
hundreds of thousands have, in the last twenty years, built the
Baltic-White Sea Canal, double-tracked the Trans-Siberian Railroad, erected engineering works in the heart of Siberia, mined
uranium, dug underground factories ; have, in a word, achieved
feats before which the construction of the Pyramids look like
child's-play. Experience has shown, however, that this method
presented certain dangers. Slave labour is cheap, since the

slaves can be made to live on a starvation diet and in crowded barracks, and it is extremely useful for work which a government might want to carry out in circumstances which no free man would dream of accepting. It was only natural, therefore, that some governments should have been tempted to acquire as vast an army of slaves as possible and as the number of criminals, particularly that of major criminals, is always small compared with the total of the population, a method had to be devised by which the number of crimes were multiplied.

Compared with the work carried out by some twentieth century slaves, that of the Utopian slaves seems very light and even pleasant. They clean the halls where the meals are taken, kill animals for human consumption, and go hunting.

In a society which admits of slavery even the " free citizen " is not free ; his chain is only longer than that of the slave. In Utopia to go out and spend a week-end in the country, without having first obtained permission from the Syphogrant and the Tranibor, and a passport from the Prince certifying that leave has been granted for travelling and how long one can stay away, is considered a crime. If " any man goes out of the city to which he belongs, without leave, and is found rambling without passport, he is severely treated, he is punished as a fugitive, and sent home disgracefully ; and if he falls again into the like fault, is condemned to slavery."

We are beginning to suspect that these Utopians are less free and happy than More would have us believe for, if the magistrates and prince are loved and respected, if the people are contented with their institutions, what need is there to punish someone who feels a sudden urge to ramble in the country? Elsewhere we are told that men are obliged " to live in full view," to make sure that they perform their ordinary tasks, which would seem un-necessary if their work was made really easy and pleasant. And again, what has the state to fear from its loyal subjects that it prevents them from meeting for a drink lest they should form themselves into parties?

Our suspicions are strengthened when we read of the manner in which the Utopians conduct wars. These paternal, modest, good-humoured people become the most ruthless, machiaevellian politicians when engaged in war. They cannot even invoke the excuse that they are obliged to defend their country against aggression, for their country is so situated as to make it unassailable. But they carry out wars of aggression and pursue, in fact, a bare-faced policy of expansion.

If there is any increase over the whole island, then they draw out a number of their citizens out of the several towns, and send them over to the neighbouring continent ; where, if they find that the inhabitants have more soil than they can well cultivate, they fix a colony, taking the inhabitants into their society, if they are willing to live with them ; and where they do that of their own accord, they quickly enter into their method of life, and conform to their rules, and this proves a happiness to both nations : for according to their constitution, such care is taken of the soil, that it becomes fruitful enough for both, though it might be otherwise too narrow and barren for any one of them. But if the natives refuse to conform themselves to their laws, they drive them out of those bounds which they mark out for themselves, and use force if they resist. For they account it a very just cause of war, for a nation to hinder others from possessing a part of that soil, of which they make no use, but which is suffered to lie idle and uncultivated ; since every man has by the law of Nature a right to such a waste portion of the earth as is necessary for his subsistence.

Their other wars are dictated by loyalty towards friendly neighbour nations. Utopia plays a role similar to that of the Great Powers to-day who, for allegedly altruistic reasons, are strongly concerned in the interests of smaller nations. The Utopians, however, " detest war as a very brutal thing " and " think that there is nothing more inglorious than that glory that is gained by war." They prefer to owe their victories to skilful diplomacy or to political manoeuvres. They have even adopted a kind of permanent Marshall Plan by which they distribute their surplus food to neighbourly nations free of charge. Though More does not explain why they behave in such an apparently philanthropic manner he may have realised that no nation, however well governed, can hope to enjoy permanent prosperity if it is surrounded by starving nations whose covetousness it would arouse.

If political methods fail to settle matters they declare war, but even then they rely more on " fifth column " activities than on battles :

As soon as they declare war, they take care to have a great many schedules, that are sealed with their common seal, affixed in the most conspicuous places of their enemies' country. This is carried out secretly, and done in many places all at once. In these they promise great rewards to such as shall kill the prince, and lesser in proportion to such as shall kill any other persons, who are those on whom, next to the prince himself, they cast the chief balance of the war. And they double the sum to him that, instead of killing the person so marked out, shall take him alive and put him in their hands. They offer not only indemnity, but rewards, to such of the persons themselves that are so marked, if they will act against their countrymen : by this means those that are named in their schedules become not only distrustful of their fellow-citizens, but are jealous of one another, and are much distracted by fear and danger ; for it has often fallen out that many of them, even the Prince himself, have been betrayed by those in whom they have trusted most : for the rewards that the Utopians offer are so unmeasurably great, that there is no sort of crime to which men cannot be drawn by them.

They also make a clever use of terrorism and are skilled in war propaganda :

They think it likewise an act of mercy and love to mankind to prevent the great slaughter of those that must otherwise be killed in the progress of the war, both on their own side and on that of their enemies, by the death of a few that are most guilty; and that in so doing they are kind even to their enemies, and pity them no less than their own people, as knowing that the greater part of them do not engage in the war of their own accord, but are driven into it by the passions of their prince.

If this method does not succeed with them, then they sow seeds of contention among their enemies, and animate the prince's brother, or some of the nobility, to aspire to the crown.

In battles they are as parsimonious with the lives of their citizens as they are liberal with those of their mercenaries whom they recruit among a nation called the Zapolets. Here More takes the opportunity of venting his contempt and hatred of the Swiss, who used to supply most armies of mercenaries in his time:

The Utopians are not at all troubled how many of these (the Zapolets) happen to be killed, and reckon it a service done to mankind if they could be a means to deliver the world from such a lewd and vicious people, that seem to have run together as to the drain of human nature.

It would take too long to describe the wars of the Utopians in detail, but it will be sufficient to say that they do to their enemies all the things they would not like to be done to themselves. Some of the most ardent admirers of More have been so shocked by his treatment of wars that they have assumed that he has not described wars as he thought they should be carried out, but that he has satirised the war methods of his contemporaries. However, though charitable, this is an improbable theory.

It would be unreasonable, however, to expect More to have described a rational and just way of waging wars. War is, as he said himself, " a very brutal thing," and the only way he could have dealt with it in a humane manner would have been by abolishing it altogether.

We can only say a few words about the religious and philosophical ideas of the Utopians. More, like Erasmus and many of the Renaissance humanists, believed that man was naturally a Christian and that his faith did not depend on divine revelation. Religion sprang from the heart and consisted in loving God and man and should therefore unite men and not divide them into sects.

The inhabitants of Utopia have not been converted to Christianity but the majority of them worship one God who made and governs the world. They tolerate all doctrines and every variety of creeds and have adopted a simple form of worship in which all can unite. They respect the law given them by their king Utopus, " that every man might be of what religion he pleased, and might endeavour to draw others to it by the force of argument, and by amicable and modest ways, but without bitterness against those of other opinions ; such as did otherwise were to be condemned to banishment or slavery."

Like the magistrates, the priests are elected by the people in secret ballot ; they are men of eminent piety " and therefore they are but a few," only thirteen in every town, one for every temple. They have no temporal power and their task is to exhort and admonish people. If their counsels are not followed, they exclude " those who are desperately wicked from joining in their worship." Their priests can marry, take part in wars, and women are not barred from priesthood.

This, then, is the constitution of that commonwealth which,

according to Raphael Hythlodaye, is not only " the best in the world, but indeed the only commonwealth that truly deserves that name. In all other places it is visible, that while people talk of commonwealth, every man only seeks his own wealth ; but there, where no man has any property, all men zealously pursue the good of the public." This is a bold claim and we prefer to admire More for his indictment of the society of his time rather than for the set of laws and institutions which he himself devised.

TOMMASO CAMPANELLA

The City of the Sun

NINETY years later another utopia was conceived by a friar, philosopher, poet and astrologer with a fanatical belief in his own ideas. There is none of More's literary elegance and fine irony in Campanella's *City of the Sun*, for unlike him he did not write in the pleasant circle of refined humanists but with his mind and limbs still aching from the tortures of the Inquisition.

Giovan Domenico Campanella was born in 1568, at Stilo, in Calabria, that province of Italy which even to-day remains a mystery to the Italians themselves and stubbornly refuses to become assimilated into Europe. He came from a poor family, and his father, when called as a witness at one of the trials of his famous son, testified with a touching simplicity : " I had heard that my son had written a book in Naples and everybody told me how fortunate I was ; now they all tell me how unlucky I am ; as for me I can neither read nor write."

Campanella was put in a monastery when he was still a child ; when he was fourteen years old he entered the order of the Dominicans and it was then that he took the name of Tommaso. He said later that he chose a monastic life more to satisfy his desire for study than from the call of religion. He soon showed an independent spirit and attacked the scholastic method and doctrines. When he was eighteen he became acquainted with the works of Bernardino Telesio, the great philosopher of the Renaissance, and felt such enthusiasm for his ideas that he left the monastery to visit him at Cosenza, but he arrived just after Telesio's death. Shortly afterwards, when he was staying at the monastery of Altomonte, he met a Rabbi who made a profound impression on him by his prophetic gifts and his knowledge of astrology. It was probably through this acquaintance that Campanella acquired a passion for astrology and prophecy which never left him. The curious combination of rationalist and scientific ideas and of a superstitious belief in supernatural phenomena, which characterises many thinkers of the Renaissance, manifests itself in a remarkably acute form throughout Campanella's writings.

His philosophical ideas very soon attracted the attention of the religious authorities. At the end of the 15th century, Italy no longer enjoyed that tolerance for new ideas which had characterised the early period of the Renaissance. The Reformation had robbed the Catholic Church of its power over a great part of Western Europe, and a state of siege had been declared in the countries which had remained under its domination. Italy was in the grip of the counter-reformation and no one, from the Pope to the most obscure monk, escaped the watchful eye of the Inquisition. In 1590 Campanella was summoned to appear before a Dominican tribunal for his writings in defence of Telesio. Three years later, while he was staying in a Dominican monastery at Bologna, he was robbed of all his manuscripts by the Pope's secret police. Campanella, suspecting the Vatican, applied to them for the return of his manuscripts but they denied all knowledge of the affair. He found them, however, thirty years later in the archives of the Holy See. In 1594 Campanella was accused of heresy for his ideas concerning universal animation, and sent for trial before the Roman Inquisition, which was unable to prove the charge, but ordered him to remain in Rome under close watch. In 1597 he returned to Naples, where he clashed once again with the religious authorities, and was obliged to retire to the monastery at Stilo.

There was a widespread belief at that time that the end of the century would bring profound changes, and even that the world might come to an end. Campanella was very much affected by these rumours, and he saw, in the unrest of Naples under Spanish rule, in events such as floods, earthquakes and the appearance of comets, a confirmation that social convulsions were imminent. A strange and powerful dream arose in his mind. He believed that the coming changes would lead to a complete reformation of society, and that the moment had come for the creation of an Universal Republic. His native Calabria, under his leadership, would be the starting-point for this movement. Until now Campanella had fought against the old ideas in his writings alone but the philosopher was now to become a man of action.

Campanella believed that a threefold reformation should take place. On the social plane, by improving the conditions of the people ; politically, by making Spain the leader of an unification of the world ; and in the sphere of religion by a reformation of the Church. But Campanella did not conceive a reformation in the sense of Calvin or Luther, who wanted to detach themselves from the domination of the Church of Rome and thereby encouraged national aspirations. Campanella was a staunch Catholic, and he wanted to unite the world under the standard of the Catholic faith. He attributed the defeats of the Catholic Church to her adherence to the old scholastic doctrines, and thought that she would neither regain nor increase her power through religious persecutions, but only in the acceptance of the new philosophical ideas. He sought to modernise the Church rather than to reform it.

The Republic of Calabria which he planned to institute would serve as an example as well as a starting-point for the creation of an universal Republic. Campanella was not, as he has sometimes been described, an Italian patriot. If he plotted against Spain, it was in order to achieve this Holy Universal Republic under the spiritual leadership of the Catholic Church, and, though he rebelled against the Spanish authorities, he believed that Spain was the only Power capable of bringing the Universal Republic into being.

In the church of the convent at Stilo he preached that the moment had come for revolt, and he persuaded some political exiles who had taken refuge in the monastery, and a number of the friars themselves, that the Holy Universal Republic would take place before the end of the world, and that it was necessary to find " propagandists " and " men of the deed " to achieve it. The friars with their tongues, the people with arms, would start a movement to create new laws and institutions for a better world. Some of the reforms and laws which he advocated at the time were later incorporated in the *City of the Sun*. The plot was discovered and Campanella and his associates were arrested. On the 8th November, 1599, they were taken to Naples, by sea, and some of Campanella's companions were quartered on the galleys, in full view of the people of Naples, who had assembled in the harbour to see their arrival.

A charge of heresy was added to that of conspiring against Spain, and out of the hundred and forty men who had been arrested (of whom 14 were friars), ten were sentenced to death. For five months Campanella was kept in a humid and dark cell, with chains on his legs. He was submitted to terrible tortures, and eventually some kind of a confession was extracted from him, which allowed the Inquisition to proceed with the charge of heresy. But a few weeks before his trial was due to begin he set fire to his cell, and began to talk and behave as if he had lost his reason. Whether he was simulating madness, as most historians are inclined to believe, or whether the tortures had really affected his mind, will never be known.

On the 10th May, 1600, the trial for heresy began again, and his madness did not protect him from being tortured once more, with greater cruelty than before and, on one occasion, for twenty-four hours without a break. The record of Campanella's ravings and cries, faithfully noted by an officer of the Inquisition, has been preserved and constitutes a truly terrifying document. This time he refused to answer any questions, and continued to behave as if he were insane. The Inquisition suspected him of simulating madness, but they had to abide by their own tests, and they could not condemn him to death because it would have meant damning his soul. After a trial which lasted a whole year he was condemned to life imprisonment.

It was just after this trial, in 1602, that Campanella wrote his *City of the Sun*. It is generally believed that this work was written at a later date, in Latin, and the circumstances in which it was first composed having been generally overlooked, it has been described as an " exotic " and " eccentric " dream, completely divorced from reality. *The City of the Sun* is in fact closely related to Campanella's unsuccessful attempt to create a Republic of Calabria. The tortures and trials had not succeeded in crushing his spirit, and he may have written it as an act of defiance, or simply to explain what would have been carried out had he been successful. It is also possible that he hoped to escape, and that he sought in this way to gain support for a renewed attempt. He himself said later that he tried to gain an ascendancy over his guardians by some magic practices which impressed them greatly. They helped to smuggle his manuscripts out of prison, and might have helped him to escape had he not been transferred to another fortress. Campanella seems to have had a considerable popular following at the time, and the sonnets, which he wrote in his cell, were recited all over Naples. The fact that he wrote *The City of the Sun* in Italian, and not in Latin, indicated that he did not consider it an academic work but wanted it to be as widely read as possible.

It has often been pointed out that Campanella has taken very little trouble to give an appearance of reality to his ideal city, and it is true that we are told practically nothing as to where it is situated or how the seaman who tells the story reached it. This is understandable if one considers that he had preached and agitated, plotted and faced torture, in order to create an ideal republic in his native Calabria. He did not wish his readers to consider his work as one of fiction and to imagine the ideal city in some distant and foreign country, but to think of it as around them and themselves as its citizens. That Campanella did not lack imagination and poetical gifts is shown by the many sonnets and poems he wrote throughout his life, yet *The City of the Sun* is as arid and uninspiring as a political blue-print, which in fact, it was meant to be.

Campanella remained a prisoner in Naples, until September, 1626, when he was freed through the intervention of the Italian Council in Madrid. After being at liberty for a month, he was arrested again, this time by order of the Pope, and was kept prisoner in the Vatican for three years. After his release he enjoyed a period of relative quiet until 1633, when the Spaniards began to persecute him anew because they held him responsible for the pro-French policy of the Pope, Urban VIII. These suspicions were probably justified, for Campanella had abandoned the hope that Spain would unify the world as he had dreamt, and believed that France should take her place. In 1636 he was obliged to flee to Paris, where he lived under the protection of Richelieu and Louis XIII, and where he was able to publish his works and lecture at the Sorbonne in spite of protests from the Vatican. He died on the 21st May, 1639, in a monastery.

Campanella has achieved fame through his tragic life and his *City of the Sun* rather than by his philosophical works, which, however, occupy an important, if not a foremost, place in the philosophy of the later Renaissance. In his own Calabria his memory still lives among the people, and it is said that he appears in dreams to reveal hidden treasures, a legend which would not have displeased the philosopher who liked sometimes to be thought a magician and a prophet.

Campanella composed most of his writings in prison, sometimes under really inhuman conditions, and he said later that he had fought death by work. Many of his manuscripts were confiscated and some of them destroyed by his jailers, and this partly explains why there are so many versions of most of his works. Some of them were composed as many as five times. *The City of the Sun* was written a second time in Italian in 1611, and for the first time in Latin in 1613-14. He wrote it for a fourth time in Latin, in a revised version, in 1630-31. The Latin versions differ considerably from the Italian, not only in style, which is more polished in the later versions, but also because his ideas altered a great deal during his imprisonment. As the years pass his ideal city becomes more and more authoritarian, and conforms more to the ideas of the Church. For example, the community of goods and of women is not abolished, but the Fathers of the Church are quoted to justify it, and sexual freedom becomes severely restricted. Astrology occupies a less important place in the later versions, probably in view of the war the Vatican was waging against astrologers.

Campanella was never a revolutionary ; he was a reformer with a rebellious spirit and when that spirit of rebellion left him he became a conformist. During his youth and the first years of imprisonment he fought for the new philosophical ideas and for a better system of society, but as the years of imprisonment went by he sought to regain his freedom by trying to make his ideas acceptable to the authorities, and at the end of his life he aspired to become a cardinal in the Church which had persecuted him and wrote flattering poems to the King of France and Richelieu.

The first version of *The City of the Sun* was written during his youth, when his body was bound but his mind was still free, and it is therefore more truly utopian than the others. Later, Campanella's vision was clouded by the fear of perpetual imprisonment and the necessity of compromise. It was, however, through the Latin versions that *The City of the Sun* became mostly known. It must have reached Germany before 1619, for it clearly influenced Andreae's *Christianopolis*, published in that year. It may have been taken there by Scioppio, a German scholar who had been converted to Catholicism and was leader of the counter-reformation in Germany. He tried hard to obtain Campanella's release, travelling from Italy to Germany in order to see the Emperor and win him to Campanella's cause, taking with him some of his manuscripts. *The City of the Sun* was published for the first time in 1623 in Frankfurt, by Tobias Adani, a German jurist who published most of Campanella's works from 1617 to 1629. An English translation (by T. W. Halliday) did not appear until 1886, when it was included in Henry Morley's *Ideal Commonwealths*. There is no indication from which Latin edition the translation was made, but it contains several obvious mistranslations which, in some cases, render the text meaningless. Some passages which have been left out are described by Morley as " one or two omissions of detail which can well be spared." These cuts seem to have been dictated by a Victorian sense of propriety rather than by considerations of space.

The passages which follow have been translated from the edition of the first Italian version which was published in Italy in 1905 and which contains, in footnotes, the variations of the 1623 and 1637 Latin editions. These variations have been mentioned when they seemed of particular interest.

The full title of the first composition clearly shows the identity between *The City of the Sun* and Campanella's dream of a Christian Republic :

City of the Sun
by
Friar Tommaso Campanella
or
Dialogue of the Republic

in which is demonstrated the idea of a reform of the Christian Republic according to the promise God made to St Catherine and St Bridget

The dialogue takes place between a Knight Hospitaller and a Genoese seaman, who describes the ideal city he has visited in the course of one of his voyages. The city is situated near Taprobane, on a large plain immediately under the equator :

Genoese : On the vast plain rises a hill on which the greater part of the City is built, but its circles extend for some distance beyond the base of the hill, which is of such size that the diameter of the city is two miles or more and its circumference about seven. But being built on a slope the city has more houses than if it were built on a plain.

The city is divided into very great circles named after the seven planets, and one passes from one to the other through four streets and four gates which look towards the four corners of the earth. It is so arranged that if the first circle were stormed, it would require more effort to storm the second, and still more for the others, so that it would be necessary to storm it seven times to capture it. But I am of the opinion that it would be impossible to seize even the first circle, so thick are the earthworks, and so well fortified with towers, artillery and ditches outside.

Entering then through the Northern Gate, which is covered with iron and which can be raised and lowered thanks to an ingenious device, one sees a level space fifty paces wide between the first and second walls. One finds places, all joined round the wall in such a manner as to appear one, and above they have ravelins supported by two columns, as in the cloisters of monasteries, and there are no entrances to be seen, for they are all on the concave side of the palaces ; the rooms are beautiful and are divided by thin walls, and have windows both on the concave and convex sides of the building. The convex wall is eight spans in thickness, the concave three, and the interior walls slightly more than one span.

And so one enters the second circle, which is two or three paces narrower than the first, and sees the second walls with ravelins and galleries for promenading, and from the inside there is another wall enclosing the palaces ; half way up the buildings there is a gallery supported by columns and containing beautiful pictures. And in this way one reaches the last circle, and the ground is always level except when one goes through the doors, which are double because of the interior and exterior walls, and going from one to the other one mounts some steps which are scarcely noticeable, as they proceed in a slanting direction and their height is hardly perceptible.

On the top of the hill there is a great flat space on which a temple has been built with wondrous art.

After the Genoese has described the temple the Knight Hospitaller expresses the desire to hear how the city is governed :

Genoese : They have among them a consecrated prince whose name is O, which in our language means *Metaphysic*. He is their spiritual and temporal head and all matters are referred to him.

He is assisted by three princes of equal rank, *Pon*, *Sin*, and *Mor* whose names signify *Power*, *Knowledge* and *Love*.

Power is in charge of all the matters related to war and peace, and to military art ; he has supreme power in wars, second only to O ; he looks after the military magistrates, the warriors, the soldiers, ammunition and fortifications.

Knowledge is in charge of all sciences and of the Doctors and Magistrates dedicated to the liberal and mechanical arts. He is assisted by as many magistrates as there are sciences, that is to say : the Astrologer, the Cosmographer, the Geometer, the Physicist, the Rhetorician, the Grammarian, the Doctor, the Political Scientist, the Moralist, and he has but one book, which contains all the sciences and which is read to all the people after the custom of the Pythagoreans. It is Knowledge who has caused all the walls, and the interior and exterior of the galleries to be covered with paintings representing all the sciences. On the exterior walls of the temple and on the curtains, which are lowered during the sermons to prevent the voice being lost, are pictures of stars and each is described in three verses. On the interior wall of the first circle are painted all the mathematical figures, more numerous than those discovered by Euclid and Archimedes, and each is accompanied by a clear explanation. On the exterior side of the wall there is map of the whole world, and beside it tablets for each province with the places, customs and laws appertaining to it and also its alphabet, against which their own is written.

In the interior of the second circle there are all the precious and common stones, the minerals and metals, both painted and in reality, with an explanation of two verses each. On the out-side there are all kind of lakes, seas, rivers, wines, oils and other liquors, with their virtues, origin and quality. And there are also vessels containing various liquors, some one hundred and others three hundred years old, which can cure all illnesses.[1]

---

[1]Hail and snow, storms and thunder, and whatever takes place in the air, are depicted and explained in little verses. The inhabitants even have the art of representing in stone all the phenomena of the air, such as wind, rain, thunder, the rainbow, etc.

In the third circle are to be found all kinds of herbs and trees of the world, some painted on the walls and some actually growing in baskets filled with earth, which are put over the ravelins, and there are explanations as to where they were first found, their virtues, their resemblances to the stars, metals, and parts of the human body, and their use in medicine. Outside the wall, there are all kinds of fishes found in rivers, lakes and the sea, and an explanation of their qualities, their ways of living and breeding, and how they can be preserved as well as of their uses and the resemblances they bear to celestial and earthly things in art and in nature. . . .

Inside the fourth circle are found pictures of all kinds of birds and the description of their qualities, size and customs, and they have a real phoenix. Outside there are all kinds of animals, reptiles, serpents, dragons, worms and insects like flies, ox-flies, and so on with their peculiarities, venoms and virtues, which are more numerous then we think.

Inside the fifth circle they have all the animals of the earth, and it is really surprising to see so many different kinds. We know not a thousandth part of them. Those which are of a bigger size are painted outside the ravelin, and of horses alone how many different breeds there are! And how cleverly are these beautiful pictures described in the verses which accompany them!

Inside the sixth circle they have all the mechanical arts and their own inventions and the different manners in which they are practised in different parts of the world. Outside are represented all the inventors in law, science and warfare. I found Moses, Osiris, Jupiter, Mercury, Mahomet and many others. In a place of great honour there was Jesus Christ and the twelve Apostles, whom they hold in high esteem ; there was also Caesar, Alexander, Pyrrhus, and all the Romans. I expressed my admiration that they should know so much history, and they told me that they knew the languages of all nations, for they were in the habit of sending ambassadors throughout the world for the purpose of learning the good and evil of all, and they greatly benefited by it.

There are also Masters who teach these things, and the children learn without any pain ; before they are ten years old they have learned all the sciences in the way of history.

Love is in charge of reproduction, and he unites men and women in such a manner that they produce a good race. They laugh at us, who show such care for the breeding of dogs and horses, and neglect our own race. *Love* also takes care of the education of children, of medicines and drugs, of sowing and the gathering of fruits, grains and herbs, and whatever else is connected with food, clothing and courtship. He is assisted by many masters and mistresses devoted to these arts.

Metaphysic looks after all these matters in co-operation with the other three ; they consult him about everything, nothing is done without him, and in whatever *Metaphysic* decides they agree....

In the following passage it will be seen that Campanella, though much influenced by Plato and Plutarch, goes further than they, for he abolishes property, not for one class only, but for the whole community :

All things are in common and are administered by the magistrates. Not only food but knowledge, honours and pleasures are common, in such a manner that no one can appropriate anything to himself.

They say that property is born out of living in separate houses and possessing a wife and children, and that from it grows self-love. For in order to raise his son to wealth and dignities, a man becomes either grasping of the public wealth, if he is strong and fearless, or avaricious and hypocritical if he is weak. But when self-love is taken away, there remains only love for the community.

Here the Knight interjects with the common objection : " In this case no one will want to work, while he will expect the others to do the work, as Aristotle argued against Plato," and the Genoese answers :

I am not able to argue, and I can only tell you that they love their fatherland with a truly amazing force. Their love is even greater than that of the Romans for their country, for they have given up property to a greater extent. And I think that if our Priests and monks had no family and friends, and no ambition to rise to greater dignities, they would have less property and would thereby be more imbued with a spirit of holiness and charity towards all....

The magistrates are very careful to see that no one receives more than another or than he deserves ; yet everyone receives whatever he needs, and friendship shows itself in wars, in illnesses or in study, when they help and teach one another. All the young men call each other brothers, and those who are fifteen years older than they, they call fathers, and those who are fifteen years younger they call sons. The magistrates, who watch carefully

over all things, see to it that no one should do injury to another
in this brotherhood.

Knight : And how?

Genoese : There are among them as many magistrates as there
are virtues among us. They are called Liberality, Magnanimity,
Chastity, Firmness, Criminal and Civil Justice, Diligence, Truth,
Kindness, Gratitude and Charity. Each one of these is chosen
when he is still a boy, and he shows at school an inclination for a
particular virtue. But as they do not have amongst them either
thefts or murders, either rape or incest, or adultery as among us,
they accuse one another of ingratitude, or malignity (when one
refuses an honest pleasure), or of deceit, which they hate more
than the plague. And those who are guilty are deprived of the
common table and of commerce with women, until the judge
thinks that they have amended themselves...

In the *City of the Sun* the study of sciences occupies an important
place but, at the same time, manual labour is highly esteemed :

Everyone is taught all the arts...After their third year, children
learn the language and the alphabet by walking round the walls
in four ranks, and four elders lead and teach them. Until the
age of seven they always go barefoot with their hair uncombed.
They are taken round the workshops of the various trades—
tailors, painters, jewellers, etc.—to discover where their inclination lies. After their seventh year all the children follow courses
in natural sciences....and when they are older they study
mathematics, medicine and other sciences ; they continually
debate among themselves and emulate one another, and
eventually they become magistrates of that science or mechanical
art in which they are most proficient...

They also go into the country to learn the work in the fields
and pastures, and he who has studied most arts, and knows how
to practise them is considered most noble. They laugh at us,
who consider our workmen ignoble and hold to be noble those
who have learned no trade and live in idleness and also keep in
idleness and lasciviousness so many servants that it is the ruin of
the republic.

The position of O, or *Metaphysic*, has often been compared to
that of the Pope, but the following passage shows that if
Campanella had modelled him on the Pope, it was an ideal Pope,
resembling more a philosopher (i.e. Campanella himself) than
the popes of the time :

No one can become O if he does not know the histories of the
peoples, their rites, sacrifices and laws ; then he must know about
all the mechanical arts, and every two days he learns a new one
(but experience and drawings make it easy for them to know
them all) ; he must know all the sciences, mathematics, physics
and astrology ; he does not need to know many languages for he
has interpreters. The most important thing is that O should be
a good metaphysician and theologian, that he should be well
acquainted with the origin and demonstration of every art and
science, the similarities and differences of all things, the object,
fate and harmony of the world, power, knowledge, love of God
and of all things. He must know the species of being and their
relation to the celestial, earthly and marine things. He must
make a careful study of the Prophets and the Astrologers. They
therefore know beforehand who must become O, and he must be
over thirty-five years of age to attain such a position, and his
office is perpetual until some man more learned, and more apt
to govern, has been found.

Knight : And who can have such knowledge? And how can
anyone devoted to all sciences be skilled in ruling?

Genoese : I asked them this question and they answered :
" We are more certain that a learned man has the ability to
govern, than you who place ignorant persons in positions of
authority because they are born nobles, or have been elected by
some powerful faction. But our O knows too much ever to be
cruel or wicked or tyrannical. Your argument is valid for the
countries which you have in mind, where a man is considered
learned if he knows more grammar or logic than Aristotle or
some other author. For that one only needs a servile memory,
and man becomes inert, for he does not observe facts but books,
his soul is degraded in the contemplation of dead things, and he
does not know how God orders all things, and the customs of
Nature and of various nations. . . .

We too are aware that he who knows only one science, does
not really know either that or any other, and he who is only
gifted for one science, and has gathered his knowledge from books
alone, is dull and unskilled. But this does not happen to alert
minds, which acquire knowledge with ease, as O's must do.
Furthermore in our city sciences are learned so quickly, that one
learns more in one year here than in ten among your people. .

The laws of the City of the Sun concerning sexual relationships
are solely dictated by the concern to produce a healthy race.
Campanella is more thorough than Plato in his eugenic theories

and believes that the magistrates should be assisted by doctors and astrologers. As an extra precaution prayers are also addressed to God asking him to grant a healthy offspring. It is rather startling to see how little Campanella conforms to the orthodox Christian morality which condemns all sexual unions whose purpose is not that of reproduction, and the idea that sexual repression in young people is harmful and must be avoided strikes one as very modern.

No woman is allowed to submit to a man before she is nineteen years old, and a man must not procreate before he is twenty-one years old...Before that age coitus is allowed with pregnant or sterile women to ease physical needs. The matrons are told in secret of those who are more tormented by Venus, and provide for their wants, not however before they have told the chief magistrate, who is a great doctor...If they are found guilty of sodomy, they are reproached and made to carry a shoe around their neck for two days, which signifies that they have perverted the order, and put the feet where the head should have been.[1]

If they abstain from coitus till they are twenty-one, they are celebrated with honours and songs. When they practice fighting, both women and men are naked, like the Greeks, and the magistrates can see who is impotent and which organs are suited to each other. Having been well washed, they give themselves to coitus every three evenings, and they couple tall and beautiful women to tall and virtuous men, and the thin with the fat to equalise them. They go to bed by order of the magistrate and the matron, and do not begin coitus, until after they have digested their food. They pray first, and have beautiful pictures of men whom the women look at. Then they go to the window and pray to God in Heaven to grant them a good offspring. They sleep in separate cells until the hour in which they must mate has come, and then the matron goes and opens the doors of both cells. The hour is fixed by the Astrologer...

If some women do not conceive with one man, they change him for another ; and if she is found to be sterile, she can go with whom she pleases, but she is deprived of the honour given to the matrons either at the common tables or in the temple, and this is done to prevent any woman from making herself sterile in order to be promiscuous.

The women of the City of the Sun share in the work of the men,

---

[1] Ed. 1623-1637 : And if they repeat the offence they are punished by death.

though they are given lighter tasks. They are trained in the use
of arms, under their own magistrates and mistresses, so that they
may be able, in case of need, to assist the men in the battles near
the city.

Military training plays an important part in the lives of the
inhabitants of the City of the Sun, but they do not engage in
wars of conquest. They only wage wars (in which they are always
the victors) when they have suffered some insult or their land has
been plundered. They also go to the assistance of nations which
are " oppressed by a tyrant of the state, for they are always the
defenders of liberty." Unlike the citizens of Plato's *Republic* they
do not despise less enlightened nations but believe that " the
whole earth will in time come to live in accordance with their
customs, and consequently they always find out whether there be
a nation whose manner of living is better and more approved
than the rest."

Agriculture is held in high esteem and is carried out scientifically. Though there are a few " feeble-minded " individuals who
are exclusively engaged in agricultural work, work on the fields
is carried out by all the citizens of the city. They go to their tasks
armed, " and with flags and drums and trumpets sounding."
Not a span of earth is left untilled, and they use " waggons fitted
with sails which are borne along by the wind even when it is
contrary, by the marvellous contrivance of wheels within wheels."

There are many other interesting " inventions " in *The City of
the Sun*, and Campanella's is the first utopia which gives a leading
role to natural sciences. It is also the first utopia which abolishes
slave labour and considers all manual work, however humble it
may appear, as an honourable duty. As in other utopias, however, there is little freedom in the City of the Sun. Women can
be condemned to death for using make-up or wearing high heels,
and crimes against the liberty of the Republic, God or the
supreme magistrates are also punished by death. But, not
unnaturally, Campanella bans prisons and torture from his ideal
city.

VALENTIN ANDREAE

Christianopolis

ANDREAE's *Christianopolis* was published in 1619, only seventeen years after Campanella wrote his *City of the Sun*, yet it bears a much closer resemblance to the reformist utopias of the 19th century than to that of the Calabrian monk. Johann Valentin Andreae, the German scholar and humanist, has much in common with the cotton manufacturer and great reformer, Robert Owen, and it is perhaps for this reason that his ideal city seems more familiar than the unreal dreams of More and Campanella. Andreae does not write with the imagination and originality of a visionary ; he discusses questions which he must have known intimately and for which he offers immediate solutions. And like most reformers he is not exempt from proselytism. His book is written in the form of a letter addressed to those who would wish to take refuge in his ideal city, and reads more like a recruiting tract than a story meant purely for edification or amusement.

Andreae was born in 1586 ; an extensive education and wide travels made him thoroughly acquainted with the thought and writings of the Renaissance. The revolution in knowledge had been accomplished ; the Aristotelian method was vanquished but the task of replacing it by a new method of education was still to be completed. Andreae devoted most of his life to this work, and already, when he was at the University, he planned a reform of the educational system, and later published several pedagogical works which were received with great interest. As a teacher he was able to put some of his ideas into practice and produced the first plan for a well-regulated gymnasium.

His interests, however, spread outside education, to more general schemes of social reform, which again he tried to put into practice. Professor Held, whose translation of *Christianopolis* is prefaced by a very interesting study of Andreae's work and influence, tells us how, when Andreae became Dekan and Spezialsuperintendent at Calw on the Nagold, he tried to establish a social system such as he had described in *Christianopolis*: "He made his own congregation the starting point of his activities,

and the children his material. Thence his efforts spread to the
working classes in the city, whether in his church or not. He
founded a mutual protective association among the workmen in
the cloth-factories and dye-works, and supported it from voluntary
subscriptions of his parishioners and friends."

It is probably thanks to Andreae's direct experience in social
reforms that his utopia has a concreteness that is absent from those
which inspired him. His scheme of education, carefully
described in *Christianopolis*, had a great influence on Comenius,
who acknowledged himself a pupil of Andreae, and on English
writers such as Hartlib, Drury, Milton and others, who were
similarly interested in educational reform. He also influenced
Samuel Gott, whose utopia, *Nova Solyma*, closely resembles
Andreae's.[1] The book did not, however, achieve the fame of
More's or Campanella's works ; a German translation did not
appear until 1741 and it was not translated into English until
1916. Little did Robert Boyle who, in a letter to Samuel Hartlib
written in 1647, expressed the wish that an English version
might be made of *Christianopolis*, suspect that it would only appear
three hundred years later, and in New York.

The neglect of this work might be attributed partly to the
troubled times in which it appeared and partly to its style, but a
further contributory cause may well have been the accusation of
some writers that it was merely a copy of More's *Utopia* and
Campanella's *City of the Sun*. Andreae was acquainted with both
works, and his ideal city bears many resemblances to that of
Campanella. But these are mostly superficial, and his scheme of
education, which occupies the greater part of the book, is entirely
original. Contrary to the previous utopias, the influence of
Greek writers hardly makes itself felt in Andreae. On the other
hand, the influence of the mediaeval city is very strong. The
conception of brotherhood, the respect for craftsmanship, the
attitude towards work and trade, the importance given to the
craft and the family, all remind us of the guilds which had been
so flourishing in the German towns of the Middle Ages.

There is also a completely new influence in Andreae's ideal
commonwealth, that of the city of Geneva, which he had visited
during his youth and which had made a very strong impression

---

[1]Regarding the influence of Andreae on Comenius, Hartlib, etc., see Prof.
Held's scholarly introduction to *Christianopolis*.

on him. He had been filled with admiration by the high moral standard of the Genevan people and he says, in his autobiography: "If differences in religion had not restrained me, the harmonious unity of their customs and morals would have bound me to the place for ever."

Andreae did not subscribe to the teachings of Calvin but wholeheartedly supported the severity of morals he had introduced in Geneva, and he would have liked to see a new reformation in the Lutheran Church carried out in the spirit of Iron Calvin. Another passage from his *Vita* showed how much he owed to his visit to Geneva :

"When I was in Geneva, I made a notable discovery, the remembrance of which and longing for which will die only with my life. Not alone is there in existence an absolutely free commonwealth, but as an object of pride a censorship of morals in accordance with which investigations are made each week into the morals and even into the slightest transgressions of the citizens —first by the supervisors of the wards, then by the aldermen, and finally by the magistrate, according as the case demands. As a result, all cursing, gambling, luxury, quarrelling, hatred, conceit, deceit, extravagance, and the like, to say nothing of greater sins, are prevented. What a glorious adornment—such purity of morals, for the Christian religion! With our bitterest tears we must lament that this is lacking and almost entirely neglected with us ; and all right-minded men must exert themselves to see that such is called back to life."

We shall see later how another Utopian, the unfrocked monk, Gabriel de Foigny, was to fare in the city which aroused such admiration in Andreae. This " free commonwealth," in which " investigations are made each week into the morals of the citizens," must have already been somewhat bleak at the time of Andreae's visit. The means by which " purity of morals " was achieved in Geneva give us an idea of what Andreae's utopia might have been like, had it not remained in the imagination of its author. In 1562, an historian tells us, twelve men were burnt alive for witchcraft, a woman was drowned in the Rhone for having committed adultery, and a bourgeois of Geneva was condemned to death for the same offence. A certain Jacques Chapellaz, who confessed that he had cursed God and said that he had eaten the devil but could not swallow his horns, and who had already been punished for a previous similar offence, was condemned to have his tongue cut out.

If the spirit of the Renaissance makes itself strongly felt in Andreae's views concerning education, it is the mentality of the religious reformers which guides his moral outlook. The freedom of the inhabitants of Christianopolis, like that of the inhabitants of Geneva, does not include the right to ignore God. Calvin's ordinances of the year 1609 and 1617 made it compulsory for all inhabitants of Geneva to attend sermons regularly and we find the same compulsion in Andreae's ideal city. The censorship of books is also there, as well as the house inspectors ; adultery is severely punished ; and though the German reformer has some very humane things to say about the death penalty and the wickedness of men who punish rather than reform, his statement that crimes against God are to be punished more severely than any other has an ominous sound.

One would feel more attracted to *Christianopolis* if Andreae's religious principles had allowed him more understanding for human feelings, and if man's nature were allowed to express itself without being suspected of falling, at every moment, into the snares of Satan. But we are reminded at every other line of the wickedness of man. " Everyone," Andreae warns us, " carries with him domestic, rustic, or even paternal and inborn evil and wickedness, and communicates these to his comrades, with so poisonous a contagion that it spares not even those who ought to be consecrated entirely to God, but winds its way with varying wickedness, deceit, and rudeness, and takes possession of them so entirely that they cannot throw it off throughout their whole lives, and among the most honourable offices...."

In order to keep Satan away Andreae accompanies his descriptions of the manners and customs of the inhabitants of Christianopolis with long sermons, of which one can truly say that " to have read one is to have read them all." There are few subjects which do not provide him with an opportunity to preach and in his godly city even dishes are seasoned with pious thoughts. These exhortations take so much space in the book that one may be forgiven for quoting one of them on Andreae's favourite theme of " light." Street lighting offers him an admirable excuse and, after stating very briefly that the inhabitants of Christianopolis " do not allow the night to be dark, but brighten it up

with lighted lanterns, the object being to provide for the safety
of the city and to put a stop to useless wandering about, but also
to render the night watches less unpleasant," he continues with
this long tirade on the symbolic significance of light :

They would strive in this way to resist the dark kingdom of
Satan and his questionable pastimes ; and they wish to remind
themselves of the everlasting light. What Antichrist expects
from the great number of wax candles, let him see for himself ;
but let us not shrink back from any system which lessens the fear
of a man working at night in the darkness, and which removes
the veil which our flesh is so anxious to draw over license and
dissoluteness...Oh, if we would but turn more to light, there
would not be such an opportunity for every sort of meanness, nor
such great number of swindlers! Would that the light of our
hearts were burning more frequently, and that we would not so
often endeavour to deceive the all-seeing eye of God! Now
that the darkness serves as excuse for the world and opens it
for all sorts of baseness, while it spreads blindness over those
things of which it is ashamed, what will be the situation when at
the return of Christ, the Sun, every fog will be dispelled and
the World's corruptness which it guards with so many covers,
shall appear, when the wantonness of the heart, the hypocrisy
of the lips, the deceitful deeds of the hands and its much
other filth shall be a disgrace to itself and a mockery to
the blessed?

The whole personality of Andreae seems to be expressed in
this passage. His goodness and consideration for his fellow men,
as well as his practical sense, asked that the city should be lighted
to provide for safety and to render night watches less tiresome,
but his moral and religious feelings made him go beyond these
practical considerations. Throughout his utopia one feels that
his love of men inclined him to trust them as sensible beings
capable of going about their lives in a reliable and honest way,
but his religion told him that man is wicked and has to be carefully guided, preached to and, if necessary, threatened, to be
kept away from sin. That is why his ideal city is a curious combination of free guilds and religious tyranny, of personal
responsibility and of complete submission to religion.

It would be perhaps more exact to describe *Christianopolis* as an
ideal community than as an ideal commonwealth. Though the

island on which it is situated is described as a world in miniature
and the city contains all the elements of a state, Andreae did not
conceive it as being inhabited by people who happened to be
there but by those who have come together, through a community
of ideals and principles.   It appears, from Andreae's introduction
to Christianopolis, that he had attempted to form a secret society
for the purpose of carrying out the religious reform which stood
so near to his heart.   This *Brüderschaft* (generally described as a
Rosicrucian brotherhood) was intended for a small élite and did
not answer the desire of the people who wanted to find a haven
of rest and safety in the midst of the horrors and confusion of the
times.   It was to fulfil their wish that the greater community of
Christianopolis was described.

Whether this Rosicrucian brotherhood was purely a mythical
organisation and whether we must believe Andreae's reasons for
presenting the plan of an ideal city are matters for speculation.
If we accept Andreae literally, *Christianopolis* was meant as a
pattern for a community which could come into existence as
soon as a sufficient number of people have gathered together for
this purpose.   This is how, two centuries later, Owen and Fourier
were to conceive the formation of their ideal communities.   Yet
Andreae begins his narrative with a purely allegorical chapter
which has led many to believe that his book was only a fable.
Here is the passage, which does not lack poetical beauty :

While wandering as a stranger on the earth, suffering much
in patience from tyranny, sophistry and hypocrisy, seeking a
man, and not finding what I so anxiously sought, I decided to
launch out once more upon the Academic Sea though the latter
had very often been hurtful to me.   And so ascending the good
ship, Phantasy, I left the port together with many others and
exposed my life and person to the thousand dangers that go with
desire for knowledge.   For a short space of time conditions
favoured our voyage ; then adverse storms of envy and calumny
stirred up the Ethiopian Sea against us and removed all hope of
calm weather.   The efforts of the skipper and the oarsmen were
exerted to the limit, our own stubborn love of life would not give
up, and even the vessel resisted the rocks ; but the force of the
sea always proved stronger.   Finally when all hope was lost and
we, rather of necessity than on account of bravery of soul, had
prepared to die, the ship collapsed and we sank.   Some were
swallowed up by the sea, some were scattered to great distances,

while some who could swim or who found planks to float upon, were carried to different islands scattered throughout this sea. Very few escaped death, and I alone, without a single comrade, was at length driven to a very minute islet, a mere piece of turf, it seemed.

The traveller lands on the island, Caphar Salama, which was " rich in grain and pasture fields, watered with rivers and brooks, adorned with woods and vineyards, full of animals, just as if it were a whole world in miniature."

Before being admitted into the city the traveller is interrogated by three examiners. Andreae is the first to make the entrance to his utopia dependent on an examination, and we can be grateful that immigration officers nowadays are not as thorough as those of Christianopolis. The first examiner satisfies himself that the traveller is not a quack, or a beggar, or a stage player. The second investigates his moral character and temperament, and the third wants to know, amongst other things, what progress he has made " in the observation of the heavens and the earth, in the close examination of nature, in instruments of the arts, in the history and origin of languages, the harmony of all the world. . ." The traveller is not very well prepared for answering these questions, but as he brings " an unsullied slate, washed clean, as it were, by the sea itself," he is admitted into the city.

The city is small but compact, and built as a unit in which each section serves a specific function. It betrays that love of perfect symmetry which characterises the architecture of the Renaissance :

Its shape is a square, whose side is seven hundred feet, well fortified with four towers and a wall. It looks, therefore, toward the four quarters of the earth. . . . Of buildings there are two rows, or if you count the seat of government and the storehouses, four ; there is only one public street, and only one market-place, but this one is of a very high order. If you measure the buildings, you will find from the innermost street, being twenty feet in width, the numbers increase by fives even up to one hundred. At this point there is a circular temple, a hundred feet in diameter. . . . . All buildings are in three stories, and public balconies lead to these . . . All buildings are made of burnt stone and are separated by fireproof walls so that a fire could not do very severe damage. . . Things look much the same all around, not

extravagant nor yet unclean ; fresh air and ventilation are
provided throughout. About four hundred citizens live here in
religious faith and peace of the highest order. Outside the walls
is a moat stocked with fish, that even in times of peace it may
have its uses. The open and otherwise unused spaces contain
wild animals, kept, however, not for purposes of entertainment
but for practical use. The whole city is divided into three parts,
one to supply food, one for drill and exercise, and one for books.
The remainder of the island serves purposes of agriculture and
for workshops.

The organisation of Christianopolis is not based on the
patriarchal family as in Amaurot, or on the monastic community
as in the City of the Sun. The city is divided into sections according to the work carried out in each of them. On the periphery
we find those devoted to the production and storing of food, as
well as that for heavy industry. The section of the corporation
which faces east is the farm quarter ; it is divided into two parts,
agriculture proper on the one side, and animal husbandry on the
other. The section which faces south is occupied by mills and
bakeries, that which faces north by the meat shops and supply
stores, and finally, the section on the west is given over to the
forge.

Inside the city craftsmen are also divided into four sections :
" For even as the city is four-cornered, so also the inhabitants
deal with four materials : metals, stones, woods and the things
that are needed for weaving ; but with this difference, that the
occupations which require more skill and innate ability are
assigned to the inner square, while those which admit of more
ease in working, to the outer or greater square."

This functional town-planning is being followed by our modern
architects and has aroused the admiration of an authority on
cities, Lewis Mumford : ". . . In planning the industrial quarters
of Christianopolis, these seventeenth century Utopians have
anticipated the best practice that has been worked out to-day,
after a century of disorderly building. The separation of the city
into zones, the distinction between heavy industries and light
industries, the grouping of similar industrial establishments, the
provision of an agricultural zone adjacent to the city, in
all this our garden cities are but belated reproductions of
Christianopolis."

For all its modernism, however, Christianopolis is based, to a certain extent, on the mediaeval city which Kropotkin describes as being " usually divided into four quarters, or into five to seven sections radiating from the centre ; each quarter corresponding to a certain trade or profession which prevailed in it, but nevertheless containing inhabitants of different social positions and occupations."

The local administration of the city is based on this division according to occupation. In the east section, that is the farm quarter, a tower dominates the buildings and under the dome of this tower " the citizens of that side of the town may come together, as often as the ordinances require, and act on sacred as well as on civil matters." Thus we see that the " guild " is based on the work performed and on the place where the worker lives.

The government is carried out by a triumvirate because, " though a monarchy has many advantages yet they prefer to preserve this dignity for Christ, and they distrust, not without cause, the self-control of human beings." The central part of the state is governed by eight men, each of whom lives in one of the larger towers and has under him eight other subordinates, distributed through the smaller towers. There are a further twenty-four councillors elected by the citizens. The members of the triumvirate, the officials and the councillors, owe their position not to their birth or wealth but to their higher virtues, their experience in public affairs, and the love and respect they inspire. The state is ruled by religion, and a double tablet, inscribed in letters of gold, sets down their confession of faith and the aims and rules of daily life, for these are " a people of Christ, whose religion agrees with that of the apostles and the state administration with the law of God."

In this Christian Republic there is no private property. Everyone receives whatever he needs from the community : " No one has any money, nor is there any use for any private money ; yet the republic has its own treasury. And in this respect the inhabitants are especially blessed because no one can be superior to the other in the amount of riches owned, since the advantage is rather one of power and genius, and the highest respect, that of morals and piety."

Work occupies an honoured place in Christianopolis, and

though Andreae echoes Campanella in abolishing slavery and
condemning the injustice that working people should support
idlers, he goes further by showing how even unpleasant work can
cease to be a burden if it is carried out in an atmosphere of
equality and freedom :

They have very few working hours, yet no less is accomplished
than in other places as it is considered disgraceful by all that one
should take more rest and leisure time than is allowed. Since in
other places it is true that ten working men with difficulty
support one idler, it will not be difficult to believe that with all
these men working there is some time of leisure left for individuals.
And yet they all together attend to their labours in such a way
that they seem to benefit rather than harm their physical bodies.
Where there is no slavery, there is nothing irksome in the human
body which weighs down or weakens.

And elsewhere he attacks the prejudice attached to manual
labour :

There are also public duties, to which all citizens have
obligation, such as watching, guarding, harvesting of grain and
wine, working roads, erecting buildings, draining ground, also
certain duties of assisting in the factories, which are imposed on
all in turn according to age and sex, but not very often nor for a
long time. For even though certain experienced men are put in
charge of all the duties, yet when men are asked for, no one refuses
the state his services and strength.   For what we are in our
homes, they are in their city, which they not undeservedly think
a home.   And for this reason it is no disgrace to perform any
public function, so long as it be not indecent. Hence all work,
even that which seems rather irksome, is accomplished in good
time and without much difficulty, since the promptness of the great
number of workmen permits them easily to collect or distribute
the greatest mass of things. Who does not believe, since we are
willing, all of us, to rejoice in and enjoy privileges and conveniences of a community, that the care and the work are
ordinarily imposed upon a few, while continual idleness and
gluttony are made permissible to the many?   On the contrary,
who denies that every citizen, in his own place and order, owes
his best efforts to the republic, not merely with his tongue but
also with hands and shoulder? With an entirely mistaken sense
of delicacy do the carnal-minded shrink from touching earth,
water, stones, coal and things of that sort ; but they think it

grand to have in their possession to delight them, horses, dogs, harlots and similar creatures.

While More thought that some trades had a degrading effect on those who carried them out, Andreae says that in Christianopolis : " Men that have to do the heavy work do not become wild and rough, but remain kindly, the guards are not gluttons, but are temperate, not evil-smelling but cleanly washed...A district on the north is devoted to the slaughter houses ..this part has no suggestion of the bestial about it. And yet in other places men become coarse from the daily custom of shedding blood, or the handling of meats, fats, hides, and the like."

He also shows that work is not a penance if it is accompanied by sufficient leisure : " While among us one is worn out by the fatigue of an effort, with them the powers are reinforced by a perfect balance of work and leisure so that they never approach a piece of work without alacrity."

Unlike Plato, he does not think that manual and intellectual work should be separated, but rather that each individual should engage in both :

..... their artisans are almost entirely educated men. For that which other people think is the proper characteristic of a few (and yet, if you consider the stuffing of inexperience as learning, the characteristic of too many men already) this the inhabitants argue should be attained by all individuals. They say neither the subtleness of letters is such, nor yet the difficulty of work, that one man, if given enough, cannot master both.

His views on the application of science to industry are interesting. Science will not merely benefit production; it will also permit the workers to understand what they are doing and thereby increase their interest in their work :

In the section given over to the forge...on the one side are seven workshops fitted out for heating, hammering, welting, and moulding metals ; while on the other side are seven others assigned to the buildings of those workmen who make salt, glass, brick, earthenware, and to all industries which require constant fire. Here in truth you see a testing of nature herself ; everything that the earth contains in her bowels is subjected to the laws and instruments of science. The men are not driven to a work with which they are unfamiliar, like pack-animals to their task, but they have been trained long before in an accurate knowledge of scientific matters, and find their delight in the inner parts of nature. If a person does not here listen to the reason and look into the most minute elements of the microcosm, they think that nothing has been proved. Unless you analyse matter by experiment, unless you improve the deficiencies of knowledge by more capable instruments, you are worthless...Here one may welcome and listen to true and genuine chemistry, free and active; whereas in other places false chemistry steals upon and imposes on one behind one's back. For true chemistry is accustomed to examine the work, to assist with all sorts of tests, and to make use of experiments. Or, to be brief, here is practical science.

This is how, in Christianopolis, production is carried out for use instead of profit :

Their work, or as they prefer to hear it called, " the employment of their hands," is conducted in a certain prescribed way, and all the things made are brought into a public booth. From here every workman receives out of the store on hand, whatever is necessary for the work of the coming week. For the whole city is, as it were, one single workshop, but of all different sorts of crafts. The ones in charge of these duties are stationed in the smaller towers at the corners of the wall ; they know ahead of time what is to be made, in what quantity, and of what form, and they inform the mechanics of these items. If the supply of material in the work booth is sufficient, the workmen are permitted to indulge and give play to their inventive genius.

If the inhabitants of Christianopolis are wise enough not to produce more than they can use they also guard themselves against unnecessary wants. The families, being small, do not need big houses, but live in small flats ; they do not require servants except on rare occasions, and, being all equals, they do not wish to impress one another by unnecessary luxury :

Almost all the houses are built after one model; they are well kept and especially free from anything unclean. There are three rooms in the average house, a bathroom, a sleeping apartment, and a kitchen. And the latter two are generally separated by a board partition. The middle part within the towers has a little open space with a wide window, where wood and heavier things are raised aloft by pulleys...The houses are kept up at the expense of the state, and provision is made by the carefulness of inspectors that nothing is thoughtlessly destroyed or changed.

No one need be surprised at the rather cramped quarters ; for their being only a very few persons, there is also need for only a very little furniture.　Other people who house vanity, extravagance, and a family of that sort, and who keep up baggage of iniquity, can never live spaciously enough.　They burden others and are burdened themselves, and no one measures their necessities, nay even their comforts, easily otherwise than by an unbearable and unmovable mass.

Now it will be easy to guess what the furnishings are.　There are none except the most necessary, and even then scant. . . . There are the necessary dishes for the table and enough cooking utensils.　For why should you want great numbers of things when all that you may reasonably desire can always be obtained at the public store-house?

They have only two suits of clothes, one for their work, one for the holidays, and for all classes they are made alike.　Sex and age are shown by the form of the dress.　The cloth is made of linen or wool respectively for summer or winter, and the colour for all is white or ashen grey, none have fancy, tailored goods.

Since grown children are brought up elsewhere, in most instances a family consists of four or five, less frequently six individuals, father, mother, and one or two children.　Servingmen and servingwomen are a rare thing, nor very noticeable, except in the case of those attending the sick, those in confinement, or babies.　The husband and wife perform together the ordinary duties of the home, and the rest is taken care of in the public workshop.

Contrary to most utopias, there are no common meals in Christianopolis, but this does not lead to inequalities, for a comprehensive rationing system is applied :

Their meals are private to all, but the food is obtained from the public storehouse.　And because it is almost impossible to avoid unpleasantness and confusion when the number of those partaking of a meal is so great, they prefer that individuals shall eat together privately in their own homes.　Even as the food is distributed according to the nature of the year, so also it is apportioned weekly according to the number of families.　But provision of wine is made for a half year, or if conditions admit, of still longer period.　They get their fresh meat from the meat shop, and they take away as much as is assigned to them.　Fish, as also game, and all sorts of birds are distributed to them according to each one's proportion, the time and age being taken into consideration.　There are ordinarily four dishes, and these after being carefully washed are prepared by the women, and are seasoned with wise and pious words. Whoever wishes to have a guest may do so, and the parties concerned, join their dishes accordingly, or if it be a foreigner, they ask from the public supplies that may be necessary.

In previous utopias one of the reasons for abolishing private meals was obviously to free the women for what were considered more worthy occupations such as, for example, military training. From Plato to Campanella, the utopian woman had been amazonian. Andreae gives her a purely feminine role, but he is not altogether Victorian. He would have women keep their place, and refuses them the " vote," but he provides girls with the same college education as boys :

The married women make use of the knowledge which they acquire while in college. For whatsoever human industry accomplishes by working with silk, wool, or flax, this is the material for woman's arts and is at her disposal. So they learn to sew, to spin, to embroider, to weave, and to decorate their work in various ways. Tapestry is their handiwork, clothes their regular work, washing their duty. In addition to this they care for the house and the kitchen and have them clean. Whatever scholarship they have, being mentally gifted, they improve diligently, not only to know something themselves, but that they may sometimes also teach. In the church and in the council they have no voice, yet none the less do they mould the piety and morals, none the less do they shine with the gifts of heaven. God has denied this sex nothing, if it is pious, of which the eternally blessed Mary is a most glorious example. If we read the histories, we shall find that no virtue has been inaccessible to women, and there is none in which they have not excelled. However rarely do many of them comprehend the value of silence. ....Women have no adornments except that mentioned by Peter ; no dominion except over household matters ; no permission to do servants' work (a thing that will surprise you), unless disease or some accident demands it. No woman is ashamed of her household duties, nor does she tire of attending to the wants of her husband. Likewise no husband of whatsoever employment thinks himself above honourable labours. For to be wise and to work are not incompatible if there is moderation.

His views on marriage are also much more conservative than those of earlier utopians. It is not carried out according to eugenic principles, but according to inclination, if this does not meet with the disapproval of the family and the state :

It is nowhere safer to get married than here. For as the unusualness of the dowry and the uncertainty of daily bread are lacking, it remains only that the value of virtues and sometimes of beauty be made. It is permitted a youth of twenty-four years to marry a girl not under eighteen, but not without the consent of the parents, consultation of the relatives, approbation of the laws, and benediction of God. There is with them the greatest reverence of relationship of blood. The factors considered in joining in marriage are for the most part conformity of natures and propriety ; but also a thing that is elsewhere so rare, recommendation of piety. The greatest fault is considered to be impurity and the laws against such offenders are severe. But by removing opportunities they easily eliminate the sins. The marriages have almost no expense or noise ; they do not at all expect worldly foolishness and senselessness...without any drunkenness, which usually initiates all sacred functions elsewhere, but not without a hymn and Christian congratulations, they are married. There is no dowry at all except the promises of Christ, the example of parents, the knowledge acquired by both, and the joy of peace. Furniture is provided together with the house out of the public store. In this summary fashion they render most safe and speedy, our cross, punishment, torment, purgatory, and however else we are accustomed to call inauspicious marriages.

The purpose of marriage is that of reproduction, and Andreae, unlike Campanella, does not admit of sexual relationships for pleasure alone :

They have the greatest desire for conjugal chastity, and they set a premium upon it, that they may not injure or weaken themselves by too frequent intercourse. To beget children is quite proper ; but passion of licence is a disgrace. Others live together like beasts ; yet even the cattle have characteristics which put such persons to shame, who might better with mutual love and mutual aid first care for heaven and later for things of the earth. So the citizens of Christianopolis believe that there may be to a certain extent fornication and pollution even in marriage. Oh, the carnal-minded who are not ashamed to make sin out of lawful as well as unlawful practices!

Religion is the keynote of education, as it is of marriage. Children are not brought up to become the soldiers of the state, but good Christians. As the family and the state are one with religion there is no need for segregating the children from their parents ; as all citizens are equal, the system of education is the same for all children, boys and girls.

Ideas on education had made enormous progress during the Renaissance, and there had been, particularly in Italy, many academies and colleges where the sons and daughters of the aristocracy and of the wealthy received a thorough and liberal education. Andreae did not concern himself, however, with the education of a small, privileged minority, the sons of princes and rich merchants who could afford tutors or private schools. For this reason his education has none of the glamour of that received by the fortunate Thelemites, but it has the advantage of being accessible to all.

The great majority of the schools of his time had not been influenced to any great extent by the ideas of the Renaissance, and radical changes were needed not only in the methods of education, but also in the schools themselves and the teaching profession. Conditions at the time of Andreae were still the same as those Erasmus denounced with such vehemence in his *Praise of Folly* :

The Grammarians...being ever hunger-starv'd, and slovens in their Schools—Schools, did I say? Nay, rather Cloisters, Bridwells or Slaughter-houses—grown old among a company of boyes, deaf with their noise, and pin'd away with stench and nastiness. And yet by my courtesie it is that they think themselves the most excellent of all men ; so greatly do they please themselves in frighting a company of fearful boyes, with a thundering voice and big looks, tormenting them with Ferules, Rods, and Whips ; and, laying about 'em without fear or wit, imitate the Ass in the Lion's skin.

In Christianopolis the school is roomy and beautiful, " all is open, sunny, and happy, so that with the sight of pictures, even, they attract the children, fashion the minds of the boys and girls, and advise the youths. They are not baked in summer nor frozen in winter ; they are not disturbed by noise nor frightened because of loneliness. Whatever is elsewhere given over to luxury and leisure of palaces, is here devoted to honourable recreation and pursuits, an investment that is nowhere more satisfactory or better paying."

Next to the appearance of the school, the greatest care must be given to the choice of masters :

Their instructors are not men from the dregs of human society nor such as are useless for other occupations, but the choice of all the citizens, persons whose standing in the republic is known and who very often have access to the highest positions in the state. The teachers who are well advanced in years and are specially remarkable for their pursuit of four virtues : dignity, integrity, activity and generosity, must spur their charges on as free agents with kindness, courteous treatment, and a liberal discipline rather than with threats, blows and like sternness.

All the children of both sexes are taken into training. When they have completed their sixth year, their parents give them over to the state. They eat and sleep at the school but parents " can visit their children, even unseen by them, as often as they have leisure." The living quarters are arranged with the same attention as the school itself to create " hygienic " conditions. " They see to it carefully that the food is appetising and whole-some, that the couches and beds are clean and comfortable, and that the clothes and attire of the whole body are clean. The pupils wash often and use linen towels for drying. The hair is also combed to prevent anything unclean from collecting. If diseases of the skin or body are contracted, the individuals in question are cared for in good time ; and to avoid the spreading of infection, they are quarantined."
Education in Christianopolis is directed towards three aims and the first is, naturally, " to worship God with a pure and faithful soul" ; the second, to strive toward the best and most chaste morals ; the third, to cultivate the mental powers. It is clear that Andreae does not conceive of education as the acquisition of knowledge in the narrow sense we give it to-day. He is more concerned with forming the mind and personality of the child and with developing his faculties than with increasing the volume of his learning.
Boys and girls follow the same courses, though not simultaneously; the boys have their study periods in the morning, the girls in the afternoon. The rest of their time is devoted to manual training, domestic art and science. Matrons as well as learned men act as instructors.

The school is divided into eight halls, which correspond to the eight departments of education. The first is the school of arts, divided into three sections according to the age of the pupils. The youngest students begin with grammar and languages, and learn to name " all sorts of things and actions in three languages, Hebrew, Greek and Latin," but Andreae reassures us by saying that they are careful not to overload delicate and fragile creatures, and that liberal recreation is allowed.

The more mature students are taught oratory, that is, to refute all sorts of arguments in accordance with the rules of the art. Though they learn how to adorn their speeches " with little flowers of elegance," more stress is laid upon natural force than artificial form. Those who are old enough also learn modern languages " not merely for the sake of knowing more, but that they may be able to communicate with many peoples of the earth —the dead as well as the living, and that they may not be compelled to put faith in every supposed scholar." But the study of languages should not be valued beyond its uses ; the important thing is what one has to say and that can be expressed just as well in one's native tongue : " If righteousness and honesty are at hand, it matters little in what tongue they are spoken, if they are absent, it is of no advantage whether one goes astray speaking Greek or Latin."

The students who have already made some progress enter the second department, where they attend lectures on logic, metaphysics and theosophy. Logic must be used as a means and not as an end in itself : " No skilled workman boasts of his sun-dial pin or his plumb-line alone, unless there is something of his own work on hand to exhibit."

In their study of metaphysics and theosophy all concern for concrete things, for investigation and invention, is left behind and knowledge is acquired by " consulting the divine sun and ascending to the known God."

In the third hall we come back to the less esoteric sciences of arithmetic, geometry and algebra, which develop mental faculties and help to solve practical matters with remarkable diligence. Here is also taught the science of mystic numbers which played such an important role in the philosophy of the Renaissance. To the planners of the Renaissance it seemed impossible that God, the arch-planner, should not have organised the world according to harmonious rules and measurements. " Surely," says Andreae, " that supreme Architect did not make this mighty mechanism haphazard, but He completed it most wisely by measures, numbers, and proportions, and He added to it the elements of time, distinguished by a wonderful harmony." This admirable plan cannot be discovered with " compasses from human philosophy " but only through God's revelation, which is not always easy to detect. The same caution must be used in the divination of the future ; Andreae does not deny the value of prophecies, but warns that " God has reserved the future for Himself, revealing it to a very limited number of individuals and then only at the greatest intervals."

To enter the fourth department, that of music, one must have a knowledge of arithmetic and geometry. Music in Christianopolis, he says, aspires to that of heaven and does not encourage " the madness of dancing, the frivolity of vulgar songs, the wickedness of roisters. All of these things have been long ago driven out of this republic and are now unheard." Their instruments, of which they have a great number and variety and which are skilfully used by practically everyone, are attuned to the instruments of God, and their chorus, which is also devoted only to solemn music, passes through the city once every week, in addition to the holidays.

The fifth department is devoted to astronomy and astrology, which are " deserving of humankind as any other art." It is unworthy of man " to look at the sky no more observantly than any beast," and those who do not know the value of astrology in human affairs, or foolishly deny it, should be condemned to dig in the earth, cultivate and work the fields, for as long a time as possible, in unfavourable weather! But astrology is far from playing here the capital role it plays in *The City of the Sun*. The inhabitants of Christianopolis say that it is an uncertain thing to make everything dependent on the stars " on the first moment of existence and birth, and from this moment to accept judgement of life or death. And so they emphasise rather this as to how they may rule the stars, and by faith shake off the yoke if any exists."

In the sixth hall are taught natural philosophy, secular and church history. The knowledge of the worlds and their creatures must be accompanied by that of the events of human tragedy.

Andreae stresses the need for historical truth, but also warns against those who merely look on the wickedness of mankind, on the monstrous deeds, the hideousness of wars, the horrors of massacres, and ignore the germs of virtue, the dignity of the human soul, the abundance of peace and restful quiet. "There are scholars who are bold enough to be unacquainted with such facts and who rank them with fables ; they are very worthy themselves to be told of in fable."

We have seen that the whole of Andreae's scheme of education is as much concerned with giving a moral education as with dispensing knowledge. In spite of this the seventh department is reserved to ethics, which includes the study of all human virtues not only in theory, but also in practice, as well as the art of government and Christian charity. The three qualities of man most valued are : equality, the desire for peace, and the contempt for riches.

The last school is devoted to theology, which teaches the "strength, elegance, efficacity, and depth" of the Holy Scriptures, and practical theology, which instructs them on how to pray and meditate. They have also a school of prophecy, not to give instruction in soothsaying, but to test those who have been favoured with the gift of prophesying, and to observe the harmony and truth of the prophetic spirit.

Besides the eight halls already described there are two rooms assigned to the study of medicine and two to jurisprudence. The study of the latter is purely academic, as there is no need for lawyers in Christianopolis. For some reason, however, lawyers and notaries have not disappeared, and Andreae informs us that, so that they may not be idle, if anything has to be copied it is entrusted to these men.

There is nothing surprising in the importance attached by Andreae to chemistry, natural sciences, anatomy, mathematics and astronomy ; they were sciences that a man of the Renaissance would not dream of neglecting any more than a Greek would have left music or gymnastics out of a system of education. What is surprising, however, is the modern and rational attitude displayed in the method of teaching. His laboratories were not reserved for great savants like Bacon's House of Salomon ; they were available to students, and if they were made as attractive as possible it was not for " show " but because " instruction enters altogether more easily through the eyes than through the ears, and much more pleasantly in the presence of refinement than among the base. They are deceived who think that it is impossible to teach except in dark caves and with gloomy brow."

Andreae is also the first to include the teaching of pictorial arts in his utopian scheme of education. The city has its studio, " a very roomy shop for pictorial art," and not merely are painting, drawing and sculpture used to decorate the city with beautiful and useful paintings and statues, but the teaching of art is encouraged, for, those who " practice with the brush, wherever they enter, bring along their experienced eyes, their hands adapted to imitation, and what is of greater importance, a judgement equal to and already trained for things, not unfruitful or mean." However, even when using a brush one may be caught in Satan's snares and the artists of Christianopolis " are seriously commanded to observe purity," so that they will not poison the eyes of the innocent with impure pictures.

Next to the work of educational reform, Andreae was interested in the formation of a " college " or society which would unite all men of learning and provide them with the necessary means to carry out their researches. Already in the *Fama*, published in 1614, and circularised in manuscript form as early as 1610, he outlined a plan for scientific investigation and had given the model for a college or society of fellows which would institute a " general reformation " of the whole civilised world. Professor Held in his introduction to *Christianopolis* has shown how Andreae's ideas influenced those writers and philosophers who laid the foundations of the Royal Society in London. It is probable also that Bacon was acquainted with Andreae's works and that they influenced his invention of the House of Salomon.

In *Christianopolis* the College is described rather briefly, and it is not clear whether it is composed of all those who wish to carry out studies or researches, or whether it is limited to a chosen few:

Now is the time when we approach the innermost shrine of the city which you would rightly call the centre of activity of the state...Here religion, justice, and learning have their abode, and theirs is the control of the city, and eloquence has been given them as an interpreter. Never have I seen so great an amount of human perfection collected into one place....

If we are left rather vague as to the exact attributes of the college, we are given on the other hand a detailed and concrete description of the library, armoury, laboratories and botanic gardens, which belong to it.

In the laboratory dedicated to chemical science " the properties of metals, minerals, and vegetables, and even the life of animals are examined, purified, increased, and united, for the use of the human race and in the interests of health...here men learn to regulate fire, make use of the air, value the water, and test the earth."

There is a pharmacy where one can find a carefully selected collection of all that can be found in nature " not only for the cause of health, but also with a view toward the advancement of education in general." They have also a place given over to anatomy, where animals are dissected, for : " The inhabitants of Christianopolis teach their youth the operations of life and the various organs, from the parts of the physical body. They show them the wonderful structure of the bones, for which purpose they have not a few skeletons and of the required variety. Meantime they also show the anatomy of the human body, but more rarely because the rather sensitive human mind recoils from a contemplation of our own suffering."

The greatest care is devoted to the Natural Science laboratory. Here we find, as in *The City of the Sun*, that natural history is painted on the walls in detail and with the greatest skill. " The phenomena in the sky, views of the earth in different regions, the different races of men, representations of animals, forms of growing things, classes of stones and gems are not only on hand and named, but they even teach and make known their nature and qualities." But the laboratory does not merely contain pictorial representations ; it is also a well-ordered museum where all the specimens of nature that can be beneficial or injurious to man's body are kept, and a competent demonstrator explains their uses and properties. The citizens of Christianopolis condemn those who acquire their knowledge merely from books and " hesitate when placed face to face with some little herb."

Mathematics of course play an important part, and there is an " excavated " workshop for astronomical instruments and a hall of mathematics, " remarkable for its diagrams of the heavens, as the hall of physics is for its diagrams of the earth."

While war or the preparations for war play such an important part in the utopias considered previously, they are mentioned extremely briefly in *Christianopolis* :

Of the Armoury...they have a still more critical opinion. For while the world especially glories in war—engines, catapults and other machines and weapons of war, these people look with horror upon all kinds of deadly and death-dealing instruments, collected in such numbers ; and they show them to visitors not without disapproval of human cruelty...However, they do bear arms, though unwillingly, for keeping off some greater evil, and they distribute them privately among the individual citizens, that they may serve in the homes in the case of sudden emergency.

Before we leave Christianopolis we shall quote these passages which express well the idealist character of Andreae's community:

You will want to know of what advantage it is for one of regular morals and excelling talent to live in this city when you hear nothing of rewards. Well, he of the Christian city solves this difficulty very easily ; for it is glory and gain enough for him to please God....The pleasure of the consciousness of having done right, the dignity of a nature that has overcome darkness, the greatness of domination over the passions, and above all, the unspeakable joy of the companionship of the saints, take possession of a refined soul far too deeply than that the renouncing of worldly pleasures should be feared.

In the same way we may say of penalties, there is no use of these in a place that contains the very sanctuary of God and a chosen state, in which Christian liberty can bear not even commands, much less threats, but is borne voluntarily toward Christ. Yet it must be confessed that human flesh cannot be completely conquered anywhere. And so if it does not profit by repeated warnings (and in case of need, serious corrections) severer scourges must be used to subdue it. For this purpose fit remedies are on hand, not of one sort only, but chosen to suit different individuals. For truly, if one withdraws the sustenance from one's carnal appetites, or substitutes the cudgel for the tickle of lust, much may be remedied. It is the art of arts to guard against permitting sin to become easy for anyone. On the other hand, how wicked it is to vent one's wrath against those towards whose ruin you hurl stones. At any rate, the judges of the Christian City observe this question especially, that they punish most severely those misdeeds which are directed straight against

God, less severely those which injure men, and lightest of all those which harm only property. How differently the world does, punishing a petty thief much more harshly than a blasphemer or an adulterer. As the Christian citizens are always chary of spilling blood, they do not willingly agree upon the death sentence as a form of punishment ; whereas the world, ever prodigal even of a brother's blood, pronounces wantonly the first sentence which occurs to it, feeling safe in this subterfuge that it has not personally employed sword, rope, wheel and fire, but only through a servant of the law. Christ be my witness, it is certainly handsome logic on the part of a government to make thieves of dissolute characters, adulterers of the intemperate, homicides of loafers, witches of courtesans, in order that it may have someone with whose blood to make expiation to God! It is far more humane to tear out the first elements and roots of vice than to lop off the mature stalks. For anyone can destroy a man, but only the best one can reform.

FRANCIS BACON
New Atlantis

THERE is some doubt as to whether the *New Atlantis* should be considered as an ideal commonwealth or as the description of an ideal scientific college, and indeed Bacon's utopia is not as many-sided as that of More or Campanella. The fact that this " fable " is described in the sub-title as a fragment would also lead one to believe that the scientific college, or House of Salomon, was only one institution, among others, which Bacon intended to depict. And Dr Rawley, his chaplain and literary executor, says that : " His Lordship thought also in the present fable to have composed a frame of Laws, or of the best state or mould of a commonwealth ; but foreseeing it would be a long work, his desire of collecting the Natural History diverted him, which he preferred many degrees before it."

Whether or not Bacon intended to write a second part to the *New Atlantis*, it is unlikely that he would have altered the fundamental character of his society, which was to give to science, and the scientists, the predominant role. Like Plato, who describes in detail the laws governing the lives of the Guardians, but tells us little about the other classes, Bacon is only interested in the institutions and work of his guardians, the fellows of Salomon's House, and says next to nothing about the lives of the rest of the people. What is left unsaid can be, however, as significant as what is said ; Plato and Bacon are only concerned with the ruling caste, because it is, in their opinion, the only one which counts. In this sense the *New Atlantis* can be considered as an ideal commonwealth.

Bacon's work has been chiefly admired, however, for being the first description of a complete scientific college based on experimental science. Whether his scheme was in fact the first of its kind or whether he borrowed it from the writings of Andreae and Campanella, or from the scientific academies which had sprung up in Italy during the Renaissance, has given rise to much controversy. Without involving oneself in it, one can fairly safely state that the idea of a college for scientific research was very much in the air at the time when Bacon conceived his scheme, and that the importance of experimental science had been appreciated by many philosophers before him. If his work is considered against the background of that which had already been done it would appear, as Harald Hoffding points out, that: " This man, who has so often been described as the founder of empirical science, does not even merit the name of a Moses who has seen the promised land. He possessed, it is true, a certain prophetic insight, and he often gave inspired utterances to thoughts which illuminated the course of human inquiry. He was, moreover, perfectly conscious of his attitude of opposition towards scholasticism; but the promised land had already been conquered, though he was not aware of it, by da Vinci, Kepler, and Galileo. He modestly declares himself to be no warrior, but merely a herald inciting to combat. The inquirers who founded modern empirical science, however, did not require the sound of his blast to inspire them for the struggle."

If too much credit has been given to Bacon for the originality of his philosophical ideas, no one, however, has disputed the fact that he was the first philosopher to envisage a renovation of society through science. In previous utopias this renovation was to be achieved through social legislation, religious reforms, or the spreading of knowledge, and even when science occupied an important place, as in *The City of the Sun* or in *Christianopolis*, the magistrates were not chosen merely for their knowledge but for their religious and moral virtues. In the *New Atlantis* the scientists form a caste endowed with a power superior to that of the King. The House of Salomon was not a society sponsored by the King and dependent on him, like the Royal Society which it inspired; it was a State within the State, with seemingly limitless funds, secret agents, and the right to withhold secrets from the rest of the community.

Bacon, furthermore, is an innovator by the almost exclusive importance which he gave to natural sciences. He carried a step forward the specialisation which had begun to take place during the Renaissance and which spelt the end of the "universal man," equally interested in philosophy and art, science and literature.

The *New Atlantis* occupies a very small place in Bacon's vast production, but it has been said that there is perhaps "no single work of his which has so much of himself in it." Bacon was not a moralist like More, a religious reformer like Andreae or a universal philosopher like Campanella ; he was a politician with a passionate interest in science and his *New Atlantis* is a " dream of compensation " where science and power unite and reign supreme. It is a dream of immense laboratories, numerous assistants and enormous funds such as any scientist, struggling alone with inadequate equipment and frustrated by lack of money and assistants, might have. But it is also the dream of a frustrated politician who, in spite of his gifts and absence of scruples, failed to secure the power he desired.

Bacon was firmly convinced that to carry out his philosophical and scientific work he needed to be in a position of power, and to this end he applied himself to politics.

But power also attracted him for its own sake. In the *New Atlantis* power and knowledge are ideally united but in his life his thirst for power and honours hindered rather than helped his scientific work. To quote Hoffding again : " He saw before him a great work which required powerful means. He admired Machiavelli and like him believed that the end justified the means, and he was not very particular in the choice of these. For him, like Machiavelli, the means gained the upper hand over the end which was to consecrate them."

The *New Atlantis* is an illustration of his famous statement " knowledge is power," but if Bacon was successful in demonstrating that science would give power to men over nature he assumed, rather than proved, that science, by satisfying man's needs, would automatically increase his happiness. Bacon's belief in science as the weapon for human improvement anticipates the modern conception of progress, which is materialistic rather than idealistic ; it assumes that happiness consists in the satisfaction of ever-increasing material needs. Plato, and other utopian writers after him, had seen, on the contrary, in the multiplication of man's needs a hindrance to his freedom and happiness.

The *New Atlantis* was written around 1624 and was published after Bacon's death in 1627. It was first written in English and later translated into Latin by Bacon himself. It appeared in the English text in the volume containing the *Sylva Sylvarum*, for which place Bacon had himself designated it, for the description of Salomon's House was meant to provide an illustration of the practical results he anticipated from the study of natural history.

The *New Atlantis* owes little to previous descriptions of ideal commonwealths, though the setting for this "fable" was suggested by the myth of Atlantis, contained in Plato's *Timaeus* and his fragmentary dialogue, the *Critias*. There is no conclusive evidence to prove that Bacon was acquainted with *The City of the Sun*, but he mentions Campanella in one of his letters and there are many resemblances of detail between the two works. It is also probable that Bacon had read Andreae's *Christianopolis*. The *New Atlantis*, however, differs considerably in all its main institutions from earlier utopias. Private property, money, and class distinctions are not abolished, and while an air of austerity pervaded most of the utopias so far considered, Bacon never tires of describing sumptuous dresses, headgear, shoes, cloaks, jewels and coaches, with a wealth of detail which is as tedious as it is superfluous.

Bacon only gives a few hints on the social and political institutions of Bensalem, as this ideal country is called. Mr Alfred B. Gough remarks that " the spirit of movement or of progress which dominates the intellectual life of the nation, appears to be totally absent from its political and moral life: the form of government is monarchical, and has been so for at least 3,000 years, the fundamental laws of the Kingdom laid down by King Solamona 1,900 years ago are still in force."

The basis of society is the patriarchal family and, though we are not told how its members spend their daily life, a long passage describes in the minutest detail what happens when a man has thirty descendants above the age of three and is given a sumptuous feast at the expense of the State (modern governments have generally recompensed the mother of large families rather than the father). Marriage is greatly respected and is unbreakable, and, though Bacon ridicules More for suggesting that men and women should see one another naked before marriage, he institutes an examination by proxy.

This is how an inhabitant of Bensalem explains to the traveller their attitude towards sex and their customs relating to marriage:

You shall understand that there is not under the heavens so chaste a nation as this of Bensalem, nor so free from all pollution or foulness. It is the virgin of the world ; I remember, I have read in one of your European books, of an holy hermit amongst you, that desired to see the spirit of fornication, and there appeared to him a little foul ugly Ethiope ; but if he had desired to see the spirit of chastity of Bensalem, it would have appeared to him in the likeness of a fair beautiful cherubim. For there is nothing, amongst mortal men, more fair and admirable than the chaste minds of this people. Know, therefore, that with them there are no stews, no dissolute houses, no courtezans, nor anything of that kind. Nay, they wonder, with detestation, at you in Europe, which permit such things. They say ye have put marriage out of office ; for marriage is ordained a remedy for unlawful con-cupiscence ; and natural concupiscence seemeth as a spur to marriage. But when men have at hand a remedy, more agreeable to their corrupt will, marriage is almost expulsed. And therefore there are with you seen infinite men that marry not, but choose rather a libertine and impure single life, than to be yoked in marriage ; and many that do marry, marry late, when the prime and strength of their years is past. And when they do marry, what is marriage to them but a very bargain; wherein is sought alliance, or portion, or reputation, with some desire (almost indifferent) of issue ; and not the faithful nuptial union of man and wife, that was first instituted. Neither is it possible that those that have cast away so basely so much of their strength, should esteem children (being of the same matter) as chaste men do. So likewise during marriage is the case much amended, as it ought to be if those things were tolerated only for necessity; no, but they remain still as a very affront to marriage. The haunting of those dissolute places, or resort to courtezans, are no more punished in married men than in bachelors. And the depraved custom of change, and the delight in meretricious embracements (where sin is turned into art), maketh marriage a dull thing, and a kind of imposition or tax. They hear you defend these things, as done to avoid greater evils ; as advoutries, deflowering of virgins, unnatural lust, and the like. But they say, this is a preposterous wisdom ; and they call it Lot's offer, who to save his guests from abusing, offered his daughters ; nay, they say further, that there is little gained in this ; for that the same vices and appetites do still remain and abound, unlawful lust being like a furnace, that if you stop the flames altogether it will quench, but if you give it any vent it will rage ; as for masculine love, they have no touch of it ; and yet there are not so faithful and inviolate friendships in the world again as are there, and to speak generally (as I said before) I have not read of any such chastity in any people as theirs. And their usual saying is that whosoever is unchaste cannot reverence himself ; and they say that the reverence of a man's self, is, next religion, the chiefest bridle of all vices.

They have also many wise and excellent laws, touching marriage. They allow no polygamy. They have ordained that none do intermarry, or contract, until a month be past from their first interview. Marriage without consent of parents they do not make void, but they mulct it in the inheritors ; for the children of such marriages are not admitted to inherit above a third part of their parents' inheritance. I have read in a book of one of your men, of a feigned commonwealth, where the married couple are permitted, before they contract, to see one another naked. This they dislike: for they think it a scorn to give a refusal after so familiar knowledge; but because of many hidden defects in men and women's bodies, they have a more civil way ; for they have near every town a couple of pools (which they call Adam and Eve's pools), where it is permitted to one of the friends of the man, and another of the friends of the woman, to see them severally bathe naked.

Of the many wise laws which the King Solamona gave to the people of Bensalem, the only ones described concern the traffic with foreign countries, which he forbade, and the considerate treatment to be meted out to travellers who happened to reach the country. The greatest achievement of this king, however, was the institution of an order, or society, which he called

Solomon's or Salomon's House. It was also sometimes called
College of Six Days' Works, " the noblest foundation, that ever
was upon the earth, and the lantern of this kingdom " and was
dedicated " to the study of the works and creatures of God "...
" for finding the true nature of all things whereby God might
have the more glory in the workmanship of them, and men the
more fruit in the use of them."

To allow the fellows of this College to gather information for
their work, the King made another ordinance :

When the king had forbidden to all his people navigation into
any part that was not under his crown, he made nevertheless this
ordinance ; that every twelve years there should be set forth out
of this kingdom, two ships, appointed to several voyages ; that
in either of these ships there should be a mission of three of the
fellows or brethren of Salomon's House, whose errand was only
to give us knowledge of the affairs and state of those countries to
which they were designed ; and especially of the sciences, arts,
manufactures, and inventions of all the world, and withal to
bring unto us books, instruments, and patterns in every kind :
that the ships, after they had landed the brethren, should return ;
and that the brethren should stay abroad till the new mission, the
ships are not otherwise fraught than with store of victuals, and
good quantity of treasure to remain with the brethren, for the
buying of such things, and rewarding of such persons, as they
should think fit. Now for me to tell you how the vulgar sort of
mariners are contained from being discovered at land, and how
they that must be put on shore for any time, colour themselves
under the names of other nations, and to what places these
voyages have been designed ; and what places of rendezvous are
appointed for the new missions, and the like circumstances of
the practice, I may not do it, neither is it much to your desire.
But thus you see we maintain a trade, not for gold, silver, or jewels,
nor for silks, nor for spices, nor any other commodity of matter ;
but only for God's first creature, which was light ; to have light,
I say, of the growth of all parts of the world.

This is the first time that we find science surrounded by such
secrecy, and this passage has a curiously modern ring. The
scientists of Bensalem act as spies on behalf of their State or
College, and though they drain the world of all its new inventions
and ideas they give nothing in exchange. Science is no longer the
property of mankind but of a particular State. This is a familiar

conception to-day, when gold and silver are guarded less jealously
than atomic secrets, but at the time it represented a break with
the universalist tradition of the humanism of the Renaissance.

The same atmosphere of secrecy surrounds the House of
Salomon itself. The arrival in the city of a father of the College
is a great event, for none of them have been seen during the past
twelve years and " his coming is in state ; but the cause of his
coming is secret."

It is true that the father of Salomon's House calls one of the
visitors to him and gives him a long description of the riches of
Salomon's House, concluding with these words : " God bless
thee my son, and God bless this relation which I have made. I
give thee leave to publish it, for the good of other nations ; for
we are here in God's bosom, a land unknown." But from the
relation, it is obvious that he gives away no secret and that he
seems more intent on impressing his guest than in helping him to
understand how the institution works. In *Christianopolis*, when
the visitor was taken round the college, nothing was hidden from
him and we gather that he was able to ask questions. Here we
have the impression of being at the fair ; the showman outside
the tent excites our curiosity with a highly-coloured description
of what goes on inside but we are not even allowed to peep
through the chink in the curtain. And what a magnificent showman Bacon is! Inventions are described with a complete disregard for order or method but with the one aim of dazzling the
reader. Many have been dazzled and have talked of his extraordinary prophetic vision, but most of the inventions he describes
as having been achieved had occupied the attention of the
philosophers and scientists of the Renaissance and of many others
long before their time. For example, an attempt at building a
flying machine had been made about 880 by the Andalusian
Abul Abbas Kasim ibn Firnas, and Leonardo da Vinci was
reputed to have invented a submarine. Burckhardt mentions that
in the fifteenth century Leon Battista Alberti " excited great
admiration by his mysterious ' Camera Obscura,' in which he
showed, at one time the stars and the moon rising over rocky hill,
at another wide landscapes with mountains and gulfs receding into
dim perspective, and with fleets advancing on the waters in
shade or sunshine." As for libraries, botanical gardens and even
zoological gardens, and the use of agents who collected manu-

scripts in foreign countries, these are all features of the Italian
Renaissance.

The *New Atlantis* is more interesting in its modern preoccupation with the practical—one could almost say industrial—
application of scientific discoveries. Bacon's description of the
manufacture of ersatz alimentary products and synthetic materials
would warm the hearts of many contemporary industrial scientists:

> We have large and deep caves of several depths ; the deepest
> are sunk 600 fathoms ; and some of them are digged and made
> under great hills and mountains ; so that if you reckon together
> the depth of the hill, and the depth of the cave, they are, some of
> them, above three miles deep. For we find that the depth of an
> hill, and the depth of a cave from the flat, is the same thing ;
> both remote alike from the sun and heaven's beams, and from the
> open air. These caves we call the lower region. And we use
> them for all coagulations, indurations, refrigerations, and
> conservations of bodies. We use them likewise for the imitation
> of natural mines and the producing also of new artificial metals,
> by compositions and materials which we use and lay there for
> many years.
>
> We have also perfume-houses, wherewith we join also practices
> of taste. We multiply smells which may seem strange : we
> imitate smells making all smells to breathe out of other mixtures
> than those that give them. We make divers imitations of taste
> likewise, so that they will deceive any man's taste. And in this
> house we contain also a confiture-house, where we make all
> sweetmeats, dry and moist, and divers pleasant wines, milks,
> broths, and salads, far in greater variety than you have.

Bacon also mentions such discoveries as perpetual motion,
elixirs to prolong life, and spontaneous generation, which had
preoccupied alchemists and philosophers for centuries and were
only abandoned when it was realised that they were based on a
false conception of science.

The organisation of scientific research is based upon a strict
division of work :

> For the several employments and offices of our fellows, we have
> twelve that sail into foreign countries under the names of other
> nations (for our own we conceal), who bring us the books and
> abstracts, and patterns of experiments of all other parts. These
> we call merchants of light.

We have three that collect the experiments which are in all books. These we call deprepators.

We have three that collect the experiments of all mechanical arts, and also of liberal sciences, and also of practices which are not brought into arts. These we call mystery-men.

We have three that try new experiments, such as themselves think good. These we call pioneers or miners.

We have three that draw the experiments of the former four into titles and tables, to give the better light for the drawing of observations and axioms out of them. These we call compilers.

We have three that bend themselves, looking into the experiments of their fellows, and cast about how to draw out of them things of use and practice for man's life and knowledge, as well for works as for plain demonstration of causes, means of natural divinations, and the easy and clear discovery of the virtues and parts of bodies. These we call dowry-men or benefactors.

Then after divers meetings and consults of our whole number, to consider of the former labours and collections, we have three that take care out of them to direct new experiments, of a higher light, more penetrating into Nature than the former. These we call lamps.

We have three others that do execute the experiments so directed, and report them. These we call inoculators.

Lastly, we have three that raise the former discoveries by experiments into greater observations, axioms, and aphorisms. These we call interpreters of Nature.

We have also, as you must think, novices and apprentices, that the succession of the former employed men do not fail ; besides a great number of servants and attendants, men and women.

This specialisation in scientific work contains certain dangers, as Mr A. B. Gough has pointed out in his introduction to the edition of *New* Atlantis which was published in 1924 :

In dealing with this new problem of the distribution of labour, to which his own experience forced him, Bacon made what in the light of later history seems the strange mistake of apportioning, not different sciences, but different stages in the general process of investigation to different workers. There must, it is true, always be subordinate workers of various kinds : explorers, collectors, field naturalists, etc., who gather the materials ; students and assistants, who perform minor experiments ; calculators and statisticians, who work out the mathematical and other details ; editors who collect, summarize and review the results of the world's scientific work in year-books and journals ; technicians who apply discoveries to practical ends. Such workers correspond roughly to some of Bacon's classes. But their functions cannot be rigidly prescribed or limited. Thus " Lamps" or " Interpreters of Nature " have often been " Dowry-men " as well. Davy invented the safety lamp, and Kelvin improved the mariner's compass and the telegraph. The higher the work the more vitally important becomes the personal factor, which Bacon almost ignored. The organisation of Salomon's House, like Bacon's logical system which it reflects, is too mechanical and inflexible to allow for the free play of genius. There is no room in Bensalem for a Copernicus, a Newton, a Darwin, or a Pasteur, they would have never been Interpreters of Nature if they had not been constantly occupied with humbler work as well. It is astonishing to find the State maintaining a constant succession of neither more nor less than three gorgeously arrayed functionaries to prosecute the work, which in reality is the crowning achievement of the patient life-work of the rarest and highest scientific genius.

What is more astonishing is that these " functionaries " are entitled to withhold their discoveries from the State ; as the Father of Salomon's House explains :

...we have consultations, which of the inventions and experiences which we have discovered shall be published, and which not : and take all an oath of secrecy for the concealing of those which we think fit to keep secret ; though some of those we do reveal sometime to the state, and some not.

To-day, when most States have their scientific colleges and research stations and keep on their pay-roll an army of scientists, we realise how impossible it would be for a society holding all the prerogatives of that conceived by Bacon to exist within the State. The existence of a dual power is impossible ; either the scientists are the instruments of the State, as they are to-day, or they rule the State, as they must have done in Bensalem.

The *New Atlantis* can have little attraction for us, since we are all living in a Salomon's House to-day and, like Bacon, we have been dazzled by the riches and marvels it contains. Now we are gradually realising that knowledge and scientific progress are not synonymous with human happiness and we begin to suspect that the enthusiastic supporters of progress were not really concerned with the happiness of mankind but with the power that this knowledge and progress gave them. And this is why Bacon talks such a great deal about the honours, privileges and power which belonged to the fellows of Salomon's House, and so little about the happiness they brought to the people. We are also in a better position to appreciate the dangers of "science without conscience." The thought that the harnessing of atomic energy may spell the end of our civilisation has deprived science of its glamorous halo. The scientist is no longer considered as a benefactor of humanity, but unwillingly assumes a sinister role and is himself sometimes overcome by feelings of guilt.

FRANÇOIS RABELAIS
The Abbey of Theleme

It would be difficult to resist the temptation to include Rabelais' Abbey of Theleme among the Utopias of the Renaissance, even knowing full well that it cannot be honestly described as an ideal commonwealth. But we shall, for once, follow the rule of the Thelemites and " do what we will," not, however, without some justification, for Rabelais' imaginary community embodies the spirit of the Renaissance, far more completely than the utopias we have considered up to now.

Rabelais himself is a typical man of the Renaissance. His encyclopaedic knowledge, his profound admiration for Greek literature, his hatred of scholastic doctrines, his pagan Christianity, his contempt for monastic life, his love of freedom and beauty, were all characteristics of the Italian humanists. Like them he had a passion for knowledge and did not only study literature and philosophy, but also medicine and law. Again, like most humanists, he was not interested in " social questions." His revolt was purely an individual one and he did not associate it with a revolt against the system of society. He saw the evils of the society of his time, but he did not try to find their cause or devise remedies for them. The Renaissance was not a movement of reform, it was a rebellion of individuals who sought freedom chiefly for themselves. In spite of their name, the humanists were not interested in humanity, they were concerned with their own individuality and the means to express it. They deeply resented any interference from civil or religious authorities and they were deeply conscious of their rights, but they did not fight for the freedom, or rights of the mass of the people.

The *Abbey of Theleme* is more than the description of an ideal court, or an ideal college, or, as Mumford saw it, an ideal country house. It is the utopia of the new aristocracy of the Renaissance, an aristocracy based on intelligence and knowledge rather than on power or wealth. Rabelais describes how these well born, well bred, gifted and handsome men and women should live. For them there is no need for laws and lawyers, politics and preachers, money and usurers, religion and monks. They do not need any rules for they know how to employ their time in the most useful and pleasant way, they do not need any external moral constraint for they are naturally honest and endowed with noble sentiments. They can enjoy complete freedom and complete equality between men and women.

Nothing can be too beautiful and sumptuous for men and women who are, so to speak, the flower of humanity. They live in a château surpassing in splendour those of Touraine, they are dressed in the richest clothes, they have a patron whose funds are apparently limitless and an army of servants and craftsmen to serve them and supply all their wants :

...there was about the wood of Theleme a row of houses of the extent of half a league, very neat and cleanly, wherein dwelt the Goldsmiths, Lapidaries, Jewellers, Embroiderers, Tailors, Golddrawers, Velvet-weavers, Tapestrie-makers and Upholsterers, who wrought there every one in his own trade, and all for the aforesaid Jollie Friars and Nuns of the new stamp...

The education received by the Thelemites is such as would suit future princes or courtiers and is indeed similar to that prescribed for the ideal courtier of the Renaissance by Castiglione[1] :

The courtier must be at home in all noble sports, among them running, leaping, swimming, and wrestling ; he must, above all things, be a good dancer and, as a matter of course, an accomplished rider. He must be master of several languages, at all events of Latin and Italian; he must be familiar with literature and have some knowledge of the fine arts....

[1]As quoted by Jacob Burckhardt in *The Civilisation of the Renaissance in Italy.*

This education, like that received by the "jollie Friars and Nuns" of the Abbey of Theleme, may create a high degree of individual perfection, but it is strangely divorced from any utilitarian purpose. The Thelemites do not seem to be destined to enter any useful profession or trade, but to have throughout their lives a body of servants at their command. It is also unlikely that they will find much pleasure in work which is merely an exercise of the body or the mind, but which never aims at creating something useful.

One cannot help feeling that, for all its splendour, life in Rabelais' Abbey would soon become monotonous, and boredom would overcome the Thelemites, as indeed it overcame many princes and courtiers even in the most brilliant courts. In fairness to Rabelais one must remember, however, that in his ideal community there is no king or prince to flatter and amuse.

These remarks would have been superfluous if many people carried away by enthusiasm for Rabelais' famous "Do what thou wilt," had not forgotten that he meant it only for :

...lively, jovial, handsom, brisk,
Gay, witty, frolick, chearful, merry, frisk,
Spruce, jocund, courteous, furtherers of trades,
And in a word, all worthy gentile blades.
....Ladies of high birth,
Delicious, stately, charming, full of mirth,
Ingenious, lovely, miniard, proper, faire.
Magnetick, graceful, splendid, pleasant, rare,
Obliging, sprightly, vertuous, young, solacious,
Kinde, neat, quick, feat, bright, compt, ripe, choice, dear,
      precious,
Alluring, courtly, comely, fine, compleat,
Wise, personable, ravishing and sweet.

In spite of its exclusive conditions of admission and of its throughly "immoral" love of luxury, the *Abbey of Theleme* remains a delightful phantasy and we are sorry that we can only reproduce here the two following chapters.

HOW GARGANTUA CAUSED TO BE BUILT FOR THE MONK THE ABBEY OF THELEME

There was left onely the Monk to provide for, whom Gargantua would have made Abbot of Seville, but he refused it ; he would have given him the Abby of Bourgueil, or of Sanct Florent, which was better, or both, if it pleased him ; but the Monk gave him a very peremptory answer, that he would never take upon him the charge nor government of Monks. For how shall I be able (said he) to rule over others, that have not full power and command of my self : if you think I have done you, or may here-after do any acceptable service, give me leave to found an Abby after my owne minde and fancie ; the motion pleased Gargantua very well, who thereupon offered him all the Countrey of Theleme by the river of Loire, till within two leagues of the great forest of Port-huaut : the Monk then requested Gargantua to institute his religious order contrary to all others. First then (said Gargantua) you must not build a wall about your convent, for all other Abbies are strongly walled and mured about : See (said the Monk, and not without cause, (seeing wall and mure signifie-but one and the same thing) ; where there is mur before, and mur behinde, there is store of murmur, envie and mutal conspiracie. Moreover, seeing there are certain convents in the world, whereof the custome is, if any woman come in (I mean chaste and honest women) they immediately sweep the ground which they have trod upon ; therefore was it ordained that if any man or woman entered into religious orders, should by chance come within this new Abbey, all the roomes should be throughly washed and cleansed through which they had passed ; and because in all other Monasteries and Nunneries all is compassed, limited, and regulated by houres, it was decreed that in this new structure there should be neither Clock nor Dial, but that according to the opportunities, and incident occasions, all their hours should be disposed of ; for (said Gargantua) the greatest losse of time, that I know, is to count the hours, what good comes of it? now can there be any greater dotage in the world then for one to guide and direct his courses by the sound of a Bell, and not by his judgement and discretion.

Item, Because at that time they put no women into Nunneries, but such as were either purblinde, blinkards, lame, crooked, ill-favoured, mis-shapen, fooles, senselesse, spoyled or corrupt ; nor encloystered any men, but those that were either sickly, subject to defluxions, ill-bred lowts, simple sots, or peevish trouble-

Houses : but to the purpose ; (said the monk) A woman that is neither faire not good, to what use serves she? To make a Nunne of, said Gargantua : Yea, said the Monk, and to make shirts and smocks ; therefore was it ordained, that into this religious order should be admitted no women that were not faire, well featur'd, and of a sweet disposition ; nor men that were not comely, personable and well conditioned.

Item, Because in the convents of women men come not but under-hand, privily, and by stealth, it was therefore enacted, that in this house there shall be no women in case there be not men, nor men in case there be not women.

Item, Because both men and women, that are received into religious orders after the expiring of their noviciat or probation-year, were constrained and forced perpetually to stay there all the days of their life, it was therefore ordered, that all whatever, men or women, admitted within this Abbey, should have full leave to depart with peace and contentment, whensoever it should seem good to them so to do.

Item, for that the religious men and women, did ordinarily make three Vows, to wit, those of chastity, poverty and obedience, it was therefore constituted and appointed, that in this Convent they might be honourably married, that they might be rich, and live at liberty. In regard of the legitimat time of the persons to be initiated, and years under, and above, which they were not capable of reception, the women were to be admitted from ten till fifteen, and the men from twelve till eighteen.

HOW THE THELEMITES WERE GOVERNED, AND OF THEIR MANNER OF LIVING

All their life was spent not in lawes, statutes or rules, but according to their own free will and pleasure. They rose out of their beds, when they thought good : they did eat, drink, labour, sleep, when they had a minde to it, and were disposed for it. None did awake them, none did offer to constrain them to eat, drink, nor to do any other thing; for so had Gargantua established it. In all their rule, and strictest tie of their order, there was but this one clause to be observed,

DO WHAT THOU WILT.

Because men that are free, well-borne, well-bred, and conversant in honest companies, have naturally an instinct and spurre that prompteth them unto vertuous actions, and withdraws them from vice, which is called honour. Those same men, when by base subjection and constraint they are brought under

and kept down, turn aside from that noble disposition, by which
they formerly were inclined to vertue, to shake off and break
that bond of servitude, wherein they are so tyrannously inslaved;
for it is agreeable with the nature of man to long after things
forbidden, and to desire what is denied us.

By this liberty they entered into a very laudable emulation, to
do all of them what they saw did please one; if any of the gallants
or Ladies should say, Let us drink, they would all drink ; if any
one of them said, Let us play, they all played ; if one said, Let
us go a walking into the fields, they went all ; if it were to go a
hawking or a hunting, the Ladies mounted upon dainty well-
paced nags, seated in a stately palfrey saddle, carried on their
lovely fists, miniardly begloved every one of them, either a Spar-
hawk, or a Laneret, or a Marlin, and the young gallants carried
the other kinds of Hawkes : so nobly were they taught, that there
was neither he nor she amongst them, but could read, write, sing,
play upon several musical instruments, speak five or sixe several
languages, and compose in them all very quaintly, both in Verse
and Prose : never were seen so valiant Knights, so noble and
worthy, so dextrous and skilful both on foot and a horseback,
more brisk and lively, more nimble and quick, or better handling
all manner of weapons then were there. Never were seene
Ladies so proper and handsome, so miniard and dainty, lesse
forward, or more ready with their hand, and with their needle,
in every honest and free action belonging to that sexe, then were
there ; for this reason, when the time came, that any man of the
said Abbey, either at the request of his parents, or for some other
cause, had a minde to go out of it, he carried along with him one
of the Ladies, namely her whom he had before that chosen for
his Mistris, and were married together : and if they had formerly
in Theleme lived in good devotion and amity, they did continue
therein and increase it to a greater height in their state of
matrimony: and did entertaine that mutual love till the very last
day of their life, in no lesse vigour and fervency, then at the very
day of their wedding.

3

Utopias of the English Revolution

WHILE on the Continent the seventeenth century saw the consolidation of absolute governments, in England the absolutism of the kings was resolutely opposed by a great section of the population, and the power of the monarchy was held in check by Parliament. At a time when Louis XIV was able to proclaim "L'Etat c'est Moi," Charles I was led to the scaffold. The doctrine of the divine right of kings, which had allowed the French monarchs to crush all political and religious freedom, had gained little support among English people who believed, on the contrary, that the power of the rulers must respect the inalienable rights of the individual and that certain limitations must be put to the power of the head of the state.

While the ideal commonwealth conceived by James Harrington tried to combine the existence of a powerful state with respect for the political rights of the citizens, Thomas Hobbes and Gerrard Winstanley, for opposite reasons, denied the possibility of power being shared between the state and the people.

We shall only say a few words here about Hobbes' *Leviathan* and Harrington's *Oceana* because, though they are often referred to as utopias, the first would be more correctly described as a treatise on government, while the second belongs to the category of ideal constitutions rather than to that of ideal commonwealths. On the other hand we shall deal at length with Winstanley's *Law of Freedom*, partly because it has generally been overlooked, and partly because it embodies the spirit of the English revolution in its more popular and revolutionary form.

Thomas Hobbes' *Leviathan*, which was published in 1651, claimed to establish the right of the State to absolute power, and denied that man possessed any "natural rights." Hobbes maintained that man is not by nature a social being, provided with moral sense, but that it was the State which had put an end to the "war of all against all." The first rulers had been given, by contract, absolute power over the rest of the people and that contract was to be respected by following generations and whoever broke it was guilty of the worst of all crimes. He recommended absolute monarchy as the best form of government and held that the individual is under obligation to submit un-questioningly to such a government. Even the Church must be denied all temporal power and religion must be recognised and taught by the state. " The name *Leviathan*," says F. A. Lange,[1] " is only too appropriate for this monster, the state, which guided by no higher consideration, like a terrestrial god orders law and justice, rights and property, according to its pleasure— even arbitrarily defines the concepts of good and evil and in return guarantees protection of life and property to those who fall on their knees and sacrifice to it."

Harrington's *Oceana* was written after the execution of Charles I, at a time when it seemed possible that far-reaching reforms might solve England's economic and political problems. While *The Law of Freedom*, which had appeared a few years earlier, is concerned mainly with improving the conditions of the landless labourers, *Oceana* offers to ameliorate the situation of the middle classes. The right of the "elder brothers" to the whole inherit-ance was concentrating property in the hands of an ever-shrinking number of people, destroying the economic balance of property in the country, and creating a class of parasites composed mainly of clergymen and lawyers, which was the refuge of the " younger sons."

Harrington believed that there could be no political power without economic power and he wished to spread this economic power over a large section of the population by the application of an agrarian law which would restrict the size of land property to that yielding a revenue of £3,000. This new balance of property was to be preserved by a Republican government in which all offices were to be filled by men chosen by ballot and holding office for a limited time. There was to be a double chamber system, one house for debate and the other for voting. This curious division was based on the assumption that there is an important distinction between the capacity for " invention " and the capacity for " judgment," and that eloquence presents a danger for the democratic state. Only the " freemen," that is to say the property owners, were to have the right to participate in the government of the Commonwealth ; the " servants " being economically dependent could not take part in the affairs

[1]Quoted in Rudolf Rocker's *Nationalism and Culture*.

of the State. Unlike the slaves of Ancient Greece, however, the " servants " could by their industry rise to the status of freemen.

Harrington had been greatly influenced by Plutarch, Plato and Aristotle, and he said himself that " Oceana was not discovered in phansy but in the archives of antient prudence." But, as H. F. Russell has pointed out in his book on *Harrington and his Oceana*, it is a work of a different type from Plato's *Republic* or More's *Utopia* : " It was meant neither for the skies nor for some spot of earth that did not exist, but for England. Its author had very clearly defined views as to the needs of his country, and his love of the picturesque prompted him to bring them forward in the form of what he called a ' political romance '. . . . The book, stripped of its allegorical trappings is little more than a magnified written constitution."

Though Harrington dedicated his *Oceana* to Cromwell, who is also the hero of the story and given the task of accomplishing for England what Lycurgus did for Sparta, the book was confiscated while it was passing through the press under the newly enacted order against " scandalous Books and Pamphlets." It was, however, allowed to appear one year later, in 1656, and immediately enjoyed a great popularity, though Cromwell's supporters tried their best to ridicule it. *Oceana*, as Russell has shown, received great attention in America and many of Harrington's ideas were embodied in the constitutions of the American colonies of the Restoration period and in particular in the constitution of Pennsylvania.

Harrington shared with the Levellers the belief that political freedom must rest on the " possession of the earth," but he only sought that freedom for a class of gentlemen farmers who were to be the " guardians " of the labouring classes.

GERRARD WINSTANLEY

The Law of Freedom

DURING the century and half which separate More's *Utopia* from Winstanley's *Law of Freedom*, the conditions of the English labourer had steadily worsened. Though commerce and industry were expanding, the seventeenth century was, in the words of Thorold Rogers, " a period of excessive misery among the mass of the people and the tenants, a time in which a few might have become rich, while the many were crushed down into hopeless and almost permanent indigence." The unemployment, homelessness and vagrancy brought about by the enclosure of the lands was continually increasing, copyhold tenants were being deprived of the strips of land they cultivated in the open fields and the landless labourers of their right to pasture their beasts and cut firewood on the commons. As during the reign of Henry VIII, the ruling class sought to crush popular discontent by increasing the severity of the laws against beggars and vagrants ; it was ordered that when apprehended for the first time they should be branded with the letter R and if found again wandering or begging they would " suffer death without benefit of Clergy."

In spite of these measures vagrancy and petty theft increased for, as More had said, " when the stomachs of those that are turned out of doors, grow keen, they rob no less keenly ; and what else can they do? " They could also revolt, and they did. Fences and hedges which enclosed the once common fields were levelled and peasants' insurrections followed one another at short intervals. Movements also came into existence which sought a remedy to the misery of the people through political action. With the fall of the Monarchy and the rise of the Independents there was a hope that radical reforms would take place, but these hopes were short lived. Discontent spread to the army and mutinies had to be crushed by wholesale cashiering. Even among the Levellers who had advocated constitutional political reforms, many began to lose faith in the Long Parliament, dominated by the landlords, who did little to relieve the increased poverty brought about by the Civil War and showed no concern for the families of those who had been maimed or killed serving in their own army. The "left wing" of the Levellers realised that a solution to the economic situation could only be found by improving the conditions of the peasantry, and they advocated the restoration of all common lands to the landless labourers and the abolition of " base tenures."

Towards 1648 a movement sprang up, of the " true levellers " or "Diggers," which went beyond the demands of even the most extreme of the Levellers. They saw that nothing, short of direct action, would give back to the peasants the lands they had lost, and eventually they even challenged the right of a few to private property in the land. This involved a complete change in the structure of society for, as Gerrard Winstanley, who became the leader and theoretician of the Diggers' Movement, expressed it, it was not enough to " remove the Conqueror's power out of the king's hand into other men's, maintaining the old laws still."

By the beginning of 1649 the " Conqueror's power " had been removed out of the King's hands, the King had been executed, the House of Commons had been purged of its " malignant members" and the Councils of State had been appointed to administer the public affairs of England. But the Diggers took it upon themselves to remove the " old Laws." On the 16th of April, 1649, the Council of State was informed that a " disorderly and tumultuous sort of people " led by " one Everard, once of the army but was cashiered," had begun to dig on St George's Hill in Surrey " and sowed the ground with parsnips, carrots and beans." The Council of State was so alarmed by the activities of the Diggers, though they only numbered twenty or thirty, that they instructed Lord Fairfax, the Lord General of the armed forces of the Commonwealth, to send some " force of horse… with orders to disperse the people so met, and to prevent the like for the future " and, so as almost to excuse themselves for their fears, they added " although the pretence of their being there may seem very ridiculous, yet that conflux of people may be a beginning to whence things of a greater and more dangerous consequence may grow, to the disturbance of the peace and quiet of the Commonwealth."

Thus at a momentous time in history the tiny Digger Movement occupied the attention of the Council of State and of the Lord General of the Armed Forces of the Commonwealth. Had they known the reasons which prompted the Diggers to occupy St George's Hill their fears would have been still greater. These reasons had been set down by Gerrard Winstanley before they began their activities :

" The work we are going about is this, To dig up Georges Hill and the waste grounds thereabouts, and sow corn, and to eat our bread together by the sweat of our brows.

" And the first reason is this, that we may work in righteousness, and lay the foundation of making the earth a common treasury for all, both rich and poor, that everyone that is born in the land may be fed by the earth his mother that brought him forth, according to the reason that rules in the creation."

Of Gerrard Winstanley, who emerges at that time as one of
the leaders of the movement, little is known until 1648 when he
published four pamphlets expressing some daring theological
views and for which he was accused, by some orthodox ministers
of the Church, of denying God, the Scriptures and the Ordinances
of God. These pamphlets were probably written before he came
in contact with William Everard and the " true Levellers," for
they do not reveal an interest in social questions, but Winstanley
had already had cause to reflect on the injustices of society. He
had been a small trader and a freeman of the City of London but,
like so many others, he had been ruined by the Civil War. As he
said later, in a letter addressed to the City of London, " I had an
estate in thee... by thy cheating sons in the thieving art of buying
and selling, and by the burdens of and for the soldiery in the
beginning of the war, I was beaten out of both estate and trade,
and forced to accept the good-will of friends, crediting of me, to
live a country life."

In January, 1649, he published *The New Law of Righteousness*,
which has been described by H. N. Brailsford " as the most
characteristic of his books...which is in reality a Communist
Manifesto written in the dialect of its day " and in which, as
George Woodcock has pointed out, " he revealed an understanding of social problems in advance of any English social thinker
before Godwin." He fiercely denounced the private ownership
of the land :

And let all men say what they will, so long as such are rulers
as call the land theirs, upholding this particular propriety of
mine and thine, the common people shall never have their
liberty, nor the land be ever freed from troubles, oppressions, and
complainings, by reason whereof the Creator of all things is
continually provoked...
The man of the flesh judges it a righteous thing that some men
who are cloathed with the objects of the earth, and so called rich
men, whether it be got by right or wrong, should be magistrates
to rule over the poor ; and that the poor should be servants,
nay, rather slaves, to the rich. But the spiritual man, which is
Christ, doth judge according to the light of equity and reason,
that all mankind ought to have a quiet subsistence and freedom
to live upon earth ; and that there should be no bondman nor
beggar in all his holy mountain.

And he advocated the end of the exploitation of man by man:

No man shall have any more land than he can labor himself, or have others to labor with him in love, working together, and eating bread together, as one of the tribes or families of Israel, neither giving nor taking hire.

Though his doctrines were revolutionary Winstanley did not incite people to violence or to the expropriation of the rich. He wanted the poor to seize the waste lands and cultivate them in common : "And let the common people, that say the earth is *ours*, not *mine*, let them labor together, and eat bread together upon the commons, mountains and hills."

During the two years which followed, the Diggers of St George's Hill were persecuted by the Lords, the soldiery and the freeholders. They were beaten up, their spades were taken away, their houses pulled down, their corn was destroyed and their carts torn to pieces. Some of them were arrested and prosecuted and, as they could not pay the heavy fine imposed upon them, their meagre possessions were taken away. After one year only a few Diggers were left, who, says Winstanley, " have made little hutches to lie in, like calf-cribs...and have planted divers acres of wheat and rye,... and nothing shall make them slack but want of food, which is not much now, they being all poor people, and having suffered so much in one expense or other since they began."

In spite of their courage and perseverance the Diggers were defeated. Winstanley had done all in his power to defend them; in several forceful pamphlets he had shown the justice of their claims and their peaceful intentions and had appealed to the Army, to Parliament, and to the City of London, that the persecutions should cease.

It was after the adventure of St George's Hill had failed to gain any support and to spread, as the pioneers had hoped, into a mass movement, that Winstanley published in 1652, *The Law of Freedom*, where he set forth the plan for an ideal commonwealth. It was written less than four years after the publication of his first pamphlet and during this short time his religious and political ideas had undergone a swift development ; they had passed from a religious mysticism to a kind of rational atheism, from agrarian reformism to integral collectivism. Winstanley was also beginning to lose faith in the methods by which he and his companions had hoped to bring about a better society. The Diggers had believed that, by explaining their aims and by their example, they could persuade the people to work the waste lands communally and that eventually even the landlords would be prepared to give up their lands. Their resistance was one of non-violence and they never employed force to defend themselves against the soldiers and the rich tenant farmers who attacked them.

The failure of the experiment at St George's Hill seems to have led Winstanley to the belief that as long as the army was against the people it would be impossible for them to seize and work the land as free men. It was perhaps for this reason that *The Law of Freedom* opens with an epistle addressed to Cromwell, who was at the time Commander in Chief of the Army, and who, more than anybody else, would have had the power to carry out far-reaching reforms. From the contents and tone of the letter, however, it is clear that Winstanley had little hope that Cromwell would carry out the programme set forth in his book and that he merely told him what he *should* do to be in a better position to criticise what he *would* do. He would not have addressed Cromwell in this way if he had seen in him a future liberator and law-giver :

That which is yet waiting on your part to be done is this, to see the oppressor's power to be cast out with his person ; and to see that the free possession of the land and liberties be put into the hands of the oppressed commoners of England...

And now you have the power of the land in your hand, you must do one of these two things. First, either set the land free to the oppressed commoners, who assisted you, and paid the Army their wages ; and then you will fulfil the Scriptures and your own engagements, and so take possession of your deserved honour.

Or secondly, you must only remove the Conqueror's power out of the King's hand into other men's, maintaining the old laws still; and then your wisdom and honour is blasted for ever ; and you will either lose yourself, or lay the foundation of greater slavery to posterity than you ever knew.

Winstanley was too acute a social thinker to think that society could be transformed through the work of one man, and he realised that a revolution from the top would be useless if man's mental and moral outlook remained the same. But he was firmly convinced that when Christ or the " spreading of light " would penetrate people's minds they would cease to covet and oppress and a new society would come into being. " He loved," says Brailsford, " to quote the Biblical prophecies which assure this triumph to ' the despised ones of the earth ' and bid the rich men ' weep and howl.' He predicts that this revolution will be accomplished ' ere many years wheel about'...The revolution he desired was to come through a change wrought by ' the spirit of Reason ' in men's hearts."

For all his Biblical quotations and biblical language Winstanley rejected all the foundations of orthodox religion. He did not believe in a personal God, and went as far as identifying God with Reason and once took the resolution, (which he did not keep) " to use the word Reason instead of the word God " in his writings. He anticipated the conception of a " socialist Christ " by declaring that he was " the true and faithful Leveller " but he did not imply by it that he was an historical figure but " the spreading power of light." He condemned the belief in miracles, in heaven and hell, and even doubted man's personal survival after death. Winstanley also rejected the doctrine of original sin. Man is born good and free : " The spirit of light in man loves freedom and hates bondage " and his nature has been warped by a system of society based on corruption and misery.

Thomas More, and most utopian writers after him, had abolished private property because they feared its corrupting influence and saw in it the greatest danger to the unity of the state. Winstanley also abolishes the private ownership of the means of production, but on the grounds that " true Freedom " cannot exist as long as men do not have economic freedom and, as he considers the land as the main source of wealth, he declares: " True commonwealth's freedom lies in the free enjoyment of the earth," and again, " A man had better to have no body than to have no food for it. Therefore this restraining of the earth from brethren by brethren is oppression and bondage ; but the free enjoyment thereof is true freedom." From the freedom to enjoy the fruits of the earth derives also the freedom of the mind, for, says Winstanley, " I am assured that if it be rightly searched into, the inward bondages of the mind, as covetousness, pride, hypocrisy, envy, sorrow, fears, desperation and madness, are all occasioned by the outward bondage that one sort of people lay upon another."

Before defining the government of a true Commonwealth Winstanley denounces the kingly government based on property, and like Proudhon he believes that " property is theft " :

Kingly government governs the earth by that cheating art of buying and selling, and thereby becomes a man of contention, his hand is against every man, and every man's hand against him. And take this government at the best, it is a diseased government and the very City Babylon, full of confusion ; and if it had not a club law to support it there would be no order in it, because it is the covetous and proud will of a conqueror, enslaving the conquered people.

This kingly government is he who beats pruning hooks and ploughs into spears, guns, swords, and instruments of war ; that he might take his younger brother's Creation birth-right from him, calling the earth his, and not his brother's, unless his brother will hire the earth of him ; so that he may live idle and at ease by his brother's labours.

Indeed this government may well be called the government of highwaymen, who hath stolen the earth from the younger brethren by force, and holds it from them by force. He sheds blood not to free the people from oppression, but that he may be king and ruler over an oppressed people. . . .

Commonwealth's government governs the earth without buying and selling and thereby becomes a man of peace, and the restorer of ancient peace and freedom. He makes provision for the oppressed, the weak and the simple, as well as for the rich, the wise and the strong. He beats swords and spears into pruning hooks and ploughs. He makes both elder and younger brother free-men in the earth. *Micah, iv, 3, 4, Isaiah, xxxiii, 1 and lxv, 17-25.*

All slaveries and oppressions which have been brought upon mankind by kings, lords of manors, lawyers, and landlords, and the divining clergy, are all cast out again by this government, if it be right in power as well as in name.

For this government is the true restorer of all long lost freedoms, and so becomes the joy of all nations, and the blessing of the whole earth ; for this takes off the kingly curse, and makes Jerusalem a praise in the earth. Therefore all you who profess religion and spiritual things, now look to it, and see what spirit you do profess, for your profession is brought to trial.

If once Commonwealth's government be set upon the throne, then no tyranny or oppression can look him in the face and live. For when oppression lies upon brethren by brethren, that is no Commonwealth's government, but the kingly government still; and the mystery of iniquity hath taken that peace-maker's name to be a cloak to hide his covetousness, pride, and oppression under.

A Commonwealth government cannot be the work of some lawgiver or saviour : " This government depends not upon the will of any particular man, or men...the great lawgiver in the Commonwealth government is the spirit of universal righteousness dwelling in mankind, now rising up to teach everyone to do to another as he would have another do to him, and is no respecter of persons, and this spirit hath been killed by the pharisaical spirit of self-love, and been buried in the dunghill of their enmity for many years past."

The laws of the true commonwealth spring from " common preservation," or what Kropotkin would call " mutual aid," which is " a principle in every one to seek the good of others as himself " :

This is the root of the tree magistracy, and the law of righteousness and peace ; and all particular laws found out by experience, necessary to be practised for common preservation, are the boughs and branches of that tree. And because, among the variety of mankind, ignorance may grow up, therefore this original law is written in the heart of every man, to be his guide or leader. So that if an officer be blinded by covetousness and pride, and that ignorance rule in him, yet an inferior man may tell him where he goes astray ; for common preservation and peace is the foundation rule of all government.

The task of the magistrates of the true Commonwealth is " to maintain the common law, which is the root of right government, and preservation and peace to everyone ; and to cast out all self-ended principles and interests, which is tyranny and oppression, and which breaks common peace."

In *The New Law of Righteousness* Winstanley had advocated a society where there would be no need for lawyers or magistrates, but in his imaginary commonwealth the administration is to be carried out by elected officers. His belief that " everyone that gets an authority into his hands tyrannises over others " did not altogether abandon him, however, and he took great precautions to ensure that this would not happen. All officers of the commonwealth must enjoy the confidence of the people and be freely elected. The first link in the magistracy is to be the father, who will rule over his family, and Winstanley argues (not very convincingly) that he has been elected by his children " because the necessity of the young children chose him by a joint consent, and not otherwise." The other links in the chain are to be the officers elected by the parish, county, shire or land.

Winstanley, being convinced that " power corrupts," particularly if enjoyed for long, advocates that new officers should be elected every year :

When public officers remain long in place of judicature they will degenerate from the bounds of humility, honesty and tender care of brethren, in regard the heart of man is so subject to be overspread with the clouds of covetousness, pride, vain glory. For though at first entrance into places of rule they be of public spirit, seeking the freedom of others as their own ; yet continuing long in such a place, where honours and greatness is coming in, they become selfish, seeking themselves and not common freedom ; as experience proves it true in these days, according to this common proverb, Great offices in a land and army have changed the disposition of many sweet-spirited men.

And nature tells us that if water stands long it corrupts ; whereas running water keeps sweet and is fit for common use.

Therefore as the necessity of common preservation moves the people to frame a law, and to choose officers to see the law obeyed, that they may live in peace : so doth the same necessity bid the people, and cries aloud in the ears and eyes of England, to choose new officers and to remove old ones, and to choose state officers every year ; and that for these reasons.

First, to prevent their own evils. For when pride and fullness take hold of an officer, his eyes are so blinded therewith that he forgets he is a servant to the Commonwealth, and strives to lift up himself high above his brethren ; and oftentimes his fall proves very great : witness the fall of oppressing kings, bishops and other state officers.

Secondly, to prevent the creeping in of oppression into the Commonwealth again. For when officers grow proud and full they will maintain their greatness, though it be in the poverty, mire and hardship of their brethren : witness the practice of kings and their laws, that have crushed the commoners of England a long time.

And have we not experience in these days, that some officers of the Commonwealth are grown so mossy for want of removing, that they will hardly speak to an old acquaintance, if he be an inferior man, though they were very familiar before these wars began, etc.?

And what hath occasioned this distance among friends and brethren but long continuance in places of honour, greatness and riches?

Thirdly, let officers be chosen new every year in love to our posterity. For if burdens and oppressions should grow up in our laws and in our officers for want of removing, as moss and weeds grow in some land for want of stirring, surely it will be a foundation of misery, not easily to be removed by our posterity ; and then will they curse the time that ever we their forefathers had opportunities to set things to rights for their ease, and would not do it.

Fourthly, to remove officers of state every year will make them truly faithful, knowing that others are coming after who will look into their ways. And if they do not do things justly they must be ashamed when the next officers succeed. And when officers deal faithfully in the government of the Commonwealth they will not be unwilling to remove. The peace of London is much preserved by removing their officers yearly.

Fifthly, it is good to remove officers every year, that whereas many have their portions to obey, so many may have their turns to rule ; and this will encourage all men to advance righteousness and good manners in hopes of honour. But when money and riches bears all the sway in the rulers' hearts there is nothing but tyranny in such ways.

Sixthly, the Commonwealth hereby will be furnished with able and experienced men, fit to govern, which will mightily advance the honour and peace of our land, occasion the more watchful care in the education of children, and in time will make our Commonwealth of England the lily among the nations of the earth.

He then determines with great care " Who are fit to choose and fit to be chosen officers in a Commonwealth " :

All uncivil livers, as drunkards, quarrellers, fearful ignorant men, who dare not speak truth lest they anger other men ; likewise all who are wholly given to pleasure and sport, or men who are full of talk ; all these are empty of substance and cannot be experienced men, therefore not fit to be chosen officers in a Commonwealth ; yet they may have a voice in the choosing.

Secondly, all those who are interested in the monarchal power and government ought neither to choose nor be chosen officers to manage Commonwealth's affairs ; for these cannot be friends to common freedom. And these are of two sorts :

First, such as have either lent money to maintain the king's army, or in that army have been soldiers to fight against the recovering of common freedom. These are neither to choose nor to be chosen officers in the Commonwealth as yet, for they have lost their freedom. Yet I do not say they should be made servants, as the conquered usually are made servants, for they are our brethren ; and what they did, no doubt they did in conscionable zeal, though in ignorance.

And seeing that but few of the Parliament's friends understand their common freedoms, though they own the name Commonwealth, therefore the Parliament's party ought to bear with the ignorance of the King's party, because they are brethren, and not make them servants ; though for the present they be suffered neither to choose nor to be chosen officers, lest that ignorant spirit of revenge break out in them to interrupt our common peace.

Secondly, all those who have been so hasty to buy and sell the Commonwealth's land, so to entangle it upon a new account, ought neither to choose nor to be chosen officers. For hereby they declare themselves either to be for kingly interests or else are ignorant of Commonwealth's freedom, or both ; therefore unfit to make laws to govern a free Commonwealth, or to be overseers to see those laws executed.

Why truly, choose such as have a long time given testimony by their actions to be promoters of common freedom, whether they be members in church fellowship or not in church fellowship, for all are one in Christ.

Choose such as are men of peaceable spirits and of a peaceable conversation.

Choose such as have suffered under kingly oppression, for they will be fellow-feelers of other bondages.

Choose such as have adventured the loss of their estates and lives to redeem the land from bondage, and who have remained constant.

Choose such as are understanding men, and who are experienced in the laws of peaceable and right ordered government.

Choose men of courage, who are not afraid to speak the truth; for this is the shame of many in England at this day ; they are drowned in the dunghill mud of slavish fear of men ; these are covetous men, not fearing God, and their portion is to be cast without the city of peace amongst the dogs.

Choose officers out of the number of those men that are above forty years of age, for they are most likely to be experienced men; and all these are likely to be men of courage, dealing truly and hating covetousness.

And if you choose men thus principled, who are poor men as times go, for the Conqueror's power hath made many a righteous man a poor man, then allow them a yearly maintenance from the common stock, until such time as a Commonwealth's freedom is established, for then there will be no need of such allowances.

As in More's *Utopia*, with which Winstanley seems to have been acquainted, the unit of society is the family and the father not only directs the education of the children but also supervises their work :

A father is to cherish his children till they grow wise and strong; and then as a master he is to instruct them in reading, in learning languages, arts and sciences, or to bring them up to labour or employ them in some trade or other, or cause them to be instructed therein, according as is shown hereafter in the education of mankind.

A father is to have a care that as all his children do assist to plant the earth, or by other trades provide necessaries, so he shall see that every one have a comfortable livelihood, not respecting one before another.

He is to command them their work, and see they do it, and not suffer them to live idle. He is either to reprove them by words, or whip those who offend, for the rod is prepared to bring the unreasonable ones to experience and moderation : that so children may not quarrel like beasts, but live in peace like rational men, experienced in yielding obedience to the laws and officers of the Commonwealth, everyone doing to another as he would have another do to him.

In the town, city or parish there are to be five kinds of officers : the peace-makers, the overseers, the soldiers (which we would call policemen), the taskmasters, and the executioner. This is how Winstanley details the tasks of each of them :

The Work of a Peace-maker

In a parish or town may be chosen three, four or six peace-makers, or more, according to the bigness of the place ; and their work is twofold.

First, in general to sit in council to order the affairs of the parish, to prevent troubles, and to preserve common peace, and here they may be called councillors.

Secondly, if there arise any matters of offence between man and man, by reason of any quarrel, disturbance, or foolish actings, the offending parties shall be brought by the soldiers before any one or more of these peace-makers, who shall hear the matter, and shall endeavour to reconcile the parties and make peace, and so put a stop to the rigour of the law, and go no further.

But if the peace-maker cannot persuade or reconcile the parties, then he shall command them to appear at the judge's court at the time appointed to receive the judgment of the law.

If any matters of public concernment fall out wherein the peace of the city, town or country in one county is concerned, then the peace-makers in every town thereabouts shall meet, and consult about it ; and from them, or from any six of them, if need require, shall issue forth any order to inferior officers.

But if the matters concern only the limits of a town or city, then the peace-makers of that town shall from their court send forth orders to inferior officers for the performing of any public service within their limits.

Thirdly, if any proof be given that any officer neglects his duty, a peace-maker is to tell that officer between them two of his neglect. And if the officer continue negligent after this reproof, the peace-maker shall acquaint either the county senate or the national Parliament therewith, that from them the offender may receive condign punishment.

And it is all to this end, that the laws be obeyed ; for a careful execution of laws is the life of government.

The Work of an Overseer

In the parish or town there is to be a four-fold degree of overseers, which are to be chosen yearly.

The first is an overseer to preserve peace, in case of any quarrels that may fall out between man and man. For though the earth with her fruits be a common treasury, and is to be planted and reaped by common assistance of every family, yet every house and all the furniture for ornament therein is a property to the indwellers ; and when any family hath fetched in from the store-house or shops either clothes, food, or any ornament necessary for their use, it is all a property to that family.

The second office of overseership is for trades. This overseer is to see that young people be put to masters, to be instructed in some labour, trade, service, or to be waiters in storehouses, that

none may be idly brought up in any family within his circuit. . .
Truly the government of the Halls and Companies in London is
a very rational and well-ordered government ; and the overseers
for trades may well be called masters, wardens, and assistants of
such and such a company, for such and such a particular trade . .
Likewise this overseer for trades shall see that no man shall be a
housekeeper and have servants under him till he hath served
under a master seven years, and hath learned his trade: and the
reason is, that every family may be governed by staid and
experienced masters, and not by wanton youth. And this office
of overseer keeps all people within a peaceful harmony of trades,
sciences or works, that there be neither beggar nor idle person
in the Commonwealth.

The third office of overseership is to see particular tradesmen
bring in their work to the storehouses and shops, and to see that
the waiters in the storehouses do their duty. . . And if any keeper
of a shop or storehouse neglects the duty of his place the overseer
shall admonish him and reprove him. If he amend, all is well ;
if he doth not, the Overseer shall give orders to the soldiers to
carry him before the peace-maker's court, and if he reform upon
the reproof of that court, all is well. But if he doth not reform,
he shall be sent by the officers to appear before the judge's court,
and the judge shall pass sentence—That he shall be put out of
that house and employment, and sent among the husbandmen
to work in the earth : and some other shall have his place and
house till he be reformed.

Fourthly, all ancient men, above sixty years of age, are general
overseers. And wheresoever they go and see things amiss in any
officer and tradesmen, they shall call any officer or others to
account for their neglect of duty to the Commonwealth's peace;
and they are called elders.

The Office of a Soldier

A soldier is a magistrate as well as any officer, and indeed all
state officers are soldiers, for they represent power, and if there
were not power in the hand of officers the spirit of rudeness would
not be obedient to any law or government, but to their own
wills.

Therefore every year shall be chosen a soldier, like unto a
marshal of a city, and being the chief he shall have divers soldiers
under him at his command, to assist in case of need.

The work of a soldier in times of peace is to fetch in offenders
and to bring them before either officer or courts, and to be a
protection to the officer against all disturbances.

The Work of a Task-master (*Prison warder*)

The work or office of a taskmaster is to take those into his oversight as are sentenced by the judge to lose their freedom, and appoint them their work and see they do it.

If they do their tasks he is to allow them sufficient victuals and clothing to preserve the health of their bodies. But if they prove desperate, wanton or idle, and will not quietly submit to the law, the taskmaster is to feed them with short diet, and to whip them. For a rod is prepared for the fool's back, till such time as their proud hearts do bend to the law.

And when he finds them subject he shall then carry a favourable hand towards them, as to offending brethren, and allow them sufficient diet and clothes in hopes of their amendment ; but withal see they do their work, till by the sentence of the law, he be set free again.

The taskmaster shall appoint them any kind of work or labour as he pleases that is to be done by man.

And if any of these offenders run away there shall be hue and cry sent after him, and he shall die by the sentence of the judge when taken again.

The Work of an Executioner

If any have so highly broke the laws, as they come within the compass of whipping, imprisoning and death, the executioner shall cut off the head, hang or shoot to death, or whip the offender according to the sentence of the law. Thus you may see what the work of every officer in a town or city is.

The Work of a Judge

The law itself is the judge of all men's actions, yet he who is chosen to pronounce the law is called judge, because he is the mouth of the law ; for no single man ought to judge or interpret the law.

Because the law itself, as it is left in the letter, is the mind and determination of the Parliament and of the people of the land, to be their rule to walk by and to be the touchstone of all actions.

And that man who takes upon him to interpret the law doth either darken the sense of the law, and so makes it confused and hard to be understood, or else puts another meaning upon it ; and so lifts up himself above the Parliament, above the law and above all people in the land.

Therefore the work of that man who is called judge is to hear any matter that is brought before him ; and in all cases of difference between man and man he shall see the parties on both sides before him, and shall hear each man speak for himself without a feed lawyer. Likewise he is to examine any witness who is to prove a matter in trial before him.

And then he is to pronounce the bare letter of the law concerning such a thing, for he hath his name judge not because his will and mind is to judge the actions of offenders before him, but because he is the mouth to pronounce the law, who indeed is the true judge. Therefore to this law and to this testimony let everyone have a regard who intends to live in peace in the Commonwealth.

But from hence hath arose much misery in the nations under kingly government, in that the man called the judge hath been suffered to interpret the law. And when the mind of the law, the judgment of the Parliament, and the government of the land is resolved into the breast of the judges, this hath occasioned much complaining of injustice, in judges, in courts of justice, in lawyers and in the course of the law itself, as if it were an evil rule.

Because the law, which was a certain rule, was varied according to the will of a covetous, envious or proud judge. Therefore no marvel though the kingly laws be so intricate, and though few knew which way the course of the law goes, because the sentence lies many times in the breast of a judge and not in the letter of the law.

And so the good laws made by an industrious Parliament are like good eggs laid by a silly goose, and as soon as she hath laid them she goes her way and lets others take them, and never looks after them more ; so that if you lay a stone in her nest she will sit upon it as though it were an egg.

And so though the laws be good, yet if they be left to the will of a judge to interpret, the execution hath many times proved bad. . . .

And surely both the judges for the law and the ministers for God's word have been both unfaithful servants to man and to God by taking upon them to expound and interpret that rule which they are bound to yield obedience to, without adding to or diminishing from.

For a whole county or shire there is to be a judge's court, or county senate, which is to be composed of a judge, of the peacemakers of every town within that circuit, and of the overseers and soldiers attending thereupon.

The Judge's Court

This court shall sit four times in the year, or oftener if need be, in the county, and four times in the year in great cities. In the first quarter of the year they shall sit in the east part of the county, and the second quarter of the year in the west, in the third in the south, and in the fourth in the north.

And this court is to oversee and examine any officer within their county or limits ; for their work is to see that everyone be faithful in his place. And if any officer hath done wrong to any, this court is to pass sentence of punishment upon the offender, according to his offence against the law.

If any grievance lie upon any man, wherein inferior officers cannot ease him, this court shall quietly hear his complaint, and ease him. For where a law is wanting, they may prepare a way of ease for the offender till the Parliament sit, who may either establish that conclusion for a law, if they approve of it, or frame another law to that effect ; for it is possible that many things may fall out hereafter, which the law-makers for the present may not foresee.

If any disorder break in among the people, this court shall set things to rights. If any be bound over to appear at this court, the judge shall hear the matter, and pronounce the letter of the law, according to the nature of the offence.

So that the alone work of the judge is to pronounce the sentence and mind of the law. And all this is but to see the laws executed, that the peace of the Commonwealth may be preserved.

For the whole land there will be a Parliament, a Commonwealth's ministry, a post-master and an army.

The Work of a Commonwealth's Parliament

A Parliament is the highest court of equity in a land, and it is to be chosen every year. And out of every city, town, and certain limits of a county through the land, two, three, or more men are to be chosen to make up this court.

This court is to oversee all other courts, officers, persons and actions, and to have a full power, being the representative of the whole land, to remove all grievances, and to ease the people that are oppressed.

First, as a tender father, a Parliament is to empower officers, and give out orders for the free planting and reaping of the Commonwealth's land, that all who have been oppressed and kept from the free use thereof by conquerors, kings, and their tyrant laws, may now be set at liberty to plant in freedom for food and raiment ; and are to be a protection to them who labour the earth, and a punisher of them who are idle.

The work of a Parliament, secondly, is to abolish all old laws and customs, which have been the strength of the oppressor, and to prepare and then to enact new laws for the ease and freedom of the people, but yet not without the people's knowledge.

For the work of a Parliament herein is three-fold.

First, when the old laws and customs of the kings do burden the people, and the people desire the remove of them, and the establishment of more easy laws.

It is now the work of a Parliament to search into reason and equity, how relief may be found out for the people in such a case, and to preserve a common peace. And when they have found out a way of debate of counsel among themselves, whereby the people may be relieved, they are not presently to establish their conclusions for a law.

But in the next place, they are to make a public declaration thereof to the people of the land who chose them, for their approbation ; and if no objection come in from the people within one month, they may then take the people's silence as consent thereunto.

And then in the third place, they are to enact it for a law, to be a binding rule of the whole land. For as the remove of the old laws and customs are by the people's consent, which is proved by their frequent petitioning and requests of such a thing, so the enacting of new laws must be by the people's consent and knowledge likewise.

And here they are to require the consent, not of men interested in the old oppressing laws and customs, as kings used to do, but of them who have been oppressed. And the reason is this : because the people must be all subject to the law, under pain of punishment ; therefore it is all reason they should know it before it be enacted, that if there be anything of the counsel of oppression in it, it may be discovered and amended.

The work of a Parliament, fourthly, is this : if there be occasion to raise an army to wage war, either against an invasion of a foreign enemy or against an insurrection at home, it is the work of a Parliament to manage that business for to preserve common peace.

So then, a Parliament is the head of power in a Commonwealth, and it is their work to manage public affairs in times of war and in times of peace ; not to promote the interests of particular men, but for the peace and freedom of the whole body of the land, viz., of every particular man, that none be deprived of his Creation rights unless he hath lost his freedom by transgression, as by the laws is expressed.

The army, in Winstanley's Commonwealth, is not to be a permanent body of hired or conscripted soldiers. It is levied only in case of emergency and is composed of the officers who form the magistracy in times of peace and, if necessary, of the whole people in arms :

A ruling army is called magistracy in times of peace, keeping that land and government in peace by execution of the laws, which the fighting army did purchase in the field by their blood out of the hands of oppression.

And here all officers, from the father in a family, to the Parliament in a land, are but the heads and leaders of an army ; and all people arising to protect and assist their officers, in defence of a right ordered government, are but the body of an army.

Winstanley saw the need to strengthen the social bonds between the various parishes and counties which compose the commonwealth and for this purpose he imagined that there should be post-masters, whose role is not dissimilar from that of our newspaper editors, though their aims seem more altruistic :

In every parish throughout the Commonwealth shall be chosen two men (at the time when other officers are chosen), and these shall be called postmasters. And whereas there are four parts of the land, east, west, north, south, there shall be chosen in the chief city two men to receive in what the postmaster of the east country brings in, and two men to receive in what the postmaster of the west brings in, and two for the north, and two for the south.

Now the work of the country postmaster shall be this. They shall every month bring up or send by tidings, from their respective parishes to the chief city, of what accidents or passages fall out, which is either to be the honour or the dishonour, hurt or profit of the Commonwealth. And if nothing have fallen out in that month worth observation, then they shall write down peace or good order in such a parish.

And when these respective postmasters have brought up their bills or certificates from all parts of the land, the receivers of those bills shall write down everything in order from parish to parish in the nature of a weekly bill of observation.

And those eight receivers shall cause the affairs of the four quarters of the land to be printed in one book with what speed may be, and deliver to every postmaster a book, that as they bring up the affairs of one parish in writing, they may carry down in print the affairs of the whole land.

The benefit lies here, that if any part of the land be visited with plague, famine, invasion, or insurrection, or any casualties, the other parts of the land may have speedy knowledge and send relief.

And if any accident fall out through unreasonable action, or careless neglect, other parts of the land may thereby be made watchful to prevent like danger.

Or if any through industry or ripeness of understanding have found out any secret in nature, or new invention in any art or trade or in the tillage of the earth, or such like, whereby the Commonwealth may more flourish in peace and plenty, for which virtues those persons received honour in the places where they dwelt ; when other parts of the land hears of it, many thereby will be encouraged to employ their reason and industry to do the like ; that so in time there will not be any secret in nature, which now lies hid (by reason of the iron age of kingly oppressing government) but by some or other will be brought to light, to the beauty of our Commonwealth.

Winstanley then goes on to describe the tasks of the Ministers of the Commonwealth who are to be laymen, elected every year by the members of the parish. Each Sunday when the parish holds its meeting the minister reads aloud the laws of the Commonwealth and the report contained in the Postmaster's gazette and this is followed by speeches and discussions on historical and scientific subjects. Thus we see that there is no room for religion in Winstanley's ideal Commonwealth and that it has been replaced by the study of nature and history. His views on experimental science, on the importance of discoveries and on education are all the more interesting since they do not come from a philosopher or a scientist, but from a man who had only received a grammar-school education :

If there were good laws, and the people be ignorant of them, it would be as bad for the Commonwealth as if there were no laws at all.

Therefore according to one of the laws of Israel's Commonwealth made by Moses, who was the ruler of the people at that time, it is very rational and good that one day in seven be still set apart, for three reasons.

First, that the people in such a parish may generally meet together to see one another's faces, and beget or preserve fellowship in friendly love.

Secondly, to be a day of rest or cessation from labour ; so that they may have some bodily rest for themselves and cattle.

Thirdly, that he who is chosen minister (for that year) in that parish may read to the people three things.

First, the affairs of the whole land, as it is brought in by the postmaster, as it is related in his office hereafter following.

Secondly, to read the law of the Commonwealth ; not only to strengthen the memory of the ancients, but that the young people also, who are not grown up to ripeness of experience, may be instructed, to know when they do well and when they do ill. For the laws of a land hath the power of freedom and bondage, life and death in its hand, therefore the necessary knowledge (is) to be known, and he is the best prophet that acquaints man therewith ; that as men grow up in years they may be able to defend the laws and government of the land. But these laws shall not be expounded by the reader, for to expound a plain law, as if a man would put a better meaning than the letter itself, produces two evils.

First, the pure law and the minds of people will be thereby confounded, for multitude of words darken knowledge.

Secondly, the reader will be puffed up in pride to condemn the law-makers and in time that will prove the father and nurse of tyranny, as at this day is manifested by our ministry.

And thirdly, because the minds of people generally love discourses ; therefore, that the wits of men both young and old may be exercised there may be speeches made in three-fold nature.

First, to declare the acts and passages of former ages and governments, setting forth the benefits of freedom by well-ordered governments, as in Israel's Commonwealth ; and the troubles and bondage which hath always attended oppression and oppressors, as the state of Pharoah and other tyrant kings, who said the earth and people were theirs and only at their dispose.

Secondly, speeches may be made of all arts and sciences, some one day, some another, as in physics, surgery, astrology, astronomy, navigation, husbandry, and such like. And in these speeches may be unfolded the nature of all herbs and plants from the hyssop to the cedar, as Solomon writ of.

Likewise men may come to see into the nature of the fixed and wandering stars, those great powers of God in the heavens above; and hereby men will come to know the secrets of nature and Creation, within which all true knowledge is wrapped up, and the light in man must arise to search it out.

Thirdly, speeches may be made sometimes of the nature of mankind of his darkness and of his light, of his weakness and of his strength, of his love and of his envy, of his sorrows and of his joys, of his inward and outward bondages, and of his inward and outward freedoms, etc. And this is that which the ministry of churches generally aim [at], but only that they confound their knowledge by imaginary study, when anyone takes upon him to speak without experience.

And because other nations are of several languages, therefore these speeches may be made sometimes in other languages and sometimes in our mother tongue ; that so men of our English Commonwealth may attain to all knowledges, arts and languages, and that every one may be encouraged in his industry, and purchase the countenance and love of their neighbourhood for their wisdom and experimental knowledge in the things which are.

Winstanley asserted that under " kingly " government education had remained the privilege of a few : " kingly bondage," he says, " is the cause of the spreading ignorance in the earth. But when Commonwealth's freedom is established, and Pharisaical or kingly slavery cast out, then will knowledge cover the earth as the waters cover the seas, and not till then." In his ideal commonwealth every child will be educated both in " book learning " and in a particular trade, and special care will also be taken to train children into good citizens :

Mankind in the days of his youth is like a young colt, wanton and foolish, till he be broke by education and correction ; and the neglect of this care or the want of wisdom in the performance of it, hath been and is, the cause of much division and trouble in the world.

Therefore the law of a Commonwealth does require that not only a father but that all overseers and officers should make it their work to educate children in good manners; and to see them brought up in some trade or other, and to suffer no children in any parish to live in idleness and youthful pleasure all their days, as many have been ; but that they be brought up like men and not like beasts, that so the Commonwealth may be planted with laborious and wise experienced men, and not with idle fools.

Mankind may be considered in a fourfold degree, his childhood, youth, manhood and old age. His childhood and his youth may be considered from his birth till forty years of age ; and within this compass of time, after he is weaned from his mother (who shall be the nurse herself if there be no defect in nature), his parents shall teach him a civil and humble behaviour toward all men. Then send him to school, to learn and to read the laws of the Commonwealth, to ripen his wits from his childhood, and so to proceed in his learning till he be acquainted with all arts and languages. And the reason is threefold.

First, by being acquainted with the knowledge of the affairs of the world, by their traditional knowledge they may be the better able to govern themselves like rational men.

Secondly, they may become thereby good Commonwealth's men in supporting the government thereof, by being acquainted with the nature of government.

Thirdly, if England have occasion to send ambassadors to any other land, we may have such as are acquainted with their language ; or if any ambassador come from other lands, we may have such as can understand their speech.

But one sort of children shall not be trained up only to book learning and no other employment, called scholars, as they are in the government of monarchy ; for then through idleness and exercised wit therein they spend their time to find out policies to advance themselves to be lords and masters above their labouring brethren ; as Simeon and Levi do, which occasions all the trouble in the world.

Therefore, to prevent the dangerous events of idleness in scholars, it is reason, and safe for common peace, that after children have been brought up at schools, to ripen their wits, they shall then be set to such trades, arts and sciences as their bodies and wits are capable of ; and therein continue till they come to forty years of age.

We have already seen that Winstanley abolished private ownership of the means of production, but unlike More, Campanella, and Andreae, he retained private ownership of " consumer goods."

If any other man endeavour to take away his house, furniture, food, wife, or children, saying, Everything is common, and so abusing the law of peace, such a one is a transgressor, and shall suffer punishment, as by the government and laws following expressed.

For though the public storehouses be a common treasury, yet every man's particular dwelling is not common, but by his consent ; and the Commonwealth's laws are to preserve a man's peace in his person, and in his private dwelling, against the rudeness and ignorance that may arise in mankind.

Nevertheless in his ideal commonwealth there is neither money nor wages and each gives according to his ability and receives according to his needs. At the end of *The Law of Freedom* he returns to the organisation of a moneyless society and explains how it will work :

The earth is to be planted and the fruits reaped and carried into barns and storehouses by the assistance of every family. And if any man or family want corn or other provision, they may go to the storehouses and fetch without money. If they want a horse to ride, go into the fields in summer, or to the common stables in winter, and receive one from the keepers, and when your journey is performed, bring him where you had him, without money. If any want food or victuals, they may either go to the butchers' shops, and receive what they want without money ; or else go to the flocks of sheep, or herds of cattle, and take and kill what meat is needful for their families, without buying and selling.

In the last chapter of *The Law of Freedom* Winstanley analyses the nature of laws and attempts to show the difference between customary, conventional and written laws, and the unwritten laws which spring from the " inward light of reason." " The King's old laws," he says, " cannot govern in times of bondage and in times of freedom too," and, with his characteristic concreteness, he compares them to " old soldiers, who will change their name, and turn about, and as they were." The law of the true commonwealth must be "a covenant of peace to whole mankind." This law " sets the earth free to all. This unites both Jew and Gentile into one brotherhood, and rejects none. This makes Christ's garment whole again, and makes the kingdoms of the world to become Commonwealths again. It is the inward power of right understanding, which is the true law that teaches people in action, as well as in words, to do as they would be done unto."

As far as the written laws of the the Commonwealth are concerned they must be " few and short and often read . . . and everyone, knowing when they did well and when ill, would be very
cautious of their words and actions : and thus would escape the
lawyer's craft." It is rather surprising, in view of this statement,
to find that Winstanley ends the description of his ideal Commonwealth with a list of sixty-two laws, many of which seem little
different from the " traditional law of kings which kills true
freedom." They appear, however, to have been put forward
tentatively, for Winstanley prefaces them with these words :
" What may be those particular laws, or such a method of law,
whereby a Commonwealth may be governed." It is disappoint-
ing, nevertheless, to see that Winstanley, like so many other
utopian writers, shows so little faithfulness to his own theoretical
views when he comes to put them into practice. He, who in the
Law of Righteousness had said : " If any man can say, he can give
life, then he hath the power to take away life. But if the power of
life and death be only in the hand of the Lord, then surely he is a
murderer of the Creation that taketh away the life of his fellow-
creature, man, by any law whatsoever," makes a free use of the
death penalty. As if he had had power to " give life," he orders :

No man shall administer the law for money or reward. He
that doth shall die as traitor to the Commonwealth ; for when
money must buy and sell justice, and bear all the sway, there is
nothing but oppression to be expected.
He who professes the service of a righteous God by preaching
and prayer, and makes a trade to get possession of the earth,
shall be put to death for a witch and a cheater.

His conception of justice is wholly barbarian :

He who strikes his neighbour shall be struck himself by the
executioner blow for blow, and shall lose eye for eye, tooth for
tooth, limb for limb, life for life ; and the reason is, that men
may be tender to one another's bodies, doing as they would be
done by.

As in More's *Utopia* slavery is prescribed as the punishment for
lesser crimes :

He who breaks any laws shall be the first time reproved in
words in private or in public, as is showed before ; the next

time whipped, the third time lose his freedom, either for a time or
for ever, and not to be any officer.

He who hath lost his freedom shall be a common servant to
any freeman who comes to the taskmasters and requires one to do
any work for him ; always provided that after one freeman hath
by the consent of the task-masters appointed him his work,
another freeman shall not call him thence till that work be done.

If any of these offenders revile the laws by words they shall be
soundly whipped and fed on coarse diet. If they raise weapons
against the laws they shall die as traitors.

When any slaves give open testimony of their humility and
diligence and their care to observe the laws of the Commonwealth,
they are then capable to be restored to their freedom when the
time of servitude is expired, according to the judge's sentence.
But if they remain opposite to the laws they shall continue slaves
till another term of time.

Winstanley was a staunch defender of the family and he had
often denounced those who, " through unreasonable beastly
ignorance, think there must be a community of all men and
women for copulation, and so strive to live a bestial life." In a
free Commonwealth " every family shall live apart, as now they
do. Every man shall enjoy his own wife, and every woman her
husband, as now they do." The laws concerning marriage are
however extremely simple and though rape is, in some cases,
punished by death, adultery is not considered a crime :

Every man and woman shall have the free liberty to marry
whom they love, if they can obtain the love and liking of that
party whom they would marry. And neither birth nor portion
shall hinder the match, for we are all of one blood, mankind.
And for portion, the common storehouses are every man's and
maid's portion, as free to one as to another.

If any man lie with a maid and beget a child, he shall marry
her.

If a man lie with a woman forcibly, and she cry out and give
no consent ; if this be proved by two witnesses, or in the man's
confession, he shall be put to death, and the woman let go free.
It is robbery of a woman's bodily freedom.

If any man by violence endeavour to take away another man's
wife, the first time of such violent offer he shall be reproved before
the congregation by the peace-maker ; the second time he shall
be made a servant under the taskmaster for twelve months ; and

if he forcibly lie with another man's wife, and she cry out, as in
the case when a maid is forced, the man shall be put to death.

When any man or woman are consented to live together in
marriage, they shall acquaint all the overseers in their circuit
therewith, and some other neighbours. And being all met
together, the man shall declare by his own mouth before them all
that he takes that woman to be his wife, and the woman shall say
the same and desire the overseers to be witnesses.

If, in the drafting of the laws of his ideal commonwealth,
Winstanley reveals an authoritarian spirit common to most
utopians he is, on the other hand, completely free from that
nationalism which characterises so many of them. Not only does
his Commonwealth not engage in wars of aggression, but he also
seems to have believed that the other nations of the world would
soon follow its example and that the whole of humanity would
live in peace :

In that nation where this Commonwealth's government shall
be first established, there shall be abundance of peace and plenty,
and all nations of the earth shall come flocking thither to see his
beauty, and to learn the ways thereof. And the law shall go forth
from that Zion, and that word of the Lord from that Jerusalem,
which shall govern the whole earth. *Micah, iv.* 1, 2.

There shall be no tyrant kings, lords of manors, tithing priests,
oppressing lawyers, exacting landlords, nor any such like pricking
briar in all this holy mountain of the Lord God our Righteousness
and Peace ; for the righteous law shall be the rule for everyone,
and the judge of all men's actions.

The whole earth would become one immense family :

And the rule of right government, being thus observed, may
make a whole land, nay the whole fabric of the earth, to become
one family of mankind, and one well governed Commonwealth ;
as Israel was called one house of Israel, though it consisted of
many tribes, nations and family.

The Law of Freedom marks the end of Winstanley's short, but
intense, literary and political activity. At the time of its appearance it must have enjoyed a certain success for it soon ran into a
second edition, and like most of his other works was widely
pirated. But with the return of the monarchy and the final
enslavement of the English working class, Winstanley's message

lost its meaning and his works were ignored both by historians and social thinkers. It was not until the beginning of this century that a comprehensive study of his activities and writings was made by L. H. Berens in *The Digger Movement in the Days of the Commonwealth*. Since then a selection from his works has been published in England and a complete edition has appeared in America. Yet Berens protests against the neglect from which Winstanley has suffered, which still applies to-day : "Its perusal (of *The Law of Freedom*) convinced us, and our subsequent investigations have only served to strengthen the belief, that Winstanley was, in truth, one of the most courageous, far-seeing and philosophical preachers of social righteousness that England has given to the world. And yet how unequally Fame bestows her rewards. More's *Utopia* has secured its author world-wide renown : it is spoken of, even if not read, in every civilised country in the world. Gerrard Winstanley's Utopia is unknown to his own countrymen."

4

Utopias of the Enlightenment

WHILE the utopias of the English Revolution are chiefly
concerned with economic and political problems, those of the
latter half of the seventeenth and of the eighteenth century are
mainly interested in philosophical and religious questions. It
was chiefly in France that utopian literature assumed its most
varied and original forms. The lack of intellectual freedom
under the absolute monarchy forced writers to hide their ideas
in the form of fantastic novels. Many of these utopias do not
purport to be complete schemes of ideal commonwealths ; the
social organisation is only roughly sketched and merely provides
the background for the discussion of non-conformist ideas.

The revolutionary influences of the Renaissance and the
Reformation had turned the minds of men towards concrete
problems of social reform, but, with the consolidation of national
states, whether Protestant or Catholic, it would have been idle to
talk of social reform. There was, however, a purpose in using
some fantastic country, or even planet, to expose and ridicule
customs and governments. In France the fashion for satirical
imaginary travels was set by Cyrano de Bergerac, whose main
works were published between 1657 and 1662. They constituted
a violent attack on religion, and Catholicism in particular, as
being the main support of the monarchy. About seventy years
later Swift used a similar formula to criticise the society of his
time, and in his turn he was imitated in France, where Gulliver's
Travels were immediately translated.

However much one may feel tempted to examine these satirical
works, they cannot be included here, for they are just the opposite
of *ideal* commonwealths. Occasionally as in Swift's *Voyage to the
Country of the Houyhnhnms* we find a brief outline of the author's
ideal society, but these descriptions are chiefly used to bring out
more vividly the stupidity and wickedness of the actual world.

The French utopias of the seventeenth and eighteenth century
are strongly influenced by Thomas More. The institutions of his
Utopia are generally transposed in a new setting with very little
change, but the discussion of philosophical and religious ideas,

which often distinguish themselves by their boldness, occupies a much greater place.

The dullest French utopia of the seventeenth century, on the other hand, is, without doubt, the *Histoire du Grand et Admirable Royaume d'Antangil*, which appeared in 1617 and has been described as the first French utopia. The author, who up to this day has remained anonymous, borrowed practically all his ideas from More, and like him, is liberal in dealing with religion. He must have been a military man, for fifteen chapters of his book are devoted to the organisation of the Police Force.

The *History of the Sevarites* by Denis Veiras, of which the first two volumes appeared in English in 1675, and the five volumes in French were published in Paris from 1677 to 1679, is also to a large extent influenced by More's *Utopia*, but contains some daring philosophical ideas and a violent attack on revealed religion. Denis Veiras, or to use his own glamourised name Veiras d'Alais, was born of a Protestant family and, after having studied law and dissipated his father's heritage, came to London, where he seems to have been successful in English society for he was sent with Buckingham, Arlington and Halifax on a diplomatic mission to The Hague. When he came back to London he wrote the first part of the *History of the Sevarites*, probably in English, which he seems to have known well.[1] The year before it appeared he had been obliged to leave London, following the disgrace of Buckingham and Arlington, and returned to Paris, where he completed his *Histoire des Sevarambes*. The first four volumes appeared with the King's privilege, while the last volume, which contains the strongest attack on religion, was published without official recognition.

The utopia of a Dijon lawyer, Claude Gilbert, met with a less happy fate. His *Histoire de Calejava* (or the Island of Reasonable Men) was printed in 1700, but before a single copy was sold the fear of prosecution led the author to destroy the whole edition,

---

[1]While in London he had met Colonel Scott, son of Thomas Scott the regicide, a former commander of the Roundheads in Holland and an associate of Aphra Behn during her career as a spy. Veiras acted as his secretary. Later Scott seems to have been instrumental in implicating Pepys in the Papist plot. To prepare his defence Pepys paid large sums of money to find witnesses who could discredit his accuser and Veiras testified against his former patron. Pepys, writing to Veiras to thank him for his testimony, told him to continue writing in English, as he knew this language as well as his own.

with the exception of one copy which he kept for himself. Like Veiras's utopia, the story by Claude Gilbert is chiefly interesting for his ideas on religion.

These utopias are significant from a social and religious point of view, particularly if one remembers the régime under which they were written, but they are, on the whole, too imitative of More's *Utopia* to make it worth while quoting extracts from them in this section. An exception has been made in the case of Gabriel de Foigny's ideal Australian land, for he has shown more originality and daring than his contemporaries.

In spite of the care taken by the utopian writers of this period to cover their ideas under the cloak of fantastic romances, they had to protect themselves against prosecution by printing their books abroad or giving them a false imprint. The utopias appertain to the clandestine literature of the time, and the fact that their authors were generally of Protestant origin must have rendered them doubly suspicious. Even Fénelon's *Télémaque*, published in 1699, which belongs to a more respectable class since it was written by an Archbishop for the edification of a future king of France, resulted in the disgrace of its author. It is probable that Louis XIV did not object to the description of the idyllic countries of La Bétique and Salente, where men led a laborious and frugal life, where gold was turned into ploughs and war was unknown, but the veiled criticisms directed against his reign did not leave him indifferent. Fénelon criticises Louis XIV for much the same reasons as More criticised Henry VIII—his passion for war, his love of luxury, and the neglect of agriculture which condemned the peasant population to live in abject poverty when the land could have been the main source of wealth for the nation.

Throughout the eighteenth century, utopias became increasingly popular and there is hardly a corner of the earth which did not provide a setting for some ideal commonwealth. The Baron de Lahontan takes us to North America, the Voyage and Adventures of François Leguat to the East Indies, Tyssot de Patot, the unorthodox teacher of mathematics at the famous school of Daventer, tells of the adventures of a " Reverend Père Cordelier " in Greenland. We are transported to an island of Military Women or to Egypt, and Australia remains, of course, extremely popular (the various ideal commonwealths supposed to have existed in Australia would alone fill an anthology). The *Memoirs of Gaudencio di Lucca*, published in 1746, is supposed to be a report to the fathers of the Inquisition at Bologna, who have arrested him, of his travels to an unknown land situated in the middle of the African desert. And when the world becomes too small to house the ever-increasing number of utopias, ideal commonwealths are imagined in some other world, or in the future, like that of L. S. Mercier.

We find also a whole literature which has many characteristics in common with the utopias, but which portrays ideal families or ideal small communities rather than whole commonwealths, and which had found its original inspiration in the story of *Robinson Crusoe*. While Defoe had created a one-man utopia, his imitators, more ambitious, shipwrecked a man and a woman, or a whole crew, on a desert island and these founded an ideal family or an ideal community. They attempted to re-constitute, in this manner, the origin and formation of society. *L'Isle Inconnue* belongs to this type of novel. The author, according to the publisher, has given in this work " the model of innocent love, the model of conjugal love, the model of domestic government, the model of a perfect education, the model of good morals, the model of an agricultural community, the model of a well-bred society."

If the purely mythical " noble savages " described by Jean-Jacques Rousseau and Bernardin de St Pierre peopled many utopias of the eighteenth century, others tried to discover "genuine savages" in countries untouched by civilisation. During the sixteenth and seventeenth centuries the dimly-known continents of America or Australia merely offered a setting into which London or Paris had been transplanted. In the eighteenth century these countries begin to have a life of their own and the customs of the people discovered there by travellers or missionaries are incorporated in the framework of the utopias. We find also that while utopias had tried to represent a society where complete equality was the rule, many of them are now concerned with building a free society. The inhabitants of Diderot's Tahiti, for example, do not know either government or laws. Utopias had provided sufficient food and clothing, comfortable houses and a good education, but in exchange they had demanded the complete submission of the individual to the state and its laws; they now sought above all these things freedom from laws and governments.

It was particularly regarding sexual relations that the eighteenth century asked for greater freedom. From Plato onwards utopians had always taken a great interest in sexual questions, but always from an eugenic or moralist point of view, and they had devised stringent laws subordinating marriages to the interests of the State or to those of religion. The French philosophers of the eighteenth century also took a lively interest in questions relating to sex, but they were far from seeing sexual relations purely as a means of reproduction ; for them sex was something to be enjoyed *per se*, and they strongly resented the restrictions put upon them by religious morality. As they tried to liberate themselves from the intellectual constraint of religion, so they also wished to overthrow all sexual moral codes. This revolt partly expressed itself in the erotic poems and novels which many of them did not think it below their dignity to write.

We shall see that Diderot showed how primitive man was free from religious and moral laws and led a happy life where luxury, property, monogamous marriage are unknown. Perhaps no writer of the eighteenth century has expressed more lucidly than the Marquis de Sade the impossibility of reconciling religion and the accepted moral code with freedom. In the *Philosophie dans le Boudoir* he put forward the principles which should guide the citizens of a free state. While many utopias had tried to reconcile the ideas of equality with the Christian faith, Sade believed that there could be no equality as long as people had not thrown off the yoke of religion and he appealed to Frenchmen to achieve their own liberation :

O! you have the axe in your hands, deliver the final blow to the tree of superstition ; do not be content to lop off the branches; uproot completely a weed whose effects are so contagious ; be absolutely convinced that your system of liberty and equality contradicts too openly the ministers of Christ's altars for there ever to be a single one of them who either accepts it in good faith, or who does not seek its downfall if he can contrive to gain a hold on people's conscience...Annihilate then for ever all that might one day destroy your work. Realise that, the fruit of your labours being reserved for your posterity alone, your duty and your integrity demands that you should not leave for them any of these dangerous germs which could plunge them once more into the chaos from which we have escaped with so much trouble.

Already our prejudices are disappearing, already the allegedly faithful, deserting the apostolic banquet, are leaving the holy bread for the mice to eat. Frenchmen, do not halt here ; the whole of Europe, one hand already upon the bandage binding its eyes, awaits from you the effort which will tear it from its brow. Hasten, do not allow to *holy Rome*—frenziedly attempting in every sphere to curb your efforts—the time to retain even now perhaps a few proselytes. Strike its haughty toppling head ruthlessly, and before two months are passed the tree of liberty, overshadowing the debris of the Chair of Saint Peter, will cover with the weight of its triumphant branches all these miserable idols of christianity, insolently erected upon the ashes of such men as Cato and Brutus.

This appeal to Frenchmen was written in 1795 when the old régime had been destroyed but not the ideas on which that régime was based. Sade saw very clearly that it is not sufficient to change the form of government to achieve freedom, but that the old ideas must also be abandoned :

Yes, citizens, religion is incompatible with the idea of liberty; you have realised that. Never shall the free man abase himself before the gods of christianity ; never shall its dogmas, its rites, its mysteries or its morality be acceptable to a republican. One more effort : since you are working to destroy all prejudices, allow none to remain. How much more certain can we be of their return if the one you leave alive is absolutely the cradle of all the others.
Let us cease to imagine that religion could be useful to mankind. Let us have good laws and we shall be able to do without religion. . .We want nothing more from an incredible author of an universe which moves of its own accord, we want nothing more from a god without dimension and who nevertheless fills everything with its immensity, a god all-powerful yet who never executes anything he desires, from a being friendly to order and in whose government all is in disorder. No, we want nothing more from a god who deranges nature, who is the father of confusion, who goads mankind to a point at which he abandons himself to horrors; such a god makes us tremble with indignation, and we relegate him for ever to the oblivion from which the infamous Robespierre wished to rescue him. . .
Frenchmen, you will strike the first blows, your national education will do the rest ; but undertake this task promptly ; let it become one of your chief cares ; above all, let it have for a

basis these essential ethics, so neglected in religious education.—
Replace the deificatory idiocies with which you have wearied the
young minds of your children by excellent social principles;
instead of teaching them to recite futile prayers, which they will
pride themselves on forgetting as soon as they are sixteen, let
them be instructed in their duties in society ; teach them to
cherish virtues of which you scarcely spoke to them previously
and which, without your religious fables, suffice for their
individual happiness ; make them realise that this happiness
consists in making others as fortunate as we ourselves desire to
be. . .

Again, while most utopians had assumed that the sole task of
marriage was that of reproduction, according to the law of nature,
Sade sees in the satisfaction of physical love a natural action
which must not be bound to marriage ceremonies or prejudices :

It is in vain that women bring up the question either of sexual
modesty or of their attachment to other men in their defence ;
these chimerical methods are worthless; we have already seen how
much modesty is in fact an artificial and contemptible feeling.
Love, which may be called *the soul's madness*, has not the right to
justify their constancy ; by satisfying only two individuals, the
loved one and the lover, it cannot be of any use for the happiness
of others, and women have been given us for the happiness of all,
not for an egotistic and privileged happiness. All men have
therefore an equal right to enjoy themselves with all women ;
and no man therefore, following the laws of nature, may set up
for himself sole and personal rights over a woman. . . .

If we admit, as we have just done, that all women should be
submitted to our desires, we should certainly allow them an equal
opportunity to satisfy fully their own desires ; with this end in
view, our laws should be partial to their fiery temperament, for
it is absurd to have put their honour and their virtue into the
anti-natural force which they exert to resist those inclinations
that they have received in far greater profusion than ourselves ;
this injustice of prevailing customs is all the more flagrant in that
we allow ourselves at the same time to weaken them by dint of
seduction and to punish them subsequently because they give in
to all the efforts we have made to provoke their downfall. The
whole absurdity of our customs is engraved, it seems to me, in
this inequitable atrocity, and this sole consideration should make
us realise the extreme need we have of changing them for one
more pure.

I say that women, having received far more violent inclinations towards the pleasures of lust than have we, should be able to surrender themselves to these pleasures as much as they wish, absolutely absolved from all marriage bonds and from all false prejudices of sexual modesty, absolutely in harmony with the principles of nature. I wish the laws to permit them to surrender themselves to as many men as may seem good to them ; I wish the enjoyment of their whole sex and of all parts of their bodies to be yielded to men ; and, under the special clause that they should give themselves equally to all who desire them, they must have the liberty likewise of enjoying all those they deem worthy to satisfy them. . . .

A new government, says Sade, necessitates new customs for " it is impossible for a free State to behave like the slave of a despotic king. . . . a mass of trifling errors and small social misdemeanours, considered extremely important under the rule of kings . . . will cease to have any meaning now ; other heinous crimes, known under the names of regicide and sacrilege, would vanish under a government which no longer knows either kings or religion, that is, in a republican State. . . . "

Laws, Sade goes on to argue, are inhuman because they cannot appreciate the motives of men's actions. They must be therefore as " mild " as possible, and in his constitution there would be no death penalty :

There follows, I feel, from this, the necessity of creating mild laws and above all of abolishing for ever the atrocity of the death penalty ; for the law, inhuman to itself, cannot have access to the passions which are able to reconcile man to the cruel action of murder. Man receives from nature the impressions which allow one to pardon him for this action, while the law, on the contrary, being always in opposition to nature and owing nothing to it, cannot be authorised to permit itself the same motives, nor is it possible for the law to have the same rights. . . The second reason for which the death penalty should be abolished is that it has never done away with crime, for this is committed every day at the foot of the scaffold. In a few words, one should suppress this penalty because there is no worse calculation than that which condemns a man to death for having killed another, for the obvious result of this process is that instead of there being one man less there are suddenly two less, and it is only executioners and congenital idiots who can be familiar with such a kind of mathematics. . .

While the writings of Foigny, Diderot and Sade break with the utopian tradition by attaching a great importance to the freedom of the individual, Mably and Morelly, on the other hand, want to establish the equality of men, which, they assert, is laid down by Nature, and to devise a stringent code of laws and institutions whose aim is to make men truly equal. They denounce property as the origin of all evils and of the unhappiness of mankind, and want the state to be the owner of everything and to distribute to the citizens all the things they require. These were familiar ideas in the eighteenth century and account for the popularity which the works of Mably and, to a lesser extent, Morelly enjoyed.

There is little that strikes one as original in the theories put forward by l'Abbé Gabriel de Bonnot de Mably, a jurist who retired from public life when still in his youth, to dedicate himself to study and the writing of innumerable books. His utopia, as he described it in his *Treatise on the Rights and Duties of Citizens*, is that of Sir Thomas More :

I am going to reveal to you one of my weaknesses. I never read a description in a travel book of a desert island where the sky is blue and the water pure without longing to go there and set up a republic in which all are equal, all are rich, all are poor, all are free, and our first law is that nothing is to be privately owned. We should bring to the public storehouses the fruit of our labours : that would be the Treasury of the State and the inheritance of every citizen. Every year the fathers of families would elect the stewards, whose duty it would be to distribute the goods according to the needs of each individual, and to instruct them as to the work required by the community.

Property, inequality and the love of riches, he   asserts continually, are the curses of mankind :

Inequality is degrading and sows division and hatred, it provokes national and civil wars. Property is the chief cause of all the unhappiness of mankind....
The more I reflect the more I feel convinced that inequality of fortunes and conditions decomposes man and alters the natural feelings of his heart...
Riches induce need, which is the most cowardly of all vices, or luxury, which gives to the rich all the vices of poverty and to the poor a covetousness which they can only satisfy by crimes and by the most degrading baseness ; voluptuousness is a consequence

of riches and while it softens and debilitates the souls of rich men who become incapable of any generous effort, it throws the people into a misery which renders them ferocious or stupid.

It is not true, Mably asserts, that private property creates the desire to work ; men will work better when all goods are common, for it is an "agreeable idea" which will inspire them. Incentives, however, will be provided by granting certain honours or distinctions to the best workers.

Like J. J. Rousseau, Mably believed that man was good when he came out of the hands of Nature, but that the human keyboard has been put out of tune. But, also like Rousseau, he did not think that it would be possible to abolish private property and return to a golden age in which reigned complete equality. "This community of goods," he says, " because of the depravity of morals, can only be a chimera in this world...it would be impossible to create such a Republic nowadays," and he puts forward a few timid reforms concerning inheritance, commerce, taxation, etc. He seemed to have recognised, however, that in some cases revolutions were justified, for he said : " To consider civil war in every case as an injustice is a doctrine contrary to *bonnes moeurs* and to the public good."

Like so many thinkers of his time, Mably reconciled an absolute belief in the goodness of human nature and the perfect equality established by Nature, with an admiration, amounting to worship, for Greek Antiquity, and for Plato and Plutarch in particular. These writers did not see the inconsistency of basing their ideal conceptions on the Sparta of Lycurgus or Plato's Republic, which represented systems based on slavery and imposed a strict hierarchy even among the citizens.

Morelly's *Code de la Nature ou le Véritable Esprit de ses Loix*, which appeared in 1755, the same year as Rousseau's *Discours sur l'Origine et les Fondements de l'Inégalité parmi les Hommes*, repeats the same commonplace ideas of the times. Man is fundamentally good but has been corrupted by institutions based on private property. Society has destroyed the harmony of Nature. No one has succeeded in identifying who Morelly was, but it is generally believed that he was the author of a poem in prose entitled *La Basiliade*, which had appeared in 1753 and expressed similar ideas. But whoever Morelly may have been, there is little doubt that he considered himself "Nature's Secretary," for in the last section of his *Code de la Nature* he set down in great detail the constitution of an ideal society according to the laws of Nature.

Nature, he informs us, thinks that the family should be the unit of society, that government should be by rotation, that goods should be stored and distributed from common store-houses, that every citizen should do agricultural work from the age of twenty to twenty-five, that children should be removed from home after the fifth year and should then be educated in public, that severe penal laws should enforce the execution of public duties. Morelly is not the first to state his belief in the innate goodness of man, but after having asserted that humanity has been perverted by lawgivers, he goes on to establish a code of laws as rigid as those which ruled the society he denounced.

Both Mably and Morelly had considerable influence on the thought of their time. Mably's most distinguished follower was probably Rousseau, while to Morelly falls the honour of having been described by Babeuf as the real instigator of the Conspiracy of the Equals. Thus they occupy an important place in the history of socialist thought, but as utopians they have contributed little that is new or original.

GABRIEL DE FOIGNY

A New Discovery of Terra Incognita Australis

GABRIEL de Foigny is perhaps not the most representative utopian of the second half of the seventeenth century, but he has the merit of having written an original and entertaining utopia, and the story of his life offers an illustration of what happens to an irreligious utopian when he lives and publishes his work in the ideal city of a christian utopian. We have seen how Andreae's Christianopolis was modelled on the city of Calvin, and we shall now see how, fifty years later, Foigny was driven from Geneva where he wrote *Les Aventures de Jacques Sadeur*, while no doubt under the influence of that satanic spirit against which both Calvin and Andreae had waged such a ruthless war.   The writing of his utopia was not Foigny's only " crime," and fortunately for him the institutions of Geneva had by this time degenerated along more liberal lines or he would have paid more dearly for his misconduct.

Gabriel de Foigny was born in a small village in the Ardennes, towards 1630, of a Catholic family.   After receiving a good education, he entered a monastery of the Order of the Cordeliers where, thanks to his gift for oratory, he became a preacher.   His scandalous behaviour, however, soon forced him to leave the Order, and he was unfrocked.   Life became difficult for him in France and he decided to change both his country and his religion.   In 1666 he went to Geneva, in a state of complete poverty, and was extremely anxious to be allowed to reside in the city.   After having examined his faith and character, the Consistory, composed of the ministers and elders of the city, accepted his conversion to the " true faith " and he was allowed to stay.

Before long the worthy citizens of Geneva had reasons to regret their decision and suspect the motives of his conversion.   The Consistory received reports on his scandalous behaviour, and after he had seduced several servant girls, broken a promise of marriage, and announced his intention to marry a widow, who had a bad reputation, he was expelled from Geneva.

From there he went to Lausanne, and then to Berne, where he led a precarious existence until, by a stroke of good luck, he became one of the masters at the College of Morges.   In the meantime he had married the disreputable widow, and would probably have settled down to a peaceful family life had he not conceived the unfortunate idea of writing a work on the Attractions of the Divine Service.   He showed the manuscript to friends and it eventually reached some members of the Consistory, who found the work infected with the Papist spirit ; their distrust of Foigny increased and attempts were made to remove him from his post.   Foigny himself soon provided them with an opportunity to do this, for he had added drunkenness to his other disorders, and one day conducted the service at the Temple " while under the influence of drink " and vomited in front of the communion table.

After being forced to leave the College, he managed to return to Geneva, where he tried to soften the hearts of the members of the Consistory and the Venerable Company by re-editing the Psalms of Marot and Beze. But he added to them some arguments and prayers of his own and these were found to smell of Papist idolatry ; the sale of the book was therefore forbidden and all the copies were seized, to be put in the public library.[1]

It seems that after this experience Foigny gave up all hope of ever becoming a good Swiss citizen, and he proceeded to write *Les Aventures de Jacques Sadeur dans la Découverte de la terre Australe,* or, to give it its English title, *A New Discovery of Terra Incognita Australis,* which was published in 1676. Foigny had no illusions as to the respectability of the book and neither asked for permission to publish it nor put his name on it, while the Genevan printer, La Pierre, appended the imprint of an imaginary Jacques Verneuil, printer at Vannes, in France.

As soon as the book appeared, the Venerable Company, created by Calvin as the guardian of the city's morals, took a lively interest in it and asked the Professors of Theology to read it and present a report. Two Professors of the Academy of Geneva perused the book and informed the Venerable Company that it was " full of extravagances, falsehoods and even dangerous, infamous and blasphemous things." They objected in particular to the chapters concerning the customs and religion of the "Australians."

Foigny was summoned to appear before the Venerable Company. He denied being the author of the book and told some unconvincing tale to explain how the manuscript had come into his hands. He also maintained that he had received permission to publish the book from one of the Syndics, who had conveniently died a few weeks before. For three months the Venerable Company investigated and discussed the case of Foigny and eventually he and his printer were put in jail. When he appeared before the syndics (or judges) Foigny confessed to being the author of the book but appealed to the pity of the

---

[1]Frederick Lachevre in his biography of Foigny, which I have used here, remarks that this meant, in reality, that the books would be destroyed, and this was in fact done so effectively that neither the Library of Geneva nor that of the Consistoire possesses a copy of this edition of the Psalms.

judges and was released "on bail." He utilised his freedom to gain the support of several members of the Consistory and that of the first syndic, and the matter was left indefinitely in abeyance.

We cannot deal here with the latter part of his stay in Geneva and his new tribulations, though they offer an interesting insight into the morals of the city of Geneva at that time. Towards the end of his life, Foigny went back to France and the Roman Catholic Church, taking with him a maid-servant (whom he had seduced), and such of his children as the inhabitants of Geneva had not succeeded in abducting. He spent his last years in a monastery, where he died in 1692.

Though Gabriel de Foigny's utopia is more edifying than his life, it is not surprising that it should have shocked the theologians of Geneva. His views on religion were " blasphemous " indeed, for he in fact attacks all the foundations of religion. The Australians do not believe in the doctrine of revelation, for they think it absurd that God should favour some of his creatures more than others. They ridicule the belief in the immortality of the soul, which is illogical because it admits that the dead could travel to the next world while the living could not and this would mean that the dead have more freedom of movement than the living, which is a contradiction. Prayers are a thoughtless action ; to pray is to suppose that God does not know our desires and this is blasphemous ; if we believe that he knows them, but that he does not wish to grant us satisfaction, we are impious, and if we think that he is indifferent we commit a sacrilege. God is beyond our feeble understanding and cannot be given any definite attributes ; one can only affirm his existence. But even assuming that the knowledge of God were possible it would only serve to divide us and to render us unhappy.

The Australians believe in God but they never mention him ; "their religion is not to speak of religion." They have no priests, and people assemble to meditate and not to pray. Religion thus deprived of all its customary attributes and functions becomes the deism of the eighteenth and nineteenth century.

Foigny also anticipates the philosophers of the eighteenth century by his belief in the innate goodness of human nature. Man is not born wicked as the Christian religion teaches, he is born free, reasonable and good. Some critics have described Foigny's utopia as Paradise before the Fall, but it would be truer to say that he did not believe in original sin, which he seems to have considered an invention of religion.

Being born good and free, the Australians do not need a government any more than they need religion. They meet to discuss the affairs of the community but they have no written laws and no rulers. They have, of course, no private property and do not even know the difference between mine and thine. The family does not threaten the unity of the community, because it does not exist.

Sexual relationships are abolished altogether, and here Foigny's thought becomes rather obscure. The Australians are a nation of hermaphrodites (or would it be more exact to say androgynes?) ; they do not indulge in sexual intercourse and children are born in a mysterious way. Did Foigny invent this " sexless " race to avoid, as Mr Lachevre suggests, the discussion of a subject on which his views would have shocked the Venerable Company? This seems unlikely, for he does not refrain from being ' shocking ' in his description of James Sadeur's feelings towards his fellow hermaphrodites. Perhaps Foigny wished to satirise the Christian attitude to sex. If sexual relations must only serve the purpose of reproduction, why not abolish them altogether! The secrecy with which the Australians surround the act of reproduction, the horror with which they regard sexual relations, is not unlike that of the Calvinists among whom Foigny lived. It is curious, however, to see how many utopias are conceived as " sexless " societies. In Plato's republic love between men and women is relegated to a purely eugenic function, Swift's Houyhnhnms regard sexual relationships with the same horror as Foigny's Australians; among the inhabitants of Hudson's *The Crystal Age* men and women know only brotherly feelings towards one another, while in the *Brave New World* of Aldous Huxley the same indifference has been achieved through a process of saturation.

Les Aventures de Jacques Sadeur appeared in an English translation in London, in 1693; the title-page describes them as :

A
New Discovery
of
Terra Incognita Australis
or the
Southern World
by
James Sadeur a Frenchman
who
Being Cast there by a Shipwreck lived 35 years in that
country, and gives a particular Description of the
Manners, Customs, Religion, Laws, Studies, and *Wars,* of
those Southern People : and some *Animals* peculiar to
that Place : with several other Rarities.

The imprimatur was that of Charles Hern, and it was printed
at the Sign of the Raven in the Poultry for John Dunton, who was
famous for his literary hoaxes, such as the publication of the
minutes of an Athenian Society which had never existed. He was
probably responsible for inserting on the title-page the following
embellishment :

These Memoirs were thought so curious that they
were kept *Secret* in the Closet of a late Great *Minister of
State,* and never Published till now since his Death.

The translation was made from the second French edition,
published with the King's Privilege (by Public Authority) in
1692, one year after Foigny's death. This edition is considerably
different from, and shorter than, the first and it is not known
whether Foigny was responsible for these alterations.

The quotations reproduced below have been taken from this
English Edition of 1693. The spelling has been modernised and
a few mis-translations have been corrected (by comparing it with
the French edition of 1692). Occasionally a few passages from
the first edition have been inserted, between brackets. The
version which appeared by authority of the King was much more
respectable than the one which appeared bearing a false imprint
in Geneva, and in justice to the learned theologians of the
Venerable Company it is necessary to quote some of the passages
which shocked them so much.

The first part of the book deals with the adventures of James
Sadeur in many parts of the world and it is the second part which is

devoted to Australia. The Australian Continent was very much
in the news at the time when Foigny wrote his book, and he
seems to have been inspired by the Relation of Ferdinand de
Quiros to the King of Spain which had been published in Latin
in 1612 or 1613 and in French in 1617. According to Foigny's
preface de Quiros described Australia as " a country much more
fertile and populous than any in Europe ; that the inhabitants
were much bigger and taller than the Europeans, and that they
lived much longer than they."

James Sadeur, who tells the story, had a troubled childhood ;
he was born during a sea voyage and every time he travelled by
sea some major misfortune befell him. His life was further
complicated by being an hermaphrodite. These peculiarities,
however, stood him in good stead on his arrival in "Australia," as
he himself shows :

If there was anything in the World which could persuade me of
the inevitable fatality of humane things, and the infallible
accomplishments of those events, the chain of which composes
the destiny of Mankind, it would certainly be this history that I
am writing ; there is not a single accident of my life, which has
not been serviceable either to direct or support me in this new
Country, where it was decreed I should one day be driven. My
often shipwrecks taught me to bear them ; both sexes were
necessary for me under pains of being destroyed at my arrival,
as I shall show in the sequel of my story. It was my good fortune
to be found naked, otherwise I had been known to be a stranger
in a Land where no one wears any covering, without that terrible
combat that I was obliged to maintain against the monstrous
Fowls and which brought me into great reputation, amongst
those that were witnesses of it, I should have been forced to have
submitted to an examination that would have been infallibly
followed by my death. In fine, the more all the circumstances of
my voyages and perils shall be considered, the more clearly it
will appear that there is a certain order of things in the fate of
man, and such a chain of effects that nothing can prevent, and
which brings us by a thousand imperceptible turnings, to the end
to which we are destined.

The custom of the inhabitants of this country is never to receive
any person amongst them, whose humour, birth and country,
they know not before : But the extraordinary courage with which
they had seen me fight ; and the great admiration they conceived
at my reviving after it, made me without any inquest be admitted

into the neighbouring quarter, where everyone came to kiss my hands [and my private parts]. They would also have carried me upon their heads, the greatest mark of high esteem that they show to any person ; but as they perceived it would not be done without incommoding me, so they omitted this ceremony. My reception being made, those that had brought and comforted me, carried me to the House of the Heb, which signifies, a House of Education ; they had provided me a lodging, and all things necessary, with such diligence, as surpassed the civility of the most polished Europeans.

The description of the country betrays the unmistakable influence of Sir Thomas More, while in the description of the buildings and apartments Foigny was probably thinking of the monastery :

What is more surprising in the Australian Dominions, is, that there is not one mountain to be seen ; the natives having levelled them all. . . this great country is flat, without forests, marshes or deserts, and equally inhabited throughout. . To this prodigy may be added the admirable uniformity of languages, customs, buildings and other things which are to be met with in this Country. 'Tis sufficient to know one quarter, to make a certain judgement of all the rest ; all which without doubt proceeds from the nature of the people, who are all born with an inclination of willing nothing contrary to one another ; and if it should happen that any one of them had anything that was not common, it would be impossible for him to make use of it.

There are fifteen thousand Seizains, in this prodigious Country. Each Seizain contains sixteen quarters, without counting the Hab, and the four Hebs ; there is twenty five houses in each quarter, and every house has four apartments which lodge four men each; so that there is four hundred houses in each Sezain, and six thousand four hundred persons, which being multiplied by fifteen thousand Seizains, will show the number of the inhabitants of the whole Australian land, to be about fourscore and 16 millions, without counting all the Youth, and the masters lodging in the Hebs, in each of which there is at least eight hundred persons ; and as in fifteen thousand Seizains there is sixty thousand Hebs, so the young men and the masters that teach them, will be found to amount to near forty eight millions.

The great house of the Seizain, which they call the Hab, that is, the House of Elevation, is built only with diaphanous and transparent stones, like to our finest crystal, only these stones are diversified with a prodigious quantity of figures of all sorts of colours, very fine and lively which by their infinite variety form sometimes human figures, sometimes represent the fields in all their beauty, and sometimes suns and other figures, of such a vivacity, as can never be too much admired. The whole building is without any artifice, except the curious cut of the stone, with seats all round it, and sixteen great tables of a much more lively red than that of our scarlet.

There is four considerable entrances, that answer to the four great ways upon which it is situated : All without is filled with very rare inventions. They ascend unto the top of it by a thousand steps, upon which there is a kind of platform, that will easily contain forty persons. . . . No one for a constancy lives in it, but each quarter take their turns to supply the tables with sufficient food for twelve persons for the refreshment of the passer-byes.

The common houses, which they call Hiebs, that is, the habitation of the men, are in number twenty five in each quarter and four score paces in circumference. They are divided like the Hebs, by two great walls, which make four distinct separations, and end each at an apartment. . . Each separation is inhabited by four persons, whom they call Cle, that is, Brethren. There is nothing to be seen in these buildings but four seats which are kind of benches, which serve them to rest themselves on, and some different seats for the same use... There is a great quantity of water that runs from the mountains and the Australians know how to conduct it so exactly, that they have brought it round and use it in a very ingenious way in all their Seizains, Quarters and Apartments which contribute much to the fruitfulness of their ground.

We pass now to a description of the Australians :

All the Australians are of both sexes, or Hermaphrodites, and if it happens that a child is born but of one, they strangle him as a monster. They are nimble, and very active ; their flesh is more upon the red than vermilion ; they are commonly eight foot high, their face pretty long, forehead large, their eyes prominent, and mouth small, their lips are of deep red coral, nose more inclined to be long than round, and beard and hair always black, which they never cut because they grow but little ; their chin is long, [cleft] and turns a little up again ; their neck slender ; their shoulders large and high ; they have very little breasts, [their breasts are round and conspicuous], placed very low, a little redder than vermilion, their arms are nervous and their hands are pretty broad and long [and with six fingers], they have a high chest, but flat belly, who appears but little when they are big with child ; their hips high ; their thighs large, and legs long [with feet with six toes]. They are so accustomed to go naked, that they think they cannot speak of covering themselves without being declared enemies of Nature, and deprived of Reason. In certain places there are some who have on their hips a kind of arm thinner but of the same length as the others and which they can extend at will and which is stronger than the others.

Everyone is obliged at least to present one child to the Heb : But they bring them forth in so private a manner, that it is accounted a crime amongst them to speak of the necessary conjunction in the propagation of mankind.

In all the time I was there, I could never discover how generation work was performed amongst them ; I have only observed, that they loved one another with a cordial love, and that they never loved any one more than another. I can affirm I neither saw quarrel or animosity amongst them. They know not how to distinguish between mine and thine and there is more perfect sincerity and disinterestment amongst them than exist between men and women in Europe.

I always used to speak what I thought ; but I was a little too free in declaring what I did not like in their manners, sometimes to a brother, sometimes to another, even by maintaining with arguments mine own opinions ; I spoke of their nakedness with certain terms of aversion, which extremely offended them. [I tried to caress some of the brothers and excite them to what we call pleasure]. In one day I stopped a brother, and waggishly demanded of him, with a seeming earnestness, where were the fathers of those children that were already born, and told him, that I thought ridiculous for them to affect such a silence in that point. This discourse and some others of the like nature gave the Australians a kind of hatred for me and many of them having maintained that I was but half a man, had concluded that they ought to destroy me.

Foigny is the first to give a description of an utopian childbirth:

As soon as an Australian has conceived, he quits his apartment, and is carried to the Heb, where he is received with testimonies of an extraordinary bounty, and is nourished without being obliged to work. They have a certain high place, upon which they go to bring forth their child, which is received upon some balsanick

leaves; after which the mother (or person that bore it) takes it
and rubs it with these leaves, and gives it suck, without any
appearance of having suffered any pain.
They make no use of swaddling clothes or cradles. The milk
it receives from the mother gives it so good nourishment, that it
suffices it without any other food for two years ; and the
excrements it voids, are in so small a quantity, that it may almost
be said, it makes none.

Education is carried out on strictly equalitarian lines and the
school-leaving age is at thirty-five!

The house of the four quarters by them called Heb ; which is
the house of education, is built of the same stone that the Hab is
paved with, except the roof of it, which is made of transparent
stone, through which the light enters into it.

This fine building is divided into four quarters, by twelve great
crossings, which are made like four semi-diameters : it is about
fifty paces diameter, and about an hundred and fifty three paces
in circuit.   Each division is allotted to the Youth of that quarter
it belongs to ; and there are at least two hundred children, whose
mothers, as soon as they have conceived of them, enter there,
and depart not till the children are two years of age, and then they
go out, leaving them to the care of certain young men, who are
there on purpose to instruct them.   These young men, whereof
there is a very great number, are divided into five Companies.
The first are employed in teaching first principles, of which there
are six Masters.   The second make it their business to give the
common reasons for natural things, among which there are four
Masters.   The third are such as are permitted to dispute, of whom
there are two Masters.   The fourth are such as can compose,
and they have but one Master.   The fifth and last are those that
expect to be chosen for Lieutenants, that is, to fill the place of the
Brethren that retire from the world.

They generally speak at eight months, they walk at a year's
end, and at two they wean them.   They begin to reason at three:
and as soon as the mother quits them, the first master of the first
company teaches them to read, and at the same time instructs
them in the first elements of a more advanced knowledge.   They
usually are three years under the conduct of the first master, and
after pass under the discipline of the second, who teaches them to
write, with whom they continue four years, and so with the others
in proportion, till they are thirty-five years of age, at which time
they are perfect in all sorts of sciences, without observing any
difference amongst them, either for capacity, genius or learning.

When they have thus accomplished the course of all their studies, they may be chosen for Lieutenants, that is to supply the place of those that would leave this life.

The problem of work is greatly simplified, in Australia, because the inhabitants nourish themselves only on fruit which grows on trees all the year round. There is some gardening to do but no cooking and as they wear no clothes and have very little furniture there is no need for industries. " They look upon our gawdy stuffs, and richest silks, as spiders' webs, they know not so much as what the names of gold or silver signifie, and in a word, all that we count precious appear in their esteem to be but ridiculous." The Australians spend the first part of the day at the school or in the study of sciences, the second part at work in their gardens which they cultivate " with such art and skill as is unknown in Europe," and the third for public exercise.

Every five days they spend one third of the day at the Hab, in meditation " without speaking one word, observing a step's distance between person and person, and are all the while so attentive upon what they are thinking upon that nothing is able in the least to distract their thoughts."

Scientific research, and discussion, play an important part :

Those days in which they go not to the Hab, they are obliged to be at the Heb, to treat of the sciences which they do with an order and method most admirably plain, and perfectly agreeing in all its parts. They propose everyone in their turn all their difficulties, which they maintain with powerful reasons, after which they answer all the objections which their antagonists oppose against them. When the dispute is ended, if anything of importance happen to have been proposed, they write it into the public book, and everyone carefully sets it down too in private. If any of them know anything that displeases him, or that he thinks may be advantageous to his Country he proposes it to the brethren, who take such resolutions thereupon, as they judge most reasonable, without aiming at anything but the public good.

The last third part of their day is allotted for three sorts of very diverting exercises, the first consists in producing what they have newly invented, or repeating the experiments of what they have already shown ; but there seldom passes a day but they propose some new invention, upon which they always take care to register the name of the inventor in their Book of Public Curiosities, which they esteem one of the greatest honours done

to them ; and in 32 years time, I observed above 5,000 of these
new inventions recorded, that would pass for so many prodigies
among us.

Their second exercise consists in managing two sorts of arms,
one of which is very like our Halberds, and the other resembles
much our organ-pipes, composed of ten or twelve pipes, which
are furnished with certain springs at one end, which being let go,
discharge bullets with so great a force, that they pierce through
the bodies of six men.

A considerable part of the book is taken up by the dialogues
between James Sadeur and an Old Man who has taken him under
his protection and who acquaints him with the philosophical
ideas and manners of the Australians.   In listening to the Old
Man one has the impression of hearing some of the Encyclopedists
and certain passages even recall the Manifesto of the Equals.

James Sadeur having said that " like care was not equally
taken throughout the world " in educating men, the Old Man
remarks that :

This irregularity caused many disorders, disputes, heats and
complaints, because he that knew least [feeling others above him
which knew more] esteemed himself the more unhappy, that birth
had made all alike.   As for us, added he, we make a profession of
being all equal, our glory consists in being all alike, and to be
dignified with the same care, and in the same manner ; all the
difference that there is, is only in divers exercises to which we
apply ourselves, so as to find out new inventions, that the
discoverers may contribute them to the public good.

After this he spoke to me of habits, which he called superfluities
amongst the Europeans and I assured him, that they had as great
an horror amongst them to see a person naked, as they Australians
had to see them in clothes ;   I alleged for reasons of this use,
modesty, the rigour of the season and custom.

To this, as I remember, he answered, that custom so much
prevails upon your minds, that one would believe everything
necessary that you practice from your birth, and that you can't
change a custom without as great a violence as changing your
own nature.   I replied, by insisting upon the reason of divers
climates and told him, that there were some countries amongst
the Europeans, where the cold was so insupportable to the body,
which was more delicate than that of the Australians, and that
there were some that even died upon it, and that it was impossible

to subsist without clothes : in fine, I told him, that the weakness of the nature of either sex was such, that there was no looking upon one that was naked without blushing, and shame and without being sensible of such emotions, as modesty obliged me to pass over in silence.

Is there a consequence in all that thou hast advanced (said he) and from whence can this custom come?   Is not this to father upon all the world what is contrary to Nature?   We are born naked, and we can't be covered without believing that it is shameful to be seen as we are : but as to what thou sayest concerning the rigour of the season, I can't, nay, I ought not to give any credit to it ; for if this country is so insupportable, what is it that obliges him that knows what reason is, to make it his country?   ...as for the weakness which thou calls modesty, I have nothing to say for it, since thou confessed with so much sincerity that it is a fault, 'tis truly a great weakness which will not permit us to look upon another without resenting the brutal motions which thou speakest of.   Beasts continually see themselves and one another but this sight causes no alteration in them: How then can you who believe yourselves of a superior order to them be more weak than they?

He said no more on this point, but without giving me time to answer, he passed to that of covetousness.

I early perceived that he knew no more of it but the name, for having desired him to explain what he meant by it, I understood that his idea of it, was a weakness of the mind, which consisted in heaping up fine things without any profit.

All the Australians possess in abundance all that is necessary to their existence, but they know not what it is to heap up, not to keep anything against to-morrow, and their manner of living thus may pass for the perfect image of the state that man first enjoyed in Paradise.

As for ambition, he had a gross idea of it ; but he defined it a desire of men being elevated above others.

Foigny is the first utopian to conceive of a society without government.   The libertarian character of this utopia has been noticed by the historian Max Nettlau who mentions it in his bibliography of anarchist utopias.   The Australians have no central government, all the decisions are taken at the local assemblies of each quarter.   Food is not provided by the state, as in previous utopias, but is brought each morning by the members of each district when they meet for the morning conference. Even in wars there are no leaders : "...that which seems to me most admirable in them, is to see them without any commanders to lead them, and without having any previous discourse or communication one with another, or receiving any direction or instruction, they know how to post themselves with so much order and discipline, that one would think they were all so many experienced captains, that were all inspired with the same design, and agreed upon the means how to execute it."

In his conversation with James Sadeur the Old Man expounds his " philosophy of anarchism " :

I told him that in Europe they held it for a maxim, that the multitude without any order begat confusion, in which there was no gust of the good things in life, and that order supposed a head, to which all others were subject. From hence the Old Man took occasion to explain a doctrine, of which I indeed conceived the meaning ; but 'tis impossible to discover the knowledge of it to others in so strong and powerful terms as these which he made use of to make me understand it. He said, that it was the Nature of Man to be born, and live free, and that therefore he could not be subjected without being despoiled of his nature, and that in such subjection man was made to descend below beasts, because a beast being only made for the service of man, subjection was after some manner natural to it. But one man could not be born for the service of another man; a constraint in this case would be a sort of violence which would even degrade a man after a certain manner from his proper existence ; he enlarged much to prove that the subjection of one man to another was a subjection of the human Nature, and making a man a sort of slave to himself, which slavery implied such a contradiction and violence as was impossible to conceive. He added that the essence of man consisting in liberty, it would not be taken away without destroying him, and therefore he that would take away another's liberty, did tacitly bid him to subsist without his own essence.

[If it happens that man is bound or made captive, he loses the exterior movement of his freedom, but the interior does not decrease. Like the stone which does not lose its heaviness when it is lifted or held up in the air, for it retains its weight and gravity since it will fall to the ground as soon as we cease to prevent it ; in the same way man only suffers his captivity because he is forced to do so. As soon as the compulsion is removed he re-appears what he really is and his glory is to die rather than to be constrained. This does not signify that he does not often do what others desire, but he does not do so because others compel or command him. The word of commandment is odious to him, he does what his reason dictates him to do ; his reason is his law, his rule, his unique guide. There is this difference between true men and half men, that all the thoughts and desires of the first, being perfectly united are the same without any difference, and it is sufficient to explain them for everyone to agree to them without any opposition as reasonable persons follow with pleasure the true road when it is pointed out to them. But because half men have only a vague knowledge and feeble lights, it happens by necessity that one thinks one thing and one, another ; and that one wants to take a certain road while the other opposes him with almost continuous objections. The reason for this is clear, for the man who can only see imperfectly is not able to avoid the dangers of making mistakes and taking one thing for another].

As we have pointed out earlier, the religion of the Australians is, in fact, a negation of religion :

There is no subject more curious and secret among the Australians, than that of their religion, 'tis a crime unheard of even to speak of it, either by dispute or a form of explanation ; even the mothers do with the first principles of knowledge, inspire into the child that of the Haab, that is to say, the Incomprehensible.

They believe that the Incomprehensible Being is everywhere, and they have all imaginable veneration for him, but they recommend carefully to the young men to adore him always, without speaking of him, and they are persuaded that it was a very great crime, to make his divine perfections the subject of their discourses, for that one may in a manner say, that their great religion is not to speak of religion.

And the Old Man points out the dangers of religious discussions :

Men cannot speak of anything that is incomprehensible, without having diverse opinions of it ; nay even such as are even contrary one to another...we better approve of an absolute silence of the matter, than to expose ourselves by putting off a many false notions concerning the nature of a Being, which is elevated so very much above our understandings. We assemble therefore together in the Hab, only to acknowledge his supreme greatness, and adore his Sovereign Power, and leave each person to their liberty of thinking what they please ; but we have made an inviolable law, never to speak of him, for fear of engaging ourselves by discourse in such errors as might offend him.

The Australians are a peaceful people and never fight against one another, but they are forced sometimes to maintain great wars to defend their country against the invasions of foreign nations. They carry out these defensive wars with a terrifying efficiency and ruthlessness, stopping only when the last enemy is killed and, in some cases, obliterating the whole country of the enemy.

One of these wars was the cause of James Sadeur being forced to leave Australia, for he had the unfortunate idea of suggesting that it would be better to take the women of the enemy than to kill them. For this " crime " he was condemned to death by the assembly of the Hab. The death penalty is carried out by asking the condemned man to eat a certain fruit, which puts an end to his life in a swift and pleasant manner, and they let him choose the moment of his own execution! Of this James Sadeur took full advantage and when he was asked " if he had anything to say " :

I made a speech and told them that I began now to look upon myself as one whose being was in a manner ceased ; that since it was the custom of our Nation, that when anyone was at the point of death, to live with great reservedness, and that my spirit would not permit me to be the same that I had been, and that knowing that I should cease to be in a little time, I would employ the moments that remained to study out some last action which should edify them much more than my first. These reasons did very much to satisfy the Assembly, and they were resolved to let me finish my life as I pleased, without speaking any more either of my words or actions. And since I ought to be reckoned in the number of the dead, they themselves named me a Lieutenant, and regarded me no more but as a dying person, who was at liberty to finish his life as himself thought fit.

In spite of an obvious incompatibility of character between the Australians and himself, James Sadeur had the most profound admiration for their perfection and we shall allow him a final comment on the superiority of their manners and customs over ours :

I could not but admire a conduct so opposite to our defective one, that I was ashamed to remember how far we were from the perfection of these People. I said in myself, can it be true that we are not all made Man? But added I, if it is not so, what is the difference of these People from us? They are by the ordinary state of life elevated to a pitch of virtue which we cannot attain but by the greatest efforts of our most noble ideas. Our best morality is not capable of better reasoning, nor more exactness, than what they practise naturally without rules, and without precepts ; this union which nothing can alter, this distance from worldly goods, this inviolable purity ; in a word, this adherence to strict reason, which unites them amongst themselves, and carries them to what is good and just, can't but be the fruits of consummate virtue, than which we can conceive nothing more perfect, but on the contrary how many vices and imperfections are we not subject to? The insatiable thirst after riches, these continual dissensions, these black treasons, bloody conspiracies, and cruel butcheries, which we are continually exercising towards one another ; don't these things force us to acknowledge that we are guided by passion rather than reason? Is it not to be wished that in this estate, one of these men which we may call Barbarians would come to disabuse us, and appear in so much virtue as they practice purely by their Natural Light, to confound the vanity which we draw from our pretended knowledge, and by the assistance of which we only live like beasts.

DIDEROT

Supplement to Bougainville's Voyage

DIDEROT believed that " Nature gave no man the right to rule over others," and he maintained his belief by refusing to become, like so many of his contemporaries, a law-giver. There is a charming anecdote which shows that he could resist the temptations of " kingship." For three successive years Diderot was made king " par la grâce du gâteau," that is to say he became " Twelfth Night King " for finding the bean in his piece of cake. As a king, he had to produce a code, which he did in a little poem in which he said :

Diviser pour régner, la maxime est ancienne
Elle fut d'un tyran, ce n'est donc pas la mienne
Vous unir est mon voeu, j'aime la liberté
   Et si j'ai quelque volonté
   C'est que chacun fasse la sienne.
          Le Code de Denis

In the third year he wrote another poem in which he renounced even the right to decree that " each should do what he wills," and declared that, as he did not wish to be given any law, neither did he wish to make one for others :

Jamais au public avantage
L'homme n'a franchement sacrifié ses droits!
La nature n'a fait ni serviteur ni maître
Je ne veux ni donner ni recevoir de lois!
Et ses mains coudraient les entrailles du prêtre,
Au défaut d'un cordon, pour étrangler les rois.

Les Eleuthéromanes ou abdication d'un roi de la fève

In a more serious mood, Diderot did, however, give a description of a free, primitive society which knows neither governments nor laws. The *Supplement to Bougainville's Voyage* is an imaginary description of the customs found by Bougainville and his companions when they first landed on the island. Louis Antoine Bougainville had explored the Archipelago of Oceania, including Tahiti, during his great voyage which lasted from 1766 to 1769. On his return he published an account of his travels (1771), which was widely read. A year later Diderot wrote his fictitious account of Bougainville's visit to Tahiti ; it was a powerful indictment of " civilisation," with its reliance on armed forces and religion, but it also provided Diderot with the opportunity to describe a primitive society, not perhaps as it was, but as it should be. As the subtitle of the *Supplement* indicates, it contains a strong attack on the accepted code of morals—" On the disadvantages of attaching moral ideas to certain physical actions incompatible therewith." The violence and the outspokenness of the criticisms prevented it from being printed. It was circulated in manuscript form during Diderot's life, and was not printed until after the Revolution, in 1796.

The *Supplement* is written in the form of a dialogue but rather than try to summarise it or quote extracts here and there, it may be better to give in full *The Old Man's Farewell,* for this gives a fairly complete idea of the customs of the inhabitants of "Tahiti".

The Old Man's Farewell

He was the father of a large family. At the arrival of the Europeans, he looked disdainfully at them, showing neither astonishment, fear, nor curiosity. They accosted him. He turned

his back on them, and withdrew into his hut. His silence and
his anxiety revealed his thoughts only too well : he lamented
within himself for the great days of his country, now eclipsed. At
the departure of Bougainville, when the inhabitants ran in a
crowd to the shore, clinging to his garments, embracing his
companions and weeping, the old man came forward with a
stern air and said :

" Weep, poor folk of Tahiti, weep! Would that this were the
arrival and not the departure of these ambitious and wicked men.
One day you will know them better. One day they will return,
in one hand the piece of wood you now see attached to the belt
of this one, and the other grasping the blade you now see hanging
from the belt of another. And with these they will enslave you,
murder you or subject you to their extravagances and vices.
One day you will serve under them, as corrupted, as vile, as
loathsome as themselves.

" But I console myself : I am reaching the end of my journey;
I shall not live to see the calamity I foretell. Oh people of Tahiti!
Oh my friends! You have a means to escape this tragic future :
but I would rather die than counsel it. Let them go their ways,
let them live."

Then, addressing himself to Bougainville, he continued :
" And you, chief of these brigands who obey you, quickly take
your vessel from our shores. We are innocent, we are happy ;
and you can only spoil our happiness. We follow the pure
instincts of nature ; and you have tried to wipe its impress from
our souls. Here everything belongs to everybody. You have
preached to us I know not what distinctions between " mine "
and " thine." Our daughters and our wives are common to us
all. You have shared this privilege with us ; and you have
lighted passions in them before unknown. They have become
maddened in your arms ; you have become ferocious in theirs.
They have begun to hate each other ; you have slain each other
for them, and they have returned to us stained with your blood.

" We are a free people ; and now you have planted in our
country the title deeds of our future slavery. You are neither god
nor demon ; who are you, then, to make slaves? Orou! You
understand the language of these men, tell us all, as you have
told me, what they have written on this sheet of metal : ' This
country is ours.' This country yours? And why? Because you
have walked thereon? If a Tahitian landed one day on your
shores, and scratched on one of your rocks or on the bark of your
trees : ' This country belongs to the people of Tahiti '—what
would you think?

" You are the strongest! And what of that? When someone took one of the contemptible trifles with which your vessel is filled, you cried out and you were revenged. Yet at the same time in the depths of your heart you plotted the theft of a whole country! You are not a slave ; you would suffer death rather than be one ; yet you want to enslave us. Do you think the Tahitian does not know how to defend his liberty and to die? The Tahitian you want to seize like a wild animal is your brother. You are both children of nature ; what right have you over him that he has not over you? When you came, did we rush upon you, did we pillage your ship? Did we seize you and expose you to the arrows of our enemies? Did we yoke you with the animals for toil in our fields? No. We respected our own likeness in you. Leave us to our ways ; they are wiser and more honest than yours. We do not want to barter what you call our ignorance for your useless civilisation. Everything that is necessary and good for us we possess. Do we deserve contempt, because we have not known how to develop superfluous wants? When we hunger, we have enough to eat ; when we are cold we have wherewith to clothe us. You have been in our huts ; what is lacking there, in your opinion? You may pursue as far as you like what you call the comforts of life ; but allow sensible people to stop, when they would only have obtained imaginary good from the continuation of their painful efforts. If you persuade us to exceed the narrow limits of our wants, when shall we ever finish toiling? When shall we enjoy ourselves? We have reduced the sum of our annual and daily labours to the least possible, because nothing seems to us preferable to repose. Go to your own country to agitate and torment yourself as much as you like ; leave us in peace. Do not worry us with your artificial needs nor with your imaginary virtues. Look on these men ; see how upright, healthy and robust they are. Look upon these women ; see how upright, healthy, fresh and beautiful they are. Take this bow ; it is my own. Call one, two, three or four of your friends to help you and try to bend it. I can bend it myself, alone. I till the soil. I climb mountains. I pierce the forest. I can run a league on the plains in less than an hour. Your young companions would be hard put to follow me, yet I am more then ninety years old.

" Woe unto this island! Woe to these people of Tahiti and to all who will come after them, woe from the day you first visited us! We should know only one disease ; that to which all men, animals and plants are subject—old age ; but you have brought us another ; you have infected our blood.

" It will perhaps be necessary to exterminate our daughters, wives, children, with our own hands ; all those who have approached your women ; those who have approached your men.

" Our fields shall be soaked with the foul blood which has passed from your veins into ours; or else our children, condemned to nourish and perpetuate the evil which you have given to the fathers and mothers, will transmit it for ever to their descendants. Villains! You will be the guilty ones ; guilty either of the ravages of disease that will follow the fatal embraces of your people, or of the murders which we shall commit to stop the spread of the poison.

" You speak of crimes ! Do you know any more enormous than your own? What is your punishment for him who kills his neighbour?—death by the sword ; what is your punishment for the coward who poisons?—death by fire. Compare your crime to his ; tell us then, poisoner of whole peoples, what should be the torment you deserve? But a short while ago, the young Tahitian girl yielded herself to the transports and embraces of the Tahitian youth ; waited impatiently until her mother, authorised by her having reached the age of marriage, should remove her veil and make naked her breast. She was proud to excite the desire and to attract the amorous glances of unknown men, of relatives, of her mother. Without dread and without shame, in our presence, in the midst of a circle of innocent Tahitians, to the sound of flutes, between the dances, she accepted the caresses of the one to whom her young heart and the secret voice of her senses urged her. The idea of crime and the peril of disease came with you. Our enjoyments, once so sweet, are now accompanied by remorse and terror. That man in black who stands near you listening to me, has spoken to our lads. I do not know what he has said to our girls. But our lads are hesitant ; our girls blush. Plunge if you will into the dark depths of the forest with the perverse companion of your pleasure ; but let the good and simple Tahitians reproduce themselves without shame, under the open sky, in the full light of day. What finer and more noble feeling could you put in place of that with which we have inspired them, and which animates them now? They think that the moment to enrich the nation and the family with a new citizen is come, and they glory in it. They eat to live and to grow; they grow in order to multiply and they find in it nothing vicious nor shameful.

" Listen to the continuation of your crimes. You had hardly come among our people than they became thieves. You had scarcely landed on our soil, than it reeked with blood. That Tahitian who ran to meet you, to receive you crying ' Taio!

friend, friend,' you slew. And why did you slay him? . . . . because he had been taken by the glitter of your little serpents' eggs. He gave you of his fruits ; he offered you his wife and daughter, he ceded you his hut ; yet you killed him for a handful of beads which he had taken without having asked. And the people? At the noise of your murderous shot, terror seized them, and they fled to the mountains. But be assured that they would not have waited long to descend again. Then you would all have perished but for me. Ah! why did I pacify them, why did I hold them back, why do I still restrain them, even now? I do not know ; for you deserve not pity ; for you have a ferocious soul which will never feel it. You have wandered, you and yours, everywhere in our island. You have been respected ; you have enjoyed all things ; you have found neither barrier nor refusal in your ways; you have been invited within, you have sat, and all the abundance of our country has been spread before you. When you desired young girls, only excepting those who had not yet the privilege of unveiling their faces and breasts, their mothers have presented to you all the others, quite naked. You have possessed the tender victim of the duties of hospitality ; flowers and leaves were heaped up for you and her ; musicians sounded their instruments ; nothing has spoiled the sweetness, nor hindered the freedom of your caresses nor of hers. They have sung the anthem exhorting you to be a man, and our child to be a woman, yielding and voluptuous. They danced around your couch. And it was when you came from the arms of this woman, after experiencing on her breast the sweetest of all intoxications, that you slew her brother, friend or father.

"You have done still worse. Look over there, see that enclosure bristling with weapons. These arms which have menaced only your enemies are now turned against our own children. See these unhappy companions of your pleasures. See their sadness, the grief of their fathers and the despair of their mothers. Why are those condemned to die, either by our hands or by the diseases you have given them?

"Away now, unless your cruel eyes revel in the spectacle of death. Go now, go ; and may the guilty seas which spared you on your voyage hither, absolve themselves and avenge us, by engulfing you before you return.

"And you, oh people of Tahiti! Go into your huts, go, all of you ; and let these strangers as they leave hear only the roar of the tide and see only the foam of its fury whitening a deserted shore."

5

Utopias of the Nineteenth Century

THE history of utopias in the nineteenth century is closely linked with the creation of the socialist movement, and it is sometimes difficult to distinguish between schemes which belong to the realm of utopian thought and those which come within the province of practical social reform. There is hardly a single work dealing with social problems, published during this period, which has not, at some time or other, been described as utopian. The word itself lost its original significance, and came to mean the opposite of scientific ; " utopian " became almost a term of abuse which self-styled scientific socialists were fond of hurling at their opponents. It is thanks to these Marxist judges that the list of nineteenth century utopias has assumed such enormous proportions.

In *Socialism, Utopian and Scientific,* Frederick Engels gave a Marxist definition of the word " utopian " which has come to be widely accepted. While until then an utopia was considered as an imaginary ideal commonwealth whose realisation was impossible or difficult, Engels gave it a much wider meaning and included all social schemes which did not recognise the division of society into classes, the inevitability of the class struggle and of the social revolution. He classified Saint-Simon, Fourier and Owen among the utopians, for " not one of them appears as a representative of the interests of the proletariat, which historical development had, in the meantime, produced. Like the French philosophers, they do not claim to emancipate a particular class to begin with, but all humanity at once."

Engels, furthermore, reproached " utopian " writers for not having understood that socialism would be possible only when the capitalist régime had achieved a certain degree of development : " To the crude conditions of capitalistic production and the crude class conditions corresponded crude theories. The solution of the social problems, which as yet lay hidden in un-developed economic conditions, the Utopians attempted to evolve out of the human brain. Society presented nothing but wrongs; to remove these was the task of reason. It was necessary, then, to discover a new and more perfect social order and to impose this upon society from without by propaganda, and, whenever it was possible, by the example of model experiments. These new social systems were foredoomed as Utopian ; the more completely they were worked out in detail, the more they could not avoid drifting off into pure fantasies."

Engels' description of socialist utopias is substantially correct. Most of them want all the means of production and distribution to be held in common, but do not think that a revolution is necessary to bring this about. They assume that the State can take over the economic machinery of a country in a peaceful manner, when the majority of the population have agreed that it is the most sensible solution. They do not think that there is an irreducible antagonism between classes, and that the proletariat is the only class able to achieve a revolution. Again, in contradiction to Marxist theories, they assert that a new society can be created at any time or place, provided governments and peoples are resolved to bring it into being ; they see no relation between the development of capitalism and the possibility of creating a new society.

Engels was not, however, justified in assuming that the " utopian " schemes were less realistic than those of the " scientific " socialists. In the light of the history of the past century it would be a difficult task to decide which school of socialism deserves the description of " utopian." The high development of capitalism, far from bringing nearer the day of the revolution, has created a new class of technicians and managers, highly paid workers and trade union leaders whose interests are identified with those of the capitalist class. The only two European countries which have, during the past thirty years, attempted to carry out social revolutions, Russia and Spain, were countries where capitalism had not yet reached a high degree of development. We have seen, furthermore, that state socialism has been partially realised in several countries, not by the militant action of the working class, but by governments holding power through an elected Parliament. More paradoxical still, from a Marxist view point, fascist governments have been obliged to adopt measures of social reform similar to those advocated by socialists.

Socialism, as we know it to-day, is nearer to the conceptions of the " utopian " socialists than to those of Karl Marx, the founder of scientific socialism. It no longer recognises the inevitability of the class struggle, and aims at gradual social reforms which will eventually eliminate the economic differences between capitalists and workers. Even in a country like Russia, which claims to have carried out a Marxist revolution, the structure of society resembles more closely that described by some utopian writers than that foreseen by Marx or Lenin. It might be wiser, therefore, to leave aside what seems to-day an arbitrary division between utopian and scientific socialists, and to consider only the most representative of those works which remain in the utopian tradition by describing ideal commonwealths in some imaginary country or in an imaginary future.

At the time of the Renaissance, utopian thought had received a strong impetus from the new philosophical ideas, the birth of national states and the discovery of the New World. At the beginning of the nineteenth century events of similar magnitude infused it with new life : these included the after-effects of the French Revolution, the rapid development of industry and the elaboration of socialist systems. The French Revolution had given power to the bourgeoisie, but at the same time it had asserted the rights of the workers and peasants, who had shown their readiness to defend them by force. The victorious bourgeoisie could not shut its eyes to social inequalities which might at any moment release a strong revolutionary movement. A few humanitarian thinkers and philanthropists tried to alleviate the growing misery of the people, and some went so far as to demand that equality which had been preached by pre-revolutionary philosophers and which was one of the supposed aims of the Revolution. But they did not trust the people, whom they feared could only change the system by revolutionary methods, and they sought a pacific solution through social reform. As Kropotkin pointed out in his introduction to *The Conquest of Bread*, "... writing during the period of reaction which had followed the French Revolution, and seeing more its failures than its successes, they did not trust the masses, and they did not appeal to them for bringing about the changes which they thought necessary. They put their faith, on the contrary, in some great ruler, some Socialist Napoleon. He would understand the new revelation ; he would be convinced of its desirability by the successful experiment of the phalansteries, or associations ; and he would peacefully accomplish by his own authority the revolution which would bring well-being and happiness to mankind. A military genius, Napoleon, had just been ruling Europe ; why should not a social genius come forward, carry Europe with him and translate the new Gospel into life? "

The industrial revolution had opened new horizons, and it seemed to many that it offered a solution to poverty and inequality. There were apparently no limits to the increase of production, and therefore there seemed no reason why everyone should not live like a bourgeois. Equality would not entail a sacrifice for anybody, since the new society would not decrease the comfort of the rich, but raise that of the poor to their level. While utopias in the past had stressed the need for detachment from material goods, those of the nineteenth century sought happiness in the satisfaction of an ever increasing number of material needs. It was not only that industrial progress now allowed greater luxury ; the whole attitude towards material pleasure was altered. In More's Utopia people led an austere life, not out of necessity, for they had gold and silver with which they could have bought goods from foreign countries and thereby improved their standard of living, but because they thought that luxury would inevitably bring corruption and moral degeneration. With a few exceptions such as Francis Bacon, utopian writers had conceived progress in terms of mental, physical and moral improvement of men, and this could not be achieved if too much importance were given to material goods. A too great indulgence of the flesh would bring corruption of the mind. We find no such moralistic preoccupations in nineteenth century utopians ; they were shamelessly materialistic and fell little short of calculating individual happiness in terms of pieces of furniture, articles of clothing or the number of courses served at each meal. Only occasionally do we find a reaction against this tendency, as in William Morris's *News from Nowhere*.

The influence of the " fathers of socialism " on the utopias of the nineteenth century was, of course, considerable. Owen, Fourier and Saint-Simon not only influenced utopias through their theoretical writings, but their concrete plans of social reform and of " villages of co-operation," parallelograms or phalansteries, have inspired many features of later utopias. In some respects, however, Owen and Fourier differ from the main trend of socialist thought of the nineteenth century, for they do not advocate a centralised government and an intensive industrialisation of the countryside but believe, on the contrary, in small autonomous agricultural communities. Owen gives the initiative of forming these small agricultural communes, not containing more than 3,000 inhabitants, to some enlightened government, but they must be self-supporting and run by autonomous administrations. All the internal affairs would be governed by a general Council, composed of all the members of the community between the ages of 30 and 40, while all the external affairs would be administered by another general council, composed of all the members from the ages of 40 to 60. All the members of the commune would be equal, and would receive an equal share of the goods produced ; the general councils would rule according to the laws of human nature. When the whole world had become covered by federations of agricultural communities, governments would become unnecessary and would disappear altogether. Owen's ideas on education are those which perhaps had the greatest influence on utopian writers. He repeatedly stated throughout his writings that " the character of man, is, without a single exception, always formed for him ; that it may be, and is, chiefly, created by his predecessors ; that they give him, or may give him, his ideas and habits, which are the powers that govern and direct his conduct." It was therefore the task of education to train men to " live without idleness, without poverty, without crime and without punishment." Owen's attempts to put his ideas into practice, first at New Lanark and later in the communities which he founded in America, inspired many similar experiments and in the nineteenth century it is not infrequent to find that utopias give birth to community movements.

The name of Fourier is often linked to that of Owen because of certain superficial resemblances between the two thinkers and in spite of the fact that Fourier always referred to Owen in the most disparaging terms. Fourier has been called, more unjustly than Owen, a " father of socialism," for he did not in fact believe in the community of goods. The idea was indeed wholly repellant to him, since he thought inequality indispensable to the smooth running of his ideal society. Though he favoured the abolition of wages, he thought that dividends should be paid according to the amount of capital invested, the results, and the talents of the individual shareholders. Fourier, however, believed that society should provide even for those who refused to work, not only to free work from its compulsory nature but because society has a duty towards its members whether they produce or not. But work was to be made so attractive and to provide so many enjoyable things that there would be very few idlers.

Fourier did not put his faith in any enlightened government, but he hoped to find some wealthy patron who would provide the necessary funds to set up a phalanstery, and that people would be so struck by its admirable results that identical phalansteries would soon cover the whole earth. The advantage of his system, he claimed, was to combine the interests of capitalists, workers and consumers by uniting all these functions in the same individual. These were ideas which were taken up by many associationists in the latter half of the nineteenth century, and even upheld by a section of the socialist movement of to-day. As Charles Gide remarks in *A History of Economic Doctrines* : " A programme which aims, not at the abolition of property, but at the extinction of the wage-earner by giving him the right of holding property on the joint-stock principle, which looks to succeed, not by advocating class war, but by fostering co-operation of capital with labour and managing ability, and attempts to reconcile the conflicting interests of capitalist and worker, of producer and consumer, debtor and creditor, by welding those interests together in one and the same person, is by no means commonplace. Such was the ideal of the French working classes until Marxian collectivism took its place, and it is quite possible that its deposition may be only temporary after all."

Charles Fourier's eccentricity prevented him from exercising a wide influence, but his writings contain such a wealth of ideas as to make them an inexhaustible source of inspiration for social reformers, and even his bitterest opponents were influenced by him. His anticipation of garden cities, which would replace the agglomeration of big cities, his advocacy of market gardening, which was to replace extensive agriculture, his study of the means by which work can be made attractive, his teachings on education and sexual questions only attracted the direct attention of a small minority, it is true, but through this medium they are known to many who have never read Fourier's writings.

Though Fourier himself was never able to realise his dream of setting up a phalanstery, communities based on his ideas were created both in France and in America. The most celebrated, although it did not last very long, was that of Brook Farm[1] in the United States. Associations of producers and consumers run according to Fourier's principles were also set up with a certain degree of success.

Among the " fathers of socialism " we should also mention Saint-Simon, for he, and perhaps even more his followers, put forward ideas which are to be found in many utopias of the latter half of the nineteenth century. While Owen and Fourier, represented, in many respects, a reaction against industrialism by wanting a return to small agricultural communities, Saint-Simon was an enthusiastic supporter of the new industrial régime and of the new ruling class created by the Great Revolution and enriched by the rapid expansion of industry. Under the old order, society was ruled by nobles and priests. These were now to be replaced by the bourgeoisie whose main task was to encourage the progress of science and industry. It would be ridiculous, said Saint-Simon, for an industrial society to be ruled by nobles who have no longer any *raison d'être*, or by politicians who know nothing of industrial problems. The old form of governments must disappear for they are completely useless to society. In the famous document which is known as *Saint-Simon's Parable* (published in 1832) he showed vividly that the vital section of society was composed of scientists, technicians, bankers and business-men and not of politicians, state officials or priests :

" Let us suppose," he said, " that France suddenly loses fifty of her first-class doctors, fifty first-class chemists, fifty first-class physiologists, fifty first-class bankers, two hundred of her best merchants, six hundred of her foremost agriculturists, five hundred of her most capable ironmasters, etc. (enumerating the principal industries). Seeing that these men are its most indispensable producers, makers of its most important products, the minute that it loses these the nation will degenerate into a mere soulless body and fall into a state of despicable weakness in the eyes of rival nations, and will remain in this subordinate position so long as the loss remains and their places are vacant. Let us take another supposition. Imagine that France retains

[1]The subject of Hawthorne's novel, *The Blithedale Romance.*

all her men of genius, whether in the arts and sciences or in the crafts and industries, but has the misfortune to lose on the same day the king's brother, the Duke of Angoulême, and all the other members of the royal family ; all the great officers of the Crown; all ministers of State, whether at the head of a department or not ; all the Privy Councillors ; all the masters of requests ; all the marshals, cardinals, archbishops, bishops, grand vicars and canons ; all prefects and sub-prefects ; all Government employees ; all the judges ; and on top of that a hundred thousand proprietors—the cream of her nobility. Such an overwhelming catastrophe would certainly aggrieve the French, for they are a kindly-disposed nation. But the loss of a hundred and thirty thousand of the best-reputed individuals in the State would give rise to sorrow of a purely sentimental kind. It would not cause the community the least inconvenience."[1]

Already in 1816 Saint-Simon had declared that politics is the science of production and that eventually it would be completely absorbed by economics ; France was to be turned into a factory and the nation organised on the model of a vast workshop. In the new society all class distinctions would disappear ; there would only be workers, the term being used in its larger sense to include manufacturers, scientists, bankers and artists. But this does not mean that all would be equal, since everyone would receive according to his capacities (and even according to the capital invested).

The originality of Saint-Simon consists in giving to the best industrial leaders, scientists, bankers, etc., the task of administering the country. In other words the old government of politicians will be replaced by a government of " managers." More than a hundred years before we began to talk of a managerial class or of a " managerial revolution," Saint-Simon had foreseen that the industrial revolution would give birth to a new ruling class. We shall see how Edward Bellamy echoes Saint-Simon, while building his utopia on a socialistic basis. The idea that the governing of men must be replaced by the administration of things, and that all the problems of society resolve themselves into that of production, became current during the nineteenth century. In one of the many schemes of government which he put forward, Saint-Simon gives the executive power to a Chamber of Deputies com-

[1]Quoted in *A History of Economic Doctrines* by C. Gide and C. Rist.

posed of representatives of commerce, industry, manufacture and agriculture, who would accept or reject the legislative proposals submitted to them by two Chambers composed of scientists, artists and engineers. The only task of this " government " would be to increase the material wealth of the country. This system left no initiative to the mass of the workers, in whom Saint-Simon had no faith whatever : " The problem of social organisation," he said, " must be solved for the people. The people themselves are passive and listless and must be discounted in any consideration of the question. The best way is to entrust public administration to the care of the industrial chiefs, who will always directly attempt to give the widest possible scope to their undertakings, with the result that their efforts in this direction will lead to the maximum expansion of the amount of work executed by the mass of the people." Though socialist thinkers professed to be shocked by Saint-Simon's high-handed way of dealing with the " proletariat," the idea that the administration of a country is a matter for experts, and that the state machine is to be composed of committees or commissariats of technicians and industrial chiefs is to be found in many socialist writings, and in Russia we have seen the creation of a managerial class endowed, as Saint-Simon would have advocated, with economic and political privileges, though he would have strongly disapproved of the retention of a political party and professional politicians.

While Owen, Fourier and Saint-Simon put little reliance on the intervention of the State to transform the structure of society, Louis Blanc is one of the first socialists to give the State the task of reforming society. He asserted that it was the duty of the State to see that the 'right to work' should be respected and thereby abolish crimes, which are all due to poverty. Only by eliminating competition can the government abolish unemployment, poverty and the moral degradation which result from them. Its task is therefore to become " the supreme regulator of production " and, to begin with, it must set up 'social workshops' in the most important branches of industry, and gradually expand them to the whole country. The State would eventually become the sole owner of all the means of production, at least so long as inequalities exist, for when perfect equality reigned the State would wither away.

Louis Blanc's proposals of reform were expounded in a booklet entitled *L'Organisation du Travail*, published in 1839, which enjoyed an immense popularity at the time. It is often described as an utopia, though it is just the opposite, being a proposal of immediate reform, and the beginning of the institution of a collectivist system of production. That Louis Blanc himself strongly believed in the practicability of his proposals is shown by the fact that, after the 1848 Revolution, he asked the General Assembly to set up a Ministry of Progress which would carry out the plan he had outlined in *L'Organisation du Travail*. The Ministry of Progress would 'set the revolution in movement' : banks railways and mines would be nationalised, and the money would be used to set up social workshops in the most important branches of industry. The State would appoint officials who would direct the factory for the first year, but once the workers would have come to know one another and take an interest in the enterprise, they would elect their own officials. Each member of the social workshop would have the right to dispose of the produce of his labour as he thought fit, but soon " the obvious economy and unquestionable excellence of community life would lead from the association of work to the voluntary association for the satisfaction of needs and pleasures." Louis Blanc also put forward a plan for the collective cultivation of the land by the creation of agricultural social workshops run upon similar principles to those of the industrial social workshops. Louis Blanc's scheme was never put into practice. The attempt to set up National Workshops in 1848 was only made by the government in order to discredit his ideas, but many productive co-operative societies arose in France at that time under the influence of his writings.

The utopias of the nineteenth century which derive their inspiration from the theories which we have briefly considered are on the whole depressingly uninspiring. They aim at setting up a vast machinery which will ensure a perfect running of society and bring material wellbeing to everyone. But in these intricate mechanisms man's individuality is completely lost. The State becomes an all-wise, all-providing God which can never make any mistakes—and if it did no one would have the power to correct them. Whether State Socialism is administered through universal suffrage, as in Cabet's *Voyage to Icaria*, or through an industrial hierarchy as in Bellamy's *Looking Backward*, the results are the same : man is unable to express his personality except through the channels provided by the State. He becomes an automaton, working the number of hours prescribed by law, fulfilling tasks which excessive industrialisation has rendered monotonous and impersonal. The produce of his labour is accumulated in gigantic storehouses, to be consumed by a community with which he has no real links, for it is too enormous and centralised to allow intimate relations. An attempt is sometimes made to create a sense of community by uniting all the people of the same district in communal restaurants, for example, but, like so many other institutions of the nineteenth century utopias, it is a purely artificial means of creating a community spirit. In utopias of the past such as Andreae's *Christianopolis* the unity of the community was a 'functional' one. Workers engaged in the same craft met to discuss the problems related to their work, the whole community assembled to discuss the quantity of food, clothing, furniture, etc, which they needed, and production was regulated according to the needs of a community which, because of its small size, they knew intimately. But in the utopias of the nineteenth century the amount of autonomy granted to factory committees or consumers' unions is mostly fictitious. There is little which the workers can discuss when everything is regulated by the State, thanks to its experts and bureaux of statistics. As Mumford has pointed out, " These utopias become vast reticulations of steel and redtape, until we feel that we are caught in the Nightmare of the Age of Machinery, and shall never escape...the means has become the end, and the genuine problem of ends has been forgotten...I doubt whether an intelligent peasant in India or China would get out of the whole batch of these utopias a single idea which would have any bearing on the life he has experienced—so little of human significance remains when the problems of mechanical and political organisation have been disposed of! "

There are fortunately a few utopias where man comes into his own again, where he is not reduced to a machine which has to be fed, clothed and housed just like any piece of machinery that requires careful handling if it is to give the maximum output, where he is not moulded from his youth into a " good citizen," that is to say, a citizen perfectly obedient to the law and incapable of thinking for himself. Of these utopias of free socialism William Morris's *News from Nowhere* is the most attractive, and has a permanent quality which allows it to be still widely read in this country as well as abroad. There are also a number of utopian romances such as W. H. Hudson's *The Crystal Age* and W. H. Mallock's *The New Republic*, which make no pretence of giving a fool-proof plan for a perfect society, but which describe the type of community in which the authors would like to live. These romances, as W. H. Hudson himself has pointed out, " however fantastic they may be, have for most of us a perennial mild interest since they are born of a common feeling—a sense of dissatisfaction with the existing order of things, combined with a vague faith in or hope of a better one to come. . . (One cannot) help asking one another, What is your dream, your ideal? What is your News from Nowhere? " However little one may feel attracted towards Hudson's sexless society, or W. H. Mallock's refined " country house," one cannot help finding these utopian writers somewhat refreshing after the numberless Messiahs with whom the path of the nineteenth century is strewn.

I would have liked to include in this section extracts from Butler's *Erewhon*, for it satirises many ideas frequently expressed in the utopias of the nineteenth century, and in particular the belief that the extensive use of machinery will automatically bring happiness to mankind, but *Erewhon* cannot properly be considered as an utopia. It belongs, as Desmond MacCarthy has remarked, " to the same class of fiction as *Gulliver's Travels* ; those books in which an imaginary civilisation is used as a device for criticising our own." I have included instead extracts from Eugene Richter's *Pictures of a Socialistic Future*, a satirical utopia which has no philosophical pretensions, but illustrates many objections which the utopias of state-socialism arouse in one's mind.

There are few utopias of the nineteenth century which can be read to-day without a feeling of utter boredom, unless they succeed in amusing us by the obvious conceit of their authors in thinking themselves the saviours of mankind. The utopias of the Renaissance contained many unattractive features, yet they had a breadth of vision which commanded respect; those of the seventeenth century presented many extravagant ideas, yet they revealed searching, dissatisfied minds with which one sympathises ; but, though we are in many ways familiar with the thought of the utopias of the nineteenth century, they are nevertheless more foreign to us than those of a more distant past. In spite of the fact that these utopian writers were no doubt inspired by the highest motives, one cannot help "feeling bitter about the nineteenth century," like the old man in *News from Nowhere*, bitter even about the love these utopian writers lavished on humanity, for they seem like so many over-affectionate and over-anxious mothers who would kill their sons with attention and kindness rather than let them enjoy one moment of freedom.

ETIENNE CABET

Voyage to Icaria

ONE may be excused a certain nervousness in dealing with a book of which its author says : " Under the shape of a novel, the *Voyage en Icarie* is a real treatise on morality, philosophy, social and political economy ; it is the fruit of long work, of immense research, of constant meditation. In order to understand it properly, it is not enough to read it ; one must read it again, read it often and study it." It is also rather disarming to be informed again, by Cabet himself, that his work " has been inspired by the most pure and burning love for Humanity." The second statement is probably more exact than the first. Etienne Cabet belonged to that type of social reformer whose love of humanity is as boundless as their faith in their own power to work out its salvation.

Cabet was born in 1788 from a working-class family, but received a good education and became a lawyer of some repute. When still young he was attracted to politics. He was a supporter of an enlightened monarchy, and when Louis Phillippe, on whom he placed great hopes, became king, he was made Attorney-General of Corsica. He was rash enough, however, to think that he could impose his counsels on the king and soon fell into disgrace and lost his post. He returned to Paris and devoted himself to the newspaper which he had founded and of which he was the editor, *Le Populaire*, and in 1834 was prosecuted for an article of which he was the author. He was condemned to two years imprisonment or five years exile. Cabet chose the latter and took refuge in England.

He arrived in London in May, 1834, and after the feverish activity which he had displayed as a lawyer, a journalist, and a deputy to the National Assembly, the enforced leisure of exile weighed heavily upon him. He was prevented from establishing contact with English people by his lack of knowledge of the language and, according to his biographer J. Prudhommeaux, " for five years London was for him an immense prison." Like other more famous exiles, he took refuge in the British Museum, and it was in the Reading Room that he carried out the "immense research " for his *Voyage en Icarie*. The amenities provided by its library are probably partly responsible for the lack of originality of his work.

The notes which Cabet took for the preparation of his utopia, and which cover a thousand small pages, have been preserved and the question of the " sources " is therefore less speculative than in most cases. Cabet did his work conscientiously. He read, if not always in the original text, at least analyses of most utopias, and he studied with particular care Harrington's *Oceana*, but, most of all, More's *Utopia*. If we are to believe him, it was the reading of More which determined him to study the system of the community of goods. Once he had discovered that " the cause of the vices and unhappiness of mankind is to be found in the *bad organisation* of society, and the radical vice of this organisation in the inequality on which it is founded," Cabet began a methodical search for thinkers, philosophers, prophets or movements of the past which had expressed a similar view. He discovered that he had a great number of allies ; not only utopian writers, but, according to him, "Jesus Christ, the Fathers of the Church, the early Christians, the Reformation Movement, the Philosophers of the eighteenth century, the American Revolution, the French Revolution, Universal Progress all proclaimed the Equality and Fraternity of men and Nations."

Though he was unwilling to admit it, Cabet had been strongly influenced, directly and indirectly, by the communist ideas of the Babouvists. He had read Philippe Buonarotti's *Conspiration pour l'égalité dite de Babeuf* which had appeared in 1828, and though this work made little impression on him at the time, he unconsciously borrowed many of the ideas which had inspired the Babouvist Movement. Besides, the scheme for establishing a society of equals and a " great national community of wealth," for giving to a centralised state all the power of administration and for putting the sovereignty in the general will of the community, which was advocated by Babeuf and his associates, had strongly influenced socialist thought of the first half of the nineteenth century in France.

As David Thompson has pointed out in his book on *The Babeuf Plot*, French socialism has always been chiefly concerned with establishing the perfect equality of men, and, to achieve it, has been prepared to sacrifice the freedom of the individual to the State. While in England even the greatest of the Levellers, Gerrard Winstanley, tried to combine equality with a great degree of personal autonomy and reduced the functions of the state to a minimum, in France the state was given the task of establishing and maintaining that " great national community of wealth " which would ensure the equality of all the citizens. While the words *community of wealth, equality, fraternity*, recur constantly in the Babouvists writings, as they did later in those of Cabet, the words *freedom* or *individual rights* are never mentioned, and the possibility of a conflict between the interests of the state and that of individuals is completely ignored.

If there is little difference between the practical programme of social reconstruction advocated by the Babouvists and that of Cabet, they differed entirely as to the means to be employed to establish their communist régime. While Babeuf wanted to overthrow the government by force with the aid of a small, well-organised party, Cabet thought that " the community (of goods) could easily come into being as soon as a Nation or its Government will adopt it...This community could not be established as Babeuf advocated by conspiracy or violence, but by means of discussion, propaganda, persuasion and the force of public opinion."

Cabet also attached a greater importance to industrial development than his precursors, and asserted that " the progress of industry renders the establishment of the community of goods easier than ever before ; the present limitless development of the power of production thanks to the use of steam and machinery can bring *equality of abundance*, and no other system is more favourable to the perfecting of arts and the reasonable pleasures of civilisation."[1]

It was probably the example of Robert Owen, with whose

[1]Preface to the second edition of *Voyage en Icarie* (1842).

work he became acquainted when he was in London, that induced Cabet to give a practical shape to his theories by founding some Icarian communities in America. His *Voyage en Icarie*, which had appeared for the first time in 1839 in a limited edition and under the title of *Voyage et Aventures de lord William Carisdall en Icarie*, was reprinted under its present title in January, 1840, and was an immediate success ; there were five editions from 1840 to 1848. In the midst of the unemployment and poverty prevalent among the French working-class at the time, Cabet's utopia was greeted with extraordinary enthusiasm. Workers who could not afford the price of the book clubbed together in order to buy it, societies adhering to Cabet's ideas of social reform sprang up all over France, and money was collected to establish some Icarian communities in America.

Towards 1847, on the eve of the 1848 Revolution, Cabet decided to put his system into practice, and began to enrol members who would form the nucleus of a new nation in America. Cabet came to London in 1847 to consult Owen as to the situation of the first colony, and he was advised to set it up in Texas. This did not prove a happy suggestion, and, after having vainly tried to settle down in Texas, the first Icarian colonisers moved to an ex-Mormon colony at Nauvoo near St. Louis, where Cabet himself took over the direction (after having played an active part in the Paris Revolution of 1848, during which he was the leader of one of the most influential socialist clubs). But he was obliged to return to Paris in 1853, and after his departure the community was weakened by internal struggles. When Cabet returned to America, he was unable to put the colony on a sound basis again, and he died a disillusioned man in 1856. Nevertheless, a number of Icarian communities persisted for some decades, the last disintegrating as late as 1898.

Cabet's *Voyage en Icarie* has been called the Bible of Icarian Communism, and in fact it is more than an utopia. The first part, which describes an imaginary country where " a great nation is organised in community," can be considered the utopia proper, but the second part explains how a Communist régime can be established, and " discusses the theory and doctrine of the Community in answering all the objections which may be raised against it," while the third part is a summary of the principles on which the community system is based.

The reasons which determine why an Utopia should be popular are as mysterious as those governing any other " best seller," but Cabet's utopia may give some indication of the qualities required. The first essential seems to be that whoever describes the imaginary country should be as uncritical as possible in his admiration and should paint a picture in outrageously bright colours. The introduction of a romance, however improbable and sentimental it may be, is a sure way to increase the chances of success, and an added charm is achieved by the fact that a young and handsome English Lord cannot conceal his admiration at the marvels of democracy, and that the dressmakers and locksmiths whom he meets in Utopia would have been under the old régime princesses and dukes. Cabet provided all this emotional background, and more, and this may explain the success of the book in spite of the lack of originality, the numerous re-petitions and its style which makes it almost unreadable nowadays.

However much the personal adventures of Lord William Carisdall, and the divine Icarian women whom he met during his voyage to the most perfect country in the world, may have contributed to the success of the book, we do not propose to deal with them here, and shall begin with a short description of the country.

Icaria is conveniently isolated from the rest of the world by mountains on the North and South, a river at the East and the sea at the West. It is divided into a hundred provinces, more or less equal in size and population. Each province is divided into ten communes of about the same size. The chief provincial town lies approximately in the centre of the province and the communal town in the centre of the commune. Each commune possesses, besides the communal town, eight villages and many farms, regularly dispersed over its territory. An extensive network of roads, railways, and water-ways connects every part of the country. As in More's Utopia the symmetrical arrangement of the cities and towns was the work of the saviour and lawgiver of the country, who has also given his name to it, Icarus.

The capital, Icara, has also been reconstructed according to a super-plan, which not only fixed its shape to an almost perfect circle but also altered the course of the river to a practically straight line and embedded it between two walls. In the centre of the city the river branches off in two arms between which there is an island whose shape is, of course, round. On the island there is a square planted with trees, in the middle of which stands the main public building of the city with a " superb " terrace garden, in the centre of which rises an " immense " column, surmounted by a " colossal " statue which dominates all other buildings. Everything in Icaria is arranged with the most scrupulous regard for symmetry. All the streets are straight and wide. Fifty main streets cross the city parallel with the river, and fifty at right angles to it. Between the streets there are squares with beautiful gardens and all the houses have gardens at the back of them, which are cultivated by the families to whom they belong.

Modern inventions have been extensively used to provide the maximum amenities for the inhabitants of the city. There are " street cars," which are an anticipation of the horse-tramcar; they run every two minutes, and there are thousands of them passing in different directions. People wait for them at covered stops, and all sorts of precautions are taken to prevent accidents, such as having pedestrian crossings, marked with the forerunners of Belisha beacons.

The cleanliness, order and efficiency, the love for planning and mathematical precision, which characterise the external life of the citizens is to be found in every aspect of their existence. Everything is carefully planned by the State with the help of experts, and after consultation with the whole nation. There is no room for spontaneity or fancy in Cabet's utopia ; everything has been fixed by law, from the plan of the cities to the shape of hats, from the rigid time-table to the menu for each day of the week. The government of Icaria is Republican and the will of the people is sovereign, but can only express itself through national assemblies or the intermediary of a deputy.

This is how a member of the Icarian commonwealth explains the " principles of the social organisation in Icaria " :[1]

Being profoundly convinced by experience that there can be no happiness without association and equality, the Icarians form together a SOCIETY founded on the basis of the most perfect EQUALITY. All of them are *associates and citizens, having equal rights and duties* ; they all share equally the *responsibilities* and the

[1]Translated from the 1st edition of 1839.

advantages of the association ; they all form a single FAMILY, whose members are united by the bonds of FRATERNITY.

We are therefore a *People* or a nation of brothers ; and all our laws must aim at establishing the most absolute equality among us, in all cases where this equality is not materially impossible. . . .

In the same way as we form a single society, one people and one family, our land, with its underground mines and external construction, forms a single estate, which is our social property,

All the personal property of the associates, with all the products of the land and industry, form a single social CAPITAL.

This social property and capital belong indivisibly to the People, who work and exploit them in common, who administer them directly or through delegates, and then share equally all the products. . .

All the Icarians are associated and equal, all must exercise a trade and work the same number of hours ; but they employ all their intelligence to find every possible means of reducing the number of hours of work and rendering it agreeable and without danger.

All the instruments of work and raw materials are provided by the social capital, and all the products of the land and of industry are deposited in public storehouses.

We are all equally provided with food, clothes, a house and furniture out of the social capital, according to the sex, age and other circumstances fixed by law.

Thus, it is the Republic or Community which alone is the owner of everything, which organises its workers, and causes its factories and storehouses to be built, which sees that the land is tilled, that houses are built, and that all the objects necessary for feeding, clothing and housing each family and each citizen are provided.

EDUCATION being considered the basis and foundation of society, the Republic provides it equally for each one of its children as it provides them equally with nourishment. All receive the same elementary education and a specialised instruction suited to their particular profession ; this education aims at forming good workers, good parents, good citizens and true men. . . .

The Icarian spokesman then goes on to describe the "principles of the political organisation of Icaria " :

As we are all associates and citizens, possessing equal rights, we all have the right to vote and to be elected and are all members of the People and of the popular guard.

United, we compose the NATION or rather the PEOPLE, for in Icaria the People includes all the inhabitants without exception.

Needless to say, the People is SOVEREIGN, and to it alone belong, together with SOVEREIGNTY, the power to draw up its own social contract, its constitution and its laws ; it is inconceivable to us that a single individual, or a family, or a class could have the absurd pretention to be our master.

The People, having the sovereign power has the right to regulate, by its constitutions and its laws, everything concerning its person, actions, property, food, clothing, houses, education, work and even its pleasures.

If the Icarian People could be assembled altogether, easily and frequently, in a hall or a valley, it could exercise its sovereignty and draw up its own constitution and laws. As it is a material impossibility to assemble in this manner, it DELEGATES the powers which it cannot exercise directly and reserves all the others for itself. It delegates to a POPULAR ASSEMBLY the power to prepare its constitution and laws, and to an EXECUTIVE the power to see that they are carried out; but it reserves the right to elect all its representatives and all the members of the executive, to approve or reject their proposals and their actions, to administer justice, to maintain order and public peace.

All public functionaries are therefore the representatives of the People, all have been elected temporarily, and are responsible to the People and subject to recall ; in order to prevent the ambitious accumulation of offices, the legislative and executive functions are incompatible.

The popular REPRESENTATION is composed of 2,000 deputies who deliberate in common in a single chamber. It is *permanent*, always or nearly always assembled, and half its members are renewed each year. Its most important laws are, like the institution, submitted to the ratification of the People.

The EXECUTIVE is composed of a President and fifteen other members, half of whom can be changed every year ; it is completely subordinated to the popular Representation.

The people exercises its rights through its *assemblies* where the elections, deliberations and judgements are also carried out.

In order to render the exercise of the People's rights easier, the country is divided into a hundred small Provinces, subdivided into 1,000 Communes of approximately the same size and population.

You know that each *Provincial* town is at the centre of its province, every *Communal* town at the centre of its commune, and everything is arranged in such a manner that all the citizens can attend the popular assembles regularly.

While all the Communes and all the Provinces deal with matters of general and national interest through their represent-atives, each Province and each Commune deals more particularly with matters related to their communal and provincial interests. In this way no question can be neglected.

Divided into 2,000 communal assemblies the People thus takes part in the discussion of its laws, either after or before the deliberations of its own Representatives.

To ensure that the People is able to discuss with a perfect knowledge of the question, everything is carried out in the full light of Publicity, all the facts are recorded by a department of *Statistics*, and everything is published in the popular *Journal* which is distributed to all citizens.

In order to make sure that every question is exhaustively treated, the popular Representation and every communal assembly, that it to say, the whole People, is divided into fifteen great principal Committees dealing with *the constitution, education, agriculture, industry, food, clothing, housing, furnishing, statistics, etc.* Each great Committee therefore comprises a fifteenth of the mass of the citizens ; and all the intelligence of a People of men well brought up and well educated is continually applied to discover-ing and putting into practice all possible ameliorations and improvements.

Our political organisation is therefore a democratic RE-PUBLIC or even an almost pure DEMOCRACY...

The unanimous will of the people is always to create political and social equality, the equality of happiness and rights, universal and absolute equality : education, food, clothing, houses and furniture, work and pleasure, rights of election, eligibility and deliberations are the same for all of us, our provinces, our communes, our towns, our villages, our farms and our houses are, as far as possible, similar. Everywhere, in a word, you will find equality and happiness.

The task of describing various aspects of Icarian life has been entrusted to a young French painter, Eugene, who has exiled himself to Icaria after the July Revolution. In the letters to his brother, who has remained in Paris, he depicts with wondrous rapture the achievements of the Icarian régime. Under cover of Eugene's pen Cabet throws overboard the little reserve he deemed necessary to observe in the case of the

English Lord, and exclamation marks, italics and capitals are used even more freely than usual.

EUGENE'S LETTER TO HIS BROTHER

" O my dear Camille, how broken-hearted I feel when I think of France and see the happiness enjoyed by the people of Icaria! You will be able to judge for yourself in learning of their institutions concerning FOOD and *clothes*.

FOOD

" Concerning this first need of man, like all the others, everything in our unfortunate country is abandoned to chance and to monstrous abuses. Here, on the contrary, everything is regulated according to the most enlightened reason and the most generous care.

" Imagine first, my dear brother, that everything concerning food has been regulated by the *law*. It is the law which accepts or rejects any type of nourishment.

" A *committee* of scientists, set up by the national representatives, with the aid of all the citizens, has made a *list* of all known foods, indicating which are good and which are bad, and the respective qualities of each of them.

" They have done more than that : among the good ones they have indicated which are necessary, useful and agreeable, and they have had this list printed in several volumes and each family possesses a copy.

" They have done still more ; they have indicated the most suitable ways of preparing each food, and each family has also a *Cookery Guide*.

" Once the list of good foods had been agreed upon, the Republic undertook the task to have them produced by its agricultural labourers and workers, and distributed them to the families ; and as none is able to get any food other than that which is distributed, you will realise that no-one can eat anything which the Republic does not approve.

" The Republic sees first that what is necessary is produced, then what is useful, and finally, in as great a measure as possible, what is agreeable.

" The Republic gives an equal share to everybody, in such a manner that each citizen will receive the same quantity of certain food if there is enough for everyone, and that everyone will receive it in turn if there is only enough, each year or each day, for a section of the population.

" Everyone has therefore an equal share of all foods without distinction, from those which we consider most plain to the most delicate ; and the whole population of Icaria is nourished not only as well, but even better, than the richest people in other countries. . .

"The Committee which I have mentioned before has also discussed and indicated the number of *meals*, the time at which they should be eaten, how long they should last, the number of courses, their nature and the order in which they should be served, varying them continuously, not only according to the seasons and the months but also according to the days, with the result that every meal of the week is different from the other.

" At six o'clock in the morning, before they begin work, all the workers, that is to say all the citizens, eat a very simple breakfast in common at their workshops, prepared and served by the factory restaurant.

" At nine o'clock, they have a luncheon in the workshop, while their wives and their children take theirs at home.

" At two o'clock, all the inhabitants of the same street eat together, in their *republican restaurant*, a dinner prepared by one of the *caterers* of the Republic.

" And every evening between nine and ten, each family has, in its own home, a supper prepared by the women of the household.

" At all these meals, the first TOAST is *to the glory of the good Icar, benefactor of the workers*, BENEFACTOR OF THE FAMILIES, BENEFACTOR OF THE CITIZENS.

" The supper consists mostly of fruits, cakes and sweets. But the *common dinner*, which is taken in superb halls elegantly decorated, and which contain from a thousand to two thousand people, surpasses by its magnificence anything you may be able to imagine. The best restaurants and cafés of Paris are nothing, in my opinion, compared with the restaurants of the Republic. You may not believe me when I tell you that, apart from the abundance and the delicacy of the meals, apart from the decorations with flowers and many other things, a delicious music charms the ear while the sense of smell enjoys delicious perfumes.

"When the young people get married, they do not need to spend their dowry in a bad marriage feast and ruin in advance their future children ; the dinners which the husband finds in the wife's restaurant, the wife in the husband's, and the two families in the home of each other, replace the most beautiful dinners of other countries.

" And yet you must realise that these common meals present a great economy compared with separate meals and can therefore afford better fare.

" You will also realise that this community of meals among workers and neighbours has other great advantages, particularly that of inducing the masses to fraternise and also to simplify the housework for women...

" You may like to know how the _distribution_ of the food is carried out : nothing is more simple : but again you must admire!

DISTRIBUTION OF FOOD

" You know firstly that the Republic is the sole grower and producer of all food and that it gathers and stores it in its innumerable and immense storehouses.

" You can easily imagine communal _cellars_ like those of Paris and London, great storehouses for flour, bread, meat, fish, vegetables, fruit, etc.

" Each republican storehouse has, like any of our bakers or butchers, the _list_ of restaurants, workshops, schools, hospitals and families which it must supply, and the quantity which must be sent to each of them.

" In the storehouse are to be found the employees, utensils, means of transport, and extremely ingenious instruments necessary to the distribution of food.

" Everything having been _prepared in advance_ in the storehouse, the provisions for the year, the month or the week and the daily provisions are delivered to the homes in the district served by the storehouse.

" The distribution of these is organised in a charming way. I will not tell you of the perfect cleanliness which reigns everywhere as a matter of course, but I will not fail to tell you that each storehouse has a _basket_, a jug, a measure for each family marked with the number of its house and holding its provision of bread, milk, etc ; and all these containers are _double_, so that when the full one has been delivered, the empty one can be brought back. Each house has, at its entrance, an _alcove_ in which the delivery man finds the empty container and replaces it by a full one. In this way, the delivery, being always made at the same time, and announced by a particular sound, is carried out without disturbing the family and with no loss of time for the delivery man.

" You can understand, my dear friend, what an economy of time and what advantages this system of mass distribution possesses.

" Besides, everything is perfect in this happy country, inhabited by men who deserve the title of *men*, since, even in the smallest things they always make full use of that sublime reason which Providence has given them for their own happiness.

CLOTHES

" As with food, so it is with the law which regulates everything connected with clothes. A committee has consulted everyone, has examined the clothes worn in every country, has made a *list* of them with their shapes and colours (a magnificent book which every family possesses), has indicated which should be adopted and which must be avoided, and has classified them according to their necessity, utility and pleasure.

" Everything that was extravagant and tasteless, has been carefully banned.... not a single shoe or head-dress is manufactured without being first discussed and adopted according to a model-plan.

" Everyone possesses the same clothes, so that there is no room either for envy or coquettishness. And yet one should not think that *uniformity* here is not without *variety* ; for, on the contrary, it is in the clothes that variety combines most happily with the advantages of uniformity. Not only are the two sexes dressed differently, but each of them changes clothes frequently, according to age and condition, for the differences in clothes always indicate the circumstances and position of the person. Childhood and youth, adolescence and maturity, the condition of celibacy or marriage, or widowhood or re-marriage, the various professions and functions are all indicated by the clothes. All the individuals belonging to the same condition wear the same *uniform* ; but a thousand various uniforms correspond to a thousand various conditions.

" And the difference between these uniforms consists sometimes in the difference between materials and colours, sometimes in the shape or a distinctive sign.

" Consider also that if the material and the shape is the same for all girls of the same age, the colour varies according to their tastes or their suitability, a certain colour being more fitting for blondes and another for brunettes.

" Consider also that the same person has a simple and comfortable suit of clothes for *work* and another for the *home*, an elegant *drawing room* suit and another for *public meetings*, and a magnificent one for the *feasts* and *ceremonies*, all of them being different. In such a way the variety in costumes is almost infinite.

" The shape of each garment has been fixed in such a manner that it can be manufactured in the most easy, rapid and economic way possible.

" Practically all the clothes, hats and shoes are *elastic*, in such a way that they can suit people of different sizes.

" They are nearly all done by *machine*, either entirely or in part and the workers have little to do to finish them.

" Nearly all clothes are made in four or five different sizes so that the workers never need to take measurements beforehand.

" All the clothes are therefore manufactured in enormous quantities, like the materials, and often at the same time ; they are afterwards deposited in immense storehouses where everyone is always sure to find immediately all the objects which he needs and which are due to him according to the law.

" I have been talking to you of the *women* : O my dear Camille, how you would love these Icarians, you so courteous and so full of passion, as I am, for this master-piece of the Creator, if you saw how they surround women with attention, respect and homages, how they concentrate all their thoughts, their solicitude and their happiness upon them, how they constantly endeavour to please them and make them happy, how they do all they can to make them more beautiful, though they are already so beautiful naturally, in order to have more pleasure in adoring them! Happy women! Happy men! Happy Icaria! Unhappy France!"

It will be unnecessary to describe in detail other aspects of social organisation in Icaria, for they are all modelled after the same pattern. There is always a *committee of experts* which, after careful study, sets forth a model-plan for the best town-house, dining-table, farm, programme of study or monument ; this is unanimously adopted by the whole nation and becomes law. The law has also fixed a rigid time-table for all inhabitants, they must all rise at 5 in the morning, work till 2 in the afternoon, enjoy themselves till 9 and after 10 o'clock scru-pulously observe the curfew which lasts until 5 the next morning.

It is the duty of every citizen to work for the Republic a certain number of hours fixed by the law. When boys leave school at the age of 18, and the girls of 17, they must choose a trade or profession. If there are too many applicants for a certain occupation the fittest are selected by a competitive examination. To become a writer one must also pass certain examinations.

Men are allowed to retire at 65 and women at 50, but work in Icaria is so light and pleasant that most of them continue in their employment after the retiring age. Work is made agreeable by allowing proper periods of rest, by keeping factories always clean and by the extensive use of machinery. (Cabet had been obviously deeply impressed by the industrial development of England at the time of his stay in this country, and though he did not underestimate the importance of agriculture, he aimed at making Icaria, even more advanced, industrially, than England. He described so many " inventions " in his utopia that one has the impression, at times, of consulting the files of a patents office).

There are no degrading trades in Icaria for the law prohibits any employment considered unhealthy or immoral—there are no tavern-keepers, for example, and no one is allowed to manufacture daggers. A shoemaker is esteemed as highly as a doctor and one of the highest magistrates in the country is a locksmith while his daughter is a dressmaker. As wages have been abolished work cannot procure a superior standard of living and thereby create a new aristocracy. Furthermore, education teaches each citizen that all trades are equally useful to the community and must be equally respected. Workers who distinguish themselves by accomplishing more than the task assigned to them or by making some useful discovery receive, however, some public distinction.

Industrial production is carried out in large factories where most work is done on the belt system. At a printing works, for example, 5,000 workers are assembled in the same building where " there are so many machines that they do practically all the work which would have required 50,000 workers. Everything is arranged in such a way that the rags are transformed into paper which is immediately used for printing, on both sides at the same time and when dry is carried to the folding department where the collating, stitching and binding takes place and where the books are made ready for despatch to the libraries."

Work in a watch factory is carried out with military discipline:

The factory given over to clock-making occupies a building of one thousand square feet and has three storeys supported by iron columns which replace the thickest walls and in this manner each floor is composed of a single room perfectly lighted.

On the ground floor there are bulky and heavy machines used

for cutting the metal and rough casting the parts. The workers are on the top floor, and are divided in as many groups as there are parts, to be manufactured, and each of them always manufactures the same parts. There is so much order and discipline that they look like an army!

One of the workers explains how this " small army " carries out the work :

" We arrive at quarter to six in the morning and leave our clothes in the cloak-room and put on our working-clothes. At six o'clock sharp we begin work as the bell sounds. At nine o'clock we go down to the refectory and have our meal in silence while one of us reads the morning paper aloud. At one o'clock the work ends and when everything is tidied up and cleaned, we go down to the cloak-room where we find everything we need to wash and where we take our outdoor clothes to go to dinner with our families and spend the rest of the day as we think fit.

" During our work we observe the most rigorous silence for two hours, but for another two hours we can talk with our neighbours and the rest of the time we all sing for ourselves or for those who may listen and we often sing together."

Compared with the conditions prevalent in the factories of the nineteenth century Cabet's ideal workshop must have seemed " utopian " indeed, but military discipline and the task of manufacturing the same piece of machinery during a lifetime can be as oppressive as unhygienic conditions.

Though there are no rich and no poor in Icaria, no professional politicians and soldiers, no policemen and no prisons, we feel strangely uncomfortable at finding that it has so many features in common with the totalitarian régimes of the twentieth century: the grandiose architecture reminiscent of Mussolini's Italy, the love of uniforms and discipline, the worship of the dead dictator Icar whose image is prominently displayed in all public places and whose name is constantly evoked in songs and speeches recall painful memories. We are not surprised to hear that books were burned in Icaria when the régime was established, and that a rigid censorship controls the production of all works of art. We look in vain for a corner of life in which man's individuality can express itself. Cabet's insistence that the " will of the people is sovereign " leaves one sceptical, for he does not tell us how a whole nation can agree in every small detail of life. The all-pervading wisdom of his " experts " is even more difficult to accept, and one may wonder according to what principles they design the uniform for an Icarian re-married widow.

The love of uniformity, centralisation and state-control is to be found in most utopias, but in *Voyage to Icaria* it is carried to such extremes as to make it resemble, in many parts, the satirical utopias of our century.

LORD LYTTON
The Coming Race

UNLIKE most utopias of the nineteenth century, Lord Lytton's *The Coming Race* does not attempt to present a scheme for social improvement in a detailed and concrete form susceptible of realisation. It is a romance of *The Shape of Things to Come* type, interesting for the bold and rather terrifying vision which it depicts. A hundred years ago, when this novel first appeared, it might have seemed altogether fantastic to imagine a race of men each provided with a " vril staff," a kind of atomic bomb, so powerful as to be able to wipe out whole populations in a few seconds; but to-day we find scientists and philosophers, journalists and the man-in-the-street earnestly discussing the problems created by such a discovery.

It is an ironical coincidence that Lord Lytton should have entrusted to an American the task of warning the world of the existence of a powerful nation, living in the bowels of the earth, capable of conquering the American people whenever it chose thanks to its " atomic " bombs. To drive home what seems to be intended as a lesson in humility, the members of this " coming race " resemble, in many respects, the Red Indians and are not only " infinitely stronger of form and grander of aspect " than the men who dwell on the surface of the earth, but they have detachable wings which enable them to fly out of windows and dance in the air.

The first contact of the American traveller with this race of super-men produces in him a state of feverish wonder, which drives him to attack his winged hosts, whereupon he is hypnotised into sleep and kept in that state for several weeks. When he is allowed to wake up he finds that, thanks to their marvellous powers, his hosts have learned his language and have taught him theirs, and an exchange of information about the world above the earth and that beneath takes place. The inhabitants of the underground world show the same contempt for the race to which the traveller belongs as Gulliver's Houyhnhnms, and they forbid him from talking about the world above the earth for fear he may corrupt them.

The language difficulty having been overcome, the traveller can now become fully acquainted with the civilisation of the " coming race." His first discovery is that they use " vril," whose amazing potency he had already been able to judge :

". . . By one operation of vril they can influence the variations of temperature—in plain words, the weather ; by other operations, akin to those ascribed to mesmerism, electro-biology, odic force, etc., but applied scientifically through vril conductors, they can exercise influence over minds, and bodies animal and vegetable. . . . This fluid is capable of being raised and disciplined into the mightiest agency over all forms of matter, animate or inanimate. It can destroy like the flash of lightning ; yet, differently applied, it can replenish or invigorate life, heal, and preserve . . . By this agency they rend way through the most solid substances, and open valleys for culture through the rocks in their subterranean wilderness. From it they extract the light which supplies their lamps, finding it steadier, softer, and healthier than the other inflammable materials they had formerly used."

It is the discovery of " vril " which has completely transformed the social organisation of the underground nation which possesses it. The " knowledge of vril and the practice of its agencies " does not belong to the whole underground population but only to certain communities which call themselves *Vril-ya*; meaning the " Civilised Nations " and which, of course, are in a position of superiority towards those nations which have not found the secret of " vril." Among the " civilised nations " the secret did not remain in the hands of the governments alone, but came into the possession of the whole people and resulted in the abolition of governments as we know them, and in a complete change of the structure of society :

The effects of the alleged discovery of the means to direct the more terrible force of vril were chiefly remarkable in their influence upon social polity. As these effects became familiarly known and skilfully administered, war between the Vril-discoverers ceased, for they brought the art of destruction to such perfection as to annul all superiority in numbers, discipline, or military skill. The fire lodged in the hollow of a rod directed by the hand of a child could shatter the strongest fortress, or cleave its burning way from the van to the rear of an embattled host. If army met army, and both had command of this agency, it could be but the annihilation of each. The age of war was therefore gone, but with the cessation of war other effects bearing upon the social state soon became apparent. Man was so completely at the mercy of man, each whom he encountered being able, if so willing, to slay him on the instant, that all notions of government by force gradually vanished from political systems and forms of law. It is only by force that vast communities, dispersed through great distances of space, can be kept together ; but now there was no longer either the necessity of self-preservation or the pride of aggrandisement to make one state desire to preponderate in population over another.

The Vril-discoverers thus, in the course of a few generations, peacefully split into communities of moderate size. The tribe amongst which I had fallen was limited to 12,000 families. Each tribe occupied a territory sufficient for all its wants, and at stated periods the surplus population departed to seek a realm of its own. There appeared no necessity for any arbitrary selection of these emigrants ; there was always a sufficient number who volunteered to depart.

The " Vril " nations are ruled by a " benevolent autocracy," but the role of the magistrate and of the Council of Sages is merely one of administration and to encourage the development of science :

This singular community elected a single supreme magistrate styled Tur ; he held his office nominally for life, but he could seldom be induced to retain it after the first approach of old age. There was indeed in this society nothing to induce any of its members to covet the cares of office. No honours, no insignia of higher rank were assigned to it. The supreme magistrate was not distinguished from the rest by superior habitation or revenue. On the other hand, the duties awarded to him were marvellously light and easy, requiring no preponderant degree of energy or intelligence. There being no apprehensions of war, there were no armies to maintain ; being no government of force, there was no police to appoint or direct. What we call crime was

utterly unknown to the Vril-ya ; and there were no courts of
criminal justice. The rare instances of civil disputes were referred for arbitration to friends chosen by either party, or decided
by the Council of Sages. . There were no professional lawyers ;
and indeed their laws were but amicable conventions, for there
was no power to enforce laws against an offender who carried
in his staff the power to destroy his judges. There were customs
and regulations to compliance with which, for several ages, the
people had tacitly habituated themselves ; or if in any instance
an individual felt such compliance hard, he quitted the community and went elsewhere. There was, in fact, quietly
established amid this state, much the same compact that is found
in our private families, in which we virtually say to any independent grown-up member of the family whom we receive and
entertain, " Stay or go, according as our habits and regulations
suit or displease you." But though there were no laws such as
we call laws, no race above ground is so law-observing. Obedience to the rule adopted by the community has become as
much an instinct as if it were implanted by nature.

Property and money have not been abolished but do not confer
any political or social advantages :

Poverty among the Ana [the name of the great family race to
which this subterranean population belongs] is as unknown as
crime : not that property is held in common, or that all are equals
in the extent of their possessions or the size and luxury of their
habitations : but there being no difference of rank or position
between the grades of wealth or the choice of occupation, each
pursues his own inclinations without creating envy or vying ;
some like a modest, some a more splendid kind of life ; each
makes himself happy in his own way. Owing to this absence of
competition, and the limit placed on the population, it is difficult
for a family to fall into distress ; there are no hazardous specula-
tions, no emulators striving for superior wealth and rank. No
doubt, in each settlement all originally had the same proportion
of land dealt out to them : but some, more adventurous than
others, had extended their possessions farther into the bordering
wilds, or had improved into richer fertility the produce of their
fields, or entered into commerce or trade. Thus, necessarily,
some had grown richer than others, but none had become
absolutely poor, or wanting anything which their tastes desired.
If they did so, it was always in their power to migrate, or at the
worst to apply, without shame and with certainty of aid, to the

rich ;   for all the members of the community considered themselves as brothers of one affectionate and united family.

The Ana attach great importance to scientific progress and
have their " House of Salomon," but, perhaps in order to revenge
himself against the Victorian contempt for feminine intellectual
powers, Lytton staffs it almost entirely with women :

The chief care of the supreme magistrate was to communicate
with certain active departments charged with the administration
of special details.   The most important and essential of such
details was that connected with the due provision of light.
Another department, which might be called the foreign,
communicated with the neighbouring kindred states, principally
for the purpose of ascertaining all new inventions ; and to a third
department, all such inventions and improvements in machinery
were committed for trial.   Connected with this department was
the College of Sages—a college especially favoured by such of
the Ana as were widowed and childless, and by the young
unmarried females... It is by the female Professors of this
College that those studies which are deemed of least use in
practical life—as speculative philosophy, the history of remote
periods, and such sciences as entomology, conchology, etc.—are
the more diligently cultivated... But the researches of the sages
are not confined to such subtle or elegant studies.   They comprise
various others more important, and especially the properties of
vril, to the perception of which their finer nervous organisation
renders the female Professors eminently keen.   It is out of this
college that the Tur, or chief magistrate, selects Councillors,
limited to three, in the rare instances in which novelty of event
or circumstances perplexes his own judgment.

The problem of work which has always greatly preoccupied
Utopian writers is here easily solved by the extensive use of
machinery, and " robots," which are to become a familiar feature
in later utopias, make here their first appearance as the servants of
man.   Work of a tedious, unpleasant or dangerous nature is, somewhat surprisingly, undertaken by children.   This idea of making
children do the " dirty work " is obviously borrowed from Fourier
who thought that the destructive instincts and love of dirt which
manifest themselves in many children should be put to some useful
purpose by giving them work for which nature had best fitted
them.   In Fourier's Phalansteries children, organised in Little
Hordes, " are always up and about at 3 o'clock in the morning,

cleaning the stables, attending to animals, working in the slaughter-houses... The Little Hordes have, as one of their duties, the incidental repairing of the highways, that is, the daily maintenance of the surface-roads," and they see to it that " no vicious reptile, serpent or viper " is discovered near the highroads.

In Lytton's utopia the bands of children perform all these tasks and many more ; most work is, in fact, carried out by them on the ground that children are more active than adults, but their work is always of a light nature for they can use machinery and "vril."

Machinery is employed to an inconceivable extent in all the operations of labour within and without doors, and it is the unceasing object of the department charged with its administration to extend it efficiently. There is no class of labourers or servants, but all who are required to assist or control the machinery are found in the children, from the time they leave the care of their mothers to the marriageable age, which they place at sixteen for the Gy-ei (the females), twenty for the Ana (the males). These children are formed into bands and sections under their own chiefs, each following the pursuits in which he is most pleased, or for which he feels himself most fitted. Some take to handicrafts, some to agriculture, some to household work, and some to the only services of danger to which the population is exposed ; for the sole perils that threaten this tribe are, first, from those occasional convulsions within the earth, to foresee and guard against which tasks their utmost ingenuity—irruptions of fire and water, the storms of subterranean winds and escaping gases. At the borders of the domain, and at all places where such peril might be apprehended, vigilant inspectors are stationed with telegraphic communication to the hall in which chosen sages take it by turn to hold perpetual sittings. These inspectors are always selected from the elder boys approaching the age of puberty, and on the principle that at that age observation is more acute and the physical forces more alert than at any other. The second service of danger, less grave, is the destruction of all creatures hostile to the life, or the culture, or even the comfort of the Ana. Of these the most formidable are the vast reptiles, of some of which antediluvian relics are preserved in our museums, and certain gigantic winged creatures, half bird, half reptile. These, together with lesser wild animals, corresponding to our tigers or venomous serpents, it is left to the young to hunt and destroy ; because, according to the Ana, here ruthlessness is wanted, and the younger a child the more ruthlessly he will destroy.

Fourier gave a very low remuneration to his Little Hordes on the ground that children do unpleasant work because of their patriotic zeal and devotion to society ; he considered them as " philanthropic bodies having a contempt for riches, and devotion to repugnant labour, which they perform as a point of honour." Lytton is more generous in dealing with children ; they receive high rates of pay and by the time they reach manhood they have accumulated sufficient capital to live in idleness for the rest of their lives if they wish :

I have said that all the human labour required by the state is carried on by children up to the marriageable age. For this labour the state pays, and at a rate immeasurably higher than our remuneration to labour even in the United States. According to their theory, every child, male or female, on attaining the marriageable age, and there terminating the period of labour, should have acquired enough for an independent competence during life. As, no matter what the disparity of fortune in the parents, all the children must equally serve, so all are equally paid according to their several ages or the nature of their work. When the parents or friends choose to retain a child in their own service, they must pay into the public fund in the same ratio as the state pays to the children it employs ; and this sum is handed over to the child when the period of service expires. This practice serves, no doubt, to render the notion of social equality familiar and agreeable.

The position of women is an unusual one, for the women of this underground nation are physically stronger than the men, and are also more skilled in the use of " vril." They could if they wished destroy the whole male population, but this would only be to their disadvantage and they never even display their superior force for fear that men may take umbrage and desert them *en masse.* Women are jealous of their right to choose their future husbands and court them, but once they are married to the men of their choice they do all they can to please them and even agree to obey them, not out of moral duty, but because they realise that this is the best way to keep their husbands. This is all the more necessary in view of the fact that marriage laws only bind men and women together for a limited period of time. When this novel appeared, the free manner in which Lord Lytton dealt with the relations between sexes, marriage and divorce, must have seemed highly immoral (if he was taken at all seriously), but it is amusing to see how akin to the position of his subterranean women is that of English and American women to-day.

The " amoralism " displayed throughout the book more resembles our modern attitude than that of the nineteenth century, when strong moral principles, and an immense love of humanity, were the fashion. Lytton does not talk of " natural rights " or of the " law of nature," but declares that " it is idle to talk of rights where there are no corresponding powers to enforce them." This axiom, which receives such wide application, particularly in political life, is rarely openly admitted in our society. The ethic of the Coming Race, on the other hand, is frankly based on power: they behave in a brotherly way towards men of the same race who are their equals, for they all have the ability to use " vril," but they have no compunction about killing barbarians, i.e. men who have not discovered the use of " vril " and who are unable to defend themselves. In this respect they are remarkably similar to non-utopian civilised nations, which have a certain code of behaviour towards other powerful nations and an entirely different one towards the " backward " races.

Lord Lytton is less convincing when he expounds the theory that the best way to avoid conflicts is for everyone to be armed to the teeth. This optimistic view has often been put forward by arms manufacturers, for obvious reasons, and also by wishful thinkers who, at the time of the discovery of the atomic bomb, for example, expressed the belief that when every nation would be able to manufacture them no one would be suicidal enough to make use of them and the world would see the end of wars. Unfortunately one may gather from past experience that even when a certain equilibrium of forces is achieved there are always men ready to gamble their own life or that of others.

The Coming Race is the kind of utopian romance which can only be treated with the greatest contempt by any scientific socialist, if indeed any of them would consent to read such petit-bourgeois literature. It is certainly a curious attempt to reconcile certain socialist principles with laissez-faire capitalism. From William Godwin, who had exerted a considerable influence on him during his youth, Lytton probably borrowed his conception of a stateless society composed of a federation of small, independent communities, and from Fourier some of his ideas concerning work, the retention of profits and his liberal attitude towards idlers. The result of conflicting influences is a society where equality is admitted on principle, but where profits are made out of capital and where therefore exploitation persists; where riches do not confer any power and never corrupt ; where there is no government to defend the interests of the privileged class. But this is an utopian romance and inconsistencies are *de rigueur* ; in spite of them, or perhaps, thanks to them, *The Coming Race* is less dull than most of the more scientific utopias of the nineteenth century.

EDWARD BELLAMY
Looking Backward

IF *Looking Backward* is, in spite of its paradoxical title, a romance about the future, it is a future with which we are already familiar. The nationalisation of industry, the conscription of labour, the importance of the managerial class, are all features which belong to the present rather than to the future, and we might be tempted to call Edward Bellamy a prophet, rather than an utopian, if he had not been sadly mistaken in thinking that these changes would bring us happiness.

The public of the 'nineties, which had not tasted the reality of state control, received Bellamy's Utopia with enthusiasm. Reviewing *Looking Backward* in *La Revolte*, at the end of 1889, two years after the book had first appeared in America Peter Kropotkin mentioned that 139,000 copies of the American edition, and 40,000 of the English edition, had already been sold and that it had achieved many " conversions." Darwin's great co-worker, Λ. R. Wallace, declared that he had only been in favour of the nationalisation of the land, but Bellamy's book had convinced him that the United States were ready for socialism.

Bellamy's clear and practical approach to economic problems was probably one of the chief causes for his success, while the sentimental romance, woven into his description of the society of the future, could not fail to appeal to the taste of the time. Bellamy was also very careful to disguise his authoritarianism in such a way as not to antagonise the individualist susceptibilities of the American bourgeoisie. Cabet wrote his Utopia thinking of the unemployed and starving masses who, he presumed, would be more interested in food and shelter than in the luxury of being allowed to decide what to eat or what to wear. Bellamy obviously wrote with an eye to the middle classes, and in seeking to attract people who did not lack the essential amenities of life, he had to emphasise other attractions than food and shelter, such as the possibility of retiring at forty-five and having no servant problems. It is also obvious that the cultured classes would not accept dictation in matters of taste or restriction in what they considered to be their intellectual freedom, and Bellamy ingeniously combined state control in matters of production and distribution with private initiative in literature and art, and allowed a greater degree of independence to the liberal professions than to the industrial workers.

Mr West, the hero of the story, lived in Boston at the end of the nineteenth century, when poverty and unemployment produced widespread industrial unrest. This wealthy young man, whose main preoccupation in life seems to have been that the building of a house for his future wife was held up by continuous strikes, suffered from insomnia and had an underground chamber specially constructed so that he could sleep without being disturbed by the noises of the town. But he had also on occasion to use the services of a doctor who sent him to sleep by hypnotism. On the night of the 30th May, 1887, his house was burnt to the ground, and, no one knowing of his underground chamber except his doctor who had left the town and his valet who had probably died in the fire, he was left to lie in his hypnotic state until the year 2,000, when he was discovered in the course of some excavation work.

Dr Leete, who is to become his host, awakens him from his long sleep and, with the help of his young and beautiful daughter, manages to reconcile the young man to his unusual experience and, furthermore, to make him into an ardent admirer of the new system. To finish with the romantic side of the book, we might mention that Edith Leete happens to be the great grand-daughter of the other Edith whom Mr. West had been prevented from marrying, firstly through the building strikes, and afterwards through his own presumed death, that the two naturally fall passionately in love, and this time no housing problem prevents their marriage. Mr West gets a chair of history at Shawmut College, Boston, and it is in his capacity of historian that he relates the story of his own experiences both in the nineteenth and twenty-first century.

The first thing which surprises Julian West, whose head is still full of the reports of strikes, lock-outs and boycotts is that, in the new society, there is no labour problem and that there are no longer, in fact, employers and employees. Dr Leete explains to him that, at the beginning of the twentieth century, a peaceful social revolution took place :

The movement toward the conduct of business by larger and larger aggregations of capital, the tendency toward monopolies, which had been so desperately and vainly resisted, was recognised at last, in its true significance, as a process which only needed to complete its logical evolution to open a golden future to humanity. Early in the last century the evolution was completed by the final consolidation of the entire capital of the nation. The industry and commerce of the country, ceasing to be conducted by a set of irresponsible corporations and syndicates of private persons at their caprice and for their profit, were intrusted to a single syndicate representing the people, to be conducted in the common interest for the common profit. The nation, that is to say, organised as the one great business corporation in which all other corporations were absorbed ; it became the one capitalist in the place of all other capitalists, the sole employer, the final monopoly in which all previous and lesser monopolies were swallowed up, a monopoly in the profits and economies of which all citizens shared. In a word, the people of the United States concluded to assume the conduct of their own business, just as one hundred odd years before they had assumed the conduct of their own government, organising now for industrial purposes on precisely the same grounds on which they had been organised for political ends. . . .
When the nation became the sole employer, all the citizens, by virtue of their citizenship, became employees, to be distributed according to the needs of industry. . . The people were already accustomed to the idea that the obligation of every citizen, not physically disabled, to contribute his military services to the defence of the nation, was equal and absolute. That it was equally the duty of every citizen to contribute his quota of industrial or intellectual services to the maintenance of the nation was equally

evident, though it was not until the nation became the employer of labour that citizens were able to render this sort of service with any pretence either of universality or equity.

Every citizen, from the age of 21, when his education ends, until the age of 45, is conscripted for some kind of national work. He is free to choose the occupation which corresponds to his tastes and capacities, unless there are too many volunteers for the needs of a particular branch of industry, in which case only the fittest are accepted. Great care is taken to render all occupations equally attractive :

It is the business of the administration to seek constantly to equalise the attractions of the trades so far as the conditions of labour in them are concerned, so that all trades shall be equally attractive to persons having natural tastes for them. This is done by making the hours of labour in different trades to differ according to their arduousness. The lighter trades, prosecuted under most agreeable circumstances, have in this way the longest hours, while an arduous trade, such as mining, has very short hours. There is no theory, nor *a priori* rule, by which the respective attractiveness of industries is determined. The administration, in taking burdens off one class of workers and adding them to other classes, simply follows the fluctuations of opinions among the workers themselves as indicated by the rate of volunteering. The principle is that no man's work ought to be, on the whole, harder for him than any other man's for him, the workers themselves to be the judges.

The problem of " who will do the dirty work " is solved by directing the new recruits for a period of three years, wherever they are needed : " It is not till after this period, during which he is assignable to any work at the discretion of his superiors, that the young man is allowed to elect a special avocation. These three years of stringent discipline none are exempt from." At the age of 45 both men and women are discharged from further service and become free to occupy themselves as they wish, or to be completely idle if they prefer, for the remainder of their lives.

The next great innovation is that the new system has established the right of each individual to an equal share of the wealth of the nation, independently of the amount of work he produces. In other words, the wage system has been abolished, and, here again, Bellamy draws a parallel between military and industrial service.

Just as in a capitalist society all the members of a nation " share
equally in the protection of the army and the prosperity it ensures,
the nation of the year 2000, all alike, whether men or women,
strong or weak, able-bodied or defective, share in the wealth
produced by the industrial army, and the share of all is equal.
This share, varying only with the general prosperity of the
national business, is the sole income and means of maintenance
of all, whether during active industrial service or after discharge
from it. Owing to the method of organising industry upon the
mutual obligation of citizen to nation, and nation to citizen, duty
has wholly taken the place of contract, as the basis of industry and
the cement of society."

The nation being the sole producer of all commodities, the
need for exchange between individuals has disappeared : " A
system of direct distribution from the national storehouses took
the place of trade, and for this money was unnecessary."
Distribution is managed on the simplest possible plan : " A
credit corresponding to his share of the annual product of the
nation is given to every citizen on the public books at the
beginning of each year, and a credit card issued him with which he
procures at the public storehouses, found in every community,
whatever he desires whenever he desires it. This arrangement
totally obviates the necessity for business transactions of any sort
between individuals and consumers." This card is issued for a
certain number of dollars ; the old word has been kept but is
merely used as an " algebraical symbol for comparing the values
of products with one another." The credit provided by the card
is so ample that it permits the satisfaction of all needs and even
many luxuries, but if a citizen happens to have some extraordinary
expense he can obtain an advance on the next year's credit,
" though this practice is not encouraged, and a heavy discount
is charged to check it."

Every citizen is at liberty to spend his allowance as he wishes:
" Although the income is the same, personal taste determines
how the individual shall spend it. Some like fine horses ; others
prefer pretty clothes ; and still others want an elaborate table.
The rents which the nation receives for these houses vary,
according to size, elegance, and location, so that everybody can
find something to suit." No one tries to impress other people by
ostentatious houses or clothes, " for everybody's income is known,

and it is known that what is spent in one way must be saved in another." On the other hand, the nation being rich, the people do not need to deprive themselves of any good thing, and parsimony is no longer regarded as a virtue.

All shopping is done in the national stores, which are run on an extremely efficient (if somewhat impersonal) system. There are no salesmen or saleswomen, but merely clerks who take the orders and punch the value of the goods purchased on the credit card. They are not expected to know, or to praise, the qualities of the goods, for all the information which the customer may require is neatly printed on a card attached to the samples on show. Shops are run on the principle of our industrial fairs rather than present-day shops ; only specimens of merchandise are shown and the orders received are transmitted to the central warehouse of the city, where they are prepared and dispatched, by means of pneumatic tubes, to the city districts and thence distributed to the houses. The sample shop of the smallest village is the exact replica of the city shop, and gives the choice of all the varieties of goods at the disposal of the nation. The " village sample shops are connected by transmitters with the central county warehouse, which may be twenty miles away," but the transmission is so swift that the time lost on the way is trifling.

Meals can be taken at home or at a public restaurant, having all the grandiosity of our Lyons' Corner Houses, but where each family in the ward can, for a small annual rent, have a room set aside for its permanent and exclusive use.

People are not obliged to spend their allowance in the United States alone but can use it in Europe, Australia, Mexico and parts of South America which are industrial republics like the United States : " An American credit card is just as good in Europe as American gold used to be, and on precisely the same condition, namely, that it be exchanged into the currency of the country you are travelling in. An American in Berlin takes his credit card to the local office of the international council, and receives in exchange for the whole or part of it a German credit card, the amount being charged against the United States, in favour of Germany on the international account."

The credit card can also be used to hire labour from the state. Although servants have disappeared it is possible to obtain cleaners or decorators from the " labour exchange " if one's house needs a spring cleaning. More important, perhaps, people can own their own newspapers by each subscribing a certain sum which will cover the cost of production, and the editor whom they have chosen is discharged from industrial service during his incumbency, for " the subscribers pay the nation an indemnity equal to the cost of his support for taking him away from the general service." The credit card also provides for the hiring of churches and clergymen.

" The religious practices of the people have naturally changed considerably in a century," says Dr Leete : " but supposing them to have remained unchanged, our social system would accommodate them perfectly. The nation supplies any person or number of persons with buildings on guarantee of the rent, and they remain tenants while they pay it. As for the clergymen, if a number of persons wish the services of an individual for any particular end of their own, apart from the general service of the nation, they can always secure it, with that individual's own consent of course, just as we secure the service of our editors, by contributing from their credit-cards an indemnity to the nation for the loss of his services in general industry. This indemnity, paid the nation for the individual answers to the salary in your day paid to the individual himself ; and the various applications of this principle leave private initiative full play in all details to which national control is not applicable."

Authors and artists are in a special category for they can use their credit card to bring out a book, or produce a work of art, and are then entitled to the royalties provided by the sale of their work.

It will be seen from this and from what we have said already, Bellamy's state socialism allows a greater degree of personal freedom than most other utopias based on the same principles. But it is the freedom which might be granted to soldiers once they have been conscripted ; no provision is made for " conscientious objectors." If a man refuses to accept the authority of the state and the inevitability of industrial service, he loses all his rights as a human being : " To speak of service being compulsory would be a weak way to state its absolute inevitableness. Our entire social order is so wholly based upon and deduced from it that if it were conceivable that a man could escape it, he would be left with no possible way to provide for his existence. He would have excluded himself from the world, cut himself off from his kind, in a word, committed suicide."

We see from this that every citizen of the new society is obliged to respect a contract, made by previous generations, between themselves and the state. No means are provided for the revision of such a contract, for the working population is deprived of all political rights. The President of the United States, who is also the commander-in-chief of the industrial army, and is " responsible for the enforcement of the laws as to all classes," is not elected by the industrial army, because that is considered prejudicial to discipline, but by the retired members. This means that up to the age of forty-five neither men nor women have the right to vote, and are ruled by the older generation.

While every citizen shares equally in the wealth of the nation, the ruling class is composed of men who distinguish themselves for their ability in industrial work. This industrial aristocracy forms what James Burnham has called the " managerial class." According to Bellamy, honours and distinctions, offices of rank and authority in the industrial army and in the nation, must be allotted to men and women according to their comparative diligence and brilliancy of achievement, to the end that the fittest may lead and rule. The reward for achievements in the industrial field not only provides a managerial class, but also serves as an incentive to produce the maximum effort. While in the old days this was chiefly provided by the desire to acquire wealth, in the new society men strive to achieve a position of authority. As in the military army, emulation is induced by the possibility of rising from the ranks to posts of command : " The line of promotion for the meritorious lies through three grades to the officer's grade, and thence up through the lieutenancies to the captaincy, or foremanship, and superintendency or colonel's rank. Next, with an intervening grade in some of the larger trades, comes the general of the guild, under whose immediate control all the operations of the trade are conducted. This officer is at the head of the national bureau representing his trade, and is responsible for its work to the administration. The general of his guild holds a splendid position, and one which amply satisfies the ambition of most men, but above his rank, which may be compared, to follow the military analogies familiar to you, to that of a general of division or major-general, is that of the chiefs of the ten great departments or groups of allied trades. The chiefs of these ten grand divisions of the industrial army may be compared to your commanders of army corps, or lieutenant-generals, each having from a dozen to a score of generals of separate guilds reporting to him. Above these ten great officers, who form his council, is the general-in-chief, who is the president of the United States."

For those who do not aspire to posts of authority merely for the sake of the power it gives them, more tangible privileges are provided :

Apart from the grand incentive to endeavour, afforded by the fact that the high places in the nation are open only to the highest class men, various incitements of a minor, but perhaps equally effective, sort are provided in the form of special privileges and immunities in the way of discipline, which the superior class men enjoy. These, while not in the aggregate important, have the effect of keeping constantly before every man's mind the desirability of attaining the grade next above his own.

On the other hand those who infringe the discipline of the industrial army are severely punished :   " For actual neglect of work, positively bad work, or other overt remissness on the part of men incapable of generous motives, the discipline of the industrial army is far too strict to allow much of that. A man able to do duty, and persistently refusing, is cut off from all human society."

The ranking system necessitates a vast bureaucratic machine and the maintenance of piece-work which might have disappeared with the abolition of the wage system :

To facilitate the testing of efficiency, all industrial work, whenever by any means, and even at some inconvenience, it is possible, is conducted by piece-work, and if this is absolutely out of the question, the best possible substitute for determining ability is adopted. The men are regraded yearly, so that merit never need wait long to rise, nor can any rest on past achievements, unless they would drop into a lower rank. The results of each annual regrading, giving the standing of every man in the army, are gazetted in the public prints.

Outside the industrial army incentive is provided by decorations :   " The highest of all honours in the nation, higher than the presidency, which calls merely for good sense and devotion to duty, is the red ribbon awarded by the vote of the people to the great authors, artists, engineers, physicians, and inventors of the generation. Not over one hundred wear it at any one time, though every bright young fellow in the country loses innumerable nights' sleep dreaming of it."

All the production and distribution of the nation is carried out by a central administration and, according to Bellamy, nothing can ever go wrong because of the simplicity and wisdom of the laws, and because all the work of direction is in the hands of " experts." Local State governments have been suppressed because " they would have interfered with the control and discipline of the industrial army, which of course, required to be central and uniform."

The tasks of government have been greatly simplified with the disappearance of the army and the navy, of the departments of state and treasury, of taxes and tax-collectors. Bellamy's society is not so ideal, however, that it does not necessitate police and judges, though their number and duties have, we are assured, been reduced to a minimum, and jails have disappeared because all cases of " atavism " are treated in the hospitals. We might mention in passing that the jury system has been abolished and that judges are nominated by the President from among citizens over forty-five years of age.

Bellamy's unlimited faith in the wisdom of experts and of the " administration " is only equalled by his confidence in technical progress. He seems to have conceived man's happiness in terms of an ever-increasing quantity of consumers' goods, of bigger and better restaurants, of a speedier delivery of goods from the stores, of sky-scrapers and streets covered with water-proof material in bad weather. Bellamy's " inventions," such as his music by telephone, are amusing to us as interesting anticipations, and if the following passage makes us aware of our good fortune, through the enthusiasm of a man of the nineteenth century for an invention which already we take for granted, we also feel that happiness cannot be found after all, in technical progress alone :

" Come, then, into the music room," she said, and I followed her into an apartment finished, without hangings, in wood, with a floor of polished wood. I was prepared for new devices in musical instruments, but I saw nothing in the room which by any stretch of imagination could be conceived as such. It was evident that my puzzled appearance was affording intense amusement to Edith.

"Please look at to-day's music," she said, handing me a card, "and tell me what you would prefer. It is now five-o'clock, you will remember."

The card bore the date " September 12, 2000," and contained the largest programme of music I had ever seen. It was as various as it was long, including a most extraordinary range of vocal and instrumental solos, ducts, quartets, and various orchestral combinations. I remained bewildered by the prodigious list until Edith's pink finger-tip indicated a particular section of it, where several selections were bracketed, with the words " 5 p.m." against them ; then I observed that this prodigious programme was an all day one, divided into twenty-four sections answering to the hours. There were but a few pieces of music in the " 5 p.m." section, and I indicated an organ piece as my preference.

She made me sit down comfortably, and crossing the room, so far as I could see, merely touched one or two screws, and at once the room was filled with the music of a grand organ anthem ; filled, not flooded, for, by some means, the volume of melody had been perfectly graduated to the size of the apartment. I listened, scarcely breathing, to the close. Such music so perfectly render-ed, I had never expected to hear.

" Grand! " I cried, as the last great wave of sound broke and ebbed away into silence. " Bach must be at the keys of that organ ; but where is the organ? "

" Wait a moment, please," said Edith ; " I want to have you listen to this waltz before you ask any questions. I think it is perfectly charming," and as she spoke the sound of violins filled the room with the witchery of summer night. When this had also ceased, she said : " There is nothing in the least mysterious about the music as you seem to imagine. It is not made by the fairies or genii, but by good, honest, and exceedingly clever human hands, We have simply carried the idea of labour-saving by co-operation into our musical service as into everything else. There are a number of music rooms in the city, perfectly adapted acoustically to the different sorts of music. These halls are connected by telephone with all the houses of the city whose people care to pay the small fee, and there are none, you may be sure, who do not. The corps of musicians attached to each hall is so large that, although no individual performer, or group of performers, has more than a brief part, each day's programme lasts through the twenty-four hours. There are on that card for to-day, as you will see if you observe closely, distinct programmes of four of these concerts, each of a different order of music from the others, being now simultaneously performed, and any one of the four pieces now going on that you prefer, you can hear merely by pressing the button which will connect your house wire with the hall where it is being rendered. The programmes are so co-ordinated that the pieces at any one time simultaneously pro-ceeding in the different halls usually offer a choice, not only between instrumental and vocal, and between different sorts of instruments ; but also between different motives from grave to gay, so that all tastes and moods can be suited."

" It appears to me, Miss Leete," I said, " that if we could have devised an arrangement for providing everybody with music in their homes, perfect in quality, unlimited in quantity, suited to every mood, and beginning and ceasing at will, we should have considered the limit of human felicity already attained, and ceased to strive for further improvements."

If we feel sceptical of the happiness which technical inventions might bring us, it also is difficult to feel very enthusiastic about the solution of the labour problem offered by Bellamy. Apart from the fact that recent experience has shown that industrial conscription does not always run as smoothly as he seems to have hoped, his rigid regimentation of men's lives takes little note of the differences in the psychological make-up of individuals. It is difficult to see why everyone should be obliged to study up to the age of 21, when many would prefer to engage in some kind of trade, and why everyone should retire at 45, when many only begin to gather the fruits of the experience acquired during their youth. Nor do we feel very comforted by the idea that after three years of " dirty work " we would be able to choose an occupation suited to our taste since, in view of the development of mass production, most of the jobs available would probably involve working in factories on some kind of belt system.

The joy with which the citizens of Bellamy's society greet their retirement is a sufficient indication that industrial conscription is resented as a burden. " We all agree," says Dr Leete, " in looking forward to the date of our discharge as the time when we shall first enter upon the full enjoyment of our birth-right, the period when we shall first really attain our majority and become enfranchised from discipline and control, with the fee of our lives vested in ourselves." Bellamy was convinced that twenty-one years of compulsory education and twenty-four years of conscripted labour was a very moderate demand on the part of the state, and that no one could possibly object to it. That life begins at forty-five is, however, an opinion with which it is permissible to disagree.

One might also feel little sympathy for the constant use Bellamy makes of compulsion. If the citizens of the new society are truly satisfied with their conditions, what need is there to compel them to do what, we are constantly assured, is light and even pleasant work? Is there not also a danger that work which can be pleasant when freely undertaken, becomes irksome when done under compulsion? Bellamy, however, was so convinced that he had found a solution to all the world's problems that he devoted the rest of his life to perfecting his system, and published several books to explain it in greater detail. That he had found a solution cannot be denied, but as we shall see in the next Utopia, there could be a more attractive one.

WILLIAM MORRIS

News from Nowhere

AFTER the stifling atmospheres of Cabet's and Bellamy's utopias, with their complicated bureaucratic machines run by an all-wise, all-pervading state, William Morris's utopian England appears like an oasis where we would like to stay, if not for ever, at least for a long time. Here we can work without having a foreman at our elbow, we can sleep without having to set the alarm clock, eat what we like and not what the experts have decided to be best suited to our constitution ; we can love without having to consider tyrannical laws or a no less tyrannical public opinion ; here we can dress as we like, read what we like and, above all, think what we like. Here we can live, because we have not been catalogued and directed, but left to arrange our lives as we think fit.

News from Nowhere was published in serial form in the *Commonweal* (the journal of the Socialist League, founded and edited by William Morris) during the year 1890. It is likely that Morris was prompted to write his Utopia after reading *Looking Backward*, which had appeared in England a few years previously and for which he could have felt little sympathy. His work too is written in the form of a romance of the future, but to the highly centralised government of Bellamy's ideal society Morris opposed a society in which government has become unnecessary, for government is " but the machinery of tyranny " and when tyranny comes to an end there is no longer need for such machinery. To the vast industrial organisation of utopian America Morris opposed a federation of agrico-industrial communities working autonomously. To the military discipline of work he opposed the right of the individual to work when and how he pleased ; to engage in machine mass-production, or in hand-made, limited, but beautifully finished goods. Indeed, there is hardly a single point on which *News from Nowhere* is not the antithesis of *Looking Backward*.

William Morris differs also from most utopian writers of the nineteenth century in his desire to break away completely not only from the misery brought about by the industrial revolution but also from faith in industrial progress. Bellamy, with the majority of utopian writers, believed that once the system of private capitalism was abolished, technical progress would bring happiness to mankind, for it would satisfy all its ever-increasing wants. Morris, on the contrary, believed that happiness had nothing to do with increased production and that most of the " progress " made in that field would be discarded when the new society came into being : " the nineteenth century saw itself as a man who has lost his clothes whilst bathing, and has to walk naked through the town."

William Morris neither believed that the new society could be the work of some Socialist Napoleon nor that it would evolve, by a kind of mechanical process, out of the old. In his opinion a free, just and happy world can only come into being when men desire freedom so strongly that they realise their strength and overthrow the old system. This is how, in *News from Nowhere*, he describes the force which brought about the Revolution : " Looking back now, we can see that the great motive-power of the change was a longing for freedom and equality, akin if you please to the unreasonable passion of the lover... It is true that the slave-class could not conceive the happiness of a free life.

Yet they grew to understand (and very speedily too) that they
were oppressed by their masters, and they assumed, you see how
justly, that they could do without them, though perhaps they
scarce knew how." And William Morris, who has often been
accused of being too unrealistic and optimistic, does not shrink
from stating that a Revolution is necessary to bring about a new
society : " the world was being brought to its second birth ;
how could that take place without a tragedy? "

If the world of to-morrow, described by William Morris,
considers the nineteenth century as an example of all that life
should not be, it is not unwilling to learn from the past and, in
particular, from the Middle Ages, when communities were still
small enough to allow bonds of friendship to exist between their
members, when workers produced for the restricted market of the
city, when craftsmen did not execute other people's plans but those
of their own creation, when all matters were settled by the guilds
and city councils and not by the impersonal authority of a centralised state. Morris's conception of life in the fourteenth century
was not perhaps completely accurate from an historical point of
view. The England of his *Dream of John Ball* may be too bright,
healthy and happy to be completely true, for, though the Middle
Ages were a period of prosperity and freedom compared with the
nineteenth century, nevertheless the mediaeval cities had to
sustain continuous struggles in order to preserve their independence. It matters little, however, if life in the Middle Ages was
not quite as idyllic as Morris liked to believe it ; what is important is that he recaptured the spirit of those times " to whom heaven
and the life of the next world was such a reality, that it became
to them a part of the life upon the earth ; which accordingly they
loved and adorned, in spite of the ascetic doctrines of their
formal creed, which bade them condemn it."

Most utopians, before William Morris, had conceived societies
where private property had been abolished, where the right of
each man to his equal share of the wealth of the community had
been recognised, but where private ownership had generally been
replaced by state ownership, the incentive of money by the
incentive of honours and decorations, the submission to the old
laws by the obedience to the new ones. And if crimes against
property had disappeared, crimes against the new institutions
were punished as severely as the former. In *News from Nowhere*

every man is his own master, and does not delegate his power to a body of men who make laws and inflict punishments if the laws are not respected. He is really the equal of his fellow men, not only because he receives the same share of food and clothing, but also because he has no authority over his neighbour or his neighbour over him.

Most utopian writers also assumed that man's happiness consisted in living in a well-regulated society which provided for all their needs. They did not appear to see the danger of man becoming utterly bored for lack of any creative expression. William Morris sought to find a guarantee for the happiness of mankind in work, which would become the means of fulfilling man's creative impulse. In his ideal society most work has become a kind of artistic activity, but this was not achieved immediately : " The art or work pleasure, as one ought to call it, sprang up almost spontaneously, it seems, from a kind of instinct amongst people, no longer driven desperately to painful and terrible overwork, to do the best they could with the work in hand, to make it excellent of its kind ; and when that had gone for a little, a craving for beauty seemed to awaken in men's minds, and they began rudely and awkwardly to ornament the wares they made ; and when they had once set to work at that, it soon began to grow...Thus at last and by slow degrees we got pleasure into our work : then we became conscious of that pleasure, and cultivated it, and took care that we had our fill of it ; and then all was gained, and we were happy."

It follows from this that, in the new society, not only the institutions but the whole of man's outlook has changed. " Human nature " is largely dependent on the nature of society, " there is the human nature of the paupers, of slaves, of slave-holders " and " the human nature of wealthy freemen," and Morris therefore peoples his free society with men who no longer have the mentality of slaves, and tries to show what the behaviour of these men would be, rather than to give us a complete picture of all the mechanisms of the new society. This may also have been dictated by the fact that Morris did not want to give his opinion on matters he knew little about, unlike so many writers of utopias who imagined themselves to be oracles in everything, from baby-rearing to town-planning, from house-work to industrial production. While William Morris does not

lose an opportunity to express his opinions on the architecture of
buildings, on painting, carving or pottery work, he observes a
discreet silence on matters with which he is not acquainted, such
as the intricacies of regulating production and distribution, or
the arrangements which are presumably made to enable scientists
to carry out their work, for, though he claims that his ideal age is
not one of invention, a new power force has been found. It is
because Morris only writes about questions which he knows
intimately and in which he is passionately interested that his book
has none of the dullness and artificiality which characterise most
utopias of that period.

One is also grateful to Morris for not claiming that his society
was the only perfect, the only desirable one. As G. D. H. Cole
has pointed out, " *News from Nowhere* was neither a prophecy nor
a promise, but the expression of a personal preference. Morris
was saying ' Here is the sort of society I feel I should like to live
in. Now tell me yours'." All utopias are, of course, the expression of personal preferences, but their authors usually have
the conceit to assume that their personal tastes should be enacted
into laws ; if they are early-risers the whole of their imaginary
community will have to get up at four o'clock in the morning ;
if they dislike women's make-up, to use it is made a crime ; if
they are jealous husbands infidelity will be punished by death.
Morris freely confesses his likes and dislikes, but no one is obliged
to accept them and there are no punishments for those who have
dissimilar tastes. He realised that the manner of life of a community cannot be artificially arranged in the mind of an individual,
but must be spontaneously created by all the members of that
community. He could dream and work for *his* ideal but he
could not achieve it for others. That could only be achieved by
the people themselves. As he said in *The Earthly Paradise* :

> Dreamer of dreams, born out of my due time
> Why should I strive to set the crooked straight?
> Let it suffice me that my murmuring rhyme
> Beats with light wing against the ivory gate,
> Telling a tale not too importunate
> To those who in the sleepy region stay,
> Lulled by the singer of an empty day.

The persuasive charm of *News from Nowhere* does not reside
so much in the admittedly convincing arguments put forward by

its various utopian inhabitants to explain why they have chosen their manner of life, but in the atmosphere of beauty, freedom, calm and happiness which pervades the whole story. Morris has neglected nothing that might seduce us ; the women are healthy, athletic and beautiful, and wear attractive silk or linen embroidered dresses, the men are handsome, strong, attentive and amorous, everybody looks younger than his age and women of forty have not a single wrinkle ; in the communal dining-halls, which, needless to say, are decorated with carvings, pictures and contain furniture beautiful in form and highly ornamented, simple but daintily prepared meals are served with a bottle of French wine, and (here we feel that Morris has really cheated) during the whole period of our stay in utopian England the weather is wonderfully fine and warm.

A few extracts from *News from Nowhere* can only give a poor idea of this work, for it should be appreciated like a painting which must be viewed as a whole.

" William Guest," after having spent an evening, up at the League, discussing with a few comrades what would happen on the Morrow of the Revolution, goes back to his home in Hammersmith dreaming of days of peace and rest, cleanness and smiling goodwill. He awakes, or dreams that he awakes, some two hundred years later to find the banks of the Thames lined with pretty houses and gardens full of flowers. We may follow him on his first trip through London, which he takes with Dick Hammond, a handsome and courteous waterman who has become his guide and is driving him in a graceful and pleasant carriage pulled by a strong grey horse. The new London bears little resemblance to the old ; it has become an agglomeration of villages separated by woods, prairies and gardens, and the ugly houses, dirty with soot, have been replaced by beautiful cottages and buildings.

We turned away from the river at once, and were soon in the main road that runs through Hammersmith. But I should have had no guess as to where I was, if I had not started from the waterside ; for King Street was gone, and the highway ran through wide sunny meadows and garden-like tillage. The Creek, which we crossed at once, had been rescued from its culvert, and as we went over its pretty bridge we saw its waters, yet swollen by the tide, covered with gay boats of different sizes. There were houses

about, some on the road, some amongst the fields with pleasant
lanes leading down to them, and each surrounded by a teeming
garden. They were all pretty in design, and as solid as might be,
but countryfied in appearance, like yeomen's dwellings ; some
of them of red brick like those by the river, but more of timber
and plaster, which were by the necessity of their construction so
like mediaeval houses of the same materials that I fairly felt as if
I were alive in the fourteenth century ; a sensation helped out by
the costume of the people that we met or passed, in whose dress
there was nothing " modern." Almost everybody was gaily
dressed, but especially the women, who were so well-looking, or
even so handsome, that I could scarcely refrain my tongue from
calling my companion's attention to the fact. Some faces I saw
that were thoughtful, and in these I noticed great nobility of
expression, but none that had a glimmer of unhappiness, and the
greater part (we came upon a good many people) were frankly
and openly joyous.

I thought I knew the Broadway by the lie of the roads that still
met there. On the north side of the road was a range of buildings
and courts, low, but very handsomely built and ornamented, and
in that way forming a great contrast to the unpretentiousness of
the houses round about ; while above this lower building rose
the steep lead-covered roof and the buttresses and higher part of
the wall of a great hall, of a splendid and exuberant style of
architecture, of which one can say little more than that it seemed
to me to embrace the best qualities of the Gothic of northern
Europe with those of the Saracenic and Byzantine, though there
was no copying of any one of these styles. On the other, the south
side, of the road was an octagonal building with a high roof, not
unlike the Baptistry at Florence in outline, except that it was
surrounded by a lean-to that clearly made an arcade or cloisters
to it : it also was most delicately ornamented.

This whole mass of architecture which we had come upon so
suddenly from amidst the pleasant fields was not only exquisitely
beautiful in itself, but it bore upon it the expression of such
generosity and abundance of life that I was exhilarated to a pitch
that I had never yet reached. I fairly chuckled for pleasure.
My friend seemed to understand it, and sat looking on me with
a pleased and affectionate interest. We had pulled up amongst
a crowd of carts, wherein sat handsome healthy-looking people,
men, women and children very gaily dressed, and which were
clearly market carts, as they were full of very tempting-looking
country produce.

I said, " I need not ask if this is a market, for I see clearly that it is ; but what market is it that it is so splendid? And what is the glorious hall there, and what is the building on the south side? "

" O," said he, " it is just our Hammersmith market ; and I am glad you like it so much, for we are really proud of it. Of course the hall inside is our winter Mote-House ; for in summer we mostly meet in the fields down by the river opposite Barn Elms. The building on our right hand is our theatre."

After crossing Kensington, which is now covered by a wood of oaks, chestnuts, planes and sycamores and where groups of children are camping, they reach Westminster :

Just as we came to the top of a rising ground, down a long glade of the wood on my right I caught sight of a stately building whose outline was familiar to me, and I cried out, " Westminster Abbey! "

" Yes," said Dick, " Westminster Abbey—what there is left of it."

" Why, what have you done with it? " quoth I in terror.

" What have *we* done with it? " said he ; " nothing much, save clean it. But you know the whole outside was spoiled centuries ago; as to the inside, that remains in its beauty after the great clearance, which took place over a hundred years ago, of the beastly monuments to fools and knaves, which once blocked it up, as great-grandfather says."

We went on a little further, and I looked to the right again, and said, in rather a doubtful tone of voice, " Why, there are the Houses of Parliament! Do you still use them?"

He burst out laughing, and was some time before he could control himself ; then he clapped me on the back and said :

" I take you, neighbour ; you may well wonder at our keeping them standing, and I know something about that, and my old kinsman has given me books to read about the strange game that they played there. Use them! Well, yes, they are used for a sort of subsidiary market, and a storage place for manure, and they are handy for that, being on the water-side. I believe it was intended to pull them down quite at the beginning of our days ; but there was, I am told, a queer antiquarian society, which had done some service in past times, and which straightway set up its pipe against their destruction, as it has done with many other buildings, which most people looked upon as worthless, and public nuisances ; and it was so energetic, and had such good reasons to give, that it generally gained its point ; and I

must say that when all is said I am glad of it : because you
know at the worst these silly old buildings serve as a kind of foil
to the beautiful ones which we build now.

The wonder of the man " from the other world " increases as
they reach Piccadilly, which is still an elegant shopping centre
where crowds like to gather, but where the shops are run by
children and no money is asked in exchange for goods :

By this time we were within the shop or booth, which had a
counter, and shelves on the walls, all very neat, though without
any pretence of showiness, but otherwise not very different to
what I had been used to. Within were a couple of children—a
brown-skinned boy of about twelve, who sat reading a book,
and a pretty little girl of about a year older, who was also sitting
reading behind the counter ; they were obviously brother and
sister.

" Good morning, little neighbours," said Dick. " My friend
here wants tobacco and a pipe ; can you help him? " . . .

" Dear neighbour," said the girl, with the most solemn
countenance of a child playing at keeping shop, " what tobacco
is it you would like ? "

" Latakia," quoth I, feeling as if I were assisting at a child's
game, and wondering whether I should get anything but
make-believe.

But the girl took a dainty little basket from a shelf beside her,
went to a jar, and took out a lot of tobacco and put the filled
basket down on the counter before me, where I could both smell
and see that it was excellent Latakia.

" But you haven't weighed it," said I, " and—and how much
am I to take? "

" Why," she said, " I advise you to cram your bag, because
you may be going where you can't get Latakia. Where is your
bag?" . . . .

Therewith she fell to cramming it with the tobacco, and laid
it down by me and said, " Now for the pipe : there are three
pretty ones just come in."

She disappeared again, and came back with a big-bowled pipe
in her hand, carved out of some hard wood very elaborately,
and mounted in gold sprinkled with little gems. It was, in short,
as pretty and gay a toy as I had ever seen ; something like the
best kind of Japanese work, but better.

" Dear me!" said I, when I set eyes on it, " this is altogether
too grand for me, or for anybody but the Emperor of the World.
Besides, I shall lose it : I always lose my pipes."

The child seemed rather dashed, and said, " Don't you like it, neighbour? "

" O yes," I said, " of course I like it."

" Well, then, take it," said she, and don't trouble about losing it. What will it matter if you do? Somebody is sure to find it, and he will use it, and you can get another."

I took it out of her hand to look at it, and while I did so, forgot my caution, and said, " But however am I to pay for such a thing as this? "

Dick laid his hand on my shoulder as I spoke, and turning I met his eyes with a comical expression in them, which warned me against another exhibition of extinct commercial morality ; so I reddened and held my tongue, while the girl simply looked at me with the deepest gravity, as if I were a foreigner blundering in my speech, for she clearly didn't understand me a bit...

I asked if children generally waited on people in the markets. " Often enough," said he, " when it isn't a matter of dealing with heavy weights, but by no means always. The children like to amuse themselves with it, and it is good for them, because they handle a lot of diverse wares and get to learn about them, how they are made, and where they come from, and so on   Besides, it is such very easy work that anybody can do it. It is said that in the early days of our epoch there were a good many people who were hereditarily afflicted with a disease called Idleness, because they were the direct descendants of those who in the bad times used to force other people to work for them— the people, you know, who are called slave-holders or employers of labour in the history books. Well, these Idleness-stricken people used to serve booths *all* their time, because they were fit for so little. Indeed, I believe that at one time they were actually *compelled* to do some such work, because they, especially the women, got so ugly and produced such ugly children if their disease was not treated sharply, that the neighbours couldn't stand it. However, I'm happy to say that all that is gone by now ; the disease is either extinct, or exists in such a mild form that a short course of aperient medicine carries it off. It is sometimes called the Blue-devils now, or the Mulleygrubs. Queer names, ain't they? "

Then they cross Trafalgar Square, which is now a large open space planted with an orchard mainly of apricot trees, " in the midst of which was a pretty gay little structure of wood, painted and gilded, that looked like a refreshment stall." Memories of Bloody Sunday assail the visitor. It was here that in 1887 a peaceful demonstration was dispersed by the police, people were bludgeoned and taken to jail ; the recollection of these incidents leads to a discussion on the behaviour of men in the nineteenth century:

" How strange to think " (said Dick) " that there have been men like ourselves, and living in this beautiful and happy country, who I suppose had feelings and affections like ourselves, who could yet do such dreadful things."

" Yes," said I, in a didactic tone : " yet after all, even those days were a great improvement on the days that had gone before them. Have you not read of the Mediaeval period, and the ferocity of its criminal laws ; and how in those days men fairly seemed to have enjoyed tormenting their fellow men?—nay, for the matter of that, they made their God a tormentor and a jailer rather than anything else."

" Yes," said Dick, " there are good books on that period also, some of which I have read. But as to the great improvement of the nineteenth century, I don't see it. After all, the Mediaeval folk acted after their conscience, as your remark about their God (which is true) shows, and they were ready to bear what they inflicted on others ; whereas the nineteenth century ones were hypocrites, and pretended to be humane, and yet went on tormenting those whom they dared to treat so by shutting them up in prison, for no reason at all, except that they were what they themselves, the prison-masters, had forced them to be. O, it's horrible to think of! "

" But perhaps," said I, " they did not know what the prisons were like."

Dick seemed roused, and even angry. " More shame for them," said he, " when you and I know it all these years afterwards. Look you, neighbour, they couldn't fail to know what a disgrace a prison is to the Commonwealth at the best, and that their prisons were a good step on towards being at the worst."

Quoth I : " But have you no prisons at all now? "

As soon as the words were out of my mouth, I felt that I had made a mistake, for Dick flushed red and frowned, and the old man looked surprised and pained ; and presently Dick said angrily, yet as if restraining himself somewhat—

" Man alive! how can you ask such a question? Have I not told you that we know what a prison means by the undoubted evidence of really trustworthy books, helped out by our own imaginations? And haven't you specially called me to notice that the people about the roads and streets look happy? and how could they look happy if they knew that their neighbours were shut up in prison, while they bore such things quietly? And if there were people in prison, you couldn't hide it from folk, like you may an occasional man-slaying ; because that isn't done of set purpose, with a lot of people backing up the slayer in cold blood, as this prison business is. Prisons, indeed! O no, no, no!"

Dick and his companion then pass in front of a factory, and, from the short description of it, one gathers that industry has been decentralised thanks to the discovery of a new power[1] :

We came by the gates of a big rambling building, in which work of some sort seemed going on. "What building is that?" said I, eagerly : for it was a pleasure amidst all these strange things to see something a little like what I was used to : "it seems to be a factory."

"Yes," he said, "I think I know what you mean, and that's what it is ; but we don't call them factories now, but Banded-workshops : that is, places where people collect who want to work together."

"I suppose," said I, "power of some sort is used there?"

"No, no," said he. "Why should people collect together to use power, when they can have it at the places where they live, or hard by, any two or three of them ; or any one, for the matter of that? No ; folk collect in these Banded-workshops to do hand-work in which working together is necessary or convenient; such work is often very pleasant. In there, for instance, they make pottery and glass,—there, you can see the tops of the furnaces. Well, of course it's handy to have fair-sized ovens and kilns and glass-pots, and a good lot of things to use them for : though of course there are a good many such places, as it would be ridiculous if a man had a liking for pot-making or glass-blowing that he should have to live in one place or be obliged to forego the work he liked."

"I see no smoke coming from the furnaces," said I.

"Smoke?" said Dick ; "why should you see smoke?"

I held my tongue, and he went on : "It's a nice place inside, though as plain as you see outside. As to the crafts, throwing the clay must be jolly work : the glass-blowing is rather a sweltering job; but some folk like it very much indeed ; and I

[1] A longer description of an ideal factory will be found in Morris's essay "A Factory as it Might Be" (in the volume of his works published by the Nonesuch Press).

don't much wonder : there is such a sense of power, when you have got deft in it, in dealing with the hot metal. It makes a lot of pleasant work," said he, smiling, "for however much care you take of such goods, break they will, one day or another, so there is always plenty to do."

The two now reach the British Museum where lives an old kinsman of Dick, who has been a custodian of the books for many years and is well versed in history. The young man leaves his guest in the company of old Hammond, while he goes out with a beautiful woman who excites both the admiration and curiosity of the visitor :

I was silent for a minute, and then I said, somewhat nervously: " Excuse me if I am rude ; but I am so much interested in Richard, since he has been so kind to me, a perfect stranger, that I should like to ask a question about him."

" Well," said old Hammond, " if he were not ' kind,' as you call it, to a perfect stranger he would be thought a strange person, and people could be apt to shun him. But ask on, ask on! Don't be shy of asking."

Said I : " That beautiful girl, is he going to be married to her? "

" Well," said he, " yes, he is. He has been married to her once already, and now I should say it is pretty clear that he will be married to her again."

" Indeed," quoth I, wondering what that meant.

" Here is the whole tale," said old Hammond ; " a short one enough ; and now I hope a happy one : they lived together two years the first time ; were both very young ; and then she got it into her head that she was in love with somebody else. So she left poor Dick ; I say *poor* Dick, because he had not found any one else. But it did not last long, only about a year, then she came to me, as she was in the habit of bringing her troubles to the old carle, and asked me how Dick was, and whether he was happy, and all the rest of it. So I saw how the land lay, and said that he was very unhappy, and not at all well ; which last at any rate was a lie. There, you can guess the rest. Clara came to have a long talk with me to-day, but Dick will serve her turn much better. Indeed, if he hadn't chanced in upon me to-day I should have had to have sent for him to-morrow."

" Dear me," said I. " Have they any children? "

" Yes," said he, " two ; they are staying with one of my daughters at present, where, indeed, Clara has mostly been. I wouldn't lose sight of her, as I felt sure they would come together again : and Dick, who is the best of good fellows, really took the matter to heart. You see, he had no other love to run to, as she had. So I managed it all ; as I have done with such-like matters before."

" Ah," said I, " no doubt you wanted to keep them out of the Divorce Court : but I suppose it often has to settle such matters."

" Then you suppose nonsense," said he. " I know that there used to be such lunatic affairs as divorce-courts but just consider; all the cases that came into them were matters of property quarrels : and I think, dear guest," said he, smiling, " that though you do come from another planet, you can see from the mere outside look of our world that quarrels about private property could not go on amongst us in our days."

Indeed, my drives from Hammersmith to Bloomsbury, and all the happy quiet life I had seen so many hints of, even apart from my shopping, would have been enough to tell me that " the sacred rights of property," as we used to think of them, were now no more. So I sat silent while the old man took up the thread of the discourse again, and said :

" Well, then, property quarrels being no longer possible, what remains in these matters that a court of law could deal with? Fancy a court for enforcing a contract of passion or sentiment! If such a thing were needed as a *reductio ad absurdum* of the enforcement of contract, such a folly would do that for us."

He was silent again a little, and then said : " You must understand once for all that we have changed these matters ; or rather, that our way of looking at them has changed, as we have changed within the last two hundred years. We do not deceive ourselves, indeed, or believe that we can get rid of all the trouble that besets the dealings between the sexes. We know that we must face unhappiness that comes of men and women confusing the relations between natural passion, and sentiment, and the friendship which, when things go well, softens the awakening from passing illusions: but we are not so mad as to pile up degradation on that unhappiness by engaging in sordid squabbles about livelihood and position, and the power of tyrannising over the children who have been the results of love or lust. . . .

" You did not seem shocked when I told you that there were no law-courts to enforce contracts of sentiment or passion ; but so curiously are men made, that perhaps you will be shocked when I tell you that there is no code of public opinion which takes the place of such courts, and which might be as tyrannical and unreasonable as they were. I do not say that people don't judge their neighbours' conduct, sometimes, doubtless, unfairly. But I do say that there is no unvarying conventional set of rules by which people are judged ; no bed of Procrustes to stretch or cramp their minds and lives ; no hyprocritical excommunication which people are *forced* to pronounce, either by unconsidered habit, or by the unexpressed threat of the lesser interdict if they are lax in their hypocrisy. Are you shocked now? "

" N—o—no," said I, with some hesitation. " It is all so different."

" William Guest " then asks the old man what is the position of women in the new society :

He laughed very heartily for a man of his years, and said : " It is not without reason that I have got a reputation as a careful student of history. I believe I really do understand ' the Emancipation of Women movement ' of the nineteenth century. I doubt if any other man now alive does."

" Well?" said I, a little bit nettled by his merriment.

" Well," said he, " of course you will see that all that is a dead controversy now. The men have no longer any opportunity of tyrannising over the women, or the women over the men ; both of which things took place in those old times. The women do what they can do best, and what they like best, and the men are neither jealous of it or injured by it. This is such a commonplace that I am almost ashamed to state it."

I said : " O ; and legislation? do they take any part in that?"

Hammond smiled and said : " I think you may wait for an answer to that question till we get on to the subject of legislation. There may be novelties to you in that subject also."

" Very well," I said ; " but about this woman question? I saw at the Guest House that the women were waiting on the men : that seems a little like reaction, doesn't it? "

" Does it ? " said the old man ; " perhaps you think house-keeping an unimportant occupation, not deserving of respect. I believe that was the opinion of the ' advanced ' women of the nineteenth century, and their male backers. If it is yours, I recommend to you an old Norwegian folk-lore tale called How the Man minded the House, or some such title; the result of which minding was that, after various tribulations, the man and the family cow balanced each other at the end of a rope, the man hanging half-way up the chimney, the cow dangling from the roof, which, after the fashion of the country, was of turf and sloping down low to the ground. Hard on the cow, *I* think. Of course no such mishap could happen to such a superior person as yourself," he added, chuckling.

The visitor then wants to know what are the new ideas on education. He has already questioned Dick, who has given some curious answers and does not seem to know the meaning of the word school. " School? " Dick said, " yes, what do you mean by that word? I don't see how it can have anything to do with children. We talk indeed, of a school of herring, and of a school of painting, and in the former sense we might talk of a school of children—but otherwise I must own myself beaten." When he tried to explain that he used the word in the sense of a system of education, the young man did not understand him any better : " Education? " he said, " I know enough Latin to know that the word must come from *educere*, to lead out, and I have heard it used ; but I have never met anybody who could give me a clear explanation of what it means." He then went on to say that children learn " whether they go through a system of teaching or not." They learn things which require skill, such as cooking, carpentering, or keeping shop. As for book learning, " most children, seeing books lying about, manage to read by the time they are four years old," but they are not encouraged to scrawl too early because it gets them into a habit of ugly writing. From this conversation the visitor concluded that children were left to run wild and were taught nothing. "In short," he tells the old man, "you have so refined your education, that now you have none."

" Then you gathered left-handed," quoth he. "But of course I understand your point of view about education, which is that of times past, when ' the struggle for life,' as men used to phrase it (i.e., the struggle for a slave's rations on one side, and for a bouncing share of the slaveholders' privilege on the other), pinched ' education ' for most people into a niggardly dole of not very accurate information ; something to be swallowed by the beginner in the art of living whether he liked it or not, and was hungry for it or not : and which had been chewed and digested over and over again by people who didn't care about it in order to serve it out to other people who didn't care about it."

I stopped the old man's rising wrath by a laugh, and said : " Well, *you* were not taught that way, at any rate, so you may let your anger run off you a little."

"True, true," said he, smiling. " I thank you for correcting my ill-temper : I always fancy myself as living in any period of which we may be speaking. But, however, to put it in a cooler way : you expected to see children thrust into schools when they had reached an age conventionally supposed to be the due age, whatever their varying faculties and dispositions might be, and when there, with like disregard to facts, to be subjected to a certain conventional course of ' learning.' My friend, can't you see that such a proceeding means ignoring the fact of *growth*, bodily and mental ? No one could come out of such a mill uninjured ; and those only would avoid being crushed by it who would have the spirit of rebellion strong in them. Fortunately most children have had that at all times, or I do not know that we should ever have reached our present position. Now you see what it all comes to. In the old times all this was the result of *poverty*. In the nineteenth century, society was so miserably poor, owing to the systematised robbery on which it was founded, that real education was impossible for anybody. The whole theory of their so-called education was that it was necessary to shove a little information into a child, even if it were by means of torture and accompanied by twaddle which it was well known was of no use, or else he would lack information lifelong : the hurry of poverty forbade anything else. All that is past; we are no longer hurried, and the information lies ready to each one's hand when his own inclinations impel him to seek it. In this as in other matters we have become wealthy : we can afford to give ourselves time to grow."

" Yes," said I, " but suppose the child, youth, man, never wants the information, never grows in the direction you might hope him to do; suppose, for instance, he objects to learning arithmetic or mathematics ; you can't force him when he *is* grown ; can't you force him while he is growing, and oughtn't you to do so? "

" Well, " said he, " were you forced to learn arithmetic and mathematics? "

" A little," said I.

" And how old are you now ? "

" Say fifty-six," said I.

" And how much arithmetic and mathematics do you know now? " quoth the old man, smiling rather mockingly.

Said I : " None whatever, I am sorry to say."

Hammond laughed quietly, but made no other comment on my admission, and I dropped the subject of education, perceiving him to be hopeless on that side.[1]

[1]Of William Morris's ideas on education, Ethel Mannin, in *Bread and Roses*, remarks : " Everything which Morris wrote of the futility of enforced school-subjects could have been written by A. S. Neill to-day."

The guest then expresses his surprise at having heard him speak of households : " That sounded to me a little like the customs of past times : I should have thought you would have lived more in public."

" Phalangsteries, eh? " said he. " Well, we live as we like, and we like to live as a rule with certain house-mates that we have got used to. Remember, again, that poverty is extinct, and that the Fourierist phalangsteries and all their kind, as was but natural at the time, implied nothing but a refuge from mere destitution. Such a way of life as that, could only have been conceived by people surrounded by the worst form of poverty. But you must understand therewith, that though separate households are the rule amongst us, and though they differ in their habits more or less, yet no door is shut to any good-tempered person who is content to live as the other house-mates do: only of course it would be unreasonable for one man to drop into a household and bid the folk of it to alter their habits to please him, since he can go elsewhere and live as he pleases."

After having heard the old man describe the new London, where slums have been demolished and covered with meadows or have been replaced by beautiful houses surrounded by gardens, the visitor wants to know about the other towns. To this Hammond replies :

" As to the big murky places which were once, as we know, the centres of manufacture, they have, like the brick and mortar desert of London, disappeared ; only, since they were centres of nothing but ' manufacture,' and served no purpose but that of the gambling market, they have left less signs of their existence than London. Of course, the great change in the use of mechanical force made this an easy matter, and some approach to their break-up as centres would probably have taken place, even if we had not changed our habits so much : but they being such as they were, no sacrifice would have seemed too great a price to pay for getting rid of the ' manufacturing districts,' as they used to be called. For the rest, whatever coal or mineral we need is brought to grass and sent whither it is needed with as little as possible of dirt, confusion, and the distressing of quiet people's lives...

"There has been but little clearance, though much rebuilding, in the smaller towns. Their suburbs, indeed, when they had any, have melted away into the general country, and space

and elbow-room has been got in their centres : but there are
the towns still with their streets and squares and market-places :
so that it is by means of these smaller towns that we of to-day
can get some kind of idea of what the towns of the older world
were like ;—I mean to say at their best...

"This is how we stand. England was once a country of
clearings amongst the woods and wastes, with a few towns
interspersed, which were fortresses for the feudal army, markets
for the folk, gathering places for the craftsmen. It then became
a country of huge and foul workshops and fouler gambling-dens,
surrounded by an ill-kept, poverty-stricken farm, pillaged by the
masters of the workshops. It is now a garden, where nothing is
wasted and nothing is spoilt, with the necessary dwellings, sheds,
and workshops scattered up and down the country, all trim and
neat and pretty."

Said I : ' That side of your change is certainly for the better.
But though I shall soon see some of these villages, tell me in a
word or two what they are like, just to prepare me."

"Perhaps," said he, "you have seen a tolerable picture of
these villages as they were before the end of the nineteenth
century. Such things exist."

"I have seen several of such pictures," said I.

"Well," said Hammond, "our villages are something like the
best of such places, with the church or mote-house of the
neighbours for their chief building. Only note that there are no
tokens of poverty about them : no tumble-down picturesque ;
which, to tell you the truth, the artist usually availed himself of
to veil his incapacity for drawing architecture. Such things do
not please us, even when they indicate no misery. Like the
mediaevals, we like everything trim and clean, and orderly and
bright ; as people always do when they have any sense of
architectural power ; because then they know that they can have
what they want, and they won't stand any nonsense from Nature
in their dealings with her."

"Besides the villages, are there any scattered country houses?"
said I.

"Yes, plenty," said Hammond ; "in fact, except in the wastes
and forests and amongst the sand-hills (like Hindhead in Surrey),
it is not easy to be out of sight of a house ; and where the houses
are thinly scattered they run large, and are more like the old
colleges than ordinary houses as they used to be. That is done for
the sake of society, for a good many people can dwell in such
houses, as the country dwellers are not necessarily husbandmen;
though they almost all help in such work at times. The life that

goes on in these big dwellings in the country is very pleasant, especially as some of the most studious men of our time live in them, and altogether there is a great variety of mind and mood to be found in them which brightens and quickens the society there."

" I am rather surprised," said I, " by all this, for it seems to me that after all the country must be tolerably populous."

" Certainly," said he ; " the population is pretty much the same as it was at the end of the nineteenth century ; we have spread it, that is all. Of course, also, we have helped to populate other countries—where we were wanted and were called for."

Even greater changes have taken place in the administration of the country, for Government has disappeared altogether.

" Now," said I, " I have come to the point of asking questions which I suppose will be dry for you to answer and difficult for you to explain ; but I have foreseen for some time past that I must ask them, will I 'nill I. What kind of a government have you? Has republicanism finally triumphed? or have you come to a mere dictatorship, which some persons in the nineteeenth century used to prophesy as the ultimate outcome of democracy? Indeed, this last question does not seem so very unreasonable, since you have turned your Parliament House into a dung-market. Or where do you house your present Parliament? "

The old man answered my smile with a hearty laugh, and said: " Well, well, dung is not the worst kind of corruption ; fertility may come of that, whereas mere dearth came from the other kind, of which those walls once held the great supporters. Now, dear guest, let me tell you that our present parliament would be hard to house in one place, because the whole people is our parliament."

" I don't understand," said I.

" No, I suppose not," said he. " I must shock you by telling you that we have no longer anything which you, a native of another planet, would call a government."

" I am not so much shocked as you might think," said I, "as I know something about governments. But tell me, how can you manage, and how have you come to this state of things? "

Said he : " It is true that we have to make some arrangements about our affairs, concerning which you can ask presently ; and it is also true that everybody does not always agree with the details of these arrangements : but, further, it is true that a man no more needs an elaborate system of government, with its army, navy, and police, to force him to give way to the will of the

majority of his *equals*, than he wants a similar machinery to make
him understand that his head and a stone wall cannot occupy the
same space at the same moment."

With the abolition of property and government people have
developed a new attitude towards their fellow-beings. Strife and
robbery are unknown and good fellowship has become a habit.
This does not mean, however, that there are not occasional
transgressions :

"But," said Hammond, "when the transgressions occur,
everybody, transgressors and all, know them for what they are:
the errors of friends, not the habitual actions of persons driven
into enmity against society."

"I see," said I; "you mean that you have no 'criminal' classes."

"How could we have them," said he, "since there is no rich
class to breed enemies against the state by means of the injustice
of the state?"

Said I : "I thought that I understood from something that fell
from you a little while ago that you had abolished civil law. Is
that so, literally? "

"It abolished itself, my friend," said he. "As I said before,
the civil law-courts were upheld for the defence of private
property ; for nobody ever pretended that it was possible to
make people act fairly to each other by means of brute force.
Well, private property being abolished, all the laws and all the
legal ' crimes ' which it had manufactured of course came to an
end. Thou shalt not steal, had to be translated into, Thou shalt
work in order to live happily. Is there any need to enforce that
commandment by violence? "

"Well," said I, "that is understood, and I agree with it ;
but how about crimes of violence? would not their occurrence
(and you admit that they occur) make criminal law necessary?"

Said he : "In your sense of the word, we have no criminal law
either. Let us look at the matter closer, and see whence crimes of
violence spring. By far the greater part of these in past days were
the result of the laws of private property, which forbade the
satisfaction of their natural desires to all but a privileged few,
and of the general visible coercion which came of those laws.
All *that* cause of violent crime is gone. Again, many violent acts
came from the artificial perversion of the sexual passions, which
caused over-weening jealousy and the like miseries. Now, when
you look carefully into these, you will find that what lay at the
bottom of them was mostly the idea (a law-made idea) of the

woman being the property of the man, whether he were husband, father, brother, or what not. *That* idea has of course vanished with private property, as well as certain follies about the ' ruin ' of women for following their natural desires in an illegal way, which of course was a convention caused by the laws of private property.

" Another cognate cause of crimes of violence was the family tyranny, which was the subject of so many novels and stories of the past, and which once more was the result of private property. Of course that is all ended, since families are held together by no bond of coercion, legal or social, but by mutual liking and affection, and everybody is free to come and go as he or she pleases. Furthermore, our standards of honour and public estimation are very different from the old ones ; success in besting our neighbours is a road to renown now closed, let us hope for ever. Each man is free to exercise his special faculty to the utmost, and every one encourages him in so doing. So that we have got rid of the scowling envy, coupled by the poets with hatred, and surely with good reason ; heaps of unhappiness and ill-blood were caused by it, which with irritable and passionate men—i.e., energetic and active, men—often led to violence."

I laughed, and said : " So that you now withdraw your admission, and say that there is no violence amongst you? "

" No," said he, " I withdraw nothing ; as I told you, such things will happen. Hot blood will err sometimes. A man may strike another, and the stricken strike back again, and the result be a homicide, to put it at the worst. But what then? Shall we the neighbours make it worse still? Shall we think so poorly of each other as to suppose that the slain man calls on us to revenge him, when we *know* that if he had been maimed, he would, when in cold blood and able to weigh all the circumstances, have forgiven his maimer? Or will the death of the slayer bring the slain man to life again and cure the unhappiness his loss has caused? "

" Yes," I said, " but consider, must not the safety of society be safeguarded by some punishment? "

" There, neighbour!" said the old man, with some exultation. " You have hit the mark. That *punishment* of which men used to talk so wisely and act so foolishly, what was it but the expression of their fear? And they had need to fear, since *they*—i.e., the rulers of society—were dwelling like an armed band in a hostile country. But we who live amongst our friends need neither fear nor punish. Surely if we, in dread of an occasional rare homicide, an occasional rough blow, were solemnly and legally to commit homicide and violence, we could only be a society of ferocious cowards. Don't you think so, neighbour?"

" Yes, I do, when I come to think of it from that side," said I.

" Yet you must understand," said the old man, " that when any violence is committed, we expect the transgressor to make any atonement possible to him, and he himself expects it. But again, think if the destruction or serious injury of a man momentarily overcome by wrath or folly can be any atonement to the commonwealth? Surely it can only be an additional injury to it."

Said I : " But suppose the man has a habit of violence, kills a man a year, for instance?"

" Such a thing is unknown," said he. " In a society where there is no punishment to evade, no law to triumph over, remorse will certainly follow transgression."

" And lesser outbreaks of violence," said I, "how do you deal with them? for hitherto we have been talking of great tragedies, I suppose?"

Said Hammond : " If the ill-doer is not sick or mad (in which case he must be restrained till his sickness or madness is cured) it is clear that grief and humiliation must follow the ill-deed ; and society in general will make that pretty clear to the ill-doer if he should chance to be dull to it ; and again, some kind of atonement will follow,—at the least, an open acknowledgment of the grief and humiliation. Is it so hard to say, I ask your pardon, neighbour?—Well, sometimes it is hard—and let it be."

" You think that enough?" said I.

" Yes," said he, " and moreover it is all that we *can* do. If in addition we torture the man, we turn his grief into anger, and the humiliation he would otherwise feel for *his* wrong-doing is swallowed up by a hope of revenge for *our* wrong-doing to him. He has paid the legal penalty, and can ' go and sin again ' with comfort. Shall we commit such a folly, then? Remember Jesus had got the legal penalty remitted before he said ' Go and sin no more.' Let alone that in a society of equals you will not find any one to play the part of torturer or jailer, though many to act as nurse or doctor."

" So," said I, "you consider crime a mere spasmodic disease, which requires no body of criminal law to deal with it?"

" Pretty much so," said he ; "and since, as I have told you, we are a healthy people generally, so we are not likely to be much troubled with *this* disease."

All the countries of the world enjoy the same freedom and equality as England, and rivalries between nations and wars exist

no longer. Within the community there are no political parties,
and if differences of opinion exist they are differences about real,
solid things which " need not, and with us do not," says
Hammond, " crystallise people into parties permanently hostile
to one another, with different theories as to the build of the
Universe and the progress of time... Amongst us, our differences
concern matters of business, and passing events as to them, and
could not divide men permanently."

Said I : " And you settle these differences, great and small, by
the will of the majority, I suppose?"

" Certainly," said he ; " how else could we settle them? You
see in matters which are merely personal which do not affect the
welfare of the community—how shall a man dress, what he shall
eat and drink, what he shall write and read, and so forth—there
can be no difference of opinion, and everybody does as he pleases.
But when the matter is of common interest to the whole community, and the doing or not doing sometimes affects everybody,
the majority must have their way ; unless the minority were to
take up arms and show by force that they were the effective or
real majority ; which, however, in a society of men who are free
and equal is little likely to happen ; because in such a community
the apparent majority *is* the real majority, and the others, as I
have hinted before, know that too well to obstruct from mere
pig-headedness ; especially as they have had plenty of
opportunity of putting forward their side of the question."

" How is that managed?" said I.

" Well," said he, " let us take one of our units of management,
a commune, or a ward, or a parish (for we have all three names,
indicating little real distinction between them now, though time
was there was a good deal). In such a district, as you would
call it, some neighbours think that something ought to be done or
undone : a new town-hall built ; a clearance of inconvenient
houses ; or say a stone bridge substituted for some ugly old iron
one,—there you have undoing and doing in one. Well, at the
next ordinary meeting of the neighbours, or Mote, as we call it,
according to the ancient tongue of the times before bureaucracy,
a neighbour proposes the change, and of course, if everybody
agrees, there is an end of discussion, except about details.
Equally, if no one backs the proposer,—' seconds him,' it used
to be called—the matter drops for the time being ; a thing not
likely to happen amongst reasonable men, however, as the
proposer is sure to have talked it over with others before the Mote.
But supposing the affair proposed and seconded, if a few of the

neighbours disagree to it, if they think that the beastly iron bridge will serve a little longer and they don't want to be bothered with building a new one just then, they don't count heads that time, but put off the formal discussion to the next Mote ; and meantime arguments *pro* and *con* are flying about, and some get printed, so that everybody knows what is going on ; and when the Mote comes together again there is a regular discussion and at last a vote by show of hands. If the division is a close one, the question is again put off for further discussion ; if the division is a wide one, the minority are asked if they will yield to the more general opinion, which they often, nay, most commonly do. If they refuse, the question is debated a third time, when, if the minority has not perceptibly grown, they always give way ; though I believe there is some half-forgotten rule by which they might carry it on further ; but I say, what always happens is that they are convinced, not perhaps that their view is the wrong one, but they cannot persuade or force the community to adopt it."

" Very good," said I ; " but what happens if the divisions are still narrow?"

Said he : " As a matter of principle and according to the rule of such cases, the question must then lapse, and the majority, if so narrow, has to submit to sitting down under the *status quo*. But I must tell you that in point of fact the minority very seldom enforces this rule, but generally yields in a friendly manner."

In the new society work has ceased to be a penance and has become, on the contrary, a pleasurable activity. Even for especially good work there are no rewards in the sense of material gain or increase in authority. The only reward is that of creation, and, says the old man, " if you are going to ask to be paid for the pleasure of creation, which is what excellence in work means, the next thing we shall hear of will be a bill sent in for the begetting of children." The use of incentives to get people to work " implies that all work is suffering, and we are so far from thinking that, that there is a kind of fear growing amongst us that we shall one day be short of work. It is a pleasure which we are afraid of losing, not a pain."

Labour which, in itself, is not pleasant has also become pleasurable because of the knowledge that it is useful. In the old society, when people were chiefly engaged in producing unnecessary goods, labour has become " the ceaseless endeavour to expend the least possible amount of labour on any article made,

and yet at the same time to make as many articles as possible."
To get rid of these goods new wants had to be created artificially,
and new markets had to be opened in "uncivilised" countries.
In the new society man does not produce useless goods for the
profit of some capitalist but only what is really needed by the
community. As in the cities of the Middle Ages, there is an
intimate relation between producer and consumer :

" The wares which we make are made because they are needed:
men make for their neighbours' use as if they were making for
themselves, not for a vague market of which they know nothing,
and over which they have no control : as there is no buying and
selling, it would be mere insanity to make goods on the chance
of their being wanted ; for there is no longer anyone who can be
compelled to buy them. So that whatever is made is good, and
thoroughly fit for its purpose. Nothing *can* be made except for
genuine use ; therefore no inferior goods are made. Moreover,
as aforesaid, we have now found out what we want, so we make no
more than we want; and as we are not driven to make a vast
quantity of useless things, we have time and resources enough to
consider our pleasure in making them. All work which would be
irksome to do by hand is done by immensely improved machinery;
and in all work which it is a pleasure to do by hand machinery is
done without. There is no difficulty in finding work which suits
the special turn of mind of everybody ; so that no man is
sacrificed to the wants of another. From time to time, when we
have found out that some piece of work was too disagreeable or
troublesome, we have given it up and done altogether without the
thing produced by it. Now, surely you can see that under these
circumstances all the work that we do is an exercise of the mind
and body more or less pleasant to be done : so that instead of
avoiding work everybody seeks it : and, since people have got
defter in doing the work generation after generation, it has
become so easy to do, that it seems as if there were less done,
though probably more is produced."

A truly happy people do not need to believe in a happier life
after death or to find solace in the love of God. The Christian
religion has been replaced by the religion of humanity, and men
love their fellows not out of duty, but because they are worthy of
their love :

" The belief in heaven and hell as two countries in which to
live, has gone, and now we do, both in word and in deed, believe

in the continuous life of the world of men, and as it were, add every day of that common life to the little stock of days which our own mere individual experience wins for us : and consequently we are happy. Do you wonder at it? In times past, indeed, men were told to love their kind, to believe in the religion of humanity, and so forth. But look you, just in the degree that a man had elevation of mind and refinement enough to be able to value this idea, was he repelled by the obvious aspect of the individuals composing the mass which he was to worship ; and he could only evade that repulsion by making a conventional abstraction of mankind that had little actual or historical relation to the race ; which to his eyes was divided into blind tyrants on the one hand and apathetic degraded slaves on the other. But now, where is the difficulty in accepting the religion of humanity, when the men and women who go to make up humanity are free, happy, and energetic at least, and most commonly beautiful of body also, and surrounded by beautiful things of their own fashioning, and a nature bettered and not worsened by contact with mankind?"

EUGENE RICHTER
Pictures of the Socialistic Future

WHEN Eugene Richter's *Pictures of the Socialistic Future* appeared in Germany, in the early eighteen-nineties, the socialist plans for the future society had more than an academic interest. The strength of the Socialist movement led many to believe that the socialist utopia would soon become a reality. This accounts for the bitterness which underlines the satire of Eugene Richter, the leader of the Liberal Party in the German Reichstag. It may also account for the success of this little book, which sold in hundreds of thousands in a few months, and was immediately translated into English.

Although the weakness of the Socialist movement in England prevented it from being considered as a serious menace either by the Liberals or the Conservatives, they must have viewed with considerable alarm the popularity which the socialist utopias had been enjoying, and the Press gave a warm welcome to Richter's book. The *National Observer* declared : " It deserves to be read by every working man with a stiver to lose, as also by many well-meaning busybodies that rank considerably higher," and the *Sydney Morning Herald* : " This will be a counter-irritant to the Bellamy remedies for Society, for it depicts the miseries of the socialistic régime and its final overthrow." While the *Spectator* more soberly stated " . . . there could be no other end to Socialism than that which he sets forth."

In view of these Press notices, it is hardly necessary to remark that Eugene Richter's satire on socialism itself is unfair, but as a satire on the utopian schemes based on state socialism which were mass produced during the nineteenth century, it stands on more solid ground. As a Liberal, Richter condemns the blind faith in the all-embracing wisdom of a Socialist State and its vast bureaucratic machinery, he asserts the right of the individual to select his own job, to eat and dress as he pleases, to leave the country if he chooses. He ridicules the idea that men can be free when all production and distribution are in the hands of the State, for who can prevent the State from directing discontented workers to unpleasant occupations or even starving them, who can prevent it from setting up a gigantic army and police to maintain " law and order "? How can there be freedom of the Press when the supplies of paper and all the printing works are in the hands of the government, and how can elections be free when there is no guarantee that the authorities will respect the secrecy of the vote? The experience of state socialism has shown that these abuses of power on the part of socialist (or communist) governments are possible—some will even say inevitable—but it can be objected, of course, that under a truly socialist régime men cannot behave in a selfish or dishonest manner as they do under capitalism. Richter, however, did not criticise an ideal society such as William Morris described (though he cannot have approved of it) where men can have a different attitude to work because they are free and know that they work for themselves and not to keep an army of bureaucrats, policemen and soldiers ; instead, he criticised a society where the authority of the capitalist state has been replaced by that of a socialist state, where people are obliged to obey the laws, made by a political party, and which are more tyrannical than the old ones. Under such a system there is nothing which can lead one to assume that the mental and moral outlook of men will change for the better instead of for the worse. Richter's polemical work naturally assumes that it would change for the worse, and he describes what would happen to Germany if the Socialist revolution were to take place, in the form of a diary by an enthusiastic socialist worker, who keeps his faith in his Party intact, until he is demoralised by personal tragedy and the general discontent around him, and eventually falls a victim to the counter-revolution.

CELEBRATION DAY

The red flag of international Socialism waves from the palace and from all the public buildings of Berlin. If our immortal Bebel could but have lived to see this! He always used to tell the bourgeoisie that " the catastrophe was almost at their very doors." Friedrich Engels had fixed 1898 as the year of the ultimate triumph of socialistic ideas. Well, it did not come quite so soon, but it has not taken much longer.

THE NEW LAWS

The *Onward*, which has hitherto been the leading organ of our party, now takes the place of the old *Imperial Advertiser*, and it is delivered at every house free of cost. All printing establishments having now become the property of the State, all the other papers have, as a matter of course, ceased to appear. In all other towns a local edition of the *Onward* is issued with a sheet of local matter for each separate place. Provisionally, and until such time as a new Parliament shall have been elected, the conduct of affairs is in the hands of the socialistic members of the late Parliament, who, in the shape of a Committee of Government, have to decide on those numerous laws it will be necessary to enact in order to establish the new era.

The old party programme which was settled upon at the Erfurt Conference in 1891, has been promulgated as an outline of the fundamental rights of the people. This promulgation proclaims that all capital, property, mines and quarries, machinery, means of communication, and all possessions whatever, have henceforth become the sole property of the State, or as it is now better called, the Community. Another decree sets forth the universal obligation there is on all persons to work; and all such persons, whether male or female, from the age of 21 to 65 years, are to enjoy precisely the same rights. Those who are below 21 years of age will be educated at the expense of the State, whilst those who are above 65 will be maintained in a similar manner. All private enterprise and productivity have, of course, ceased.

Pending, however, the new regulations as to supply, all persons are to retain their old posts, and to go on working for the State, as their master.

The new Government, thanks to the smart Chancellor at its head, proceeds with no less energy than directness of purpose. Every precaution in the first place is to be taken against any possibility of capital ever regaining its old ascendency. The army is disbanded; no taxes will be collected, as the Government proposes to raise that which is required for public purposes out of the revenue yielded by State trade transactions.

It is quite evident that entirely new and glorious times are in store for us.

THE CHOICE OF TRADES

Big red placards on all the hoardings remind people that in accordance with the regulations of the new Labour Law, all persons of both sexes between the ages of twenty-one and sixty-five years, are required within three days to register themselves with a view to being told off to some trade. The old police stations and various other public offices come in nicely for this purpose. The attention of women and girls is especially called to the fact that on their entering upon work in one of the numerous State workshops, they are forthwith relieved from all household toil, such as taking care of children, the preparation of meals, nursing the sick, washing, etc., etc. All children and young people are to be brought up in State maintenance houses and in public schools. The chief meal of each day will be taken at the State cookshop of the district. Sick people must all be sent to the hospitals. Washing can be done solely at the great central washhouses of the State. The hours of work, for both sexes, both in trades and in State or public departments, are fixed at eight hours for the present.

ASSIGNMENT OF WORK

The union between Franz and Agnes is suddenly put off indefinitely. The police have to-day distributed the orders relating to the occupations of the people, which orders are based partly upon the registration lately made, and partly upon the plan organised by the Government for regulating production and consumption.

True, Franz is to remain a compositor, but, unfortunately, he can't stay in Berlin, but is sent to Leipsig. Berlin requires now hardly one-twentieth part of the number of compositors it formerly employed. None but absolutely reliable Socialists are allowed on the *Onward*. Now Franz, through some unguarded expressions in Palace Square over that unfortunate savings bank business, is regarded with some suspicion. Franz will have it, too, that politics have had something to do with the assignment of labour ; and he says, for instance, that in Berlin the Younkers have been completely scattered as a party. One had to go as a paperhanger to Inowrazlaw because there was a scarcity of paperhangers there, whereas in Berlin there are too many. Franz quite lost all patience, and said it seemed to him that the old law against the Socialists, with its expatriation, had come to life again. Well, we must excuse a little haste in an engaged young man who sees himself suddenly, and for an indefinite period, cut off from the girl of his heart.

I tried to offer Franz a little comfort by remarking that in the very next house a married couple had been separated by the action of this law. The wife goes to Oppeln in the capacity of nurse, the husband to Magdeburg as a bookkeeper. This set my wife going, and she wanted to know how anyone dared to separate husband and wife? It was infamous, and so on. The good soul entirely forgot that in our new community marriage is a purely private relationship, as Bebel lucidly explained in his book on woman. The marriage knot can at any time, and without the intervention of any official whatever, be tied and again untied. The Government is hence not at all in a position to know who is married, and who is not. In the registries of names we find, therefore, as might be logically expected, that all persons are entered in their Christian names, and the maiden names of their mothers. In a well-considered organisation of production and consumption, the living together of married couples is clearly only practicable where the scale of occupation allows of such an arrangement ; not *vice versa*. It would never do to make the organisation of labour in any way dependent upon a private relationship which might be dissolved at any moment.

In order to pacify them somewhat, I read to them out of the *Onward* a statement in tabular form dealing with the selections of trades people had made, and with the labour assignments to them. A greater number of persons had registered themselves as gamekeepers than there are hares within forty miles' circumference of Berlin. From the number of entries made the Government would have no difficulty in posting a hall-porter at every single door in Berlin : every tree could have its forester, every horse its groom. There are a great many more nurse-girls than kitchen-maids registered ; more coachmen than ostlers. The number of young women who have put their names down as

waitresses and public singers is very considerable, but this super-
abundance is balanced by the paucity of those who desire to
become sick-nurses. There is no lack of salesmen and saleswomen. The same remark applies to inspectors, managers,
foremen, and similar positions ; there is even no scarcity of
acrobats. The entries for the more arduous labours of the pavior,
the stoker, the smelter are more sparse. Those who have
manifested a desire to become cleansers of sewers are, numerically
not a strong body.

Under these circumstances, what has the Government to do in
order to bring their scheme for organising production and
consumption into some sort of harmony with the entries made by
the people?

For the present no other plan seemed feasible than that of a
lottery. The entries for each trade were set apart by themselves,
and from these entries the appointments required for each branch
of trade by the Government organisation scheme were settled by
a simple drawing of lots. Those who drew blanks in the first
lottery cast lots again and again until they got a trade ; and in
this way the vacancies were filled up in these branches of labour
for which there had been a scarcity of applicants. I understand
that a kind of labour they do not at all relish, has, in this way,
fallen to the lot of a good many people.

Franz says there always have been horse-raffles and dog-raffles
and all kinds of raffles, but this is the first time that man-raffles
have taken place.

NEWS FROM THE PROVINCES

All young men of the age of twenty are required to enrol
themselves within three days. The " National Bulwark," as it
is called, is to be organised and armed with all speed . . .

The internal affairs of the country render it necessary that the
National Bulwark should be called out earlier than had been
intended, and also that the organisation be on a far larger scale
than had been at first contemplated. The New Provincial
Councillors are constantly sending urgent requests for military
assistance to aid them in the work of establishing the new laws
in country districts and in small towns. Hence, it has been
decided to establish at convenient centres all over the country,
a battalion of infantry, a squadron of cavalry, and a battery.
In order to ensure better security the troops are composed of
men chosen from districts lying far asunder.

These country boors and louts must be brought to reason.

They actually go the length of objecting to the nationalisation—
or as the official term runs, the communalisation—of their private
means, their possessions in the shape of acres, houses, cattle, farm
stock and the like. Your small owner in the country will insist on
remaining where he is, and sticking fast to what he has got, in
spite of all you can tell him of the hard lot he has from sunrise to
sunset. People of this sort could be left quietly where they are,
but then the mischief is, it would greatly interfere with the vast
scheme for the organisation of production. So there is no other
way than to compel these thick-headed people by sheer force to
see what is to their advantage. . . .

It would unquestionably have been better if those regulations
which have only just been issued had been issued at the very first.
According to these regulations no one can now temporarily leave
his place of residence without first providing himself with a leave-
of-absence ticket ; and no one can make a permanent removal
without receiving such directions from higher quarters. It is,
of course, intended that Berlin shall still remain a much-visited
capital ; but people are not to come and go in a capricious
aimless way, but only, as the *Onward* simply and clearly sets
forth, in a manner which shall accord with the carefully
prepared calculations and plans of the Government. The socialistic State or, as we now say, the Community, is in earnest
as respects the obligation on all persons alike to work ; and it,
therefore, is fully determined not to permit any vagabondism of
any kind, not even any railway vagabondism.

THE NEW DWELLINGS

The universal dwelling-house lottery has taken place, and we
are now in possession of our new home ; but I cannot exactly say
that we have bettered our position. We used to live S.W., at the
front of the house, on the third storey. Oddly enough, a dwelling
has fallen to our lot on the very same premises, only it happens to
be at the back of the house, and quite in the back-yard, in fact.
It is likewise on the third storey. My wife's disappointment is
considerable. She had given up all thought of a small villa, but
she still clung to the hope of getting a neat suite of rooms on an
elegant flat.

At the commencement of the new régime it was found, as
already stated, that in round numbers one million rooms were at
the disposal of the authorities. Of these, after deducting the
requirements of the various public institutions, some 600,000
more or less smallish rooms remain, to which, however, must be

added several hundred thousand kitchens (now become superfluous), attics, and garrets. As there are one million persons to
provide for, it is at once seen that the space allotted is about one
room per head ; and in order to observe the utmost impartiality
in the disposal of these rooms, they were assigned by lottery, each
person from the age of twenty-one to sixty-five years, irrespective
of gender, receiving a lottery ticket. And, indeed, this system of
raffling is an excellent means of regulating the principle of
equality wherever the essential features are disproportionate.
The social democrats in Berlin, even under the old régime, had
introduced this system of raffling for seats at the theatres.

THE NEW STATE COOKSHOPS

It was, indeed, a wonderful achievement that to-day, in Berlin,
one thousand State cookshops, each one capable of accommodat-
ing 1,000 persons, should have been opened at one stroke.   True,
those persons who had imagined that it would be like the *table
d'hôte* of the great hotels of the past days, where a pampered upper
class continually revelled in every refinement of culinary art—
such persons, I say, must feel some little disappointment.   As a
matter of course, we have here likewise no trim, swallow-tailed
waiters, no bills of fare a yard long, and no such paraphernalia.

In the State cookshops everything, even to the smallest details,
has been anticipated and settled beforehand.   No one person
obtains the smallest preference over others.   The picking and
choosing amongst the various State cookshops cannot, of course,
be tolerated.   Each person has the right to dine at the cookshop
of the district in which his dwelling is situated.   The chief meal
of the day is taken between 12 o'clock and 6 in the evening.
Everyone has to report himself at the cookshop of his district,
either during the mid-day rest or at the close of the day.

I am sorry to say that I can now no longer take my meals with
my wife except on Sundays, as I have been accustomed to do for
the last twenty-five years, inasmuch as our hours of labour are
now entirely different.

Upon entering the dining-room an official detaches the dinner
coupon from your book of money certificates, and hands you a
number which indicates your turn.   In the course of time others
get up and go away, and your turn comes, and you fetch your
plate of victuals from the serving tables.   The strictest order is
maintained by a strong body of police present.   The police to-
day—their number has now been augmented here to 12,000—
rather gave themselves airs of importance in the State cookshops,

but the fact is, the crowd was a very big one. It seems to me that Berlin proves itself to be on too small a scale for the vast undertakings of Socialism.

As each one takes his place as he comes from his work the groups sometimes have a somewhat motley appearance. Opposite to me to-day sat a miller, and his neighbour was a sweep. The sweep laughed at this more heartily than the miller. The room at the tables is very cramped, and the elbows at each side hinder one much. However, it is not for long, the minutes allowed for eating being very stingily measured. At the expiration of the meagrely apportioned minutes—and a policeman with a watch in his hand stands at the head of each table to see that time is strictly kept—you are remorselessly required to make room for the next.

It is an inspiring thought to reflect that in every State cookshop in Berlin on one and the same day exactly the same dishes are served. As each establishment knows how many visitors it has to count upon, and as these visitors are saved all the embarrassment of having to choose from a lengthy bill of fare, it is clear that no time is lost ; whilst there is also none of that waste and loss consequent upon a lot of stuff being left, which circumstance used so much to enhance the price of dining at the restaurants of the upper classes. Indeed, this saving may well be reckoned amongst the most signal triumphs of the socialistic organisation. .

All the portions served out are of the same size. One insatiable fellow to-day who asked for more was rightly served by being heartily laughed at ; for what more deadly blow could be levelled at one of the fundamental principles of equality? For the same reason the suggestion to serve out smaller portions to women was at once indignantly rejected. Big, bulky men have to put up with the same sized portions, and to do as best they can. But, then, for such amongst them who, in their former easy circumstances, used to stuff themselves, this drawing in of their belt is quite a good and wholesome thing.

EMIGRATION

The ministerial crisis called forth by the boot-polishing question is not yet over. Meantime, a decree has been issued against all emigration without the permission of the authorities. Socialism is founded upon the principle that it is the duty of all persons alike to labour, just as under the old régime the duty to become a soldier was a universally recognised one. And just as in the old days young men who were ripe for military service were never allowed to emigrate without authority, so can our Government similarly not permit the emigration from our shores of such persons as are of the right age to labour.. . .

Under these circumstances the Government is to be commended for stringently carrying out its measures to prevent emigration. In order to do so all the more effectually, it has been deemed expedient to send strong bodies of troops to the frontiers, and to the seaport towns. The frontiers towards Switzerland have received especial attention from the authorities. It is announced that the standing army will be increased by many battalions of infantry and squadrons of cavalry. The frontier patrols have strict instructions to unceremoniously shoot down all fugitives.

THE ELECTION STIR

The general election is at last to take place, and next Sunday is fixed as the polling day. This choice of a day of rest and leisure deserves the highest commendation, as nowadays a hundred times more issues depend upon the result of an election than was formerly the case. Laws are everything in a socialistic State; the law has to prescribe to each separate individual how long he must labour, how much he has to eat and drink, how he must be dressed, housed and what not.

The Opposition parties complain bitterly of the scarcity of persons who, when it comes to the test, have the requisite courage to boldly face the Government as opponents, either as candidates for Parliament or as speakers at election meetings. The fact that every obnoxious person may be unceremoniously told off by the Government to some other occupation, or sent away to a distant part of the country, may have something to do with this hanging back. Such sudden changes involve frequently the endurance of many unpleasantnesses and hardships, particularly to people of riper years. Of course everybody has the right to protest against a transfer which looks like mere caprice on the part of the Government. But how can an individual undertake to prove that the transfer was not a well-advised step, and not justified by other alterations elsewhere in the general labour scheme, which rendered this particular appointment necessary?

The voting takes place by means of voting-papers, which bear the official stamp, and which are handed in in sealed envelopes. But in view of the system of espionage in the hands of the Government, which penetrates into everyone's most private affairs ; in view of the publicity which everybody's life now has, and the system of control that all are subject to ; in view of these things, many persons seem to mistrust the apparent security and secrecy of the voting-papers, and not to vote according to their inmost convictions. In former times, somewhat of this sort of thing prevailed in small electoral districts. Now, however, every single individual is a spy on his neighbour.

THE RESULT OF THE ELECTIONS

Franz has proved to be right in his forecast of the results of the elections. In his last letter he expressed his belief that, in a community in which there was no longer any personal or commercial freedom, even the freest form of government would fail to restore any political independence. He considered that those subjects who are so dependent upon the Government, even in the most ordinary affairs of life, as is now the case with us, would only in very rare instances have the courage to vote, no matter how secret that voting might be, in opposition to the known wishes of those in power. The right of voting, Franz wrote, could have no more serious significance in our socialistic State of society than such a right has for soldiers in barracks, or for prisoners in gaol.

The result of the elections shows that the Government party, in spite of all the wide-spread discontent there is, has secured two-thirds of the votes recorded.

Weighed down by the load of adversity which has befallen us as a family, I relinquished my original intention of giving an adverse vote, and sided with the Government. Whatever would have become of my wife and me if, in our present frame of mind, I had been sent away to some far-off little place in the provinces?

GREAT STRIKE AND SIMULTANEOUS OUTBREAK OF WAR

All the iron-workers in Berlin and the neighbourhood came out on strike this morning, upon the refusal of their demands to receive the full reward of their labour. The Government met the strike with a prompt order to at once stop the dinners and suppers of all those on strike. In all the State cookshops the officials have the strictest instructions not to honour the coupons of the iron-workers. The same suspension of the coupons applies to all restaurants, and all shops whence, in accordance with the Government regulations, these persons in ordinary times derive their supplies. The various shops and places in question are closely watched by strong detachments of police. By these means it is hoped that those on strike will, in a very short time, be starved into submission, inasmuch as the few crumbs and parings which their wives and friends will be able to give them from their rations will be of very little avail.

There is more bad news to follow. An order has just been issued to reduce the bread rations of the entire population by one half, and to do away with the meat rations altogether. It is hoped by these measures to effect such a saving as will enable the Government to, at least to some extent, provision the frontier fortresses. For, in the meantime, the threatened distraints in Germany have actually begun to take place. From the Grand Duchy of Luxemburg, French cavalry has advanced across the German frontier...

The police force has of late been fixed at 30,000 men. None but fanatical Socialists may serve, and these are chosen from all parts of the country. The foree is also supported by strong detachments of artillery and cavalry...

Detachments of police, some on foot and some mounted, are continually hurrying with all possible speed towards the centre of the city. From all appearance the whole of the armed force available is being drawn together in the neighbourhood of the palace and unter den Linden. What will be the end of it all?

6

Modern Utopias

THE fashion for Utopian schemes so prevalent in the nineteenth century seems to be dying out. The utopias written after 1900 are mostly hang-overs from the nineteenth century, pale, or sometimes, elaborate versions of past ideal commonwealths, but bringing little that is new and causing none of the stir that the works of Cabet, Bellamy or Morris had created in their time. The two first mentioned were dull works, yet they arrested the attention of the public, for they crystallised a certain trend of social thought. No comparable impression has been made by the utopias published in the last fifty years. Anatole France's utopian sketch in *La Pierre Blanche* has been rightly ignored, as it is one of his dullest pieces of writing; Gabriel Tarde's *Underground Man* was more concerned with the discussion of philosophical ideas than the presentation of an ideal commonwealth, while Sebastien Faure's *Le Bonheur Universel* had a limited appeal as a piece of sentimental propaganda.

H. G. Wells made a more important contribution to utopian literature with *A Modern Utopia* and *Men Like Gods*, but the former is, in spite of its title, very much indebted to the utopias of the past.

In his *Modern Utopia* Wells, however, breaks with the utopian tradition by refusing to describe a perfect society : " In a modern Utopia," he says, "there will, indeed, be no perfection ; in Utopia there must also be friction, conflicts, and waste, but the waste will be enormously less than in our world." His utopia is " a state of affairs at once possible and more desirable than the world in which we live," but it will be " most distinctly impracticable by every scale that reaches only between today and to-morrow."

A Modern Utopia appeared in 1905 ; in *Men Like Gods*, published in 1923, Wells did in fact describe a society where there are no conflicts, friction or waste. Unlike the ageing Plato, Wells may have been more optimistic later in life than in his youth, or he may have considered his " modern utopia " or second-best state as a necessary transition to a perfect society.

With *A Modern Utopia* we leave behind the national utopias or even federations of utopias. Wells claims that the time has passed for frontiers and barriers created by languages ; only a whole planet can serve the purpose of a modern utopia, for : " A State powerful enough to keep isolated under modern conditions would be powerful enough to rule the world, would be, indeed, if not actively ruling, yet passively acquiescent in all other human organisations, and so responsible for them altogether. World-state, therefore, it must be." This World-state, to which we are transported by an effort of imagination, is on a planet identical to ours ; every river, lake or mountain of our Earth has its equivalent in Utopia and each earthly inhabitant has his counterpart among the population of the utopian planet which is located somewhere beyond Sirius. The difference between Utopia and our Earth is that, at some fairly recent period, its social organisation has rapidly improved and reached a level considerably superior to ours.

Into the imagining of this new social organisation goes a great deal of knowledge of the utopias of the past. Some of their features are criticised, and this is by no means the least interesting part of the book. Others are incorporated in the Wellsian scheme. Plato and Auguste Comte provide much of the psychological structure, while Theodor Hertzka provides the economic. But Wells claims that there is a need for an entirely new scheme, on the grounds that the utopias of the past did not give enough freedom to the individual. He rightly remarks that : " To the classical Utopias freedom was relatively trivial. Clearly they considered virtue and happiness as entirely separable from liberty, and as being altogether more important things. But the modern view, with its deepening insistence upon individuality and upon the significance of its uniqueness, steadily intensifies the value of freedom, until at last we begin to see liberty as the very substance of life, that indeed it is life, and that only the dead things, the choiceless things, live in absolute obedience to law. To have free play for one's individuality is, in the modern view, the subjective triumph of existence, as survival in creative work and offspring is its objective triumph." From this, however, Wells goes on to assert : " Individual liberty in a community is not, as mathematicians would say, always of the same sign. To ignore this, is the essential fallacy of the cult called Individualism.

But in truth, a general prohibition in a state may increase the sum of liberty, and a general permission may diminish it. It does not follow, as these people would have us believe, that a man is more free where there is least law and more restricted where there is most law."

This assumption that laws are the best guardians of freedom is at the basis of nearly all utopias, and in spite of his plea for freedom, Wells commits the fault of his forerunners by introducing a vast amount of legislation into his utopia. He puts forward the childish view that murders are avoided by " the loss of the common liberty to kill," as if people would start butchering one another if all punishment for murder were suddenly abolished. While most previous utopias had pointed out that the aim of legislation should be to remove the *cause* of crime, Wells sees the only corrective in punitive legislation.

Wells's conception of freedom turns out to be a very narrow one. He deprecates the " suppression of individualities to a common pattern"; also : " The ideal community of man's past (which) was one with a common belief, with common customs and common ceremonies, common manners and common formulae ; men of the same society dressed in the same fashion, each according to his defined and understood grade, behaved in the same fashion, loved, worshipped, and died in the same fashion." But after having condemned this ideal, he goes on to elaborate a similar one by describing a ruling class having all the characteristics mentioned before. The freedom of creative work is only possible for those who have private means or happen to choose work which is useful to the State. Wells's freedom is the result of a compromise between socialism and *laisser faire* capitalism, and it is unsatisfactory, like all compromises : " To the onlooker," he says, "both Individualism and Socialism are, in the absolute, absurdities : the one would make men slaves of the violent and the rich, the other the slaves of the State official, and the way of sanity runs, perhaps even sinuously, down the intervening valley...We have to provide not only for food and clothing, for order and health, but for initiative."

This ideal compromise between Individualism and Socialism was the aim of the Austrian economist Theodor Hertzka, whose plan for a better society, put forward in *Freeland* : *A Social Anticipation* (published in 1891) was received with great enthusiasm in this country. In the preface to his book Hertzka explained the synthesis which he had attempted : " If it is possible for the community to provide the capital for production without thereby doing injury to either the principle of perfect individual freedom or to that of justice, *if interest can be dispensed with without introducing communistic control in its stead, then there no longer stands any positive obstacle in the way of the free social order.*" Theodor Hertzka proposed that the land, capital and means of production should belong to the State, and that every inhabitant should have an equal right to the common land and to the means of production provided by the State. Invalids and old people would be at the charge of the State, wages would vary according to the value of the work done, a technician being paid more than a labourer, dividends would be distributed to the members of the company after putting aside a portion for re-payment of capital and tax to the State. If an association of men wished to devote themselves to industry or agriculture they could obtain land and capital on demand from the State. Personal objects, houses and gardens would be considered as private property.

H. G. Wells's scheme presents similar features. " The world State in this ideal presents itself as the sole land-owner of the earth, with the great local governments...the local municipalities, holding, as it were, feudally under it as landlords....The trend in modern thought is entirely against private property in land or natural objects or products and in Utopia these things will be the inalienable property of the World State. Subject to the right of free locomotion, land will be leased out to companies or individuals, but—in view of the unknown necessities of the future —never for a longer period than, let us say, fifty years." The State, or the local governments and municipalities, " holds all the sources of energy, and either directly or through its tenants, farmers and agents, develops these sources, and renders the energy available for the work of life. It or its tenants will produce food, and so human energy, and the exploitation of coal and electric power, and the powers of wind and wave and water will be within its right. It will pour out of this energy, by assignment and lease and acquiescence and what not, upon its individual citizens. It will maintain order, maintain roads, maintain cheap and rapid locomotion and be the common carrier of the planet, convey and distribute labour, control, let, or administer all natural productions, pay for and secure healthy births and a healthy and vigorous new generation, maintain the public health, coin money and sustain standards of measurement, subsidise research, and reward such commercially unprofitable undertakings as benefit the community as a whole : subsidise when needful chairs of criticism and authors and publications, and collect and distribute information."

Though the State is the source of all energy, and the final legatee, it is essential that private property should be maintained for, according to Wells, " a man without some negotiable property is a man without freedom, and the extent of his property is very largely the measure of his freedom. . . The object of Modern Utopian statesmanship will be to secure a man the freedom given by all his legitimate property, that is to say, by all the values his toil or skill or foresight and courage have brought into being. Whatever he has justly made he has a right to keep, that is obvious enough ; but he will also have a right to sell and exchange. . ." The State will limit the right of a man's property when it reaches such proportions that his freedom oppresses the freedom of others. Wells does not tell us when " exploitation " begins to become " oppression," and on this question, as on many others, he is guilty of much loose thinking.

Money is also considered essential to freedom, and H. G. Wells's utopia reverses the general attitude of utopias, which consider money as the source of all evil, by making an apology for money : " Money, did you but use it right, is a good thing in life, a necessary thing in civilised human life, as complicated, indeed for its purposes, but as natural a growth as the bones in a man's wrist, and I do not see how one can imagine anything at all worthy of being called a civilisation without it. It is the water of the body social, it distributes and receives, and renders growth and assimilation and movement and recovery possible. It is the reconciliation of human interdependence with liberty." And he indignantly condemns the undignified use to which Sir Thomas More put gold. Labour credits, or free demand of commodities from a central store, or similar devices, " give ten thousand times much more scope for that inherent dross in man " than the use of money. Gold, however, is not used as the standard of value since its value is too changeable, but productive energy is used instead. The available energy is reckoned in physical units and tends to become uniform because of the automatic adjustment of labour power.

In this modern Utopia work is a necessity but, as in our present society, a privileged few can afford to live without working if they wish : " If, under the restricted Utopian scheme of inheritance, a man inherited sufficient money to release him from the need to toil, he would be free to go where he pleased and do what he liked." This is justified on the grounds that : " A certain proportion of men at ease is good for the world ; work as a moral obligation is the morality of slaves, and so long as no one is overworked there is no need to worry because so few are underworked."

The Utopian worker has a greater choice of occupations than his equivalent on the earth today ; he is also able to move much more freely from one place to another thanks to the rapid means of transport. Unemployment is unknown, for the State absorbs all surplus labour by setting on foot some permanent special works of its own, " paying the minimum wage and allowing them to progress as slowly or just as rapidly as the ebb and flow of labour dictated." The State may also absorb the excess by reducing the working day. Though the extensive use of machinery tends to create surplus labour, the careful control of the increase of the population prevents any major unemployment. It is however in the interest of the State to have always at its disposal a pool of surplus labour which it can employ at a minimum wage.

The State is able to keep a check on all the inhabitants of the Utopian planet, since they are all obliged to register and notify any change of address, even a temporary one. An elaborate system is necessary, which concentrates the records of 1,500,000,000 people, their index numbers, their finger-prints, notes concerning their movements hither and thither, marriage, parentage, criminal convictions and the like. This colossal central index is housed, as a tribute " to the distinctive lucidity of the French mind," in a vast series of buildings at or near Paris. All the incidents of a man's life are thus recorded, and " at last, when the citizen died, would come the last entry of all, his age and the cause of his death and the date and place of his cremation, and his card would be taken out and passed on to the universal pedigree, to a place of greater quiet, to the ever-growing galleries of the records of the dead."

H. G. Wells is not prepared to let this scheme be considered a caprice of his fancy, but asserts that " such a record is inevitable if a Modern Utopia is to be achieved " ; he seems to believe that without it the migratory workers of a modern Utopia would all emulate Monsieur Verdoux by becoming " base men who subsist and feed their heavy imaginations in the wooing, betrayal, ill-treatment, and sometimes even the murder of undistinguished women." Having been shown dramatically the dangers of being able to adopt aliases, we are also told not to fear the loss of our privacy. " Only the State," says Wells, " would share the secret of one's little concealment. To the eighteenth-century Liberal, to the old-fashioned nineteenth-century Liberal, that is to say to all professed Liberals, brought up to be against the Government on principle, this organised clairvoyance will be the most hateful of dreams...But suppose we do not assume that government is necessarily bad, and the individual necessarily good— and the hypothesis upon which we are working practically abolishes either alternative—then we alter the case altogether. The government of a modern Utopia will be no perfection of intentions ignorantly ruling the world..."

As we learn more about his modern Utopia we realise that Wells's scheme for universal registration is due not only to what appears to be an inordinate love for index files, but that it is indeed, as he says, indispensable to his utopian scheme. The State would be unable to control the world population if it did not have such a machinery at its disposal. This is indispensable, not only to regulate labour, but also to control the increase in the population and the improvement in the quality of the people. Wells rejects State breeding of the population, which " was a reasonable proposal for Plato to make, in view of the biological knowledge of his time and the purely tentative nature of his metaphysics ; but for anyone in the days after Darwin, it is preposterous." But while rejecting compulsory pairing, he gives the State the right to maintain certain general limiting conditions :

The State is justified in saying, before you may add children to the community for the community to educate and in part to support, you must be above a certain personal efficiency, and this you must show by holding a position of solvency and independ-ence in the world ; you must be above a certain age, and a certain minimum of physical development, and free of any transmissible disease. You must not be a criminal unless you have expiated your offence. Failing these simple qualifications, if you or some person conspire and add to the population of the State, we will, for the sake of humanity, take over the innocent victim of your passions, but we shall insist that you are under a debt to the State of a peculiarly urgent sort, and one you will certainly pay, even if it is necessary to use restraint to get the payment out of you ; it is a debt that has in the last resort your liberty as a security, and, moreover, if this thing happens a second time, or if it is disease or imbecility you have multiplied, we will take an absolutely effectual guarantee that neither you nor your partner offend again in this matter.

When citizens fulfil the conditions set by the State before marriage is permissible, i.e., ability to earn a certain income, age (21 for women, 26-27 for men), minimum physical development and lack of transmissible diseases, the State blesses their marriage. The card-index plays, of course, an important part here ; each of the parties to a projected marriage " would be supplied with a copy of the index card of the projected mate, on which would be recorded his or her age ; previous marriages, legally important diseases, offspring, domiciles, public appointments, criminal convictions, registered assignments of property, and so forth. Possibly it might be advisable to have a little ceremony for each party, for each in the absence of the other, in which the record could be read over in the presence of witnesses, together with some prescribed form of address of counsel in the matter. There would then be a reasonable interval for consideration and withdrawal on the part of either spouse. In the event of the two people persisting in their resolution, they would after this minimum interval signify as much to the local official and the necessary entry would be made in the registers." Men and women who chose to ignore these conditions before uniting would be ignored by the State unless illegitimate children were born.

The State is entitled to lay down in the completest fashion " what things a man or a woman may be bound to do, and what they cannot be bound to do " after their marriage, for " it is of primary importance to the State, first in order to secure good births, and secondly good home conditions, that these unions should not be free, nor promiscuous, nor practically universal throughout the adult population." Since the aim of marriage is primarily that of reproduction, childless marriages are allowed to lapse after a period of years, but unions which result in children would continue, since children are brought up in the most favourable conditions when in the family.

In the modern Utopia motherhood is considered a service of the State, and a mother receives a certain gratuity upon the birth of a child. The State also pays her at regular intervals sums sufficient to keep her and her child in independence. Wells imagines a curious system of bonuses by which the State would pay more when the child rises markedly above certain minimum qualifications, physical or mental. This is supposed to make thoroughly efficient motherhood a profession worth following, and if the child falls below the minimum standard of health and physical and mental development, the state allowance is discontinued.

Wells's Utopian state will do all in its power to eliminate inferior people : " For Nature's process of having the strong murder the weak in cold blood will be substituted the ways and means of the modern men." The Utopian society must eliminate the idiots and lunatics, perverse and incompetent persons, drunkards, drug addicts, persons tainted with transmissible diseases, thieves, cheats and criminals, but it will not resort to capital punishment and there will be no jails in Utopia. The State will send its exiles to islands lying apart from the ocean highways, and will make sure that they cannot have children, for women will be segregated from men and there will be "island monasteries and island nunneries."

The complexity of Utopian organisation demands a more powerful and efficient method of government than the electoral system can give. As in Plato's *Republic*, a class of guardians, the *Samurai*, are entrusted with the task of governing the country. They owe their position neither to elections or to inheritance ; they are a " voluntary nobility."

All the real power of the world resides in the hands of the samurai. All head teachers and disciplinary heads of colleges, all judges, barristers, employers of labour beyond a certain limit, all medical men and legislators, must be samurai ; all the executive committees which play an important role in running the affairs of the society are drawn by lot exclusively from them.

The samurai are volunteers, " any intelligent adult in a reasonably healthy and efficient state may, at any age after five-and-
twenty, become one of the samurai, and take a hand in the
universal control." The samurai must be willing and able to
follow the Rule, designed to exclude the dull, and to be unattractive to the base. The Rule aims " to discipline the impulses
and emotions, to develop a moral habit and sustain a man in
periods of stress, fatigue, and temptation, to produce the
maximum co-operation of all men of good intent, and, in fact,
to keep all the samurai in a state of moral and bodily health and
efficiency."

The Rule consists of three parts. There is the list of qualifications which include the passing of college examinations as a proof
of steadiness of purpose, self-control and submission ; there is
the list of things that must not be done, and the list of things that
must be done. Many small pleasures which do no great harm
are forbidden so as to weed out self-indulgence. The samurai
must follow a regimen of food, never indulge in tobacco, alcoholic
drinks or drugs. They are forbidden to engage in commerce,
which tends to bring out unsocial human qualities ; acting,
singing, or reciting are also forbidden them as they tend to weaken
the soul. They may neither be servants nor keep any, they may
not bet nor play games or watch them being played. There is a
Rule of Chastity, but not of Celibacy—marriage between equals
is considered the samurai's duty to the race, but if a samurai loves
a woman who does not belong to the order he must either leave
the samurai to marry her, or induce her to accept the Woman's
Rule. The portion of the Rule dealing with the things that the
samurai are obliged to do prescribes a simple, even Spartan life
and a number of minor obligations, such as reading the Book of
the Samurai for at least ten minutes every day, which " serve to-
break down isolations of sympathy, all sorts of physical and
intellectual sluggishness and the development of unsocial preoccupations of many sorts." Every year the samurai must go
out alone for a week in the mountains, the forests, or some far-
away place where they sleep under the open sky, " they must go
bookless and weaponless, without pen or paper, or money."
They come back fortified in body and spirit.

We have no room to describe here other aspects of the modern
Utopia, the system of education, the industrial regions and

residential towns, the changes which have taken place in architecture and industrial design ; the synthesis of cultures and races into one World State. To all these questions Wells brings interesting suggestions without attempting to give the *only* and *final* solution, unlike so many utopian writers before him. His utopia is not static, and admits of other utopias, and he concludes by saying : " There will be many Utopias. Each generation will have its new version of Utopia, a little more certain and complete and real, with its problems lying closer and closer to the problems of the Thing in Being. Until at last from dreams Utopias will have come to be working drawings, and the whole world will be shaping the final World State, the fair and great and fruitful World State, that will only not be a Utopia because it will be this world."

H. G. Wells himself fulfilled this prophecy by describing another utopia in *Men Like Gods*, which is written in the form of a romance, and in which he leaves behind many of the practical considerations which had been present in his former book. In *A Modern Utopia* he had said : " Were we free to have our untrammelled desire I suppose we should follow Morris to his Nowhere, we should change the nature of man and the nature of things together ; we should make the whole race wise, tolerant, noble, perfect—wave our hands to a splendid anarchy, every man doing as it pleases him, and none pleased to do evil, in a world as good as its essential nature, as ripe and sunny, as the world before the Fall." *Men Like Gods* is Wells's *News from Nowhere*, a Nowhere which would have been too scientific and streamlined for Morris's taste, but which gets rid of much of the bureaucracy, coercion and moral compulsion that pervade *A Modern Utopia*.

The Utopia of *Men Like Gods* is also on another planet similar to our own. It is a sister universe a little advanced in time in relation to our own, but unlike the Modern Utopia, it has no central government at all. There is no " council or bureau with which the final decision rests in cases of collective action for the common welfare...no ultimate seat and organ of sovereignty...no concentration of authority... ; in the past there had been, but it had long since diffused back into the general body of the community." Decisions in regard to any particular matter are made by the people who know most about it. There are no laws as we know them, and no power to enforce them : " If someone refused to observe a regulation concerning public health, for example, the regulation would not be enforced but if they would enquire why he or she did not conform it might be found that there is some exceptional reason ; failing that an enquiry would be made into his mental and moral health."

The ruling class of the samurai has no equivalent in this utopia, where all men have the same rights and duties and where property, which was before considered essential to freedom, has disappeared :

" The activities of our world," said the Utopian Spokesman, " are all co-ordinated to secure the general freedom. We have a number of intelligences directed to the general psychology of the race and to the interaction of one collective function upon another."

" Well, isn't that group of intelligences a governing class? " said one of the Earthlings.

" Not in the sense that they exercise any arbitrary will," said the Utopian. " They deal with general relations, that is all. But they rank no higher, they have no more precedence on that account than a philosopher has over a scientific specialist...

" We found at last that private property in all but very personal things was an intolerable nuisance to mankind. We got rid of it. An artist or a scientific man has complete control of all the materials he needs, we all own our tools and appliances and have rooms and places of our own, but there is no property for trade or speculation. All this militant property, this property of manoevre, has been quite got rid of."

This utopian society had been made possible by a change in the thought of the whole people :

A growing number of people were coming to understand that amidst the powerful and easily released forces that science and organisation had brought within reach of man, the old conception of social life in the State, as a limited and legalised struggle of man and women to get the better of one another, was becoming too dangerous to endure, just as the increased dreadfulness of modern weapons was making the separate sovereignty of nations too dangerous to endure. There had to be new ideas and new conventions of human association if history was not to end in disaster and collapse...

The idea of competition to possess, as the ruling idea of intercourse, was, like some ill-controlled furnace, threatening to consume the machine it had formerly driven. The idea of creative service had to replace it. To that idea the human mind and will had to be turned if social life was to be saved. Propositions that had seemed, in former ages, to be inspired and exalted idealism began now to be recognised not simply as sober psychological truth but as practical and urgently necessary truth.

The Utopian society was not brought in by a sudden revolution, but by a gradual increase of light, a dawn of new ideas. Slowly the race had improved, both physically and intellectually, and continued to improve, thanks to the betterment in economic conditions and the progress made in the study of eugenics and education. One of the " Earthlings " who found themselves suddenly transported to Utopia was struck by the beauty of the unclothed bodies of its inhabitants, but after a few hours' conversation with them he realised that the superiority of their bodies was nothing compared with that of their minds :

Innately better to begin with, the minds of these children of light had grown up uninjured by any such tremendous frictions, concealments, ambiguities and ignorances as cripple the growing mind of an Earthling. They were clear and frank and direct. They had never developed that defensive suspicion of the teacher, that resistance to instruction, which is the natural response to teaching that is half aggression. They were beautifully unwary in their communications. The ironies, concealments, insincerities, vanities and pretentions of earthly conversation seemed unknown to them.

The social organisation of *A Modern Utopia* revealed Wells's distrust of human nature and of " instinctive life," but in *Men Like Gods* he condemns the suppression of animal instincts and appetites :

Very slowly Utopia had evolved its present harmony of law and education. Man was no longer crippled and compelled ; it was recognised that he was fundamentally an animal and that his daily life must follow the round of appetites satisfied and instincts released. The daily texture of Utopian life was woven of various and interesting foods and drinks, of free and entertaining exercise and work, of sweet sleep and of the interest and happiness of fearless and spiteless love-making. Inhibition was at a minimum. But where the power of Utopian education began was after the animal had been satisfied and disposed of.

The jewel on the reptile's head that had brought Utopia out of the confusion of human life, was curiosity, the play impulse, prolonged and expanded in adult life into an insatiable appetite for knowledge and an habitual creative urgency. All Utopians had become as little children, learners and makers.

Education no longer aims at developing self-control, and submission in the child, but " its natural impulses to play and learn are gratified... the growth of its imagination is watched and encouraged... it goes to work that attracts it and chooses what it will do." This is not to say that all instincts are allowed to follow their natural course. Wells makes a liberal use of what psycho-analysts would call "sublimation" : " The sexual passions of the child are turned against its selfishness, its curiosity flowers into scientific passion, its combativeness is set to fight disorder, its inherent pride and ambition are directed towards an honourable share in the common achievement."

The crude methods of regulation of *A Modern Utopia* have been replaced by " the subtlest educational methods." For example, there is no punishment for idlers in Utopia, but they will find no lovers, " because no one in Utopia loves those who have neither energy nor distinction." Strict marriage laws are non-existent here ; unions are contracted freely and freely terminated, women have no obligation to bear children and do so only after due thought and preparation. " In Utopia there are no bonds." Physical love is regarded as something natural and beautiful, and children talk about it without any feeling of self-consciousness.

Education, in Utopia, has replaced government :

Utopia has no parliament, no politics, no private wealth, no business competition, no police nor prisons, no lunatics, no defectives nor cripples, and it has none of these things because it has schools and teachers who are all that schools and teachers can be. Politics, trade and competition are the methods of adjustment of a crude society. Such methods of adjustment have been laid aside in Utopia for more than a thousand years. There is no rule nor government needed by adult Utopians because all the rule and government they need they have had in childhood and youth.

Children are brought up on large educational estates where they are carefully sheltered from fear, evil suggestions, or shocks to the imagination, and are taught habits of cleanliness, truth, helpfulness, confidence in the world and a sense of belonging to the great purpose of the race. After nine or ten the children go out into the world, and while up to that age their education is largely in the hands of nurses and teachers, after that time the parents play a larger part in the education of their children. Though parents have practically no power over a son or daughter, they become naturally the advocates and friends of their children.

Every young Utopian learns the Five Principles of Liberty. The first is the Principle of Privacy : " This is, that all individual personal facts are private between the citizen and the public organisation to which he entrusts them, and can be used only for his convenience and with his sanction. . . such facts are available for statistical uses, but not as individual personal facts." This principle is made all the more necessary because, as in *A Modern Utopia*, Wells insists on everyone being indexed and noted, and the whereabouts of every soul upon the planet has to be known to the Utopian organisation. The obvious dangers of interference and blackmail on the part of people in possession of the intimate facts concerning individuals has to be obviated by making privacy a sacred right.

The second principle is that of Free Movement : " A citizen, subject to the due discharge of his public obligations, may go without permission or explanation to any part of the Utopian planet. All the means of transport are freely at his service. Every Utopian may change his surroundings, his climate and his social atmosphere as he will."

The third principle is that of Unlimited Knowledge : " All that is known in Utopia, except individual personal facts about living people, is on record and as easily available as a perfected series of indices, libraries, museums and inquiry offices can make it."

The fourth principle of liberty is that " Lying is the Blackest Crime " ; the inexact statement of facts and even the suppression of a material fact is considered as a lie in Utopia.

The fifth principle is that of Free Discussion and Criticism ; any Utopian is free to criticise and discuss anything in the whole universe provided he tells no lies ; he can be as disrespectful as he pleases and propose anything, however subversive.

Though in *Men Like Gods* Wells sacrifices many of his

" bourgeois " conceptions, he cannot reconcile himself to adopting a system of communism. Money in the form of coins or notes is no longer used, as all transactions are done through banks. Every child receives from the common fund at his birth a sum sufficient to educate and maintain him up to the age of twenty-five, but then he is expected to choose some occupation and replenish his account. Energetic and creative people are often given big grants to carry out their work, and artists sometimes grow rich if there is a great demand for their work. The retention of wages appears to play a small role in Utopia, and seems merely due to Wells's unwillingness to give in to communists like William Morris.

He seems however to have surrendered on an equally fundamental question, for, in spite of what he had said in *A Modern Utopia*, he has described a wise, tolerant, noble, perfect race which is not however, fundamentally different from our own. In Utopia " there had been," he says, "a certain deliberate elimination of the ugly, malignant, narrow, stupid and gloomy types during the past dozen centuries or so ; but except for the fuller realisation of his latent possibilities, the common man in Utopia was very little different from the ordinary energetic and able people of a later stone-age or early bronze-age community. They were infinitely better nourished, trained and educated, and mentally and physically their condition was clean and fit, but they were the same flesh and nature as we are."

Men Like Gods is the last utopia in the " classical " tradition, and one may well ask oneself if Wells will not prove to be the last of utopian writers. The interest in utopian literature, on the other hand, is far from dying out. Lewis Mumford has dedicated a comprehensive study to *The Story of Utopias*, combining a critical analysis with some interesting suggestions of his own. More recently, Ethel Mannin in *Bread and Roses* has surveyed various conceptions of Utopias and given us the vision of her own utopia. These writers continue to assert the will to utopia, and echo Oscar Wilde's famous remark : " A map of the world that does not include Utopia is not worth even glancing at, for it leaves out the one country at which Humanity is always landing. And when Humanity lands there, it looks out, and seeing a better country, sets sail. Progress is the realisation of Utopias." Nevertheless, the trend of modern literature is becoming increasingly anti-utopian. Utopia is no longer considered as an ideal and impossible dream, but as having been partly realised already or as being in process of realisation. It no longer spells happiness, perfection and progress ; for many the dream has become a nightmare.

The prediction of Nicholas Berdiaev seems to be coming true: " Utopias," he said, " appear to be much more capable of realisation than they did in the past. And we find ourselves faced by a much more distressing problem : How can we prevent their final realisation?...Utopias can be realised. Life advances towards utopia. And perhaps a new century is beginning, a century in which the intellectuals and the cultivated classes will dream of the means by which utopias can be avoided and how we can return to a non-utopian society, less 'perfect ' and more free."

It is perhaps unjust to say that the twentieth century is living the utopias of the past. A world which has experienced two major wars in the span of thirty years, a world ravaged by epidemics and starvation, can hardly be compared with the utopias which claim to abolish poverty, unemployment, and even establish a world government that would put an end to wars. But it is true to say that, to a large extent, the *structure* of the societies advocated by past utopians has become a reality, and as the results bear little resemblance to those which they had led us to expect, one may be justified in thinking that the structure is a faulty one. When the twentieth century has tried to carry out the utopian plans of the past it has failed miserably ; it has created all-powerful States which control the means of production and distribution, but which have not abolished starvation ; States encouraging scientific discoveries and developing production, but failing to give to every citizen a decent standard of life ; States which claimed to institute perfect equality, but which have given birth instead to new privileged classes and new inequalities perhaps more appalling than the old ; States which have made people into Taylorised robots, subordinated by the machines they serve, brutalised by propaganda ; States which have created conditions where all individual thought is regarded as criminal, where literature, music and art cease to be the expression of the individual and instead eulogise the régime where servitude to the old religion is replaced by that to the State and its new gods.

Have these utopias really betrayed the spirit of the men who conceived them? These men loved authority, they were convinced that the " people " had to be told what was good for them, they wanted order at any price, even that of bureaucracy, they hated individuality, they had narrow, " inhuman " minds. We can imagine Cabet accompanying Beatrice and Sidney Webb in their journey to the land of the Soviets, and, in all likelihood, his report would have been as enthusiastic as theirs. One feels that Bellamy would have been seduced by many features of Fascist Italy and Nazi Germany, and would have certainly been filled with admiration for Britain's industrial conscription, nationalisation of industries, rationing system and other recent developments.

But these " utopias " have not always been seen through the eyes of the successors of the nineteenth century utopians, well-meaning Fabians or Communist clergymen. They have sometimes been seen by journalists in search of facts, who have given accounts of their " Assignment in Utopia", or by writers endowed with critical minds regarding social questions who, like André Gide, did not hesitate to express their painful disappointment in the land where they had believed that " Utopia was in process of becoming reality". These books enraged those whose " love of order is indistinguishable from their partiality to tyrants",[1] but they also created a widespread distrust of the State Socialism advocated by the Utopians of the nineteenth century.

The main trend of literature between the two wars has been one of extreme scepticism regarding the power of the State to transform society. The rise of new régimes, frankly communistic or vaguely socialistic, but always totalitarian and ready to sacrifice the individual to the interests of the State, forced intellectuals to adopt either an attitude of complete subservience to the State and become little more than paid propagandists, or to claim defiantly the rights of the individual.

There has also been a turning-away from the faith in the inevitability of progress. For most writers of the nineteenth century, scientific discoveries and industrial development were going to increase automatically the happiness of mankind, but modern generations see the dangers as well as the advantages which " progress " can bring. The machines no longer appear

---

[1]Tocqueville, on Democracy in America quoted by André Gide in *Back from the U.S.S.R.*

as the liberators of mankind by becoming, as Oscar Wilde had dreamt, the slaves of men ; they appear more often as the masters of men. The modern worker recognises himself in Charlie Chaplin fighting desperately against the infernal machinery of *Modern Times*. And we fear that even Lord Lytton's obedient robots may get out of hand ; that fear has been expressed in scores of novels, films, plays, and even " comic strips," from Capek's *R.U.R.* to a recent American story entitled *Folded Hands* which described the invasion of the earth by robots belonging to another planet. They obey a " prime directive " which compels them to take over all the unpleasant and dangerous tasks carried out by men. Humanity becomes free to idle, but is overcome by despair.

This is not the place to discuss the problem of " man versus the machine," but merely to point out that the faith in the machine as an agent of human happiness, which plays such an important role in the utopias of the nineteenth century, has been displaced by a distrust in and even fear of the machine, and has deprived these utopias of much of their glamour.

Another blow has been dealt to utopian literature by the insistence of modern writers on discussing the problem of " man versus the State". The majority of utopias assumed that the interests of the individual coincided with those of the State and that a conflict between the two was unthinkable. Modern writers have dealt, on the contrary, with all kind of possible conflicts between the State and the individual. The individual may be one of the " cafoni " described by Ignazio Silone, or one of the starving, malaria-stricken peasants whom Carlo Levi had known in Southern Italy ; he may be a poet committing suicide rather than becoming a clog in the propaganda machine ; he may be a Soldier Schweik ; he may be an old revolutionary reduced to betraying his ideals ; he may be a civil servant or a storm trooper ; or he may be one of Kafka's characters fighting against authority, against the blind stupidity of the law and bureaucracy. All of us have, at some time or other, felt like K. in *The Trial*, lost and defenceless, completely unable to comprehend the meaning of the machinery which regulates, and often dominates, our lives. Kafka's criticism of society is not directed against any particular State, but the struggles of K. are those of any modern man.

Utopians have been apt to forget that society is a living orgainsm and that its organisation must be an expression of life and not a dead structure. The realisation of this fact has led contemporary writers to attack the State, and any form of authority, whether springing from religion or from political parties, and to return to the ideal of independent communities, united in a free federation and offering the greatest opportunity for the development of man's personality. They have reasserted the need for a true ethic, not taught at school like a catechism and based on obedience to authority, not justifying sacrifices and compromises for the " good of the community", but asserting the right of the individual to think for himself and to defend his freedom, since a man who is not free cannot be a worthy member of the community ; if he sacrifices his individuality, his spirit of initiative and even of revolt, he harms the community instead of serving it.

This passage from Silone's *The School for Dictators*, though aimed at actual institutions, reads like a condemnation of authoritarian utopias : " Machines, which ought to be man's instrument, enslave him, the state enslaves society, the bureaucracy enslaves the state, the church enslaves religion, parliament enslaves democracy, institutions enslave justice, academies enslave art, the army enslaves the nation, the party enslaves the cause, the dictatorship of the proletariat enslaves Socialism."

Even more forcibly, Herbert Read says : " I believe that the only idea of a society which is capable of guaranteeing the integrity of the person is the negation of the idea of society. Every advance towards community must be countered by an affirmation of individual freedom. Every law must allow for its violation. The greatest power must be vested in the humblest men. Every act of government must involve a limit of service and an impermanency of office. The continuity of life should be as invisible as the prevailing wind. No drums to bang, no flags to wave ; no salutes or genuflections, no armies marching or choirs singing ; but only the still small voice and the orient wheat."

Politicians and statesmen bring us every day nearer to the realisation of utopias by supervising more and more thoroughly the lives of the individuals. In this country the Government has not gone as far as issuing a list of the foods the nation should eat

and those it should avoid, as in Icaria, but through rationing and
the control of imports it determines to a great extent what we
should eat ; during the war it restricted women's fashions more
on utilitarian than on aesthetic grounds, and even altered men's
clothes ; through the control of paper it has a considerable say
on what should be printed, and industrial conscription, though
presenting more loop-holes than were allowed in Utopia,
establishes the duty of every citizen to work. National Insurance
is another application of the principle dear to most utopias, that
the community is responsible for the sick, the old, the unemployed
and children—reduced, of course, to the niggardly scale of the
Beveridge plan. In the industrial and scientific field utopian
inventions have been equalled and very often surpassed. But as
the world becomes more and more " utopian " Berdiaev's prediction is coming true : intellectuals are dreaming of avoiding the
realisation of utopias and of returning to a less " perfect " but
more free society.

The writers quoted above are not isolated fighters for an anti-
utopian world ; in France Jean-Paul Sartre, André Breton and
Camus, in America Henry Miller and a score of young poets and
writers, Catholics like Eric Gill and Georges Bernanos; sociologists
and biologists like Lewis Mumford and Patrick Geddes, novelists
like E. M. Forster, Rex Warner and Graham Greene, have all
fought the battle of the individual against the State. Some have
gone as far as elaborating satirical utopias, visions of the future
world where man has completely lost a sense of his uniqueness,
perfect societies where men have become efficient machines,
incapable of experiencing any strong emotion. It would be
difficult to estimate to what extent these anti-utopias are directed
against the utopias of the past, or against the realisations and
trends in our modern society. Zamyatin's *Nous Autres*, which
appeared in Russia in the late twenties, was obviously inspired
by the Soviet régime, and Aldous Huxley's *Brave New World*, which
was first published in 1932, and which bears many resemblances
to Zamyatin's novel, aims at satirising modern America. *Animal
Farm*, by George Orwell (1945), could only be considered as a
satirical utopia by those who have not followed the history of
Russia during the past thirty years.

Zamyatin's anti-utopia is one of anticipation. He describes the
society which is supposed to exist a thousand years after the

establishment of the Unique State over the whole world, on the
eve of the conquest of the whole universe, thanks to a formidable
machine which can travel to the other planets. In the Unique
State life is regulated with a mathematical precision, everything
has been reduced to mathematical equations, men and women
all wear a conspicuous gold plate bearing their number : " No
member of the society is ' one ' but ' one amongst,' 'one of ', we
are so much alike." The State is ruled by the ' Benefactor,' whose
agents 'the Guardians,' are considered as real guardian angels ;
they know every movement and even every thought of each
citizen, for they fulfil both the role of the confessor and that of
the police spy. A time-table has replaced the icon in every
room ; working, eating, sleeping, sexual intercourse, are all
strictly regulated by the time-table. The gold plate carried by
each citizen has a watch at the back of it which has almost become
integrated to the human mechanism ; even when under the stress
of great emotions he can estimate the time to within a few
minutes. There is not such a thing as the private life of the
individual ; not only is his mail opened before it reaches him,
not only is he obliged to report to the Guardians any irregularity,
but an acoustic apparatus, artistically concealed, records all
conversations in the street for the Office of the Guardians. The
Task of the Guardians is further simplified by the fact that all
houses are made with glass walls and they see at a glance what goes
on in each apartment. Only during the " sexual hour " is permission given to lower the curtains : " We are only entitled to
the curtains on the sexual days. Otherwise, we always live
openly in our transparent walls, which seem woven of sparkling
air, bathed in light, for we have nothing to hide, and this mode of
life renders less irksome the difficult task of the Benefactor.
Otherwise, who knows what could happen? Maybe that the
opaque homes of the Ancients were responsible for creating in
them their miserable cellular psychology."

Sexual life is carried out according to scientific principles.
The Sexual Bureau analyses the hormones of each citizen and
establishes a table of sexual days. A person declares afterwards
that he or she wants to use such or such a number or numbers,
and a booklet with pink tickets is delivered, each entitling to
one sexual hour. This pink ticket can be used for any " No.",
for the principle that one belongs to all and all to one is applied.

Women are only allowed to have children if they conform to certain standards, and if they disobey they are punished by death.

In this society of the future the ideal is to become " perfect like a machine " ; the Taylor system is applied not merely to work but to the whole of life, to each step, to each movement. Men eat synthetic food, dress in a synthetic uniform, are taught at school by robots, listen to synthetic music produced by a " musicometre", thanks to which, by turning a handle, anyone can produce up to three sonatas per hour.

Elections are still held, but one gathers that the Benefactor always gets a hundred per cent of the votes, and the day of the elections is appropriately called " the Day of Unanimity". Freedom is not only considered unnecessary but dangerous : " Freedom and crime are as intimately linked as, for example, the movement of an aeroplane and its speed. If the speed of the plane is nil, it remains motionless ; if man's freedom is nil, clearly he does not commit any crime. The only means to deliver man from crime is to deliver him from freedom."

However, even a thousand years after the establishment of the Unique State there are rebels against the system, men who break the rules or utter unorthodox ideas, women who desire children even though they are an inch under the precribed norm, but no pity is shown to these refractories. If they are unwilling to confess their crimes they are placed under enormous bell jars in which the air is sometimes rarefied, sometimes replaced by special gases. This leads either to confession or death. More spectacular executions are carried out in public by the Machine of the Benefactor, a kind of monumental electric chair which reduces the human body to a few drops of water in a few seconds. It is operated by the Benefactor himself, who fills the rôle of the executioner.

One of the most curious features of the Unique State is that each city is surrounded by a Green Wall and no one is allowed outside it. In the no-man's-land which separates the various cities live men and women who seem to belong to a different species, remnants of the old civilisation. They are the survivors of the free, instinctive life, and they have their allies inside the walls of the city, men and women possessed of a longing for the past, of a desire for dangers, suffering and excitement. When these attempt to revolt, the State applies a long overdue reform—the compulsory destruction of man's imagination, a simple operation of the brain which eradicates for ever any longing for freedom, any unsatisfied desire, any scruple or remorse.

Zamyatin's satire has a violence and bitterness which is not to be found in Huxley's _Brave New World_, and which suggests that it was more than an academic anticipation. The rôle played by the police, the methods of torture and execution, the oppressing atmosphere of official and not-so-official informers, are described with what seems to amount to almost intimate knowledge. Though the book ends with the complete victory of the Unique State, which succeeds in destroying the imagination of all its citizens, the recourse to this extreme measure shows the weakness of totalitarianism. A thousand years of propaganda have not succeeded in transforming men into perfect machines ; an operation on their brain is necessary to carry this out.

The stability of Huxley's _Brave New World_ is obtained by even more drastic means : there is first the conditioning of the " bottled babies," then the conditioning by " Hypnopaedia," the teaching of moral education during sleep, the neo-Pavlovian conditioning of reflexes in infants, and for grown-ups, the use of _soma_, the wonderful drug which cures all discontent, ill-humour, resentment or bitterness. The result is that corrective methods can be much milder than in Zamyatin's Unique State ; there are no instruments of torture or executioners, the offenders against the State are despatched to some far-away island where, one gathers, life is unattractive, riots are suppressed by the use of _soma_ gas and recorded " pep " talks.

Utopias had often instituted rigid time-tables for their inhabitants and had even planned their leisure. In _Brave New World_ a man is, in theory, free to use his leisure as he thinks fit, but, because of his " conditioning " he is incapable of remaining alone with himself or using his own initiative to seek a personal pleasure. All pleasures are enjoyed passively. Even the effort of imagination which is required to enjoy a love scene on the screen is rendered unnecessary for, through certain apparatus, the visual images are automatically translated into sensations of touch, hearing or smell. Love must, of course, disappear in a society where strong passions are regarded as a danger to the stability of the State ; it is replaced by promiscous sexual intercourse, carried out as a hygienic measure or merely " for fun " rather than any strong passion.

But even the marvellous system of " conditioning " is not always completely successful and there are a few people dissatisfied with society, an occasional individual who wants to feel more himself, more on his own, " not just a cell in the social body". There is also a Savage who has by chance come out of the reserves where the remnants of the old civilisation are kept in the interest of science. The Savage is, of course, very much like a modern, civilised man with an unnatural desire for suffering, a belief in self-inflicted frustration, a contempt for the flesh which finally drive him to hang himself.

Both Zamyatin and Huxley are extremely successful in their satire on the compulsory happiness decreed by the totalitarian states, but instead of demanding the right to free happiness which would result from the expression of man's personality, they ask for the right to suffer. The idea that suffering and frustration are necessary to creation, that the soul needs to be mortified, lies at the bottom of their criticisms of utopia. They would like to see a return to the past, or the present, when men believe in atonement, when physical love is considered sinful, when jealousy, ambition, and other base passions spur men to action. These writers criticise utopia because there is no room for Hamlet or Othello in it, forgetting that between Hamlet and a robot-like man there is room for an individual who would neither have Hamlet's neurotic temperament nor be a robot.

The authoritarian utopias of the nineteenth century are chiefly responsible for the anti-utopian attitude prevalent among intellectuals to-day. But utopias have not always described regimented societies, centralised states and nations of robots. Diderot's *Tahiti* or Morris's *Nowhere* gave us utopias where men were free from both physical and moral compulsion, where they worked not out of necessity or a sense of duty but because they found work a pleasurable activity, where love knew no laws and where every man was an artist. Utopias have often been plans of societies functioning mechanicaly, dead structures conceived by economists, politicians and moralists ; but they have also been the living dreams of poets.

LONDON, *January-July* 1948

A TRAMP'S UTOPIA *

The Big Rock Candy Mountains

One evenin' as the sun went down
And the jungle fire was burnin',
Down the track came a hobo hikin',
And he said : ' Boys, I'm not turnin',
I'm headed fer a land that's far away
Beside the crystal fountains,
So come with me, we'll all go see
The Big Rock Candy Mountains.'

In the Big Rock Candy Mountains,
There's a land that's fair and bright,
Where the handouts grow on bushes,
And you sleep out every night.
Where the boxcars are all empty,
And the sun shines every day
On the birds and the bees and the cigarette trees,
And the lemonade springs where the bluebird sings,
In the Big Rock Candy Mountains.

In the Big Rock Candy Mountains,
All the cops have wooden legs,
The bulldogs all have rubber teeth,
And the hens lay soft-boiled eggs.
The farmers' trees are full of fruit,
And the barns are full of hay.
Oh, I'm bound to go where there ain't no snow,
Where the rain don't pour, the wind don't blow,
In the Big Rock Candy Mountains.

---

*The anonymous literature of the underprivileged in all ages has contained songs and fables of a society without hunger and oppression. The slaves of the ancient world looked back to a legendary Golden Age of equality, and the Negroes of nineteenth-century America placed in a future life their dreams of a respite from incessant toil for which they could not hope in this one. Much of the Utopian folklore is of great beauty and poignancy, but there is nothing other-worldly in this amusing song of the American ' hoboes,' or migratory workers, of this century. The hobo is not concerned with governments or juridical systems,—he knows what *he* wants in his shamelessly materialistic ' ideal commonwealth.'

In the Big Rock Candy Mountains,
You never change your socks,
And the little streams of alcohol
Come tricklin' down the rocks.
There the brakemen have to tip their hats
And the railroad bulls are blind.
There's a lake of stew and of whisky too,
You can paddle all around 'em in a big canoe,
In the Big Rock Candy Mountains.

In the Big Rock Candy Mountains,
All the jails are made of tin,
And you can bust right out again
As soon as you are in.
There ain't no short-handled shovels,
No axes, saws or picks.
I'm going to stay where you sleep all day,
Where they hung the Turk that invented work,
In the Big Rock Candy Mountains.

Bibliography

THE aim of this book has been to present a general survey of utopian thought from Ancient Greece to the present day, and such a survey has to include those utopias which have enjoyed the greatest popularity or which have influenced utopian thought, to the exclusion of many interesting but little-known ones. The following bibliography will give an idea of the immense, and partly unexplored field of utopias.

Though my choice of utopias has been made on the whole on orthodox lines, it may be felt that some works classified as utopias should not be considered as such, while others which have been included should have been left out. The difficulty of any classification arises from the fact that though most definitions of utopias agree with one another, the word has been used to cover very varied forms of literature. An utopia has been defined, in the *Encyclopedia Britannica*, as " an ideal commonwealth whose inhabitants exist under perfect conditions." This definition applies closely to More's *Utopia*, and in the preceding selection I have tried to present works which come as near as possible within the scope of this definition. The ideal commonwealth may be found on some imaginary island or continent, some far-away planet, in the past or in the future.

But a utopia has been also defined as " an imaginary conception of an ideal government " (*Dictionnaire Général de la Langue Française*). This is a definition which has been less frequently adopted, and would apply more to works describing ideal constitutions, such as Harrington's *Oceana*, or theoretical works on government as Hobbes's *Leviathan*. Though these works did not seem to come within the scope of this book, they have sometimes been mentioned briefly and have been included in the bibliography.

Any classification is bound to be somewhat arbitrary, but I have tried to avoid the obvious pitfalls of classifying as utopian whatever seemed to me impossible of realisation. Curiously, this is a criterion of classification which has often been adopted. Marxists have classified as utopian any " unscientific " scheme, while non-Marxists tend to include socialist programmes among

320

utopias. Ironically, while Engels wrote a book to demonstrate the difference between utopian (that is to say pre-marxist, unscientific thought) and scientific socialism, Marx has sometimes been included among utopian writers, as in the Rev. M. Kaufmann's *Utopias: or, Schemes of Social Improvement.* (P. J. Proudhon, who is included along with Marx, would have equally resented the classification.)

There is hardly any scheme of social betterment which has not, at some time or other, been described as utopian. Even political programmes, such as the Babeuvist *Manifesto of the Equals* figures sometimes in bibliographies of utopias. Though occasionally the difference between utopias and political programmes is a tenuous one, works which are concerned with setting down a plan of immediate action and defining the means to be used to reach a certain end, cannot be considered as utopias. The fact that a political programme has not proved to be capable of realisation does not justify its inclusion among utopian works.

Another difficulty is presented by writers who claim to have written utopias, while neither the form nor the contents of their books bears any relation to an utopia. One may consider it a tribute to More that so many writers should have tried to cash in on the success of his work, by using its title for all kinds of writings which have little in common with the original production. The name *utopia* has been given, for example, to "key" romances whose aim was to describe exactly the opposite from an ideal society. Women have been particularly unscrupulous in that respect : Mrs Manley used the title of *New Atlantis* for a collection of libellous anecdotes aimed chiefly at the Duchess of Marlborough, which was published in 1711, and for which she was arrested together with the printer and publisher on a warrant from the Earl of Sunderland. Mrs Eliza Haywood also wrote a key romance, entitled *Memoirs of a certain Island adjacent to the Kingdom of Utopia*, which was published in 1725-26. The title of *Utopia* seems to have been particularly fashionable at the time and is found in titles of satirical poems and plays, sometimes imitative of Aristophanes, such as *Canary-Birds Naturaliz'd in Utopia. A Canto*, 1709 or '10, and *The Six Days Adventure or the New Utopia*, a play which was acted at the Duke of York's Theatre in 1671, and which purported to describe an " Attempt at a common-wealth of women." A curious political pamphlet

published in 1647 claims to be a letter from the " King of Utopia
to the Citizens of Cosmopolis, the Metropolitan City of Utopia,"
and to have been " Translated out of the Utopian Tongue, into
broken English by 'tis no matter who. But *Why Broken English?*
O Sir! What here's spoken, Imports that England is by th'
English broken." One even finds a religious tract for some
mysterious reason called, *A charge from Utopia*, and a magazine,
which seems to have had a precarious existence, called *The
Utopian.*

Many descriptions of ideal imaginary commonwealths are to
be found in the stories of imaginary travels so popular in the
seventeenth and eighteenth century. The precise definition given
by Geoffrey Atkinson of the imaginary travel or " extraordinary
voyage " brings out their close relationship to the utopias : the
" extraordinary voyage is," he says, " a fictitious narrative
purporting to be the veritable account of a real voyage made by
one or more Europeans to an existent but little known country
—or several countries—together with a description of the happy
condition of society there found, and a supplementary account of
the traveller's return to Europe." Sometimes the description of
the ideal country is very vague, while at other times, as in Gabriel
de Foigny's *Adventures of James Sadeur*, it occupies a more important
place than the relation of adventure and travels. Only the
latter type have been included in the bibliography.

I have also included in this bibliography only a few works which
may be considered the precursors of utopias, for it would have
been impossible to present a complete list. Dr J. O. Hertzler, in
his *History of Utopian Thought*, considers the Hebrew prophets as
the fathers of utopian thought. For him, the prophet Amos
(middle of the eighth century B.C.), and the unbroken line of
prophets for three centuries before, during and after the Babylon-
ion exile of the Hebrews, are the equals, if not the peers of Plato,
as social critics and social architects. Though the influence of
Greece on utopian thought has been most important, other
cultures and literatures have played a considerable rôle.

I have also mentioned some works which have influenced utopias
by their description of actual societies and communities. The
description of the Jewish communities of the Essenes, on the
Western shores of the Dead Sea, by the historian Josephus, those
of more or less mythical communities in the islands of the

Mediterranean by Diodorus Siculus, the accounts of the Inca civilisation and of the Jesuit republic set up in the second half of the sixteenth century, and which lasted for over a hundred years, all provided raw material for the edification of utopias.

Charles Gide, in his book *Communist and Co-operative Colonies*, asked himself if he should not include utopias in a study of communities, since some of the utopias are more real than actual experiments. One may ask oneself, on the other hand, if the stories of some of these communities should not be paralleled with those of utopias. The communities which were set up mostly in the nineteenth century were the expression of the will to utopia, they were, or, rather, were intended to be, utopias in miniature and the constitutions of some of these communities strongly resemble those of some utopian commonwealths. In many cases utopias inspired the founders of communities, while the results of these practical experiments were incorporated in some of the modern utopias.

This bibliography also includes some of the critical works on utopias which have been published during the past hundred years. Though most of them considered utopias from a Marxist viewpoint, more recent works, like Lewis Mumford's *The Story of Utopias*, adopt a less partisan attitude and contain much interesting criticism and appreciation. Finally, I have included in the bibliography books such as Rudolf Rocker's *Nationalism and Culture*, Kropotkin's *Mutual Aid* and Alexander Gray's *The Socialist Tradition*, which, though not dealing specifically with utopias, contain much material relevant to the discussion of the subject. I have tried throughout to avoid footnotes as much as possible but all the sources used will be found in the bibliography.

GENERAL

Kaufmann, Moritz: *Utopias: or, Schemes of Social Improvement, from Sir Thomas More to Karl Marx*, London, 1879.

Nettlau, Max: *Bibliographie de l'Anarchie*, (Utopies Libertaires), Paris, 1897.

Hoffding, Harald: *A History of Modern Philosophy*, translated by B. E. Meyer, London, 1900.

Kropotkin, Peter: *The Conquest of Bread*, Introduction to 1913 Edition, London. *Mutual Aid, A Factor of Evolution*, London, 1902.

Burckhardt, Jacob: *The Civilisation of the Renaissance in Italy*, London, 1904.

Gide, Charles: *Communist and Co-operative Colonies*, London, 1930. *A History o, Economic Doctrines*, London, 1917.

Mumford, Lewis: *The Story of Utopias*, New York, 1922.
Hertzler, Joyce Oramel: *The History of Utopian Thought*, London, 1923.
Rocker, Rudolf: *Nationalism and Culture*, U.S.A., 1937.
Read, Herbert: *Poetry and Anarchism*, London, 1938. *A Coat of Many Colours*, London, 1945.
Mannin, Ethel: *Bread and Roses, an Utopian Survey and Blue-Print*, London, 1944.
Gray, Alexander: *The Socialist Tradition, Moses to Lenin*, London, 1946.
Thompson, David: *The Babeuf Plot, The Making of a Republican Legend*, London, 1947.

Chapter I

UTOPIAS OF ANTIQUITY

Plato: *The Republic*, translated by A. D. Lindsay. Everyman edition, London, 1935.
The Dialogues of Plato, translated into English by Benjamin Jowett, 5 vols., Oxford, 1875.
Dickinson, G. Lowes: *Plato and his Dialogues*, London, 1931.
Aristophanes: *The Clouds* and the *Ecclesiazusae*, translated by B. B. Rogers, London, 1852 and 1915. *The Archians, The Knights and The Birds*, A metrical version with an occasional comment by John Hookham Frere, with an introduction by Henry Morley, London, 1886.
Zeno: Fragment from *The Republic*, in Diogenes Laertius' *Life of Zeno*, Loeb Edition, Vol. 2, London, 1924.
Plutarch: *Life of Lycurgus*, in *Ideal Commonwealths*, edited by Henry Morley, London, 1885.
Strabo: *Geography*, Crete, Book 10, Sect. 4.
Diodorus Siculus, Loeb Edition, Vol. 3, Books 2 and 5, London, 1939.
Aristotle: *Politics*, translated by William Ellis, Everyman edition, London, 1912.

Chapter II

UTOPIAS OF THE RENAISSANCE

Saint Brendan: *St Brandan: a medieval legend of the sea*, London, 1844.
The Anglo-Norman Voyage of St Brendon by Benedeit, Oxford, 1928.
St Thomas Aquinas: *De Regimine Principum*, translated by Gerald B. Phelan, New York.
More, Thomas: *Libellus vere Aureus nec minus salutaris quam festivus de optimo reip. statu deque noua Insula Vtopia*, Louvain, 1516.
Utopia; or, the best state of a republic weal, first English translation by Ralph Robynson, 1551.
Sir Thomas More's Utopia, in *Ideal Commonwealths*, edited with an introduction by Henry Morley, London, 1885.
More's Utopia, translated into Modern English by G. C. Richards, Oxford, 1923.
Dermenghem, Emile: *Thomas Morus et les Utopistes de la Renaissance*, Paris, 1927.
Donner, H. W.: *Introduction to Utopia*, Stockholm and London, 1945.

Erasmus, Desiderius: *Moriae Encomium*, 1511. *The Praise of Folly*, translated by John Wilson, 1668, edited with an introduction by Mrs P. S. Allen, Oxford, 1913.
The Epistles of Erasmus, from his earliest letters to his 51st year, translated by F. M. Nichols, London, 1901-18.
Morgan, Arthur E.: *Nowhere is Somewhere*, North Carolina, 1948.

Bodin, Jean: *Les six livres de la Republique de Iean Bodin Angeuin*, Lyon, 1557. Latin translation: Io Bodini... *De Republica Libri sex*, latine ab autore redditi, multo quam antea locupletiores, etc., 1586.
The Six Bookes of a Commonweale, Out of the French and Latine copies, done into English by Richard Knolles, London, 1606.
Chauviré, R.: *Jean Bodin, auteur de la Republique*, 1914.
Lavie, J. C. de: *Abrégé de la République de Bodin*, London, 1755.

Campanella, Tommaso: *Civitas Solis Poetica: Idea Reipublicae Philosophiae*, Frankfurt, 1623. First English translation, with a few omissions, by Thomas W. Halliday, in *Ideal Commonwealths*, edited by Henry Morley, London, 1885.
Quotations in this volume have been translated from *La Città del Sole*, Edita per la prima volta nel testo originale, con introduzione e documenti, da Edmondo Solmi, Modena, 1904.
Le Piu belle Pagine di Tommaso Campanella, scelte da Corrado Alvano, Milano, 1935.
Dentice di Accadia, C.: *Tommaso Campanella*, with a bibliography and a portrait, Italy, 1921.
Amabile, L.: *Fra Tommaso Campanella, la sua congiura, i suoi processi e la sua pazzia*, 1882.

Andreae, Johann Valentin: *Reipublicae Christianopolitanae Descriptio*, 1619. First English translation: *Christianopolis, An Ideal State of the Seventeenth Century*, translated from the Latin of Johann Valentin Andreae, with an historical introduction by Felix Emil Held, New York, 1916.

Bacon, Francis: *New Atlantis*, first published by William Rawley, in the same volume with *Sylva Sylvarum: or a Naturall Historie*, London, 1627. A Latin version of the *New Atlantis* was published by Rawley in 1638. Edition in Modern English, in the third volume of the standard edition of Bacon's works edited by R. L. Ellis, J. Spedding & D. D. Heath, 1857-74.
Bacon's New Atlantis, in *Ideal Commonwealths* edited by Henry Morley, 1885.
New Atlantis, by Francis Bacon, Lord Verulam, Viscount St Albans, edited with introduction and notes by Alfred B. Gough, Oxford, 1924.

Hartlib, Samuel: *A Description of the famous Kingdom of Macaria: showing its excellent Government, wherein the Inhabitants live in great Prosperity, Health and Happiness: the King obeyed, the Nobles honoured, and all good Men respected: Vice punished, and Virtue rewarded. An Example to other Nations: In a Dialogue between a Scholar and a Traveller*. First Edition, London, 1641. Reprinted in the Harleian Miscellany, Vol. I., 1744.

Gott, Samuel: *Nova Solyma*. First published in Latin, anonymously in 1648, under the title: *Novae Solymae Libri Sex*. (In the second edition, 1649, the title was supplemented by the words: *Sive Institutio Christiani*.) First English translation, with a long introduction by Rev Walter Stephen K. Jones, who attributed the work to Milton. In 1910 he discovered that the author was Samuel Gott.

Rabelais, François: *Gargantua and Pantagruel*, translated into English by Sir Thomas Urquhart and Peter Le Motteux, 1653-1694; published with an introduction by David Nutt, London, 1900.

Chapter III

UTOPIAS OF THE ENGLISH REVOLUTION

Winstanley, Gerrard: *The New Law of Righteousness*, 1649.
The Law of Freedom in a Platform: Or True Magistracie Restored, London. 1652
Berens, Lewis H.: *The Digger Movement in the Days of the Commonwealth as revealed in the writings of Gerrard Winstanley, the Digger*, London, 1906.
Gerrard Winstanley, Selections from his works, edited by Leonard Hamilton, with an introduction by Christopher Hill, London, 1944.
The Works of Gerrard Winstanley, edited by G. H. Sabine, New York, 1941.
H. N. Brailsford: *Winstanley, The Digger*.
Woodcock, George: *Anarchy or Chaos*, Chapter IV, London, 1944.
Hobbes, Thomas: *Leviathan, or The Matter, Forme and Power of A Commonwealth Ecclesiasticall and Civil*, London, 1651. Edited with an introduction by Michael Oakeshott, Blackwell's Political texts, Oxford, 1946.
Harrington, James: *The Common-Wealth of Oceana*, first published, London, 1656. Edited with an introduction by Henry Morley, London, 1883.
Smith, Hugh F. R.: *Harrington and his Oceana. A study of a seventeenth century Utopia and its influence in America*, 1914.

Chapter IV

UTOPIAS OF THE ENLIGHTENMENT

T.I.D.M.G.: *Histoire du Grand et Admirable Royaume d'Antangil*, 1617. *La Première Utopie Francaise, Le Royaume d'Antangil*, Avec des éclaircissements de F. Lachèvre, 1933.
Cyrano de Bergerac: *Histoire Comique—Voyage dans la Lune*, first published, 1657. *Histoire des Etats et Empires du Soleil*, first published, 1662. *Voyages to the Moon and the Sun*, translated by Richard Aldington, London, 1923.
Vairasse, d'Allais, (Denis Veiras): *The History of the Sevarites or Sevarambi a nation inhabiting a part of the third continent commonly called Terrae Australes Incognitae*. With an account of their admirable Government, Religion, Customs and Languages. Written by one Captain Siden, London, 1675. A further account of their Government, Religion, Customs and Language. The second part more wonderful and delightful than the first, London, 1679. (The second part is an abridged version of the French edition). *L'Histoire des Sévarambes, peuples qui habitent une partie du troisième Continent*, etc., 5 vols., Paris, 1677-79.
Gabriel de Foigny: *La Terre Australe connue, c'est à dire la description de ce pays inconnu jusques ici, de ses moeurs et de ses Coutumes*, par M. Sadeur. Avec les aventures qui le conduisirent en ce Continent et les particularitez du séjour qu'il y fit durant trente-cinq ans et plus, et de son retour. Réduites et mises en lumière par les soins et la conduite de G. de F. Vannes, Par Jacques Verneuil (in reality printed at Geneva by La Pierre), 1676.
A New Discovery of Terra Incognita Australis or the Southern World, by James Sadeur a Frenchman, London, 1693.
Fénelon, François de Salignac de la Mothe: *Les Aventures de Télémaque*, Suite du quatrième livre de l'Odyssée d'Homère, Paris, 1699.
Gilbert, Claude: *Histoire de Calejava ou de l'isle des Hommes raisonnables*. Avec le parallele de leur morale et du Christianisme, Dijon, 1700.
Lesconvel, Pierre: *Voyage de l'Isle de Naudely, ou l'idée d'un regne heureux* (sometimes known as *Voyage du Prince Montberaud*), Cazeres, 1703.

Lom d'Arce, L. A. de Baron de Lahontan: *Nouveaux voyages de M. le baron de Lahontan dans l'Amérique septentrionale*, etc..., La Haye, 1703.
Mémoires de l'Amérique septentrionale ou la suite des voyages de M. le baron de Lahontan, etc...T. II. id.
Supplément aux Voyages du baron de Lahontan ou l'on trouve des dialogues, curieux entre l'auteur et un sauvage de bon sens qui a voyagé. T. III, id.
Dialogues curieux et Memoires de l'Amérique Septentrionale, edited by Gilbert Chinard, Paris, 1931.

Tyssot de Patot, S. (Ps.: Pierre de Mésange) : *La Vie, les Aventures, et le Voyage de Groenland du Révérend Père Cordelier P. de Mésange*, (2 vols), Amsterdam, 1720.

Swift, Jonathan: *Gulliver's Travels*, London, 1726.
Voyages de Gulliver, Tome I and II, translated by l'Abbé Desfontaines, Paris, 1726-27.

Rostaing, L. de Saint-Jory: *Les Femmes Militaires. Relation Historique d'une Isle nouvellement découverte*, par le sieur C.D., Amsterdam, 1736.

Berington, Simon (?): *Mémoires de Gaudencio di Lucca où il rend compte aux Pères de l'Inquisition de Bologne qui l'ont fait arreter, de tout ce qui lui est arrivé de plus remarquable dans sa vie; où il les instruit d'un pays inconnu, situé au milieu des vastes deserts de l'Afrique, dont les habitants sont aussi anciens, aussi nombreux et aussi civilisés que les Chinois.* First published 1746, enlarged edition, 1753 Reprinted under the title: *Les Mémoires de Gaudence de Luques* in *La Collection des Voyages Imaginaires*.

Morelly: *Naufrage des isles flottantes, ou Basiliade*, du célèbre Pilpai, poeme héroique (en prose) traduit de l'Italien par M.M——Tome 1er et 2nd A Messine par une Société de Libraires 1753
Le Code de la Nature ou le Véritable Esprit de ses lois, first published 1755. Publié avec notice et table analytique par Edouard Dolléas, Paris, 1910.

Voltaire: *Candide*, first published, Geneva, 1758.
Candide or Optimism, translated by John Butt, Penguin Books, 1947.

Roche, Tiphaigne de la: *Giphantie*, 1ère et 2ème partie, La Haye (Paris), 1760.
Histoire des Galligènes ou Mémoires de Duncan, 1ère et 2ème partie, 1765.

Burgh, James: *Account of the Cessares*, 1764.

Fontenelle, M. de: *La Republique des Philosophes ou Histoire des Ajaoiens*, Genève, 1768.

Mercier, Louis Sébastien: *L'An deux mille quatre cent quarante*, reve s'il en fut jamais, etc., Amsterdam, 1770.
Memoirs of the year two thousand five hundred, translated from the French, 1772. A new edition corrected, to which is now prefixed some account of the author, Liverpool, 1802.

Bernardin de Saint Pierre: *L'Arcadie*, Livre 1er, Angers, 1781.

Restif de la Bretonne: *La Découverte Australe, par un Homme volant, ou le Dédale francois:* Nouvelle très philosophique: Suivie de la Lettre d'un Singe, etc. 1er à 4ème vols., Leipsick, 1781.
Les Gynographs, La Haye, 1777.
L'Andrographe, La Haye, 1782.

Author unknown: *L'Isle inconnue, ou Mémoires du Chevalier de Gastines*, Recueillis et publiés par M. Grivel, Paris et Bruxelles, 1784, Reprinted in *La Collection des Voyages Imaginaires*.

Mably, Gabriel Bonnot de: *Des Droits et des Devoirs du Citoyen*, 1794-5.
De la Legislation, ou Principe des Loix, 1794-5.

Hodgson, W.: *The Commonwealth of Reason*, 1795.

Spence, Thomas: *Description of Spensonia*, London, 1795. Privately printed at the Courier Press, Leamington Spa, 1917.

Marquis de Sade, Donatien Alphonse François Comte de: *La Philosophie dans le Boudoir*, London, 1795. A chapter entitled: *Frenchmen! One more effort if you want to be Republicans*, translated by Simon Watson Taylor was published in *Free Unions*, London, 1946.

Diderot: *Supplément au Voyage de Bougainville. Dialogue sur l'inconvénient d'attacher des idées morales à certaines actions physiques qui n'en comportent pas*, Paris, 1796.

Les Eleuthéromanes, Paris, 1884.

Say, J. B.: *Olbie*, 1800.

La Collection des Voyages Imaginaires, 28 vo's, Paris, 1787-89.

Atkinson, Geoffroy: *The Extraordinary Voyage in French Literature before 1700*, New York 1920.

The Extraordinary Voyage in French Literature from 1700 to 1720, Paris, 1922.

Chapter V

UTOPIAS OF THE NINETEENTH CENTURY
Socialist and Scientific Utopias

Fourier, Charles: *Traité de l'Association domestique agricole*, 2 vols, 1822.

Le Nouveau Monde Industriel, 2 vols, 1829.

Selections from the works of Fourier, translated by Julia Franklin, with an introduction by Charles Gide, London, 1901.

Blanc, Louis: *L'Organisation du Travail*, Paris, 1839.

Cabet, Etienne: *Voyage en Icarie*, First Published under the title *Voyage et Aventures de Lord William Carisdall en Icarie*, traduits de l'Anglais de Francis Adams Par Th., Dufruit, Paris, 1840. Second edition, with preface by the author, Paris, 1842.

Prudhommeaux, J.: *Etienne Cabet et les Origines du Communisme Icarien*, 1907.

Saint-Simon, Henri-Claude de Rouvroy de: *Catéchisme Politique des Industriels, Parabole*, in Oeuvres Choisies, Brussels, 1859.

Oeuvres de Saint-Simon, edited by Rodrigues, Paris, 1841.

Owen, Robert: *The Book of the New Moral World*, New York, 1845.

Dolléans, Edouard: *Robert Owen* (1771-1858), Paris, 1905.

Buckingham, James Silk: *National Evils and Practical Remedies*, London, 1848.

Lytton, Lord Edward George EarleBulwer-: *The Coming Race: or the New Utopia*, London, 1870.

Butler, Samuel: *Erewhon*, London, 1872.

Erewhon Revisited, London, 1901.

Mallock, William Hurrell: *The New Republic*, London, 1877.

Bellamy, Edward: *Looking Backward—If Socialism Comes*, 2000-1887, Boston, 1888.

Kropotkin, Peter: *Le Vingtième Siècle*, articles published in *La Révolte*, Paris, 30 Nov-28 Dec, 1889.

Engels, Frederick: *Socialism, Utopian and Scientific*, translated by Edward Aveling, 1892.

Morris, William: *News from Nowhere: or, an Epoch of Rest*, Being some chapters from a Utopian Romance. First published in serial form in *Commonweal*, London, 11th Jan-4th Oct, 1890; reprinted in one volume, London, 1891.

A Dream of John Ball, first published in *Commonweal* and as a pamphlet, 1892.

The Earthly Paradise, a poem, first published 1872. *A Factory as it Might Be, How we live and how we might live*, reprinted in *William Morris, Stories in Prose, Stories in Verse, Shorter Poems, Lectures and Essays*, edited by G. D. H. Cole, London, 1934.

Richter, Eugene: *Pictures of the Socialistic Future* (freely adapted from Bebel), authorised translation by Henry Wright, with an introduction by T. Mackay, London, 1893.

Howard, (Sir) Ebenezer: *Garden Cities of To-morrow* (first published under the title: *To-morrow—a Peaceful Path to Real Reform*), London, 1898.

Hudson, William Henry: *A Crystal Age*, with an introduction by the author, London, 1906.

Chapter VI

MODERN UTOPIAS

Hertzka, Theodor: *Freiland: ein sociales Zukunftsbild*, first German edition, 1890 First English edition: *Freeland, A Social Anticipation*, translated by Arthur Ransome, London, 1891.

Wells, H. G.: *Anticipations*, London, 1901.
A Modern Utopia, London, 1905.
New Worlds for Old, London, 1908.
Men Like Gods, London, 1923.

France, Anatole: *Sur la Pierre Blanche*, Paris, 1905.

Tarde, Gabriel: *Underground Man*, translated by Cloudesley Brereton, with a preface by H. G. Wells, London, 1905.

Faure, Sebastien: *Mon Communisme (Le Bonheur Universel)*, Paris, 1921.

Capek, Carel: *R.U.R.*, a play, first shown in London, 1923.

Zamyatin, Eugeny Ivanovich: *Nous Autres*, traduit de Russe par B. Cauvet. Duhamel, Paris, 1929.

Huxley, Aldous: *Brave New World*, London, 1932.

Index of Persons

[references in italics are to the bibliography].

Subject Index

The name of an author indicates a reference to his work ('Wells *U*' and 'Wells *G*' refer to *A Modern Utopia* and *Men Like Gods*, respectively).

Agriculture
  in Sparta, 36, 53; Aristophanes, 48; Aquinas, 53; monastic, 55; More, 64, 70–71; Campanella, 102; 17th century, 146; Winstanley, 147–150, 169; Harrington, 144; Fourier, 212; Owen, 211, 213; Cabet, 225, 228; Morris, 273.
Anarchism, 46, 197, 198, see *also* *Government*.
Architecture and Town Planning
  Mumford, 5, 110; Wells, 5; in Sparta, 37; More, 69; Campanella, 95; Andreae, 109, 110, 114; Rabelais, 138, 140; Foigny, 191–192, 194; Cabet, 223–224, 232, 234; Morris, 261–263, 266, 272–273; Richter, 287–288.
Armies
  Plato, 22–23; in Sparta, 38; More, 85–87; Campanella, 102; Winstanley, 159, 163, 164; Foigny, 200; Richter, 282.
Army, New Model, 146, 147, 149, 150.
Aristocracies see *Ruling Classes*
Art
  in totalitarian states, 8, 31, 309, 317; Plato, 8, 24, 30, 33; More, 56; Andreae, 123; Rabelais, 138; Morris, 258–259, 260; Bellamy, 247.
Athens, 9, 10, 33, 53, 77.
Atomic energy, 133, 137, 235.
Austerity
  Plato, 16; in Sparta, 37–38, 42; Aristophanes, 50; More, 76–77; Andreae, 115; in the modern state, 38.
Authoritarian Nature of Utopias
  2–4, 6–8; Plato, 9, 11, 15, 29, 31–33, 62; of Sparta, 39, 45; More, 62, 84–85; Campanella, 102; Andreae,

107; Winstanley, 172; Cabet, 216–217, 224, 252–255; Bellamy, 216–217, 243, 254–255; Wells *U.*, 295, 298–301; Zamyatin, 313–316; Huxley, 316–317.
  authoritarian nature of the modern state, 311–313.

Bolshevism, 46, see also *Marxism, Communism, U.S.S.R.*
Bloody Sunday, 264.
Brook Farm, 213.

Calvinism, 90, 105, 106, 184, 185, 186.
Capitalism, 207, 208, 212, 245, 256.
Capital Punishment
  of beggars, 2, 146; of thieves, 63, 64; More, 72; Campanella, 101, 102; in Calvinist Geneva, 105; Andreae, 106; Winstanley, 160, 170, 171; Sade, 181; Morris, 276; Wells *U.*, 295, 301; Zamyatin, 315.
Catholic Church, 61, 88–94, 174, 185–188, see also *Inquisition*.
Censorship
  Plato, 30, 31; of Campanella, 89, 93, 94; in 17th century, 145; of Gilbert, 175; of 18th century Utopias, 176; of Foigny, 186, 189; of Diderot, 202; Richter on press freedom, 282.
Childbirth
  Plato, 18–21; Campanella, 100–101; Andreae, 117; Winstanley, 171; Foigny, 193; Wells *U.*, 299–300, 301; Zamyatin, 315; Huxley, 316.
Children
  Plato, 18–21; in Sparta, 42–44; Aristophanes, 48; More, 78, 82; Campanella, 97, 99; Andreae, 117–119; Bacon, 130–131; Winstanley, 154, 155, 157, 168; Morelly, 184;